HERE ARE THE STEPS WE TOOK

HERE ARE THE STEPS WE TOOK

HOW TO COMPLETE THE 12 STEPS OF A.A. IN EIGHT SESSIONS

Alex M.

My basic flaw had always been dependence—almost absolute dependence—on people or circumstances to supply me with prestige, security, and the like. Failing to get these things according to my perfectionist dreams and specifications, I had fought for them. And when defeat came, so did my depression... If we examine every disturbance we have, great or small, we will find at the root of it some unhealthy dependency and its consequent unhealthy demand. Let us, with God's help, continually surrender these hobbling demands. Then we can be set free to live and love; we may then be able to Twelfth Step ourselves and others into emotional sobriety.

Bill W., The Next Frontier: Emotional Sobriety, A.A. Grapevine January 1958

A.A.'s Twelve Steps are a group of principles, spiritual in their nature, which, if practiced as a way of life, can expel the obsession to drink and enable the sufferer to become happily and usefully whole.

Foreword, Twelve Steps and Twelve Traditions, p.15

Here we begin to practice all Twelve Steps of the program in our daily lives so that we and those about us may find emotional sobriety. When the Twelfth Step is seen in its full implication, it is really talking about the kind of love that has no price tag on it.

Step Twelve, Twelve Steps and Twelve Traditions, p.106

Spirituality refers to the raison-d'être of one's existence, the meaning and values to which one ascribes. Thus everyone embodies a spirituality. It should be seen in a wider context to refer to the deepest dimension of the human person. It refers therefore to the ultimate values that give meaning to our lives.

Celia Kourie, The Turn to Spirituality, Acta Theologica   Supplementum 8 (2006):19–38

A.A. is no success story in the ordinary sense of the word. It is a story of suffering transmuted, under grace, into spiritual progress.

As Bill Sees It, p.35

PREFACE

I never believed that I was born an alcoholic, but modern science suggests that I was born "a quart low" in some of the reward chemicals in my brain. Not only that, but my neurological reward pathways behave differently than those of normal people.

My brain function defects did not make me alcoholic, but they increased the odds that I would become one. It has been helpful for me to understand that my addictive behavior has some medical basis, because I never understood why I never felt a part of those around me, as much as I wanted to.

I spent years trying to find a way to fit in. I just wanted to feel normal, so I looked for any way to feel included and accepted by my herd. Like Bill Wilson, I wanted to prove to the world I was important—that I mattered.

Efforts to be the smartest guy in the room, or the funniest guy, or the most handsome guy, or the toughest guy, or the nicest guy, or the best at sports guy—all failed. None of my endeavors helped me fit in, until I discovered alcohol.

Drinking let me fit in with those I drank with, and enough alcohol made me forget how much I needed anyone's approval. When I drank I felt normal; I no longer felt a quart low.

I soon discovered that other drugs and activities could replenish my missing quart of magic leading to acceptance and self-esteem. Sex, gambling, hashish, pills, shopping and exercise were able to change my brain chemistry enough to let me feel a part of the human race and remove my dumpster full of fears about what happened yesterday and what might happen tomorrow.

So when I'm summoned by whichever addiction or compulsion is in charge of chairing the committee in my head today, I jog over to the feel good Dopamine Café to choose which activity or drug I'm going to use to deal with it.

Maybe I'll drown out the emotional squealing in my head with alcohol today, or should I toss back a few narcotic pills, or perhaps a handful of benzodiazepines or amphetamines? Maybe I should go gambling, or shopping, or to the gym, or look for sex in sordid places.

My dopamine-boosting concoction of choice was always alcohol. When it stopped working after several decades, I slinked back to the Dopamine Café to review my other options. On the way over, I got sidetracked by A.A., and never needed to visit that café again.

Here Are The Steps We Took—How to Complete the 12 Steps of A.A. in Eight Sessions was written to help any A.A. member, or sponsor and sponsee read through the Big Book *Alcoholics Anonymous* and complete the work of A.A.'s 12 Step program.

While there are many 12 Step Study books available on how to take a sponsee through the step work, I've tried to organize, condense and simplify the process by combining everything needed into one book.

To begin with, going through the 12 Steps requires studying the main text of the Big Book. So how do we do that?

As a sponsor, I ask myself what part of the Big Book chapters should I emphasize with my sponsee? Which specific areas should I make certain my sponsee reads and understands?

The bulk of the time and energy spent working the 12 Steps is studying the first 164 pages of the Big Book. I know my sponsee and I can't realistically read aloud face-to-face and discuss every sentence of the main text, but we can read the chapters on our own and then review the highlights together. *

But what are the highlights? Which key words, phrases, sentences or passages are best reviewed together? What questions should we ask or focus on as we read through the material in preparation for our step work?

In that spirit I've **bolded** the Big Book words and phrases which have been shared in the rooms as being significant to our recovery. I've commented on the sections of the readings which in my experience are important in recovery, acknowledging that every A.A. member and newcomer will have their own preference. In some cases my comments may seem gender specific to men, but they obviously apply to both men and women.

I've also tried to be sensitive to the multitude of ways each of us defines and relates to the terms God, God of our understanding, Higher Power, religion and spirituality, since the Big Book mixes all these terms together in an often confusing manner. While many A.A. members believe in God, not all of us do, and I have attempted to be sensitive and respectful of that fact in my writing.

The study guide questions for consideration that are noted in *italics* are taken from the Eight Week Step Study Guide printed in full in the back of the book.

Sharing key words, sentences and phrases with a sponsee for each of the eight step study sessions sets the foundation for the sponsee's step work, and hopefully prevents them from becoming so frustrated and overwhelmed that they give up on A.A. altogether.

My experience has shown me that the sooner newcomers get relief from their obsession to drink and find a new design for living, the higher the odds they will stay permanently sober and remain in A.A.

Years ago five of us, all with long-time sobriety and extensive experience hosting Step Study groups, experimented by going through one 4, 8 and 18 week study session each. We concluded that the optimal duration of a step study session was eight weeks, and that time period should permit any newcomer to get relief from their obsession and angst not drinking.

Here Are The Steps We Took is divided into eight working sessions.

The first 164 pages of the Big Book are included, with key text bolded and comments presented.

With my sponsees, I suggest we both follow the Eight Week Step Study Guide included at the end of this book, completing one session per week. For each week's assignment we read the text separately, review the questions for consideration, note items requiring further explanation or clarification, and then discuss together.

We often focus on the highlighted text of each chapter in the book, which gives us common ground for discussion, and adequate time to do so.

Preceding the session section in the book are some general thoughts on sponsorship, including an outline of what I discuss with sponsees before agreeing to sponsor them. There is also a sample sponsee commitment test, some potential red flags and a few frequently asked questions on sponsorship.

Several historical sponsorship guides are included, along with additional references.

Following the session section, just for fun since we aren't a glum lot, some items that were heard in the rooms of A.A. are presented, as well as some other materials and information about the author and his other publications.

* For years I have participated in a weekly Big Book study meeting where members read and discuss a few paragraphs of the first 164 pages at each meeting. On average, it takes our group two and one-half years to review the first 164 pages of the main text of the book in such detail.

As a footnote, I have not included the details of my journey into A.A. in *Here Are The Steps We Took*, since they are well documented in my other three books which are listed in the "About The Author" section at the end of this book.

"My Story" was published in December, 2018 on the "AA Agnostica" website at: https://aaagnostica.org/2018/12/02/my-aa-story

Acknowledgements

As always, I thank the A.A. Fellowship for welcoming me and all alcoholics who have a desire to stop drinking, and for every A.A. member who continually tries to practice the A.A. spiritual 12 Step principles and carry the message of hope and recovery to the alcoholic who still suffers.

Many thanks goes to my first sponsor, Dean J., who took me through all 12 Steps and the Big Book, and to my current sponsor, Greg B., who shows me daily how to practice the principles of the 12 Steps.

And a very special thanks to all my sponsees and those who have allowed me to work with them on the 12 Step program. You have taught me more than you know.

And of course, I thank my exceptional and cantankerous family and friends, both inside and outside of A.A.

TABLE OF CONTENTS

SPONSORSHIP

In Step Twelve it is suggested that we in A.A. have two duties: to try to carry the message of hope and recovery to other alcoholics, and to practice the spiritual principles of the 12 Steps in all our affairs.

There are many ways to try to carry the A.A. message to others. The most important is to demonstrate to those about us that we have a legitimate message to carry by demonstrating the positive change in our attitudes and actions brought about by the spiritual awakening we experienced after completing the 12 Steps ourselves.

Carrying the message also requires that we attempt to help other willing alcoholics by guiding them through their personal 12 Step work. Those efforts are usually labeled as sponsorship, which is defined as one alcoholic who has made progress in the recovery program sharing their experience on a continuous, individual basis with another alcoholic who is attempting to attain or maintain sobriety through A.A.

In other words, it's two people simply trying to stay sober by helping each other. It's two people connecting with each other based on sharing our mutual problem of alcoholism and the common solution we find in A.A.

Both parties benefit from sponsorship. Sharing our journey through sobriety makes it easier to live without alcohol and inspires us to maintain our sobriety as we encounter the daily challenges of life that inevitably arise.

The sponsor passes on how they have maintained their physical sobriety and grown in emotional sobriety, and encourages the sponsee to find their own way using the spiritual tools of the A.A. program, which consist of the Fellowship, Big Book and 12 Steps.

A good sponsor may share some of their personal beliefs with their sponsee, but will never impose those beliefs on them. The sponsor admits they don't know everything, and does not attempt to replace or discourage other needed medical treatment, or cultural or religious activities which may help the sponsee.

The sponsor is not a substitute for A.A., and reminds their sponsees they need to rely on the A.A. Fellowship rather than one person for their recovery. Nor does a sponsor object if the sponsee asks for guidance from other A.A. members or decides to change sponsors.

INITIAL CONVERSATION

When a man asks me to be his sponsor, our conversation usually goes something like this:

Him: Will you be my sponsor?

Me: Why?

Him: They said I need a sponsor.

Me: Do you want to stop drinking?

Him: Yes.

Me: What are you willing to do to stop drinking?

Him: Anything.

Me: Give me your two minute *Reader's Digest* version of God.*

Him: I believe in God and have no problem with him.

Me: What do you expect from a sponsor?

Him: I'm not sure. I think I need help with the Big Book readings and 12 Step work, and I want to better understand how the A.A. program can help me.

Me: I'm glad to talk to you some more about sponsorship, and we can go from there.

At that point I tell the potential sponsee that there is technically only one job I have as a sponsor, and that is to help another alcoholic through the work of the 12 Steps and answer any questions or discuss any concerns they may have about A.A. and their illness.

I tell the potential sponsee that what we will have is a simple business arrangement. You agree to do all the 12 Step work, and I agree to help you with that.

I remind them that my job is not to become their friend or counselor, although we may end up friends at some point. My job is not to be their mother, wife, girlfriend, counselor, lawyer, psychiatrist, banker or employer. We're simply equals among equals, both trying not to drink and maintain a new, sober way of living as best we can.

This question is not meant to qualify or disqualify a potential sponsee. I ask it only to get an idea of how much work I may have ahead of me as we go through the 12 Steps, which is heavily God-laden. If a potential sponsee is one of the 20% of Americans who has no relationship with God, it takes more time and work to get through the religious and spiritual aspects of the Big Book and 12 Steps.

COMMITMENT TEST

At some point during our discussion on sponsorship, I test him to see how committed he is to doing the program work. I ask him to read "The Doctor's Opinion," in the Big Book, which is only eight pages long, and to call me the following day to discuss it. I suggest he make notes in his Big Book of any questions, concerns, misunderstandings, or disagreements he may have with the reading, and then we will review over the phone.

And I wait.

I rarely get a return call. Even when I do get a response and we start on the step work, I know the odds of my sponsee staying sober and remaining in A.A. are very low. Having worked with almost one hundred men helping them through the 12 Step work, only five or so finished their step work with me and have attained long term sobriety, as far as I know.

I do not chase down potential sponsees, but I make it clear in meetings and elsewhere that I am willing to work with any man who wants to stop drinking and is willing to do the work required in the program.

I firmly believe men should sponsor only men and women only women. Gay men and women should find and use a heterosexual same-sex sponsor.

If the sponsee is illiterate and unable to read, they can listen to the free audio recording of the Big Book available on the AAWS website at: https://www.aa.org/pages/en_US/alcoholics-anonymous-audio-version

EXPECTATIONS

In the early days of A.A., all responsibility for the sponsee fell on the sponsor. He or she was expected to call the sponsee daily, make certain they attended meetings regularly and transport them to those meetings, ensure they read the Big Book, take them through the 12 Steps and regularly meet with their spouse and family.

My experience has shown me that if someone really wants to get sober, there is nothing I can do that will prevent it. If someone does not want to get sober, or is not ready to do the work required to get sober, there is nothing I can do to make it happen. My sole responsibility is to be available by phone and in person for my sponsee.

I do not give orders to my sponsees. I tell them I am available if they want to call me, but that I will not be calling them daily. I do not insist my sponsee call me every day. It is always the sponsee's job to get themselves to their A.A. meetings, just as they were able to get themselves to the bar and liquor store when they were drinking. I'm glad to meet them before or after any meeting I'm able to attend, and meet them one-on-one for their step study work. I rarely meet with any of the sponsee's family members, but I'm willing to speak with them if there is a good reason and it would be beneficial.

I expect that once my sponsee has completed his 12 Step work, he will start living his life based on our 12 Step principles, and begin sponsoring other alcoholics.

FREQUENTLY ASKED QUESTIONS

How do I know if the newcomer is a real alcoholic?

This is a tough topic because being a real alcoholic is *not* an A.A. membership requirement. According to Tradition Three, the only requirement for A.A. membership is a desire to stop drinking.

However, if I'm asked to spend my time to take a newcomer through the 12 Steps, I want to qualify him as a real alcoholic so I'm not wasting my time.

I naturally assume any suffering newcomer who regularly shows up at A.A. meetings has a real problem with drinking, and is probably alcoholic. But I do ask him the two questions presented in the first paragraph of the chapter "We Agnostics," which are:

1) Are you able to stop drinking forever?

2) Once you take that first drink, are you able to control the amount you drink afterwards—every single time?

If the newcomer answers no to either question, in my opinion they qualify as an alcoholic, and are worth working with on the 12 Steps.

> In the preceding chapters you have learned something of alcoholism. We hope we have made clear the distinction between the alcoholic and the non-alcoholic. If, when you honestly want to, you find you cannot quit entirely, or if when drinking, you have little control over the amount you take, you are probably alcoholic. If that be the case, you may be suffering from an illness which only a spiritual experience will conquer. [Big Book, p.44]

When should a newcomer start their 12 Step work?

As soon as possible, so the sponsee or new member can get relief from their obsession to drink and find a better way of living as rapidly as they can. If newcomers don't get relief quickly, many mistakenly decide A.A. doesn't work, and two-thirds of them exit the program, never to return.

Be aware that it takes time for the damaged brain to heal and the physiological effects of withdrawal from alcohol or drugs to diminish. It can take months or even years for the brain the heal completely, as described in the Post-Acute Withdrawal Syndrome (PAWS). *

However, a few weeks of abstinence is usually adequate for most alcoholics' minds to clear enough to begin their 12 Step work.

* PAWS

https://drugabuse.com/drug-withdrawal/post-acute-withdrawal-syndrome

What is a sponsor?

The sole job of the same-sex sponsor is to guide the sponsee through the 12 Steps of A.A. and answer any questions related to A.A. and the fellowship the sponsee may have, based on the sponsor's best knowledge and experience.

What are the qualifications to be a sponsor?

A sponsor is an active A.A. member who is dedicated to service work and growing in their own emotional sobriety. The sponsor has completed the 12 Steps of A.A., has a sponsor, has studied the Big Book and is willing to devote the time and energy required to mentor another alcoholic. How long a sponsor has been sober is less important than how deeply involved in the A.A. fellowship the sponsor is.

What are the traits of a good sponsor?

Ideal traits include honesty, reliability, empathy, patience, tolerance, understanding and compassion. The sponsor can share only their experience, strength and hope, and share with newcomers what works for them in a non-judgmental manner. Sponsors should use their moral compass, their own sponsor, the Fellowship, the Big Book and the principles of the 12 steps to guide them.

Sponsors often re-read the chapter "Working With Others" in the Big Book before accepting a new sponsee to remind them of their role.

What are the traits of a good sponsee?

Honesty, meaning the sponsee tells his sponsor the truth at all times. I tell my sponsees if they lie to me, and if they lie about lying, I will no longer be their sponsor. Sponsees need to be open-minded and willing to completely change the way they think and act. They must be willing to devote the time and effort to doing the work required in A.A. without whining, and must attend A.A. meetings regularly, which is at least three times or more a week for most people located in urban areas where there are sufficient A.A. meetings. They should be willing to read the Big Book, do the 12 Step work and start practicing the principles of the steps to the best of their ability.

How do I choose a sponsor?

A.A. is a program of attraction, not promotion. Many have found that it is better to choose a sponsor based as much on their gut as their head. Does that person have what you want? Is he honest? Do his actions match his words? Does he walk the talk? Does he do the next right thing right? Is he kind, humble, patient and tolerant?

If the person feels right to you, just go up to him and ask him to be your sponsor. That will start the conversation going.

I chose both my sponsors in A.A. by wanting what they had. Their length of sobriety, what their day job was, their bleeding deacon or elder statesman status, who else they sponsored, what they looked like, what their I.Q. was, which meetings they attended, which home group they had, or whether or not other A.A. members liked them—was irrelevant.

My sponsor had to be someone I felt I could completely trust with whatever we discussed. I had to feel some type of personal and emotional connection with him. I had to feel safe taking a chance on that person, knowing that if things did not work out I could always terminate the relationship.

I also suggest asking a potential sponsor how many other sponsees he is *actively* working with to get an idea if he will have enough time for me. If a sponsor has more than two or three *active* sponsees, meaning he is going through the steps with each of them, he probably will *not* have enough time to take on another needy sponsee.

Most sponsors have an additional group of stable, long term sponsees. Those folks have done all the 12 Step work, and not much time is required for the sponsor to work with them.

What if I'm gay?

Should I get a sponsor of the same or opposite sex? Can an opposite sex partner be gay? I've seen all types of sponsor-sponsee pairings in the gay community. My suggestion is if you're gay, work with same-sex sponsors or sponsees who are *not* LGBTQ. The bottom line is to work with people you are not sexually attracted to.

What if I'm agnostic or atheist?

Bill Wilson got sober with God, as did most of his fellow Christian alcoholics in the early days of A.A. He wrote about that experience in the Big Book, which is not only a textbook for recovery, but a historical document.

The suggestion that we choose our "own concept of God," does little to ease concerns of agnostics or atheists because God still remains the preferred Higher Power in A.A., regardless of one's concept.

Some freethinkers, humanists and secular members in A.A. refer to their guiding spiritual force or power as G-O-D: "Group of Drunks," "Good Orderly Direction," or just "Good," as the Buddhists suggest.

Other secular members do not think of a Higher Power as an *entity*, but as the moral *values* embedded in the spiritual principles of the 12 Steps.

The bottom line is that agnostics, atheists and any secular alcoholic can get sober in A.A. They do *not* need to seek out a like-minded sponsor; any qualified same-sex member will do. My own sponsor was an enthusiastic born-again Christian, and he did a superb job of taking me through the steps, despite my atheistic beliefs.

Secular members will likely need extra patience and tolerance to withstand the constant God references in the Big Book and discussed in the meeting rooms, but it should not prevent them from working with any sponsor to complete their 12 Step work.

Should I be a co-sponsor for someone?

Never. Sponsorship is not parenting, where the sponsee can run back and forth between mommy and daddy, playing off both when they are told something they don't like. It's a recipe for disaster.

What about relapse?

If your sponsor relapses, immediately get another sponsor. If your sponsee relapses and they are still sincere about their recovery and willing to do the work of the A.A. program, it is suggested that they return to Step One, and start over with their 12 Step work.

How do I deal with sponsees or sponsors I no longer want to work with?

Leaving Sponsors:

During all my years in A.A. I have had only two sponsors. I left my first sponsor because after he got married, had a child and started his own business he stopped attending A.A. to focus on those life changes. I thanked him for taking me through the 12 Steps and supporting me in my journey, but said that I needed a sponsor who was very active in the fellowship to help me stay sober. He understood, and there were no hard feelings.

The sponsee should never put their sponsor on a pedestal, and if they feel the relationship isn't working for whatever reason, they should say so and find another sponsor. The bottom line is if my sponsor is not helping me stay sober, then it's time for a change.

Leaving Sponsees:

I need sponsees who help me stay sober, are willing to do the work of the A.A. program and are willing to engage with our fellowship to the best of their ability. My sponsees must be willing to read the Big Book, complete the 12 Step work, and sponsor other alcoholics.

If they are unwilling or unable to do so, for whatever reason, then we part ways in our formal relationship. I explain that, through no fault of their own, they are not helping me stay sober. I am always available to discuss anything with them as a general member of the fellowship, but they need to seek out a different sponsor. I'm terminating the sponsee-sponsor relationship, not our fellowship relationship.

What is the ideal sponsor-sponsee relationship?

There is no ideal; there is only the one that works for both parties. Although the sponsor may be considered the teacher and the sponsee the student, both must meet on equal terms and footing. Both are trying to stay sober using the tools of A.A., and neither can honestly claim to be better or worse than the other.

Problems in the sponsor-sponsee relationship:

Obvious hazardous areas are sex (don't), mental or physical abuse (get out), deliberate dishonesty by omission or commission (be careful), making ultimatums or becoming threatening in ways that make you feel unsafe (get out), or demonstrating they can't be trusted (get out).

Other reasons to probably terminate the relationship:

Terminating Sponsors: the sponsor isn't available at your agreed-upon time on a regular basis. The sponsor only gives you part of your allocated meeting time. The sponsor is multi-tasking and not listening to you. You feel like you have to walk on eggshells and do not feel safe with your sponsor. The sponsor launches in with their own problems without being asked. The sponsor attempts to control your life. The sponsor is nasty, yells at you, or consistently criticizes you.

Terminating Sponsees: the sponsee regularly misses your meetings entirely or frequently calls in late. The sponsee is malicious, vicious or abuses you. The sponsee does not respect boundaries of when to text or call, such as late at night or early morning unless it is an emergency. The sponsee lies to you, and lies about lying to you.

https://gettingoutfromgoingunder.wordpress.com/2014/02/01/sponsorsponsee-breakups/

HISTORICAL SPONSORSHIP GUIDES

A.A. Sponsorship... Its Obligations and Its Responsibilities

The "A.A. Sponsorship Pamphlet" by Clarence Snyder was the first pamphlet ever written concerning sponsorship. It was published by the Cleveland Central Committee in 1944 under the title "A.A. Sponsorship... Its Opportunities and Its Responsibilities."

http://silkworth.net/pages/aahistory/aapamplet_clarences.php

Akron Manual For Alcoholics Anonymous

Dr. Bob said the "Akron Manual" was written and distributed within one year of the publication of the Big Book, which would date it to 1940. On the basis of a number of statements made within the text, it probably was not produced much later than that. This pamphlet assumes hospitalization at St. Thomas Hospital under the care of Sister Ignatia and the overall supervision of Dr. Bob as the normal first step in recovery, and gives recommended readings (e.g. *The Upper Room*) for morning meditation.

Bible and other Christian readings dropped out of A.A. practice within a few years, but parts of the manual are still relevant today. We can assume Dr. Bob and Sister Ignatia gave their approval to the statements made in this booklet. (Akron Group #1, 1940)

http://silkworth.net/pages/aahistory/akron_manual.php

https://aaagnostica.org/wp-content/uploads/2015/01/A-Manual-for-Alcoholics-Anonymous-Compressed.pdf

An Interpretation of the Twelve Steps: The Detroit Pamphlet

Detroit Beginners Meetings were started in 1943, when a group of members with some time in the program would read introductory material they had written and allow newcomers to ask questions. The beginner needed to go to four meetings to receive the complete set of introductory lessons. The Beginners Meetings worked so well that they were adopted by other groups in Detroit and then in many other communities throughout the country. The materials which the Detroit people had written were originally called "The Table Leaders Guide," and were first published by the Washington, D.C. groups in a pamphlet called "An Interpretation of the Twelve Steps." Detroit quickly came out with their own printed version of the pamphlet, which is still in print today.

http://silkworth.net/pages/aahistory/print/detroit_pamphlet1_2.html

<u>Alcoholics Anonymous—An Interpretation of our Twelve Steps</u>

This pamphlet titled "Alcoholics Anonymous—An Interpretation of our Twelve Steps," was published in September, 1944 by the Washington, D.C. group who borrowed it from the Detroit Pamphlet (Washington, D.C. Pamphlet, 1944).

https://www.nwarkaa.org/washingtondcguideto12steps.pdf

A.A. Sponsorship Pamphlet

Clarence Snyder (1944)

This is the first pamphlet ever written concerning sponsorship. It was written by Clarence H. Snyder in early 1944. Its original title was to be "A.A. Sponsorship... Its Obligations and Its Responsibilities." It was printed by the Cleveland Central Committee under the title: "A.A. Sponsorship... Its Opportunities and Its Responsibilities."

PREFACE

Each member of Alcoholics Anonymous is a potential sponsor of a new member and should clearly recognize the obligations and duties of such responsibility.

The acceptance of an opportunity to take the A.A. plan to a sufferer of alcoholism entails very real and critically important responsibilities. Each member, undertaking the sponsorship of a fellow alcoholic, must remember that he is offering what is frequently the last chance of rehabilitation, sanity or maybe life itself.

13

Happiness, health, security, sanity and life of human beings are the things we hold in balance when we sponsor an alcoholic.

No member among us is wise enough to develop a sponsorship program that can be successfully applied in every case. In the following pages, however, we have outlined a suggested procedure, which supplemented by the member's own experience, has proven successful.

PERSONAL GAINS OF BEING A SPONSOR

No one reaps full benefit from any fellowship he is connected with unless he whole-heartedly engages in its important activities. The expansion of Alcoholics Anonymous to wider fields of greater benefit to more people results directly from the addition of new, worthwhile members or associates.

Any A.A. who has not experienced the joys and satisfaction of helping another alcoholic regain his place in life has not yet fully realized the complete benefits of this fellowship. On the other hand, it must be clearly kept in mind that the only possible reason for bringing an alcoholic into A.A. is for that person's gain. Sponsorship should never be undertaken to:

1) Increase the size of the group.

2) For personal satisfaction and glory.

3) Because the sponsor feels it his duty to re-make the world.

Until an individual has assumed the responsibility of setting a shaking, helpless human being back on the path toward becoming a healthy useful, happy member of society, he has not enjoyed the complete thrill of being an A.A.

SOURCE OF NAMES

Most people have among their own friends and acquaintances someone who would benefit from our teachings. Others have names given to them by their church, by their doctor, by their employer, or by some other member who cannot make a direct contact.

Because of the wide range of the A.A. activities, the names often come from unusual and unexpected places.

These cases should be contacted as soon as all facts such as marital status, domestic relations, financial status, drink habits, employment status and others readily obtainable are at hand.

IS THE PROSPECT A CANDIDATE?

Much time and effort can be saved by learning as soon as possible if:

1) The man really has a drinking problem.

2) Does he know he has a problem?

3) Does he want to do something about his drinking?

4) Does he want help?

Sometimes the answers to these questions cannot be made until the prospect has had some A.A. instruction, and an opportunity to think. Often we are given names, which upon investigation, show the prospect is in no sense an alcoholic, or is satisfied with his present plan of living. We should not hesitate to drop these names from our lists. Be sure, however, to let the man know where he can reach us at a later date.

WHO SHOULD BECOME MEMBERS?

A.A. is a fellowship of men and women bound together by their inability to use alcohol in any form sensibly, or with profit or pleasure. Obviously, any new members introduced should be the same kind of people, suffering from the same disease.

Most people can drink reasonably, but we are only interested in those who cannot. Party drinkers, social drinkers, celebrators, and others who continue to have more pleasure than pain from their drinking are of no interest to us.

In some instances an individual might believe himself to be a social drinker when he definitely is an alcoholic. In many such cases more time must pass before that person is ready to accept our program. Rushing such a man before he is ready might ruin his chances of ever becoming a successful A.A. Do not ever deny future help by pushing too hard in the beginning.

Some people, although definitely alcoholic, have no desire or ambition to better their way of living, and until they do A.A. has nothing to offer them.

Experience has shown that age, intelligence, education, background, or the amount of liquor drunk, has little, if any, bearing on whether or not the person is an alcoholic.

PRESENTING THE PLAN

In many cases a man's physical condition is such that he should be placed in a hospital, if at all possible.

Many A.A. members believe hospitalization, with ample time for the prospect to think and plan his future, free from domestic and business worries, offers distinct advantage. In many cases the hospitalization period marks the beginning of a new life. Other members are equally confident that any man who desires to learn the A.A. plan for living can do it in his own home or while engaged in normal occupation. Thousands of cases are treated in each manner and have proved satisfactory.

SUGGESTED STEPS

The following paragraphs outline a suggested procedure for presenting the A.A. plan to the prospect, at home or in the hospital.

QUALIFY AS AN ALCOHOLIC

1) In calling upon a new prospect, it has been found best to qualify oneself as an ordinary person who has found happiness, contentment, and peace of mind through A.A. Immediately make it clear to the prospect that you are a person engaged in the routine business

of earning a living. Tell him your only reason for believing yourself able to help him is because you yourself are an alcoholic and have had experiences and problems that might be similar to his.

TELL YOUR STORY

2) Many members have found it desirable to launch immediately into their personal drinking story, as a means of getting the confidence and whole-hearted cooperation of the prospect.

It is important in telling the story of your drinking life to tell it in a manner that will describe an alcoholic, rather than a series of humorous drunken parties. This will enable the man to get a clear picture of an alcoholic which should help him to more definitely decide whether he is an alcoholic.

INSPIRE CONFIDENCE IN A.A.

3) In many instances the prospect will have tried various means of controlling his drinking, including hobbies, church, changes of residence, change of associations, and various control plans. These will, of course, have been unsuccessful. Point out your series of unsuccessful efforts to control drinking, their absolute fruitless results and yet that you were able to stop drinking through application of A.A. principles. This will encourage the prospect to look forward with confidence to sobriety in A.A. in spite of the many past failures he might have had with other plans.

TALK ABOUT "PLUS" VALUES

4) Tell the prospect frankly that he cannot quickly understand all the benefits that are coming to him through A.A. Tell him of the happiness, peace of mind, health, and in many cases, material benefits which are possible through understanding and application of the A.A. way of life.

SHOW IMPORTANCE OF READING THE BOOK

5) Explain the necessity of reading and re-reading the A.A. book. Point out that this book gives a detailed description of the A.A. tools and the suggested methods of application of these tools to build a

foundation of rehabilitation for living. This is a good time to emphasize the importance of the twelve steps and the four absolutes.*

The Oxford Group's Four Absolutes were Honesty, Unselfishness, Love and Purity. They were felt to be the distilled, uncompromising moral principles taught by Jesus.

QUALITIES REQUIRED FOR SUCCESS IN A.A.

6) Convey to the prospect that the objectives of A.A. are to provide the ways and means for an alcoholic to regain his normal place in life. Desire, patience, faith, study and application are most important in determining each individual's plan of action in gaining full benefits of A.A.

INTRODUCE FAITH

7) Since the belief of a Power greater than oneself is the heart of the A.A. plan, and since this idea is very often difficult for a new man, the sponsor should attempt to introduce the beginnings of an understanding of this all-important feature.

Frequently this can be done by the sponsor relating his own difficulty in grasping a spiritual understanding and the methods he used to overcome his difficulties.

LISTEN TO HIS STORY

8) While talking to the newcomer, take time to listen and study his reactions in order that you can present your information in a more effective manner. Let him talk too. Remember—Easy Does It.

TAKE TO SEVERAL MEETINGS

9) To give the new member a broad and complete picture of A.A., the sponsor should take him to various meetings within convenient distance of his home. Attending several meetings gives a new man a chance to select a group in which he will be most happy and comfortable, and it is extremely important to let the prospect make his own decision as to which group he will join.

Impress upon him that he is always welcome at any meeting and can change his home group if he so wishes.

EXPLAIN A.A. TO PROSPECT'S FAMILY

10) A successful sponsor takes pains and makes any required effort to make certain that those people closest and with the greatest interest in their prospect (mother, father, wife, etc.) are fully informed of A.A., its principles and its objectives. The sponsor sees that these people are invited to meetings, and keeps them in touch with the current situation regarding the prospect at all times.

HELP PROSPECT ANTICIPATE HOSPITAL EXPERIENCE

11) A prospect will gain more benefit from a hospitalization period if the sponsor describes the experience and helps him anticipate it, paving the way for those members who will call on him.

CONSULT OLDER MEMBERS IN A.A.

These suggestions for sponsoring a new man in A.A. teachings are by no means complete. They are intended only for a framework and general guide. Each individual case is different and should be treated as such. Additional information for sponsoring a new man can be obtained from the experience of older men in the work. A co-sponsor, with an experienced and newer member working on a prospect, has proven very satisfactory. Before undertaking the responsibility of sponsoring, a member should make certain that he is able and prepared to give the time, effort, and thought such an obligation entails. It might be that he will want to select a co-sponsor to share the responsibility, or he might feel it necessary to ask another to assume the responsibility for the man he has located.

IF YOU ARE GOING TO BE A SPONSOR—BE A GOOD ONE!

SPONSORSHIP REFERENCES

"Questions & Answers On Sponsorship," Alcoholics Anonymous World Services (1983)

https://www.aa.org/assets/en_US/aa-literature/p-15-questions-and-answers-on-sponsorship

Hamilton B., *Twelve Step Sponsorship*, Hazelden (1996)

https://www.goodreads.com/book/show/165959.Twelve_Step_Sponsorship

Robert Fitzgerald, *The Soul of Sponsorship: The Friendship of Fr. Ed Dowling and Bill Wilson in Letters*, Hazelden (2011)

https://www.goodreads.com/book/show/1121119.The_Soul_of_Sponsorship

Tonigan & Rice, "Is it Beneficial to Have an Alcoholics Anonymous Sponsor?" Psychol Addict Behav. 2010 September; 24(3): 397–403.

https://www.ncbi.nlm.nih.gov/pmc/articles/PMC5512698/pdf/nihms-173128.pdf

Paul Whelan, "The Role of AA Sponsors: A Pilot Study" Alcohol and Alcoholism, Vol. 44, #4, July-August 2009, Pgs. 416–422. https://doi.org/10.1093/alcalc/agp014

Clarence Snyder, "A.A. Sponsorship...Its Opportunities and Its Responsibilities," Cleveland Central Committee (1944)

http://silkworth.net/pages/aahistory/aapamplet_clarences.php

TWELVE WAYS TO TELL THE DIFFERENCE BETWEEN YOUR SPONSOR AND YOUR THERAPIST

1) Your sponsor isn't all that interested in the "reasons" you drank.

2) Your therapist thinks your root problem is your lack of self-esteem and your negative self-image. Your sponsor thinks your problem is yourself.

3) Your therapist wants to pamper your inner child. Your sponsor thinks it's time for him to grow up.

4) Your sponsor thinks your inventory should be about you, not your parents.

5) Speaking of your parents, your sponsor tells you not to confront them, but to make amends to them.

6) The only time your sponsor uses the word "closure" is before the word "mouth."

7) Your sponsor thinks "boundaries" are things you need to take down, not build up.

8) Your therapist wants you to love yourself first; your sponsor wants you to love others first.

9) Your therapist prescribes medication. Your sponsor prescribes prayer, meditation and service work.

10) Your sponsor thinks "anger management skills" are numbered 1 through 12.

11) Now that you haven't had a drink in six months, your therapist thinks you should make a list of all your goals and objectives for the next five years, starting with finishing up that college degree. Your sponsor thinks you should start today by cleaning coffee pots and helping them carry a heavy box of literature to the jail.

12) Your sponsor will not lose their license if they talk about God.

STEP STUDY ORIENTATION

BIG BOOK EIGHT WEEK STUDY GUIDE

WK	STEP	BIG BOOK CHAPTER READINGS	BB PGS
		STUDY GROUP ORIENTATION	
1	1	PREFACE, FOREWORDS, DOCTORS OPINION, BILLS STORY, THERE IS A SOLUTION, MORE ABOUT ALCOHOLISM	1 - 43
2	2,3	WE AGNOSTICS	44 - 64
3	4	HOW IT WORKS – Inventory: Grudge / Resentments	64 - 67
4	4	HOW IT WORKS – Inventory: Fears / Sex	67 - 71
5	5,6,7	INTO ACTION – Complete Fifth Step	72 - 76
6	8,9	INTO ACTION	76 - 84
7	10,11	INTO ACTION	84 - 88
8	12	WORKING WITH OTHERS	89 - 103

1) Appoint a Chairperson, which is usually the member that organized the Step Study.

2) Have each member introduce himself and BRIEFLY share their reasons for joining the Step Study.

3) Read the PURPOSE below.

4) Review the MATERIALS needed and make sure all members have a Sponsor.

5) Review the COMMITMENTS section. This is what is expected from each team member.

6) Agree on the meeting FORMAT.

7) Read the Assignment for the next meeting.

8) Choose a Chairperson for the next meeting.

PURPOSE
To complete the Twelve Steps of Alcoholics Anonymous, as outlined in the books *Alcoholics Anonymous* & the *Twelve Steps and Twelve Traditions.*

MATERIALS
1) Books: *Alcoholics Anonymous* (Big Book) & the *Twelve Steps and Twelve Traditions*

2) Get a <u>Notebook</u> for writing
3) Get a <u>Sponsor</u>

STRUCTURE

Remember that a Step Study group is NOT an "A.A. meeting" under the formal definition of the Traditions, and therefore does NOT fall under AAWS guidelines. It is simply a group of alcoholics who have decided to meet for a few months to treat their illness.

1) Ideally, each group should be a mixture of experienced members and newer members.
2) The group members agree on a time and place for a weekly meeting and the length of the meeting.
3) The group usually exchanges full names, telephone numbers and e-mail addresses.
4) The group needs to decide if they will allow new members (late-comers) to join after the orientation meeting. It is usually inadvisable to admit new members late.
5) Each member will commit to completing the weekly assignment including the written work as outlined in the Step Study Guide.
6) For the written assignment, each member, in turn, will share <u>only from what they have written</u>. If you did not complete the written assignment we ask that you <u>not</u> participate in this part of the meeting.

YOUR RESPONSIBILITY & COMMITMENT

- I commit to attend each weekly meeting.
- If I am unable to attend a meeting due to unforeseen events, I will inform the meeting Chair or another group member prior to the meeting so as not to keep the group waiting.
- I commit to completing all the steps, including the Fifth Step (the step is not done with the group so details need not be revealed).
- I will communicate <u>regularly</u> with my sponsor during the study on my progress and activity.
- I am expected to prepare for the weekly meeting by completing the assignment for that week.
- If I <u>relapse</u> during the Step Study, I will withdraw and start over at Step One with my sponsor.

POSSIBLE MEETING FORMAT

1) Open meeting with a moment of silence or the Serenity Prayer.
2) Around the room introductions.
3) Review the COMMITMENTS.
4) Each member will read his assignment and then we will go around the room with other members reading their material.
5) Once all members have read their assignment and time permits the Chair may ask if anyone wants to discuss anything from the Study Guide that calls for further attention.

Close discussion soon enough before the agreed end time in order to:

1) Read the assignment for next week.
2) Pick a Chairperson for the next meeting. No sobriety time requirement to chair.
3) Collect Tradition VII donations if needed.
4) Close the meeting with an optional prayer or reading of the Chairperson's choice.

WEEKLY ASSIGNMENTS

The Eight Week Study Guide has a section for each week, and includes READING & WRITING assignments.

CONSIDERATIONS may be used to help you reflect on what you have read and guide your writing. Write as much as you want, but read only what you are comfortable reading at the meeting within the allowed timeframe. Depending on the size of the group and the time available, each member's reading may need to be limited to three or four minutes or so (use a timer if needed).

Suggestion: Since writing requires focus and is best done when free of distraction, you may want to schedule at least an hour of "quiet time" each week to do your writing. Ensure your writings remain securely stored so that no one can read them without your permission, such as spouses, family members or friends.

SESSION ONE

STEP 1

Preface, Forewords, Dr.'s Opinion, Bill's Story, There Is A Solution, More About Alcoholism

Pages 1 – 43

STEP 1 -- *We admitted we were powerless over alcohol—that our lives had become unmanageable.*

<u>READ</u> from the beginning (Facepage) of *Alcoholics Anonymous* through "More About Alcoholism" (Chapter 3, <u>p.43</u>).

<u>WRITE</u> down your reactions to the readings as to <u>how they apply to you and your illness</u>, incorporating as much as possible of the considerations into your work. Think about:

1) Any reservations you may have that in fact, you are powerless over alcohol.
2) How the writings apply to your life.
3) How you are powerless over alcohol and begin to consider <u>what</u> you can truly "manage" in your life.
4) Have you listed those things you attempted to do to control your use of alcohol?
5) Did you have a reservation of any kind or lurking notion that you will someday be immune to alcohol?

<u>CONSIDERATIONS – Preface, Foreword, Doctor's Opinion</u>

1) Were you aware that your illness affected both your mind and your body?
2) Have you ever experienced the phenomena of "craving?" – <u>p.xxviii</u>
3) Did you reach the point where you could not differentiate the "true" from the "false?"
4) Did your alcoholic life seem normal?
5) The Doctor seems to say that a "psychic change" must occur – What is a psychic change? (Spiritual Awakening)
6) Can you accept the fact that alcoholism "has never been, by any treatment with which we are familiar, permanently eradicated?"

25

CONSIDERATIONS – Bill's Story

1) Did you ever ask "Was I crazy?" – p.5
2) Did you ever feel the remorse, horror and hopelessness of the next morning? – p.6
3) Did your mind ever race uncontrollably? – p.6
4) Did you ever seek oblivion? – p.6
5) Did you ever feel lonely? – p.8
6) Did you ever feel fear? – p.8
7) What was your reaction to religion, the church and God? – p.10
8) Note what happened to Bill's prejudice against "their God" when he began to apply his own concept of God – p.12
9) Did you know that "nothing more was required of me" to make my beginning than "willingness," or a "willingness to believe?"
10) Doesn't Bill essentially take the First through the Eleventh Steps at this time? – p.13
11) Notice how Bill was instructed to find God's will and pray. – p.13
12) Has your common sense become "uncommon sense" in manner? – p.13
13) Bill really takes the Twelfth Step on p.14, doesn't he?
14) The Program worked in all of Bill's affairs – p.15.
15) What was of particular significance to you in this chapter?
16) What did you find that you could not accept?

CONSIDERATIONS – There Is A Solution

1) What is your reaction to the membership of A.A.? -- p.17
2) Did your alcoholism "engulf all whose lives touched the sufferer's?" – p.18
3) What was their reaction?
4) Did you see how you can reach another alcoholic? – p.18
5) Note on p.20, the book answers the question, "What do I have to do?"
6) Have you been asked the questions of p.20 by yourself or other people? What were the answers?
7) From your examination of yourself in the past weeks and your reading of this chapter, are you a "real alcoholic?" – p.21 If not, why not?
8) Did you have control over alcohol? Did you do absurd and

incredible and tragic things while drinking? Were you a Jekyll and Hyde?

9) Did the questions and observations on p.21 help you in answering the questions you have been writing and talking about? *For example:*
- Why did we drink the way we did? – p.22
- Why do we take that one drink?
- Why can't we stay on the wagon?
- What has become of the common sense and the will power that we still sometimes display with respect to other matters?
- Did you ask yourself these questions?
- Had you lost the power of choice described on p.24?
- Have you ever said – "What's the use anyhow" or something similar?

10) Go to "There is a Solution" (p.25). Read "The great fact is just this and nothing less: that we have had deep and effective spiritual experiences."

11) Read and understand the rest of this paragraph and Appendix II because it is an outstanding summary of what happens in the program.

12) Our alternative to the solution is to "go on blotting out the consciousness of our intolerable situation as best we could or to accept spiritual help" (p.25). Note that Appendix II is referred to again on p.27.

CONSIDERATIONS – More About Alcoholism

1) Did you have the "great obsession?" -- p.30

2) Has your writing in your handbook listed those things you attempted to do to control your use of alcohol? -- p.33

3) Did you have a reservation of any kind or lurking notion that you will someday be immune to alcohol? -- p.33

4) Can you identify with the mental states that precede a relapse into drinking?

5) Do you understand that these mental states are the crux of the problem? -- p.35

6) Do you understand why an actual or potential alcoholic will be absolutely unable to stop drinking on the basis of self-knowledge? -- p.39.

7) Note the doctor's reaction to alcoholism on p.43.

8) Also note the solution at the top of p.43.

BIG BOOK TEXT FOR STEP 1

Chapters 1,2,3

PREFACE, FOREWORDS, DR'S OPINION, BILL'S STORY, THERE IS A SOLUTION, MORE ABOUT ALCOHOLISM

Pages 1 – 43

ALCOHOLICS ANONYMOUS

The Story of How Many Thousands of Men and Women Have Recovered from Alcoholism

PREFACE

What follows is the second edition of the book "Alcoholics Anonymous," which made its first appearance in April 1939. More than 300,000 copies of the first edition are now in circulation.

Because this book has become the basic text for our Society and has helped such large numbers of alcoholic men and women to recovery, there exists a sentiment against any radical changes being made in it. Therefore, the first portion of this volume, describing the A.A. recovery program, has been left largely untouched.

But the personal history section has been considerably revised and enlarged in order to present a more accurate representation of our membership as it is today. When the book was first printed, we had scarcely 100 members all told, and every one of them was an almost hopeless case of alcoholism. This has changed. A.A. now helps alcoholics in all stages of the disease. It reaches into every level of life and into nearly all occupations. Our membership now includes many young people. Women, who were at first very reluctant to approach A.A., have come forward in large numbers. Therefore the range of the story section has been broadened so that every alcoholic reader may find a reflection of him or herself in it.

As a souvenir of our past, the original Foreword has been preserved and is followed by a second on describing Alcoholics Anonymous of 1955.

Following the Forewords, there appears a section called "The Doctor's Opinion." This also has been kept intact, just as it was originally written in 1939 by the late Dr. William D. Silkworth, our Society's great medical benefactor.

Besides Dr. Silkworth's original statement, there have been added, in the Appendices, a number of the medical and religious endorsements which have come to us in recent years.

On the last pages of this second edition will be found the Twelve Traditions of Alcoholics Anonymous, the principles upon which our A.A. groups function, together with the directions for getting in touch with A.A.

FOREWORD TO THE FIRST EDITION

This is the Foreword as it appeared in the first printing of the first edition in 1939.

WE, of Alcoholics Anonymous, are more than one hundred men and women who have **recovered from a seemingly hopeless state of mind and body. To show other alcoholics precisely how we have recovered is the main purpose of this book**.

> We can't recover from our alcoholism as we would from a bout of pneumonia, but we can recover from the hopelessness and despair which led us into the rooms of A.A. Our bodies were beaten and pickled, and our minds brimming with anger, fear and self-absorption. Many of us had reached that jumping off place where suicide appeared to be the only way out. Here we are presented with textbook testimony for our recovery.
>
> *Were you aware that your illness affected both your mind and your body? Do you believe you have a way out?*

For them, we hope these pages will prove so convincing that no further authentication will be necessary. We think this account of our experiences will help everyone to better understand the alcoholic.

Many do not comprehend that the alcoholic is a very sick person. And besides, we are sure that our way of living has its advantages for all.

It is important that we remain anonymous because we are too few, at present to handle the overwhelming number of personal appeals which may result from this publication. Being mostly business or professional folk, we could not well carry on our occupations in such an event. We would like it understood that our alcoholic work is an avocation.

When writing or speaking publicly about alcoholism, we urge each of our Fellowship to omit his personal name, designating himself instead as "a member of Alcoholics Anonymous." Very earnestly we ask the press also, to observe this request, for otherwise we shall be greatly handicapped.

We are not an organization in the conventional sense of the word. There are no fees or dues whatsoever. The only requirement for membership is an honest desire to stop drinking. We are not allied with any particular faith, sect or denomination, nor do we oppose anyone. We simply wish to be helpful to those who are afflicted.

We are reminded that anonymity applies not only to how we share our names in A.A., but how we learn to live life on a more humble, less egotistical basis by putting the 12 Step spiritual principles before our naturally selfish and self-centered personality. Anonymity means it not all about me.

Our fellowship is open to all who have a desire to stop drinking. The original A.A. Preamble was published in the *A.A. Grapevine* in 1947, and modified over the next decade. Our current A.A. Preamble was finalized in 1958 after the word "honest" was removed from "desire to stop drinking."

A.A. PREAMBLE: Alcoholics Anonymous is a fellowship of men and women who share their experience, strength and hope with each other that they may solve their common problem and help others to recover from alcoholism. The only requirement for membership is a desire to stop drinking.

There are no dues or fees for A.A. membership; we are self-supporting through our own contributions. A.A. is not allied with any sect, denomination, politics, organization or institution; does not wish to engage in any controversy; neither endorses nor opposes any causes. Our primary purpose is to stay sober and help other alcoholics to achieve sobriety.

Tip: one easy way to remember personal anonymity at the public level is:

a) If I use my *full* name then I *don't* say I'm in A.A. I can say I'm "in a 12 Step recovery program," or I'm just "in recovery."

b) If I use my *first* name only, I *can* say I'm an A.A. member, *unless* I'm so famous and well recognized that everyone knows my full name without me stating it.

We shall be interested to hear from those who are getting results from this book, particularly form those who have commenced work with other alcoholics. We should like to be helpful to such cases.

Inquiry by scientific, medical, and religious societies will be welcomed.

When Bill W. was writing the Big Book, he felt it was essential not to offend any of the influential medical or religious leadership of the day. He did not want those groups attacking A.A., the Big Book or its suggestions, which could damage the growth of the fellowship and reduce book sales. This is why Bill took great pains to get the pre-publication buy-in of the Catholic Church and the respected medical societies of the time.

FOREWORD TO SECOND EDITION

Since the original Foreword to this book was written in 1939, a wholesale miracle has taken place. Our earliest printing voiced the hope that every alcoholic who journeys will find the Fellowship of Alcoholics Anonymous at his destination. Already, continues the early text, twos and threes and fives of us have sprung up in other communities.

Sixteen years have elapsed between our first printing of this book and the presentation in 1955 of our second edition. In that brief space, Alcoholics Anonymous has mushroomed into nearly 6,000 groups whose membership is far above 150,000 **recovered alcoholics.**

Groups are to be found in each of the United States and all of the provinces of Canada. A.A. has flourishing communities in the British Isles, the Scandinavian countries, South Africa, South America, Mexico, Alaska, Australia and Hawaii. All told, promising beginnings have been made in some 50 foreign countries and U.S. possessions. Some are just now taking shape in Asia. Many of our friends encourage us by saying that this is but a beginning, only the augury of a much larger future ahead.

Estimates of A.A. membership in 2017 were 2.1 million members in more than 120,000 groups residing in 180 countries worldwide.

The spark that was to flare into the **first A.A. group** was struck at **Akron, Ohio in June 1935**, during a talk between a New York stockbroker and an Akron physician. Six months earlier, **the broker had been relieved of his drink obsession by a sudden spiritual experience** following a meeting with an alcoholic friend who had been in contact with the **Oxford Groups** of that day. He had also been greatly helped by the late **Dr. William D. Silkworth**, a New York **specialist in alcoholism** who is now accounted no less than a medical saint by A.A. members, and whose story of the early days of our Society appears in the next pages. From this doctor, the broker had learned the grave nature of alcoholism. Though he could not accept all the tenets of the Oxford Groups, **he was convinced of the need for moral inventory, confession of personality defects, restitution to those harmed, helpfulness to others, and the necessity of belief in and dependence upon God.**

Bill W. became involved in the Oxford Group, who called themselves a First Century Christian Fellowship, after group member and boyhood friend Ebby Thacher visited him in November 1934, sharing how he had gotten sober in the group.

After Bill got sober in December, 1934, he shared the Oxford Group message with Dr. Bob in May, 1935, who was already attending Oxford Group meetings in Akron with his wife Anne.

Bill said later that the 12 Steps of A.A. came straight from the Oxford Group and directly from the Reverend Sam Shoemaker, the group's former leader in America, and from nowhere else.

The Oxford Group promoted and practiced absolute surrender, guidance by the Holy Spirit, belief in God, sharing and asking for guidance from their fellowship and daily prayer. Members sought the group's Four Absolute standards of Unselfishness, Love, Honesty and Purity, which were incorporated into the first A.A. programs in Akron, Cleveland and New York City.

A.A. members in New York left the Oxford Group in 1937, and Akron members left in 1939 to focus exclusively on helping alcoholics.

Prior to his journey to **Akron**, the broker had worked hard with many alcoholics on the theory that **only an alcoholic could help an alcoholic**, but he had succeeded only in keeping sober himself. The broker had gone to Akron on a business venture which had collapsed, leaving him greatly in fear that he might start drinking again. He suddenly realized that **in order to save himself he must carry his message to another alcoholic**. That alcoholic turned out to be the Akron physician [Dr. Bob].

This physician had repeatedly tried spiritual means to resolve his alcoholic dilemma but had failed. But when the broker gave him Dr. Silkworth's description of alcoholism and its hopelessness, the physician began to pursue the **spiritual remedy** for his malady with a willingness he had never again up to the moment of his death in 1950. This seemed to prove that one alcoholic could affect another as no nonalcoholic could. It also indicated that **strenuous work, one alcoholic with another, was vital to permanent recovery**.

Before Bill W.'s white flash religious conversion experience in

Towns Hospital in December 1934, he described himself as an agnostic and never attended church regularly.

Dr. Bob had always been a practicing Christian, and later an Oxford Group member, but admitted his religious efforts and beliefs could not get him sober. Both men initially turned to religion and the church to get them sober, but it did not work.

After Bill W. chose his own conception of God following Ebby's suggestion, Bill did not return to the church of his childhood, but did label his conversion a religious "spiritual experience" allowing him to connect with the Christian God of his current understanding.

Dr. Bob had no similar conversion or spiritual experience, and struggled for almost three years with a powerful daily obsession to drink. Service work with other alcoholics kept him sober though those rough times, as did his weekly A.A. meetings which were essentially Christian religious meetings, involving Bible study and devotional literature readings, prayer, acceptance of Christ, emphasis on church affiliation, and Christian outreach efforts.

Bill W. became a spiritual person, whereas Dr. Bob remained a religious person.

Hence the two men set to work almost frantically upon alcoholics arriving in the ward of the Akron City Hospital. Their very first case [Bill Dotson], a desperate one, recovered immediately and became A.A. number three. He never had another drink. This work at Akron continued through the summer of 1935. There were many failures, but there was an occasional heartening success. When the broker returned to New York in the fall of 1935, the first A.A. group had actually been formed [in Akron], though no one realized it at the time.

A second small group promptly took shape at New York, to be followed in 1937 with the start of a third at Cleveland. Besides these, there were scattered alcoholics who had picked up the basic ideas in Akron or New York who were trying to form groups in other cities.

By late 1937, the number of members having substantial sobriety time behind them was sufficient to convince the membership that a new light had entered the dark world of the alcoholic.

It was now time, the struggling groups thought, to place their message and unique experience before the world. This determination bore fruit in the spring of 1939 by the publication of this volume. The membership had then reached about 100 men and women. The fledgling society, which had been nameless, now began to be called Alcoholics Anonymous, from the title of its own book. The flying-blind period ended and A.A. entered a new phase of its pioneering time.

With the appearance of the new book a great deal began to happen. Dr. Harry Emerson Fosdick, the noted clergyman, reviewed it with approval. In the fall of **1939**, Fulton Oursler, the editor of *Liberty* printed a piece in his magazine, called "Alcoholics and God." This brought a rush of 800 frantic inquiries into the little New York office which meanwhile had been established. Each inquiry was painstakingly answered; pamphlets and books were sent out. Businessmen, traveling out of existing groups, were referred to these prospective newcomers. New groups started up and it was found, to the astonishment of everyone, that A.A.'s message could be transmitted in the mail as well as by word of mouth. By the end of 1939 it was estimated that 800 alcoholics were on their way to recovery.

In the spring of **1940**, John D. Rockefeller, Jr. gave a dinner for many of his friends to which he invited A.A. members to tell their stories. News of this got on the world wires; inquiries poured in again and many people went to the bookstores to get the book Alcoholics Anonymous.

By March, **1941** the membership had shot up to 2,000. Then **Jack Alexander wrote a feature article in the *Saturday Evening Post*** and placed such a compelling picture of A.A. before the general public that alcoholics in need of help really deluged us. By the close of 1941, A.A. numbered 8,000 members. The mushrooming process was in full swing, A.A. had become a national institution.

Our Society then entered a fearsome and exciting adolescent period. The test that it faced was this:

Could these large numbers of erstwhile erratic alcoholics successfully meet and work together? Would there be quarrels over membership, leadership and money? Would there be strivings for power and prestige? Would there be schisms which would split A.A. apart? Soon A.A. was beset by these very problems on every side and in every group. But out of this frightening and at first disrupting experience the conviction grew that **A.A.'s had to hang together or die separately. We had to unify our Fellowship** or pass off the scene.

As we discovered the principles by which the individual alcoholic could live, so **we had to evolve principles by which the A.A. groups and A.A. as a whole could survive and function effectively**. It was thought that no alcoholic man or woman could be excluded from our Society; that our leaders might serve but not govern; that each group was to be autonomous and there was to be no professional class of therapy. There were to be no fees or dues; our expenses were to be met by our own voluntary contributions. There was to be the least possible organization, even in our service centers. Our public relations were to be based upon attraction rather than promotion. It was decided that all members ought to be anonymous at the level of press, radio, TV and films. And in no circumstances should we give endorsements, make alliances, or enter public controversies.

The above paragraph formed the basis of A.A.'s Preamble.

In the September 1958, *A.A. Grapevine*, the preamble was first published in its present form: "Alcoholics Anonymous is a fellowship of men and women who share their experience, strength and hope with each other that they may solve their common problem and help others to recover from alcoholism. The only requirement for membership is a desire to stop drinking. There are no dues or fees for A.A membership; we are self-supporting through our own contributions. A.A. is not allied with any sect, denomination, politics, organization or institution; does not wish to engage in any controversy, neither endorses nor opposes any causes. Our primary purpose is to stay sober and help other alcoholics achieve sobriety."

However, the Preamble today is not exactly like the one below which was published in the *A.A. Grapevine* in June, 1947 by then-editor Tom Y. The original version differed in two ways: 1) It stated that "the only requirement for membership is an *honest* desire to stop drinking," and 2) its description of self-support consisted only of the brief phrase "A.A. has no dues or fees."

"Alcoholics Anonymous is a fellowship of men and women who share their experience, strength and hope with each other that they may solve their common problem and help others to recover from alcoholism. The only requirement for membership is an honest desire to stop drinking. AA has no dues or fees. It is not allied with any sect, denomination, politics, organization or institution; does not wish to engage in any controversy, and neither endorses nor opposes any causes. Our primary purpose is to stay sober and to help other alcoholics to achieve sobriety." [1947]

This was the substance of **A.A.'s Twelve Traditions**, which are stated in full on page 564 of this book. Though none of these principles had the force of rules or laws, they had become so **widely accepted by 1950** that they were confirmed by our first International Conference held at Cleveland.

Today the remarkable **unity of A.A.** is one of the greatest assets that our Society has.

A.A.'s Twelve Traditions are an exceptional set of suggested guidelines for promoting inter-group unity and managing the relationship between the A.A. groups, members, other groups, the global fellowship and society at large. Questions concerning finance, public relations, donations and group purpose are addressed in the Traditions.

Between 1945 and 1949, Bill W. published a comprehensive series of essays in the *A.A. Grapevine* magazine which formed the basis of the Twelve Traditions. Those original Grapevine essays can be found in the A.A. book *The Language of the Heart.*

While the internal difficulties of our adolescent period were being ironed out, public acceptance of A.A. grew by leaps and bounds. For this there were two principal reasons: the large numbers of recoveries, and reunited homes. These made their impressions everywhere. **Of alcoholics who came to A.A. and really tried, 50% got sober at once and remained that way; 25% sobered up after some relapses, and among the remainder, those who stayed on with A.A. showed improvement**. Other thousands came to a few A.A. meetings and at first decided they didn't want the program. But great numbers of these—about two out of three—began to return as time passed.

> No one knows how many people have gotten sober, or are currently getting sober in A.A., since personal records are no longer kept as they were in the early days.
>
> Of interest was that the results of the A.A. member headcount in November, 1937 was *not* "100 or so with 75% sober," but 45 members with 29 sober (64%). When A.A. was two years old, only 8 of 18 (44%) members were sober in New York City, and 21 of 27 members were sober in Akron, Ohio (78%).
>
> By the time Bill W. published the Big Book in April 1939, an estimated 74 members were in A.A., and 41 (55%) of them were thought to have been sober at that time.
>
> Remember that A.A. had existed for only a few years when all the head-counting was occurring, so "long-term sobriety" could never have been more than several years.
>
> Akron had much higher sobriety rates than New York because in Akron alcoholics were intensely prescreened and had to qualify for A.A. membership. Before being permitted in the fellowship by Dr. Bob, Akron alcoholics required hospitalization for five days while A.A. members visited the newcomer and told him their story.

Women and young alcoholics were not allowed in A.A. at that time.

On the fifth day the new man had to get down on his knees and say a prayer surrendering himself to Christ and God.

It was only then that the A.A. candidate could begin attending A.A. meetings and become an A.A. member. No such requirements were imposed on the New York fellowship.

If anyone wants to fire up an argument among alcoholics in the fellowship, start discussing the recovery rate in A.A., which Bill W. claimed to be 75%.

By Wilson's earlier admission, no more than two-thirds had been sober for only two years when he did his 1937 headcount. Two years is not long term sobriety.

A.A. Membership surveys cannot determine an accurate sobriety rate, since they survey only members who are currently in A.A., not those who have come and gone in A.A.

Multiple medical and research studies of A.A. and addiction treatment in general suggest a long term recovery rate of between 4% and 8%. Recovery means complete, lifelong abstinence from alcohol and drugs. Personal observation and experience confirms these low rates.

Clinical studies have *not* demonstrated that A.A. is a better program to treat alcoholics than other legitimate addiction treatment programs. What clinical studies have discovered is that A.A. works best for the "severe" alcoholic who is *totally committed* to recovery and *heavily involved* in A.A.

In other words, the sicker we are and the more deeply involved in A.A. we are, the better our chances for lifelong abstinence and recovery.

As for newcomers who visit A.A. and quickly leave, recent research studies have disputed Bill W.'s observation that two-thirds return over time. The fact is, two-thirds *never* return to A.A.

Another reason for the wide acceptance of A.A. was the ministration of friends—friends in medicine, religion, and the press, together with innumerable others who became our able and persistent advocates. Without such support, A.A. could have made only the slowest progress. Some of the recommendations of A.A.'s early medical and religious friends will be found further on in this book.

Alcoholics Anonymous is not a religious organization. Neither does A.A. take any particular medical point of view, though we cooperate widely with the men of medicine as well as with the men of religion.

> Even though A.A. as an international fellowship does not get involved in public discourse, it does have a historic religious and medical view.

> In the chapter "The Doctor's Opinion," Dr. Silkworth made it clear alcoholism was a medical illness, and throughout the Big Book alcoholism is referred to as a disease, illness or malady.

> Although A.A. is not an official religious organization, A.A.'s doctrines and practices have been determined to be religious by multiple U.S. state and federal courts. Like the Oxford Group, A.A. is undeniably a Christian and God-centric fellowship, despite denials by some members and A.A. leadership.

> The Big Book repeatedly states that our recovery is dependent on God, and that God will do for us what we cannot do for ourselves. Even when we choose our own conception of God, God remains the Higher Power of choice in A.A.

> Many today perceive A.A. as a non-denominational Christian mutual aid society for alcoholics.

Alcohol being no respecter of persons, we are an accurate cross section of America, and in distant lands, the same democratic evening-up process is now going on.

By personal religious affiliation, we include Catholics, Protestants, Jews, Hindus, and a sprinkling of Moslems and Buddhists. More than fifteen per cent of us are women.

At present, **our membership is increasing** at the rate of about seven per cent a year. So far, upon the total problem of several million actual and potential alcoholics in the world, we have made only a scratch.

In all probability, we shall never be able to touch more than a fair fraction of the alcohol problem in all its ramifications. **Upon therapy for the alcoholic himself, we surely have no monopoly**. Yet it is our great hope that all those who have as yet found no answer may begin to find one in the pages of this book and will presently **join us on the high road to a new freedom**.

Because of anonymity, and the fact that no formal or reliable membership records are kept, A.A. membership estimates are inconsistent and vary markedly, depending on the source.

What is accurate is that membership exploded after the Jack Alexander article in the *Saturday Evening Post*, published in March of 1941. Membership increased from that time forward until 1990, when it started to flatten and has remained essentially flat for the past three decades, despite increases in the population and in the number of alcoholics worldwide.

In the 2014 "A.A. Membership Survey," 89% of members were Caucasian with an average age of 50. Nineteen percent were retired and 41% were married or had a life partner. Almost two-thirds of members were being treated with outside counseling. Half were sober less than five years.

https://www.aa.org/assets/en_US/p-48_membershipsurvey.pdf

For unclear reasons, A.A. membership in the U.S. and worldwide has grown little over the past thirty years. Some note that even though the total number of registered A.A. groups has increased, each A.A. group has gotten smaller, reflecting no significant growth in overall membership.

Estimated A.A. United States membership, from AAWS and other sources:

1935 - 5
1936 - 15
1937 - 45
1938 - 73
1939 - 800
1940 - 2,000
1945 - 13,000
1950 - 96,000
1955 - 94,000
1960 - 108,000
1965 - 134,000
1970 - 167,000
1975 - 293,000
1980 - 414,000
1985 - 676,000
1990 - 1,012,600
1995 - 1,153,800
2000 - 1,162,100
2005 - 1,068,500
2010 - 1,279,700
2015 - 1,262,500
2017 - 1,124,500

THE DOCTOR'S OPINION

WE of Alcoholics Anonymous believe that **the reader will be interested in the medical estimate of the plan of recovery described in this book**. Convincing testimony must surely come from medical men who have had experience with the sufferings of our members and have witnessed our return to health. A well-known doctor, chief physician at a nationally prominent hospital specializing in alcoholic and drug addiction, gave Alcoholics Anonymous this letter:

To Whom It May Concern:

I have specialized in the treatment if alcoholism for many years. In late 1934 I attended a patient who, though he had been a competent businessman of good earning capacity, was an alcoholic of a type I had come to regard as hopeless.

In the course of his third treatment he acquired certain ideas concerning a possible means of recovery. As part of his rehabilitation he commenced to present his conceptions to other alcoholics, impressing upon them that they must do likewise with still others. This has become the basis of a rapidly growing fellowship of these men and their families. This man and over one hundred others appear to have recovered.

I personally know scores of cases who were of the type with whom other methods had failed completely.

These facts appear to be of extreme medical importance; because of the extraordinary possibilities of rapid growth inherent in this group they may mark a new epoch in the annals of alcoholism. These men may well have a remedy for thousands of such situations.

You may rely absolutely on anything they say about themselves.

Very truly yours, William D. Silkworth, M.D.

The patient Dr. Silkworth, a neuro-psychiatrist, was describing was Bill Wilson, who eventually recognized the hopelessness of his illness during his third and final admission to New York's Towns Hospital in December, 1934:

"But it was not, for the frightful day came when I drank once more. The curve of my declining moral and bodily health fell off like a ski-jump. After a time I returned to the hospital. This was the finish, the curtain, it seemed to me. My weary and despairing wife was informed that it would all end with heart failure during delirium tremens, or I would develop a wet brain, perhaps within a year. We would soon have to give me over to the undertaker or the asylum." [Bill's Story, p.7]

In 1934, there was no effective program or treatment for alcoholism. Alcoholics were left on their own to cycle through jails and usually ended up warehoused in institutions until they died.

The book *Alcoholics Anonymous*, published in 1939, was the first document to describe a fellowship of alcoholics and a spiritual 12 Step program of recovery based on the recognition that alcoholism was a treatable medical illness, rather than a result of an individual's moral failure and lack of self-will.

The physician who, at our request, gave us this letter, has been kind enough to enlarge upon his views in another statement which follows. In this statement he confirms what we who have suffered alcoholic torture must believe that **the body of the alcoholic is quite as abnormal as his mind**. It did not satisfy us to be told that we could not control our drinking just because **we were maladjusted to life**, that we were **in full flight from reality**, or were outright **mental defectives**. These things were true to some extent, in fact, to a considerable extent with some of us. But we are sure that **our bodies were sickened as well**. In our belief, any picture of the alcoholic which leaves out this physical factor is incomplete. The doctor's theory that **we have an allergy to alcohol** interests us. As laymen, our opinion as to its soundness may, of course, mean little. But as ex-problem drinkers, we can say that his explanation makes good sense. It explains many things for which we cannot otherwise account.

Dr. Silkworth's hypothesis that alcoholics have a physiological allergy to alcohol was a simple way to describe a complex problem. He felt alcoholics had some inherent, physical abnormality which prevented them from reacting as normal people when they ingested alcohol. Whatever that was led to a loss of control once the alcoholic started drinking.

Little did Silkworth know he on the right track. Today, clinical studies have discovered that alcoholics are physically and genetically different from normal drinkers. Our brain chemistry and how some of us process alcohol are abnormal, due to a combination of genetics and historical environmental circumstances. Knowledge of our abnormalities, however helpful, is unfortunately not enough to stop us from drinking once we start.

Though we work out our solutions on the spiritual as well as an altruistic plane, we favor hospitalization for the alcoholic who is very jittery or befogged. More often than not, **it is imperative that a man's brain be cleared before he is approached**, as he has then a better chance of understanding and accepting what we have to offer.

The doctor writes:

The subject presented in this book seems to me to be of paramount importance to those afflicted with alcoholic addiction.

I say this after many years' experience as Medical Director of one of the oldest hospitals in the country treating alcoholic and drug addiction.

There was, therefore, a sense of real satisfaction when I was asked to contribute a few words on a subject which is covered in such masterly detail in these pages.

We doctors have realized for a long time that some form of **moral psychology** was of urgent importance to alcoholics, but its application presented difficulties beyond our conception. What with our ultra-modern standards, our scientific approach to everything,

45

we are perhaps not well equipped to apply the powers of good that lie outside our synthetic knowledge.

Moral psychology has multiple definitions, but involves how people make moral decisions based on their interpretation of right and wrong, and their behavior related to those decisions.

For example, an alcoholic might believe that it is morally wrong to always be drunk and disrupt the lives of others, but they get drunk anyway. Unfortunately, their moral will power is rarely adequate to overcome their mental obsession and physical allergy of craving after taking that first drink.

There is nothing moral or psychological about A.A.'s 12 Steps other than the principles they reflect. The Steps are a spiritual program of action which allows us to recover from our hopeless state of mind and body. This recovery, not simply abstinence from alcohol, is what enables us to change our attitudes and actions, which results in the discovery of a new and rewarding design for living in sobriety.

Many years ago one of the leading contributors to this book came under our care in this hospital and while here he acquired some ideas which he put into practical application at once.

Later, he requested the privilege of being allowed to tell his story to other patients here and with some misgiving, we consented. The cases we have followed through have been most interesting; in fact, many of them are amazing.

The unselfishness of these men as we have come to know them, the entire absence of profit motive, and their community spirit, is indeed inspiring to one who has labored long and wearily in this alcoholic field. They believe in themselves, and still more in the Power which pulls chronic alcoholics back from the gates of death.

Of course an alcoholic ought to be freed from his **physical craving** for liquor, and this often requires a definite hospital procedure, before psychological measures can be of maximum benefit.

We believe, and so suggested a few years ago, that **the action of alcohol** on these chronic alcoholics **is a manifestation of an allergy**; that the **phenomenon of craving is limited to this class** and never occurs in the average temperate drinker. These allergic types **can *never* safely use alcohol in any form at all**; and once having formed the habit and found they cannot break it, once having lost their self-confidence, their reliance upon things human, their problems pile up on them and become astonishingly difficult to solve.

Dr. Silkworth describes the obsession in our mind for alcohol that drives us to drink, and once we start drinking, the physical craving for more alcohol takes over. At that point, once we have taken that first drink, our most principled willpower cannot stop us from continuing to drink, even if we really want to stop. We become truly powerless over alcohol, as our first step suggests.

I never comprehended the danger of that first drink, although I had the same experience with cigarettes long before my addiction to alcohol. After I started smoking at age ten, I quickly became addicted and decided to quit when I was in college. I stopped cold-turkey after high school, and remained abstinent for three years.

In college I was offered a cigarette at a party, and thought there could be no harm if I had just one. Little did I know. The nicotine craving set in, and after smoking the rest of the evening on donated cigarettes, I bought a pack on the way home. That sad night occurred almost fifty years ago, and I have been smoking ever since because I have no desire to stop.

So whenever I think about taking that first drink, I remember what happened to me after I smoked that first cigarette.

Have you ever experienced the phenomena of craving?

Frothy emotional appeal seldom suffices. The **message** which can interest and hold these alcoholic people **must have depth and weight**. In nearly all cases, **their ideals must be grounded in a power greater than themselves**, if they are to re-create their lives.

If any felt that as psychiatrists directing a hospital for alcoholics we appear somewhat sentimental, let them stand with us a while on the firing line, see the tragedies, the despairing wives, the little children; let the solving of these problems become a part of their daily work, and even of their sleeping moments, and the most cynical will not wonder that we have accepted and encouraged this movement. We feel, after many years of experience, that we have found nothing which has contributed more to the rehabilitation of these men than the altruistic movement now growing up among them.

Men and women drink essentially because they like the effect produced by alcohol. The sensation is so elusive that, while they admit it is injurious, **they cannot after a time differentiate the true from the false**. To them, **their alcoholic life seems the only normal one**.

> Alcoholics not only like the effect of alcohol, but we *need* the effect to get through whatever fear or anxieties we are experiencing at the present moment. Despite knowing that once we start drinking we won't be able to stop whenever we wish, we start anyway. Over time, we learn to rationalize this abnormal behavior and accept it as normal.
>
> *Did you reach the point where you could not differentiate the "true" from the "false?" Did your alcoholic life seem normal?*

They are **restless, irritable and discontented**, unless they can again experience the **sense of ease and comfort** which comes at once by taking a few drinks—drinks which they see others taking with impunity. After they have succumbed to the desire again, as so many do, and the **phenomenon of craving develops**, they pass through the well-known stages of a **spree**, emerging remorseful, with a firm **resolution not to drink again**. This is **repeated over and over**, and **unless this person can experience an entire psychic change there is very little hope of his recovery**.

On the other hand—and strange as this may seem to those who do not understand—**once a psychic change has occurred**, the very same person who seemed doomed, who had so many problems he despaired of ever solving them, **suddenly finds himself easily able to control his desire for alcohol**, the only effort necessary being that **required to follow a few simple rules**.

Dr. Silkworth is presenting us alcoholics with a hook, or teaser. He says we are hopelessly doomed to an alcoholic death and will never be able to lick our illness on our own. But, he adds, if we have some mysterious psychic change   and follow a few simple rules, our obsession to drink will disappear and we can recover.

The Doctor seems to say that a "psychic change" must occur. What is a psychic change? (Spiritual Awakening)

Men have cried out to me in sincere and despairing appeal: "Doctor, I cannot go on like this! I have everything to live for! I must stop, but I cannot! You must help me!"

Faced with this problem, if a doctor is honest with himself, he must sometimes feel his own inadequacy. Although he gives all that is in him, it often is not enough. One feels that **something more than human power is needed to produce the essential psychic change**. Though the aggregate of recoveries resulting from psychiatric effort is considerable, we physicians must admit we have made little impression upon the problem as a whole. Many types do not respond to the ordinary psychological approach.

I do not hold with those who believe that alcoholism is entirely a problem of **mental control**. I have had many men who had, for example, worked a period of months on some problem or business deal which was to be settled on a certain date, favorably to them. They took a drink a day or so prior to the date, and then the **phenomenon of craving** at once became paramount to all other interests so that the important appointment was not met. **These men were not drinking to escape; they were drinking to overcome a craving beyond their mental control**.

Earlier Dr. Silkworth said that we drink because we like the effect produced by alcohol whenever we become irritable,

49

restless and discontented. Then he says we drink to overcome a craving beyond our control. Which is it?

It's both. When we get agitated and anxious, we search our memory for what gave us relief from those unwanted feelings in the past. Since alcohol worked before, we always believe it will work again, even if we know it might not work this time. So we develop an obsession to take a drink.

Once we take that drink, our obsession is relieved, but now we must deal with our physical allergy to alcohol, which causes us to crave even more alcohol after our obsession has been relieved and our anxiety has been reduced.

This cruel reality of our illness propels us into a pattern of constant drinking, because we are always irritated, restless and discontented about something every day. We have the obsession, we drink for relief, we get relief, but we must continue to drink because we have triggered our craving.

After a while, we just give up trying to control our drinking because it doesn't work. We just drink and drink and drink, often until we blackout or pass out. We eventually come to, and repeat the cycle, over and over and over.

There are many situations which arise out of the phenomenon of craving which cause men to make the supreme sacrifice [suicide] rather than continue to fight. The **classification of alcoholics** seems most difficult, and in much detail is outside the scope of this book. There are, of course, the **psychopaths** who are emotionally unstable. We are all familiar with this type. They are always "going on the wagon for keeps." They are over-remorseful and make many resolutions, but never a decision.

There is the type of **man who is unwilling to admit that he cannot take a drink**. He plans various ways of drinking. He changes his brand or his environment. There is the type who always **believes that after being entirely free from alcohol for a period of time he can take a drink without danger**.

There is the **manic-depressive** type, who is, perhaps, the least understood by his friends, and about whom a whole chapter could be written.

Then there are **types entirely normal** in every respect except in the effect alcohol has upon them. They are often able, intelligent, friendly people.

All these, and many others, have **one symptom in common**: they **cannot start drinking without developing the phenomenon of craving**. This phenomenon, as we have suggested, may be the manifestation of an **allergy** which differentiates these people, and sets them apart as a distinct entity. **It has never been, by any treatment with which we are familiar, permanently eradicated**. The **only relief** we have to suggest **is entire abstinence**.

> According to the good doctor, there are five types of alcoholics. Most of us fall into either the normal category or the delusional category of thinking we will someday be able to drink normally if we just go on the wagon long enough.
>
> If we have a mental illness in addition to our alcoholism, we may require separate medical treatment for that as well.
>
> Dr. Silkworth says the *only* solution for all of us, besides the earlier psychic change he mentioned, is to stop drinking *forever*.
>
> *Can you accept the fact that alcoholism "has never been, by any treatment with which we are familiar, permanently eradicated?"*

This immediately precipitates us into a seething caldron of debate. Much has been written pro and con, but among physicians, the general opinion seems to be that **most chronic alcoholics are doomed**.

What is the solution? Perhaps I can best answer this by relating one of my experiences. About one year prior to this experience a man was brought in to be treated for chronic alcoholism. He had but partially recovered from a gastric hemorrhage and seemed to be a case of pathological mental deterioration. He had lost everything worthwhile in life and was only living, one might say, to drink. He frankly admitted and believed that for him there was no hope.

Following the elimination of alcohol, there was found to be no permanent brain injury. **He accepted the plan outlined in this book**. One year later he called to see me, and I experienced a very strange sensation. I knew the man by name, and partly recognized his features, but there all resemblance ended. From a trembling, despairing, nervous wreck had emerged a man brimming over with self-reliance and contentment. I talked with him for some time, but was not able to bring myself to feel that I had known him before. To me he was a stranger, and so he left me. A long time has passed with no return to alcohol.

> The second member of A.A. in New York City was Hank Parkhurst. His story in the first edition of the Big Book was titled "The Unbeliever," and he is credited with writing the Big Book chapter "To Employers." Hank was a fervent promoter who had worked for Standard Oil of New Jersey before getting fired for his drinking.
>
> He had a long and stormy relationship with Bill W., but with the help of Jim Burwell, the two men were responsible for the 12 Step compromise phrase "God as we understood Him" being added to Steps Three and Eleven.
>
> Hank stayed sober for four years after he met Bill, but relapsed in 1939 and died still drinking in 1954.
>
> Hank's tenacity and drive was responsible for getting *Alcoholics Anonymous* published. As Bill W.'s secretary Ruth Hock said about the Big Book: "It wouldn't have been written without Bill, and it wouldn't have been published without Hank."

When I need a mental uplift, I often think of another case brought in by a physician prominent in New York.

The patient had made his own diagnosis and deciding his situation hopeless, had hidden in a deserted barn determined to die.

He was rescued by a searching party, and, in desperate condition, brought to me. Following his physical rehabilitation, he had a talk with me in which he frankly stated he thought the treatment a waste of effort, unless I could assure him, which no one ever had, that in the future he would have the "will power" to resist the impulse to drink.

His alcoholic problem was so complex and his depression so great, that we felt his only hope would be through what we then called "moral psychology," and we doubted if even that would have any effect.

However, he did become "sold" on the ideas contained in this book. He has not had a drink for a great many years. I see him now and then and he is as fine a specimen of manhood as one could wish to meet.

> The third New York A.A. member was John Henry Fitzhugh Mayo, nicknamed "Fitz," and his story was recorded in the Big Book as "Our Southern Friend." He was twelve stepped by Bill W. at Towns Hospital and got sober in October, 1935. The son of a minister, Fitz was very active in A.A. He helped research and select the formal name for the Big Book, and founded multiple A.A. meetings in and around Washington, D.C. He died sober in 1943 from cancer.

I earnestly advise every alcoholic to read this book through, and though perhaps he came to scoff, he may remain to pray.

William D. Silkworth, M.D.

> One of the most important contributions Dr. Silkworth made to A.A. was not automatically dismissing Bill W.'s hot flash experience at Towns Hospital in December of 1934. He told Bill: "Something has happened to you I don't understand. But you had better hang on to it. Anything is better than the way you were."

> Had he told Bill his white light hot flash event was nothing more than a drug-induced, hallucinatory side-effect of his belladonna treatment, Bill may not have stayed sober or ever created our A.A. fellowship.

One of the finest and most comprehensive books about the life of Dr. Silkworth is titled *Silkworth: The Little Doctor Who Loved Drunks*, by Dale Mitchel. The author is an alcoholic who has appeared on numerous radio and television shows throughout the country offering his analysis of alcoholism, its treatment and recovery.

BILL'S STORY

The first chapter in the Big Book is called "Bill's Story." It is unclear why he begins his life story when he was already 22 years old. Neither in this chapter or elsewhere in the book does Bill speak of his childhood upbringing, which had a profound impact on his personality, behavior, relationships, alcoholism and later life events.

William G. Wilson was born to Emily Griffith and Gilman Wilson at their home, the Mount Aeolus Inn and Tavern, on November 26, 1895, in East Dorset, Vermont.

By the time Bill was ten years old, his parents' marriage had fallen apart, aggravated by his father's hard drinking, and his parents divorced when Bill was twelve. Gilman moved to British Columbia, Canada, and Emily left to study osteopathic medicine in Boston. Bill remained in Vermont to be raised by his maternal grandparents, Fayette and Ella Griffith.

As an aside, Bill's paternal grandfather, William C. Wilson, was an alcoholic who suddenly stopped drinking after having a religious conversion experience during a soul searching hike on nearby Mount Aeolus a few miles from East Dorset. Interestingly, Wilson described his own religious conversion experience in Towns Hospital using almost exactly the same words as his grandfather had when describing his experience.

Chapter 1

BILL'S STORY

War fever ran high in the New England town to which we new, young officers from Plattsburg were assigned, and we were flattered when the first citizens took us to their homes, **making us feel heroic**. Here was love, applause, war; moments sublime with intervals hilarious. **I was part of life at last**, and in the midst of the excitement **I discovered liquor**. I forgot the strong warnings and the prejudices of my people concerning drink. In time we sailed for "Over There." **I was very lonely and again turned to alcohol**.

We landed in England. I visited **Winchester Cathedral**. Much moved, I wandered outside. My attention was caught by a doggerel on an old tombstone:

"Here lies a Hampshire Grenadier who caught his death drinking cold small beer. A good soldier is ne'er forgot, whether he dieth by musket or by pot."

Ominous warning—which I failed to heed.

Twenty-two, and a veteran of foreign wars, I went home at last. **I fancied myself a leader**, for had not the men of my battery given me a special token of appreciation? My talent for leadership, I imagined, would place me at the **head of vast enterprises** which I would manage with the utmost assurance.

I took a night law course, and obtained employment as investigator for a surety company. **The drive for success was on. I'd prove to the world I was important**. My work took me about Wall Street and little by little I became interested in the market. Many people lost money—but some became very rich. Why not I? I studied economics and business as well as law. Potential alcoholic that I was, I nearly failed my law course. At one of the finals I was too drunk to think or write. Though **my drinking was not yet continuous**, it disturbed my wife. We had long talks when I would still her forebodings by telling her that men of genius conceived their best projects when drunk;

that the most majestic constructions philosophic thought were so derived.

> Bill began drinking in 1917 at the age of 22, and married his sweetheart Lois Burnham the following year, just prior to being shipped overseas in World War I, which ended four months after Bill arrived in England.
>
> Bill discovered liquor could fuel his ego and dreams of glory in civilian life as he tried to prove to the world he was important. Bill was drinking alcoholically within four years, and by 1922 he was unable to control his drinking, suffering academic and professional consequences.
>
> Not only had Bill quickly become powerless over alcohol, but his life was becoming increasingly unmanageable, both hallmarks of Step One.

By the time I had completed the course, I knew the law was not for me. **The inviting maelstrom of Wall Street had me in its grip**. Business and financial leaders were my heroes. Out of this ally of drink and speculation, I commenced to forge the weapon that one day would turn in its flight like a boomerang and all but cut me to ribbons. Living modestly, my wife and I saved $1,000. It went into certain securities, then cheap and rather unpopular. I rightly imagined that they would someday have a great rise. I failed to persuade my broker friends to send me out looking over factories and managements, but my wife and I decided to go anyway. I had developed a theory that most people lost money in stocks through ignorance of markets. I discovered many more reasons later on.

We gave up our positions and off we roared on a motorcycle, the sidecar stuffed with tent, blankets, a change of clothes, and three huge volumes of a financial reference service. Our friends thought a lunacy commission should be appointed. Perhaps they were right. **I had had some success at speculation**, so we had a little money, but we once worked on a farm for a month to avoid drawing on our small capital. That was the last honest manual labor on my part for many a day.

We covered the whole eastern United States in a year. At the end of it, my reports to Wall Street procured me a position there and the use of a large expense account. The exercise of an option brought in more money, leaving us with a profit of several thousand dollars for that year.

For the next few years **fortune threw money and applause my way**. **I had arrived**. My judgment and ideas were followed by many to the tune of paper millions. The great boom of the late twenties was seething and swelling. **Drink was taking an important and exhilarating part in my life**. There was loud talk in the jazz places uptown. Everyone spent in thousands and chattered in millions. Scoffers could scoff and be damned. I made a host of fair-weather friends.

My drinking assumed more serious proportions, continuing all day and almost every night. The remonstrances of my friends terminated in a row and **I became a lone wolf**. There were many unhappy scenes in our sumptuous apartment. There had been **no real infidelity**, for loyalty to my wife, helped at times by extreme drunkenness, kept me out of those scrapes.

In 1929 I contracted golf fever. We went at once to the country, my wife to applaud while I started out to overtake Walter Hagen. **Liquor caught up with me** much faster than I came up behind Walter. **I began to be jittery in the morning**. Golf permitted drinking every day and every night. It was fun to carom around the exclusive course which had inspired such awe in me as a lad. I acquired the impeccable coat of tan one sees upon the well-to-do. The local banker watched me whirl fat checks in and out of his till with amused skepticism.

Abruptly **in October 1929 hell broke loose on the New York stock exchange**. After one of those days of inferno, I wobbled from a hotel bar to a brokerage office. It was eight o'clock—five hours after the market closed. The ticker still clattered. I was staring at an inch of the tape which bore the inscription XYZ-32. It had been 52 that morning. **I was finished** and so were many friends. The papers reported men jumping to death from the towers of High Finance.

That disgusted me. I would not jump. **I went back to the bar**. My friends had dropped several million since ten o'clock—so what? Tomorrow was another day. As I drank, the old fierce determination to win came back.

> The crash of the stock market at the end of the Roaring Twenties in 1929 drove many to suicide, but it drove Bill to the bottle. Alcohol soothed his anger and fear over his financial ruin. Displaying symptoms of daily alcohol withdrawal tremors and drinking around the clock confirmed he had become a hopeless alcoholic twelve years after he took his first drink.

Next morning I telephoned a friend in Montreal. He had plenty of money left and thought **I had better go to Canada**. By the following spring we were living in our accustomed style. I felt like Napoleon returning from Elba. No St. Helena for me! **But drinking caught up with me again** and my generous friend had to let me go. This time **we stayed broke**.

We went to live with my wife's parents. I found a job; then lost it as the result of a brawl with a taxi driver. Mercifully, no one could guess that **I was to have no real employment for five years**, **or hardly draw a sober breath**.

> After the market crash in 1929, Bill and Lois could no longer afford their apartment and moved in with Lois's parents at 182 Clinton Street in Brooklyn Heights, where they stayed until 1939. During that time, Lois's mother died and her father remarried and moved away. No longer able to afford the rent, Bill and Lois began a two-year period of moving from house to house staying with friends. By Lois' count, it amounted to fifty-four moves. In 1941, after 23 years of marriage, they moved into their first home in Bedford Hills, NY, which they named Bill-Lo's Break and later renamed Stepping Stones.

My wife began to work in a department store, coming home exhausted to find me drunk. I became an unwelcome hanger-on at brokerage places.

Failing to get sober during a geographic cure attempt, Bill's drinking worsened as he became unable to work. His wife had to support the family as he sat at home drinking day and night. Most alcoholics progress through their illness like Bill. They squirm and struggle, hoping to recover in different towns or diverse employment, but never succeed.

Liquor ceased to be a luxury; it became a necessity. Bathtub gin, two bottles a day, and often three, got to be routine. Sometimes a small deal would net a few hundred dollars, and I would pay my bills at the bars and delicatessens. **This went on endlessly**, and I began to waken very early in the morning shaking violently. A tumbler full of gin followed by half a dozen bottles of beer would be required if I were to eat any breakfast. Nevertheless, **I still thought I could control the situation**, and there were periods of sobriety which renewed my wife's hope.

> Our peculiar alcoholic mental twist forces us to deny the obvious unmanageability of our life, which is the second half of the first step. We have long known we were powerless over alcohol, but still delude ourselves into thinking our life is manageable—or will be tomorrow. It is this second part of the first step that seems to give many of us the most trouble.

Gradually **things got worse**. The house was taken over by the mortgage holder, my mother-in-law died, my wife and father-in-law became ill.

Then I got a promising business opportunity. Stocks were at the low point of 1932, and I had somehow formed a group to buy. I was to share generously in the profits. Then I went on a prodigious bender, and that chance vanished.

> Bill's stock scheme failure was described perfectly by Dr. Silkworth in "The Doctor's Opinion" when he said: "I have had many men who had, for example, worked a period of months on some problem or business deal which was to be settled on a certain date, favorably to them. They took a drink a day or so

prior to the date, and then the phenomenon of craving at once became paramount to all other interests so that the important appointment was not met." [Doctor's Opinion, p.xxvii]

No matter how hard we try to manage our lives, once we pour alcohol on it, we become powerless and our life always gets worse. Welcome to Step One.

I woke up. This had to be stopped. **I saw I could not take so much as one drink**. I was through forever. Before then, I had written lots of sweet promises, but my wife happily observed that **this time I meant business**. And so I did.

Shortly afterward **I came home drunk. There had been no fight. Where had been my high resolve?** I simply didn't know. It hadn't even come to mind. Someone had pushed a drink my way, and I had taken it. **Was I crazy?** I began to wonder, for such an appalling lack of perspective seemed near being just that.

Renewing my resolve, **I tried again**. Some time passed, and confidence began to be replaced by cock-sureness. I could laugh at the gin mills. Now I had what it takes! One day I walked into a cafe to telephone. **In no time I was beating on the bar** asking myself how it happened. As the whisky rose to my head **I told myself I would manage better next time**, but I might as well get good and drunk then. And I did.

Bill's peculiar mental twist in the above paragraph is reflected in the four stories by the Jaywalker, the Man of Thirty, Jim the car salesman and Fred the accountant in "More About Alcoholism." All those men failed to accept the first step; they suddenly thought they could take a drink after a spell of abstinence and control the outcome. Even if we alcoholics accept the fact that we are powerless over our drinking, most of us simply give up and yield to our obsession and craving after indulging. We stop trying to control our drinking and cease fighting, still believing that the next time will be different.

Did you ever ask "Was I crazy?"

60

The remorse, horror and hopelessness of the next morning are unforgettable. The courage to do battle was not there. My brain raced uncontrollably and there was a terrible sense of impending calamity. I hardly dared cross the street, lest I collapse and be run down by an early morning truck, for it was scarcely daylight. An all-night place supplied me with a dozen glasses of ale. My writhing nerves were stilled at last. A morning paper told me the market had gone to hell again. Well, so had I. The market would recover, but I wouldn't. That was a hard thought. **Should I kill myself? No—not now**. Then a **mental fog** settled down. **Gin would fix that**. So two bottles, and—**oblivion**.

> Bill is in the terminal stage of his alcoholism, close to the jumping off place where we are faced with the ultimate decision: death or destruction by our own hand to end our misery, or admitting complete defeat and becoming willing to accept help. This is the crux of Step One.
>
> *Did you ever feel the remorse, horror and hopelessness of the next morning? Did your mind ever race uncontrollably? Did you ever seek oblivion?*

The mind and body are marvelous mechanisms, for mine endured this agony two more years. Sometimes I stole from my wife's slender purse when the morning terror and madness were on me. Again **I swayed dizzily before an open window, or the medicine cabinet where there was poison**, cursing myself for a weakling.

There were **flights from city to country and back**, as my wife and **I sought escape**. Then came the night when the physical and mental torture was so hellish I feared I would burst through my window, sash and all. Somehow I managed to drag my mattress to a lower floor, lest I suddenly leap. A doctor came with a heavy sedative. **Next day found me drinking both gin and sedative**. This combination soon landed me on the rocks. People **feared for my sanity**. So did I. I could eat little or nothing when drinking, and I was forty pounds under weight.

My brother-in-law is a physician, and through his kindness and that of my mother I was placed in a nationally known hospital for the mental and physical rehabilitation of alcoholics. Under the so-called **belladonna treatment** my brain cleared. Hydrotherapy and mild exercise helped much. Best of all, I met a kind doctor who explained that though certainly selfish and foolish, I had been seriously ill, bodily and mentally.

> Fortunately for Bill and for all of A.A., he was cared for by a remarkable physician who believed alcoholism was a medical illness rather than a moral failing, which was not the accepted dogma in the medical community of that time. Unfortunately, no known medical treatments were available to help alcoholics recover. The alcoholic of the 1930s was truly doomed to die, and everyone knew it.

It relieved me somewhat to learn that **in alcoholics the will is amazingly weakened when it comes to combating liquor**, though it often remains strong in other respects. My incredible behavior in the face of a desperate desire to stop was explained. Understanding myself now, I fared forth in high hope. For three or four months the goose hung high. I went to town regularly and even made a little money. **Surely this was the answer—self-knowledge**.

But it was not, for the frightful day came when **I drank once more**. The curve of my declining moral and bodily health fell off like a ski-jump. After a time I returned to the hospital. This was the finish, the curtain, it seemed to me. My weary and despairing wife was informed that **it would all end with heart failure during delirium tremens, or I would develop a wet brain**, perhaps within a year. **We would soon have to give me over to the undertaker or the asylum**.

> Even when we are at the worst stage of our drinking, somehow down deep we know that we are slowly killing ourselves. We know in our head we won't be able to stop once we take that first drink, but it doesn't matter; we drink regardless because we can't help ourselves. That is the cruel tragedy of our illness—self-knowledge is useless. It is never powerful enough to keep us from taking that first drink.

They did not need to tell me. I knew, and almost welcomed the idea. It was a devastating blow to my pride. I, who had thought so well of myself and my abilities, of my capacity to surmount obstacles, was cornered at last. Now I was to plunge into the dark, joining that endless procession of sots who had gone on before. I thought of my poor wife. There had been much happiness after all. What would I not give to make amends. But that was over now.

No words can tell of the loneliness and despair I found in that bitter morass of self-pity. Quicksand stretched around me in all directions. **I had met my match**. I had been overwhelmed. **Alcohol was my master**.

Trembling, I stepped from the hospital a broken man. **Fear sobered me for a bit**. Then came the **insidious insanity of that first drink**, and on Armistice Day 1934, **I was off again**. Everyone became resigned to the certainty that I would have to be shut up somewhere, or would stumble along to a miserable end. How dark it is before the dawn! In reality that was the beginning of my last debauch. **I was soon to be catapulted into what I like to call the fourth dimension of existence**. I was to know happiness, peace, and usefulness, in a way of life that is incredibly more wonderful as time passes.

> Bill gives us another teaser. He is standing at the edge of the abyss, but plants a seed of hope: How dark before the dawn! Most of us felt as Bill did when we were at the end of our line, full or fear, misery, shame and depression, praying someone or something would emerge to save us.

> *Did you ever feel lonely? Did you ever feel fear?*

Near the end of that bleak November, I sat drinking in my kitchen. With a certain satisfaction I reflected there was enough gin concealed about the house to carry me through that night and the next day. My wife was at work. I wondered whether I dared hide a full bottle of gin near the head of our bed. I would need it before daylight.

My musing was interrupted by the telephone. The cheery voice of an **old school friend** asked if he might come over. **He was sober**. It was years since I could remember his coming to New York in that condition. I was amazed. Rumor had it that he had been committed for alcoholic insanity. I wondered how he had escaped. Of course he would have dinner, and then I could drink openly with him. Unmindful of his welfare, I thought only of recapturing the spirit of other days. There was that time we had chartered an airplane to complete a jag! His coming was an oasis in this dreary desert of futility. The very thing— an oasis! Drinkers are like that.

The door opened and he stood there, fresh-skinned and glowing. There was something about his eyes. He was inexplicably different. **What had happened?**

I pushed a drink across the table. He refused it. Disappointed but curious, I wondered what had got into the fellow. He wasn't himself.

"Come, **what's all this about?** I queried. He looked straight at me. Simply, but smilingly, he said, "**I've got religion**."

I was aghast. So that was it—last summer an alcoholic crackpot; now, I suspected, a little cracked about religion. He had that starry-eyed look. Yes, the old boy was on fire all right. But bless his heart, let him rant! Besides, my gin would last longer than his preaching.

But he did no ranting. In a matter of fact way he told how two men had appeared in court, persuading the judge to suspend his commitment. They had told of **a simple religious idea and a practical program of action**. That was two months ago and the result was self-evident. **It worked!**

He had come to pass his experience along to me—if I cared to have it. I was shocked, but interested. Certainly **I was interested**. I had to be, **for I was hopeless**.

He talked for hours. Childhood memories rose before me. I could almost hear the sound of the preacher's voice as I sat, on still Sundays, way over there on the hillside; there was that proffered temperance pledge I never signed; my grandfather's good natured contempt of some church fold and their doings; his insistence that the spheres really had their music; but his denial of the preacher's right to tell him how he must listen; his fearlessness as he spoke of these things just before he died; these recollections welled up from the past. They made me swallow hard.

That war-time day in old Winchester Cathedral came back again.

I had always believed in a Power greater that myself. I had often pondered these things. **I was not an atheist**. Few people really are, for that means blind faith in the strange proposition that this universe originated in a cipher and aimlessly rushes nowhere.

My intellectual heroes, the chemists, the astronomers, even the evolutionists, suggested vast laws and forces at work. Despite contrary indications, I had little doubt that a might purpose and rhythm underlay all. How could there be so much of precise and immutable law, and no intelligence? **I simply had to believe in a Spirit of the Universe**, who knew neither time nor limitation. But that was as far as I had gone.

With ministers, and the world's religions, I parted right there. **When they talked of a God personal to me**, who was love, superhuman strength and direction, I became irritated and **my mind snapped shut** against such a theory.

> Bill's excitement while his old childhood friend Ebby Thacher visited him allowed him to pay attention to Ebby's story. After Ebby told Bill he had gotten religion, somehow Bill continued to listen to him, rather than dismissing him or getting too drunk to remember what Ebby was telling him.

> Bill was agnostic, meaning he was on the fence about a personal God. His discussion with Ebby caused him to reflect on what God, or a Spirit of the Universe actually meant to him.

> All of us who stick with A.A. are forced to have the same type of honest, internal discussion with ourselves on what we can and cannot believe about God, Higher Power, religion, the

church, and what spirituality means to us.

Bill's religious ruminating reflects Step Two: Came to believe that a Power greater than ourselves could restore us to sanity, and easily leads to Step Three: Made a decision to turn our will and our lives over to the care of God as we understood him.

Is there something out there or within ourselves, which is intangible, spiritual or religious in nature, that we can use to help us overcome our alcoholism?

What was your reaction to religion, the church and God?

To Christ I conceded the certainty of a great man, not too closely followed by those who claimed Him. His moral teaching—most excellent. For myself, I had adopted those parts which seemed convenient and not too difficult; the rest I disregarded.

Most of us, like Bill, even if we are atheist or agnostic, recognize that many of the Christian teachings reflect the moral values embedded in the principles of 12 Steps.

The wars which had been fought, the burnings and chicanery that religious dispute had facilitated, made me sick. I honestly doubted whether, on balance, the religions of mankind had done any good. Judging from what I had seen in Europe and since, the power of God in human affairs was negligible, the Brotherhood of Man a grim jest. If there was a Devil, he seemed the Boss Universal, and he certainly had me.

But **my friend sat before me, and he made the point-blank declaration that God had done for him what he could not do for himself. His human will had failed**. Doctors had pronounced him incurable. Society was about to lock him up. Like myself, **he had admitted complete defeat. Then he had**, in effect, **been raised from the dead**, suddenly taken from the scrap heap to a level of life better than the best he had ever known!

Had this power originated in him? Obviously it had not. There had been no more power in him than there was in me at that minute; and this was none at all.

That floored me. **It began to look as though religious people were right after all**. Here was something at work in a human heart which had done the impossible. My ideas about miracles were drastically revised right then. Never mind the musty past; **here sat a miracle** directly across the kitchen table. He shouted great tidings.

I saw that my friend was much more than inwardly reorganized. He was on different footing. **His roots grasped a new soil**.

Despite the living example of my friend **there remained in me the vestiges of my old prejudice**. The word God still aroused a certain antipathy. When the thought was expressed that there might be a God personal to me this feeling was intensified. I didn't like the idea. I could go for such conceptions as Creative Intelligence, Universal Mind or Spirit of Nature but **I resisted the thought of a Czar of the Heavens**, however loving His sway might be. I have since talked with scores of men who felt the same way.

My friend suggested what then seemed a novel idea. He said, "**Why don't you choose your own conception of God?**"

That statement hit me hard. It melted the icy intellectual mountain in whose shadow I had lived and shivered many years. I stood in the sunlight at last.

It was only a matter of being willing to believe in a power greater than myself. Nothing more was required of me to make my beginning. I saw that growth could start from that point. Upon a foundation of complete willingness I might build what I saw in my friend. Would I have it? Of course I would!

> In the above paragraph Bill takes Step Two: Came to believe that a power greater than ourselves could restore us to sanity.

Thus was I convinced that God is concerned with us humans when we want Him enough. At long last I saw, I felt, I believed.

Scales of pride and prejudice fell from my eyes. A new world came into view.

Ebby visited Bill in late November, 1934, just two months after he got sober in the Oxford Group he had recently joined. He returned several times to visit Bill, once bringing with him the non-alcoholic Sheppard Cornell, and they both spoke to Bill about the benefits of the Oxford Group, a non-denominational Christian organization.

Despite Bill's enthusiasm about Ebby's religious conversion experience, Bill continued to drink. On December 11, 1934, Bill was admitted drunk to Towns Hospital for the third and last time. Three days later, on December 14, he had his second spiritual experience—his hot flash event. His first spiritual experience was during his 1918 visit to Winchester Cathedral in London during the war, where he felt the presence of God.

Note what happened to Bill's prejudice against "their God" when he began to apply his own concept of God. Did you know that "nothing more was required of me" to make my beginning than willingness, or a willingness to believe?

The real significance of my **experience in the Cathedral** burst upon me. **For a brief moment, I had needed and wanted God**. There had been a humble willingness to have Him with me—**and He came**. **But soon the sense of His presence had been blotted out by worldly clamors**, mostly those within myself. And so it had been ever since. How blind I had been.

Bill W.'s first spiritual, or religious experience occurred at the Winchester Cathedral he mentioned on the first page of "Bill's Story."

Bill described that event in more detail in several drafts of his story that predated the final Multilith Edition of the Big Book. On lines 209 to 233 of "W.G. Wilson's Original Story," Bill wrote:

"I stood in Winchester Cathedral... with head bowed, for

something had touched me then I had never felt before... Where could the Deity be? Could there be such a thing? Where now was the God of the preachers, the thought of which used to make me so uncomfortable when they talked about Him? A feeling of despair settled down on me. Where was He? Why did he not come?

And suddenly in that moment of darkness, He was there. I felt an all enveloping, comforting, powerful presence. Tears stood in my eyes, and as I looked about, I saw on the faces of others nearby, that they too had glimpsed the Great Reality...

And after going outside the cathedral, reading the doggerel on the tombstone and seeing the airplane squadron flying overhead, I cried to myself 'Here's to adventure' and the feeling of being in the Great Presence disappeared, never to return for many years."

At the hospital I was separated from alcohol for the last time. Treatment seemed wise, for I showed signs of delirium tremens.

There **I humbly offered myself to God**, as I then I understood Him, to do with me as He would. **I placed myself unreservedly under His care and direction**. I admitted for the first time that of myself I was nothing; that without Him I was lost. **I ruthlessly faced my sins and became willing to have my new-found Friend take them away**, root and branch. **I have not had a drink since**.

> In the above paragraph Bill takes Steps 3, 6 and 7: Made a decision to turn our will and our lives over to the care of God as we understood him (Step 3); Were entirely ready to have God remove all these defects of character (Step 6); and Humbly asked Him to remove our shortcomings (Step 7).

My schoolmate visited me, and I fully acquainted him with my problems and deficiencies. We made a list of people I had hurt or toward whom I felt resentment. I expressed my entire willingness to approach these individuals, admitting my wrong. Never was I to be critical of them. I was to right all such matters to the utmost of my ability.

> The above paragraph reflects Steps 4, 5, 8 and 9: Made a searching and fearless moral inventory of ourselves (Step 4); Admitted to God, to ourselves and to another human being the exact nature of our wrongs (Step 5); Made a list of all persons we had harmed, and became willing to make amends to them all (Step 8); Made direct amends to such people wherever possible, except when to do so would injure them or others (Step 9).

I was to test my thinking by the **new God-consciousness within**. Common sense would thus become uncommon sense. I was to sit quietly when in doubt, asking only for direction and strength to meet my problems as He would have me. Never was I to pray for myself, except as my requests bore on my usefulness to others. Then only might I expect to receive. But that would be in great measure.

> The above paragraph reflects Steps 11: Sought through prayer and meditation to improve our conscious contact with God as we understood Him, praying only for knowledge of His will for us and the power to carry that out.

> *Doesn't Bill essentially take the First through the Eleventh Steps at this time? Notice how Bill was instructed to find God's will and pray. Has your common sense become "uncommon sense" in manner?*

My friend promised when these things were done I would enter upon a new relationship with my Creator; that I would have the elements of a way of living which answered all my problems. **Belief in the power of God, plus enough willingness, honesty and humility to establish and maintain the new order of things, were the essential requirements.**

Simple, but not easy; a price had to be paid. **It meant destruction of self-centeredness**. I must turn in all things to the Father of Light who presides over us all.

These were **revolutionary and drastic proposals**, but the moment I fully accepted them, **the effect was electric**. There was a sense of victory, followed by such a peace and serenity as I had never known. There was utter confidence. **I felt lifted up, as though the great clean wind of a mountain top blew through and through**. God comes to most men gradually, but His impact on me was sudden and profound.

For a moment I was alarmed, and called my friend, the doctor, to ask if I were still sane. He listened in wonder as I talked.

Finally he shook his head saying, "Something has happened to you I don't understand. But you had better hang on to it. Anything is better than the way you were." The good doctor now sees many men who have such experiences. He knows that they are real.

We will never know what caused Bill to have his white light, hot flash episode in Towns Hospital. Was it due to the hallucinatory effects of his belladonna treatment? Did he dream it? Did he make it up? Was he hallucinating for some other reason? Was he really touched by the hand of God? Who knows? The only thing that mattered was that Bill believed God had reached out to him personally and directly.

On December 15, while still in Towns Hospital and one day after his white flash conversion experience, Ebby brought Bill a copy of *The Varieties of Religious Experience* by William James.

As Bill read the book, he discovered James's beliefs about spiritual experiences and how they might totally transform a person's life. Conversion experiences could come in many forms, ranging from sudden and profound insights, as Wilson had seemingly experienced the day prior, to more gradual changes over time. What struck Wilson most clearly from the book was that those experiences nearly always came to people in dire circumstances, such as those in the grips of severe anguish or a calamity.

The book listed three key elements Bill later recognized were necessary for recovery through a conversion experience: 1) calamity or complete defeat in some vital area of life, 2) admission of that defeat, and 3) an appeal to a higher power for help.

While I lay in the hospital the thought came that there were **thousands of hopeless alcoholics** who might be glad to have what had been so freely given me. **Perhaps I could help some of them. They in turn might work with others**.

My friend had emphasized the absolute necessity of demonstrating these principles in all my affairs. Particularly was it **imperative to work with others** as he had worked with me. **Faith without works was dead**, he said. And how appallingly true for the alcoholic!

> The above two paragraphs reflect Step 12: Having had a spiritual awakening as the result of these Steps, we tried to carry this message to alcoholics, and to practice these principles in all our affairs.

> What makes A.A. unique is one alcoholic passing on the message of hope and recovery one-on-one to another alcoholic.

For **if an alcoholic failed to perfect and enlarge his spiritual life through work and self-sacrifice for others, he could not survive the certain trials and low spots ahead**. If he did not work, he would surely drink again, and if he drank, he would surely die. Then faith would be dead indeed. With us it is just like that.

> What is truly amazing is that Bill did not hoard his sudden gift of sobriety. Somehow he understood that staying sober required him to pass on his experience to others, just as Ebby had passed his experience to him. Bill never tried to rationalize his way out of his obligation to help others.

> Trying to carry *this* message—that we can recover from our hopeless state of mind and body—to *alcoholics* is a mandate of our Twelfth Step.

Bill really takes the Twelfth Step on page 14, doesn't he? The Program worked in all of Bill's affairs.

My wife and I abandoned ourselves with enthusiasm to the idea of helping other alcoholics to a solution of their problems. It was fortunate, for my old business associates remained skeptical for a year and a half, during which I found little work. **I was not too well at the time**, and was **plagued by waves of self-pity and resentment**. This sometimes nearly drove me back to drink, but I soon found that **when all other measures failed, work with another alcoholic would save the day**. Many times I have gone to my old hospital in despair. On talking to a man there, I would be amazingly lifted up and set on my feet. **It is a design for living that works in rough going**.

> We know today that Bill W. probably suffered from the Post Acute Withdrawal Syndrome (PAWS), which is common after abstinence and due to our brain chemistry gradually returning to normal.
>
> Symptoms include mood swings, anxiety, irritability, fatigue, low enthusiasm, poor concentration and disturbed sleep patterns, and can last from a few months to as long as five years, as mine did.
>
> Directing our energy to becoming more deeply involved in A.A. and trying to carry the message of hope and recovery to others worked for both Bill W. and Dr. Bob, who had to deal with his constant obsession to drink for almost three years after he stopped drinking.

We commenced to make many fast friends and **a fellowship has grown up among us** of which it is a wonderful thing to feel a part. **The joy of living we really have, even under pressure and difficulty**. I have seen hundreds of families set their feet in the path that really goes somewhere; have seen the most impossible domestic situations righted; feuds and bitterness of all sorts wiped out. I have seen men come out of asylums and resume a vital place in the lives of their families and communities.

Business and professional men have regained their standing. There is scarcely any form of trouble and misery which has not been overcome among us. In one western city and its environs there are one thousand of us and our families. **We meet frequently so that newcomers may find the fellowship they seek**. At these informal gatherings one may often see from 50 to 200 persons. We are growing in numbers and power.

An alcoholic in his cups is an unlovely creature. Our struggles with them are variously strenuous, comic, and tragic. **One poor chap committed suicide in my home**. He could not, or would not see our way of life.

> Bill C., a Canadian lawyer and compulsive professional bridge player, lived with the Wilsons at their Clinton Street home for almost a year. In October, 1936 after returning home from visiting Fitz Mayo and others in Maryland, Bill opened the door to the strong smell of the natural gas that had ended the "poor chaps" life. Over the next few months, Bill and Lois discovered that he had been selling off their good dress clothes to finance his drinking and gambling.

There is, however, a vast amount of fun about it all. I suppose some would be shocked at our seeming worldliness and levity. **But just underneath there is deadly earnestness**. Faith has to work twenty-four hours a day in and through us, or we perish.

Most of us feel **we need look no further for Utopia**. We have it with us right here and now. Each day my friend's simple talk in our kitchen multiplies itself in a widening circle of peace on earth and good will to men.

Bill W., co-founder of A.A., died January 24, 1971.

> Bill recognized that just because we get sober, it doesn't mean life will treat us any differently. We will be dealing with the same type of problems sober that we disregarded while we were drunk. The good news is that it is a lot easier to deal with

life's slings and arrows sober than it is drunk.

Our 12 Step program is the gateway to learning how to live life on life's terms—sober.

What was of particular significance to you in this chapter? What did you find that you could not accept?

Chapter 2

THERE IS A SOLUTION

We, of Alcoholics Anonymous, know thousands of men and women who were once just as hopeless as Bill. Nearly all have recovered. They have solved the drink problem.

We are average Americans. All sections of this country and many of its occupations are represented, as well as many political, economic, social, and religious backgrounds. **We are people who normally would not mix. But there exists among us a fellowship**, a friendliness, and an understanding which is indescribably wonderful. **We are like the passengers of a great liner the moment after rescue from shipwreck** when camaraderie, joyousness and democracy pervade the vessel from steerage to Captain's table. Unlike the feelings of the ship's passengers, however, our joy in escape from disaster does not subside as we go our individual ways. The **feeling of having shared in a common peril is one element in the powerful cement which binds us**. But that in itself would never have held us together as we are now joined.

The tremendous fact for every one of us is that **we have discovered a common solution. We have a way out** on which we can absolutely agree, and upon which we can join in brotherly and harmonious action. This is the great news this book carries to those who suffer from alcoholism.

Soon after we join A.A. we are drawn closer to our fellows as we recognize how much we have in common. None of us could control our drinking, and our lives ended up a mess in one way or another. It takes time to appreciate that we also have a common solution beyond the support and camaraderie of the fellowship. We have discovered a new design for living, which consists of the 12 Step program and the Big Book instructions and testimony.

It is farfetched to say that all of us absolutely agree on the way out, but most of us agree on the basic tenant of the A.A.

program: our need to connect with the human power of the fellowship, and our additional need to connect with some sort of spiritual force or power of our own understanding and acceptance.

This is what the first three steps are all about. Those three steps are spiritual in nature, requiring nothing more than an honest willingness to admit defeat and be open to some type of solution that has worked for millions of alcoholics and might work for us.

What is your reaction to the membership of A.A.?

An illness of this sort—and **we have come to believe it an illness—** involves those about us in a way no other human sickness can. If a person has cancer all are sorry for him and no one is angry or hurt. But not so with **the alcoholic illness**, for with it there goes annihilation of all the things worthwhile in life. **It engulfs all whose lives touch the sufferer's**. It brings misunderstanding, fierce resentment, financial insecurity, disgusted friends and employers, warped lives of blameless children, sad wives and parents—anyone can increase the list.

Most of us initially believed that our drinking did not affect anyone but ourselves. After all, we were the ones who were drunk, and we couldn't make anyone else drunk. At the end we usually isolated, hiding in dark corners as we quietly drank ourselves into oblivion.

So what if we forgot a few appointments, paid our bills late if at all, missed work from time to time, emotionally neglected our spouses and children, ignored our friends, wasted money and had a head full of anger and fear? It's not that big a deal, and things could always be worse.

Denying our selfish and self-centered behavior was just another element of our illness, as was our apathy and self-pity which kept us in defiance over the extent of our illness and discouraged us from changing.

Did your alcoholism engulf all whose lives touched the sufferer's?

77

What was their reaction? Did you see how you can reach another alcoholic?

We hope this volume will inform and comfort those who are, or who may be affected. There are many.

Highly competent psychiatrists who have dealt with us have found it sometimes impossible to persuade an alcoholic to discuss his situation without reserve. Strangely enough, wives, parents and intimate friends usually find us even more unapproachable than do the psychiatrist and the doctor.

But the ex-problem drinker who has found this solution, who is properly armed with facts about himself, **can generally win the entire confidence of another alcoholic in a few hours.** Until such an understanding is reached, little or nothing can be accomplished.

That the man who is making the approach has had the same difficulty, that he obviously knows what he is talking about, that his whole deportment shouts at the new prospect that **he is a man with a real answer**, that he has no attitude of Holier Than Thou, nothing whatever except the sincere desire to be helpful; that there are no fees to pay, no axes to grind, no people to please, no lectures to be endured—these are the conditions we have found most effective. After such an approach many take up their beds and walk again.

None of us makes a sole vocation of this work, nor do we think its effectiveness would be increased if we did. We feel that **elimination of our drinking is but a beginning. A much more important demonstration of our principles lies before us in our respective homes, occupations and affairs**. All of us spend much of our spare time in the sort of effort which we are going to describe. A few are fortunate enough to be so situated that they can give nearly all their time to the work.

If we keep on the way we are going there is little doubt that much good will result, but the surface of the problem would hardly be scratched. Those of us who live in large cities are overcome by the reflection that close by hundreds are dropping into oblivion every day. **Many could recover if they had the opportunity** we have enjoyed. **How then shall we present that which has been so freely given us?**

We have concluded to **publish an anonymous volume** setting forth the problem as we see it. We shall bring to the task our combined experience and knowledge. This should **suggest a useful program** for anyone concerned with a drinking problem.

> Nothing is more effective than speaking with a person who knows how we think and feel as an alcoholic. Since they have stood in our shoes we will listen to them, even if we do not agree with them.

> What we hear those who have gone before us say is that stopping drinking isn't our goal; it's becoming the person we, down deep, always wanted to be—a decent and honorable citizen of society.

> Of course this requires that we stop drinking, but more importantly, to begin to behave in ways that will allow us to better fit in among our fellows. That ideal behavior is reflected in the principles of the 12 Steps, to which we can aspire.

> Although the fellowship is necessary to guide and support us on our journey, there is an ebb and flow to it. A.A. members come and go, but our book *Alcoholics Anonymous* does not. It remains constant and available for us to use any time of day or night. Its message of hope and recovery remains consistent and undiluted.

Of necessity **there will have to be discussion of matters medical, psychiatric, social, and religious**. We are aware that **these matters are** from their very nature, **controversial**. Nothing would please us so much as to write a book which would contain no basis for contention or argument. We shall do our utmost to achieve that ideal. Most of us sense that real tolerance of other people's shortcomings and viewpoints and a respect for their opinions are attitudes which make us more useful to others.

Our very lives, as ex-problem drinkers, depend upon our constant thought of others and how we may help meet their needs.

You may already have asked yourself why it is that all of us became so very ill from drinking. Doubtless **you are curious to discover how and why**, in the face of expert opinion to the contrary, **we have recovered from a hopeless condition of mind and body**. If you are an alcoholic who wants to get over it, you may already be asking— "**What do I have to do?**"

It is the purpose of this book to answer such questions specifically. We shall tell you what we have done. Before going into a detailed discussion, it may be well to summarize some points as we see them.

How many times have people said to us: "I can take it or leave it alone. Why can't he?" "Why don't you drink like a gentleman or quit?" "That fellow can't handle his liquor." "Why don't you try beer and wine?" "Lay off the hard stuff." "His will power must be weak." "He could stop if he wanted to." "She's such a sweet girl, I should think he'd stop for her sake." "The doctor told him that if he ever drank again it would kill him, but there he is all lit up again."

Now these are commonplace observations on drinkers which we hear all the time. Back of them is a world of ignorance and misunderstanding. We see that these expressions refer to people whose reactions are very different from ours.

> Here is another Bill W. Big Book teaser that touts there is a solution for dealing with our alcoholism, and the answer will be revealed shortly, so keep on reading.
>
> *Note that on pg. 20 above the book answers the question, "What do I have to do?" Have you been asked the questions of pg. 20 by yourself or other people? What were the answers?*

Moderate drinkers have little trouble in giving up liquor entirely if they have good reason for it. They can take it or leave it alone. Then we have a certain type of **hard drinker**. He may have the habit badly

80

enough to gradually impair him physically and mentally. It may cause him to die a few years before his time. If a sufficiently strong reason— ill health, falling in love, change of environment, or the warning of a doctor—becomes operative, this man can also stop or moderate, although he may find it difficult and troublesome and may even need medical attention.

But **what about the real alcoholic?** He may start off as a moderate drinker; he may or may not become a continuous hard drinker; but **at some stage of his drinking career he begins to lose all control of his liquor consumption, once he starts to drink**.

Here is a fellow who has been puzzling you, especially in his lack of control. He does absurd, incredible, tragic things while drinking. He is a real **Dr. Jekyll and Mr. Hyde**. He is seldom mildly intoxicated. **He is always more or less insanely drunk**. His disposition while drinking resembles his normal nature but little. He may be one of the finest fellows in the world.

Yet let him drink for a day, and **he frequently becomes** disgustingly, and even dangerously **anti-social. He has a positive genius for getting tight at exactly the wrong moment**, particularly when some important decision must be made or engagement kept. He is often perfectly sensible and well balanced concerning everything except liquor, but in that respect he is incredibly dishonest and selfish. He often possesses special abilities, skills, and aptitudes, and has a promising career ahead of him. He uses his gifts to build up a bright outlook for his family and himself, and then pulls the structure down on his head by a senseless series of sprees.

He is the fellow who goes to bed so intoxicated he ought to sleep the clock around. Yet early next morning he searches madly for the bottle he misplaced the night before. If he can afford it, he may have liquor concealed all over his house to be certain no one gets his entire supply away from him to throw down the wastepipe. As matters grow worse, **he begins to use a combination of high-powered sedative and liquor to quiet his nerves** so he can go to work.

Then comes the day when he simply cannot make it and gets drunk all over again. Perhaps he goes to a doctor who gives him **morphine** or some **sedative** with which to taper off. Then **he begins to appear at hospitals and sanitariums**.

This is by no means a comprehensive picture of the **true alcoholic**, as our behavior patterns vary. But this description should identify him roughly.

> Most of us have progressed through the stages of moderate drinking into hard drinking before reaching our final stage of full-blown alcoholism. We yearn for the days before our alcoholism took hold. Why can't we go backwards in time and capacity?
>
> If we are doubly unfortunate, we started using drugs in addition to alcohol to change the way we felt, and help us forget that we have already passed the point of no return. We may or may not have been sentenced to rehabilitation, either by courts or family members. Regardless, nothing helped.
>
> *From your examination of yourself in the past weeks and your reading of this chapter, are you a "real alcoholic?" If not, why not? p. 21*
>
> *Did you have control over alcohol? Did you do absurd and incredible and tragic things while drinking? Were you a Jekyll and Hyde? p.21*

Why does he behave like this? If hundreds of experiences have shown him that one drink means another debacle with all its attendant suffering and humiliation, **why is it he takes that one drink?** Why can't he stay on the water wagon? What has become of the common sense and will power that he still sometimes displays with respect to other matters?

Perhaps **there never will be a full answer to these questions**. Opinions vary considerably as to why the alcoholic reacts differently from normal people.

We are not sure why, once a certain point is reached, little can be done for him. We cannot answer the riddle.

Because of advances in understanding the neurophysiology of addiction, medical researchers have a very good idea of why we take that first drink, and why we can't stop drinking afterwards.

Despite our extensive clinical knowledge of the chemical changes in our brain caused by addiction, that knowledge fails to help us stop drinking in any practical way. As Bill related in his story, self-knowledge is not the answer (Big Book, p.7).

Did the questions and observations on p.21 help you in answering the questions you have been writing and talking about?

For example: Why did we drink the way we did? Why do we take that one drink? Why can't we stay on the wagon? What has become of the common sense and the will power that we still sometimes display with respect to other matters?

Did you ask yourself these questions?

We know that while the alcoholic keeps away from drink, as he may do for months or years, he reacts much like other men. We are equally positive that **once he takes any alcohol whatever into his system, something happens, both in the bodily and mental sense, which makes it virtually impossible for him to stop**. The experience of any alcoholic will abundantly confirm this. These observations would be academic and pointless if our friend never took the first drink, thereby setting the terrible cycle in motion.

Therefore, **the main problem of the alcoholic centers in his mind**, rather than in his body. If you ask him why he started on that last bender, the chances are he will offer you any one of a hundred alibis. Sometimes these excuses have a certain plausibility, but none of them really makes sense in the light of the havoc an alcoholic's drinking bout creates. They sound like the philosophy of the man who, having a headache, beats himself on the head with a hammer so that he can't feel the ache.

If you draw this fallacious reasoning to the attention of an alcoholic, he will laugh it off, or become irritated and refuse to talk.

Once in a while he may tell the truth. And the truth, strange to say, is usually that **he has no more idea why he took that first drink than you have**. Some drinkers have excuses with which they are satisfied part of the time. But in their hearts they really do not know why they do it. **Once this malady has a real hold, they are a baffled lot. There is the obsession that somehow, someday, they will beat the game**. But they often suspect they are down for the count.

How true this is, few realize. In a vague way their families and friends sense that these drinkers are abnormal, but everybody hopefully awaits the day when the sufferer will rouse himself from his lethargy and assert his power of will. The tragic truth is that if the man be a real alcoholic, the happy day may not arrive. He has lost control. **At a certain point in the drinking of every alcoholic, he passes into a state where the most powerful desire to stop drinking is of absolutely no avail**. This tragic situation has already arrived in practically every case long before it is suspected.

The fact is that **most alcoholics, for reasons yet obscure, have lost the power of choice in drink**. Our so-called will power becomes practically nonexistent. We are unable, at certain times, to bring into our consciousness with sufficient force the memory of the suffering and humiliation of even a week or month ago. **We are without defense against the first drink**.

> Once again, through repetition, we are reminded that we have an illness of both mind and body, just as Dr. Silkworth observed in "The Doctor's Opinion."
>
> Our obsession to drink is clearly centered in our mind. Our allergic reaction to alcohol is centered in our body. Despite our explanations and excuses, we really do know why we take that first drink—we don't want to feel the emotional pain of the moment. It doesn't matter why we are hurting, or who caused it. The only thing that matters is getting immediate relief.

Since alcohol provided us with a rapid reprieve in the past, why would we seek any other solution? When the alcohol later stopped working, we were astonished, angry and disbelieving.

Yet we continued to believe in our hearts that just because alcohol didn't work the last time to change the way we felt, it would surely work this time. We will beat the game because we deserve to win. With this type of thinking, we remain stuck on Step One.

Had you lost the power of choice described on p. 24?

The almost certain consequences that follow taking even a glass of beer do not crowd into the mind to deter us. If these thoughts occur, they are hazy and readily supplanted with **the old threadbare idea that this time we shall handle ourselves like other people**. There is a complete failure of the kind of defense that keeps one from putting his hand on a **hot stove**.

The alcoholic may say to himself in the most casual way, "**It won't burn me this time, so here's how!**" Or perhaps he doesn't think at all. How often have some of us begun to drink in this nonchalant way, and after the third or fourth, pounded on the bar and said to ourselves, "For God's sake, how did I ever get started again?" Only to have that thought supplanted by "Well, I'll stop with the sixth drink." Or **"What's the use anyhow?"**

> Driven by false hope and insane thinking, we readily and willingly delude ourselves into believing the next time we take a drink things will be different. If our hand was burned on that first stove, we'll move over here and try to see if we'll get burned on this other hot stove, and on and on.
>
> When our hand emerges black and scarred from hundreds of stovetop burners, instead of being convinced we can't drink normally, we give up and give in to the next drink anyway, adopting the fatalistic attitude that since we are doomed, why not just drink our fear and woe away once again?

When this sort of thinking is fully established in an individual with alcoholic tendencies, **he has probably placed himself beyond human aid**, **and unless locked up, may die or go permanently insane**. These stark and ugly facts have been confirmed by legions of alcoholics throughout history. But for the grace of God, there would have been thousands more convincing demonstrations. So many want to stop but cannot.

There is a solution. Almost none of us liked the self-searching, the leveling of our pride, the confession of shortcomings which the process requires for its successful consummation. But **we saw that it really worked in others**, and we had come to believe in the hopelessness and futility of life as we had been living it. When, therefore, we were approached by those in whom the problem had been solved, **there was nothing left for us but to pick up the simple kit of spiritual tools laid at our feet**. We have found much of heaven and we have been **rocketed into a fourth dimension of existence** of which we had not even dreamed.

> The Big Book keeps telling us there is a solution for our alcoholism, and when we attend A.A. meetings we hear that same message. Looking around us in the rooms, we see so many alcoholics who appear to have happily recovered, and we can't help being curious as to how they did it.
>
> Our book says all we need to do is to pick up the simple kit of spiritual tools laid at our feet. Personally, I never had anything laid at my feet and I was never rocketed anywhere, but I did come to slowly comprehend the basic tenets of the A.A. program.
>
> Bill W. does not define, identify or list any kit of spiritual tools in A.A. He does suggest that once we have completed all twelve steps, we will have had a spiritual awakening, but we won't be receiving any toolbox at our graduation.
>
> Some oldtimers have suggested that the A.A. kit of spiritual

tools consists of two items which reflect the dual power we need for sobriety and our new way of life.

The first item in our toolbox is the *Fellowship*, which consists of a home group, sponsor, sponsees, A.A. meeting attendance and service work.

The second item in our toolbox is our *Design For Living*, as outlined in the Big Book and the 12 Steps.

These are the tools, or the *power* we need for recovery. The power of the Fellowship is human; the power of the Big Book and 12 Steps is spiritual.

Grasping and using those two powers may not rocket us anywhere, but they will slowly lead us into a new sober and satisfying life, which is completely different from our old life.

The **great fact is** just this, and nothing less: That **we have had deep and effective spiritual experiences [see Appendix II] which have revolutionized our whole attitude toward life, toward our fellows and toward God's universe**. The central fact of our lives today is the absolute certainty that **our Creator has entered into our hearts** and lives in a way which is indeed miraculous. He has commenced to accomplish those things for us which we could never do by ourselves.

If you are as seriously alcoholic as we were, we believe **there is no middle-of-the-road solution**. We were in a position where life was becoming impossible, and if we had passed into the region from which there is no return through human aid, **we had but two alternatives**: One was **to go on to the bitter end**, blotting out the consciousness of our intolerable situation as best we could; **and the other, to accept spiritual help**. This we did because we honestly wanted to, and were willing to make the effort.

Go to "There is a Solution" on page 25. Read "The great fact is just this and nothing less: that we have had deep and effective spiritual experiences." Read and understand the rest of that paragraph and Appendix II because it is an outstanding summary of what happens in the program. Our alternative to the A.A. solution is to "go on blotting out the consciousness of our intolerable situation as best we could or to accept spiritual help." Note that Appendix II is referred to again on p. 27.

My experience was that I needed both human and spiritual help, motivation and direction to recover. I needed to feel connected to be free. I needed a human connection with other alcoholics through the Fellowship as well as some type of undefinable spiritual connection to the world about me. I had to feel worthy of acceptance into the human race, and worthy of my existence in this universe.

Once I accepted I was unable to recover by myself and that I needed help, direction and support, I became willing to ask for that help from A.A., and A.A. responded. I now had a true choice of either accepting help or dying from my alcoholism.

Appendix II—Spiritual Experience

Had the "Appendix II" on page 567 below not been added to the Big Book, I would never have joined A.A., and would most certainly be dead by now from my alcoholism. I thought I had to be God-struck just like Bill W. had been in order to recover.

What I learned was that my journey among the Fellowship and through the 12 Steps provided me with a psychic change, or personality change, sufficient to bring about my recovery from alcoholism.

My slow, educational William James variety transformation from a hopeless and suicidal alcoholic into a hopeful and grateful member of the A.A. Fellowship took time, work and a change in my general attitudes and actions. I needed to change my way of thinking and acting, and I did, through the help of my A.A. comrades and an experienced sponsor who took me through the Big Book and 12 Steps.

My spiritual awakening was secular in nature, not a religious spiritual experience. My awakening resulted in an attitude and action change which I ascribe to having done all the work outlined in our 12 Step program, and my continuation of the daily spiritual maintenance suggested in Steps Ten through Twelve in our book.

My religious friends speak of their spiritual experience as given to them by the God of their understanding, but their results were the same as mine, with no God required.

Whatever we call it, any and all of us can have that personality change sufficient to bring about our recovery from alcoholism, provided we are willing to work for it.

APPENDIX II—SPIRITUAL EXPERIENCE

Page 567

The terms "**spiritual experience**" and "**spiritual awakening**" are used many times in this book which, upon careful reading, shows that **the personality change sufficient to bring about recovery from alcoholism has manifested itself among us in many different forms**.

Yet it is true that our first printing gave many readers the impression that **these personality changes, or religious experiences**, must be in the nature of sudden and spectacular upheavals. Happily for everyone, this conclusion is erroneous.

In the first few chapters a number of sudden revolutionary changes are described. Though it was not our intention to create such an impression, many alcoholics have nevertheless concluded that in order to recover they must acquire an **immediate and overwhelming God-consciousness** followed at once by a vast change in feeling and outlook.

Among our rapidly growing membership of thousands of alcoholics such transformations, though frequent, are by no means the rule. **Most of our experiences are** what the psychologist William James calls **the "educational variety"** because **they develop slowly over a period of time**. Quite often friends of the newcomer are aware of the difference long before he is himself. He finally realizes that **he has undergone a profound alteration in his reaction to life**; that such a change could hardly have been brought about by himself alone. What often takes place in a few months could hardly be accomplished by years of self-discipline. With few exceptions our members find that **they have tapped an unsuspected inner resource which they presently identify with their own conception of a Power greater than themselves**.

Most of us think this awareness of a **Power greater than ourselves is the essence of spiritual experience**. Our more **religious members call it "God-consciousness."**

Most emphatically we wish to say that **any alcoholic** capable of honestly facing his problems in the light of our experience **can recover, provided he does not close his mind to all spiritual principles**. He can only be defeated by an attitude of intolerance or belligerent denial.

We find that no one need have difficulty with the spirituality of the program. **Willingness, honesty and open mindedness are the essentials of recovery**. But these are indispensable.

There is a principle which is a bar against all information, which is proof against all arguments and which cannot fail to keep a man in everlasting ignorance—that principle is contempt prior to investigation. [Herbert Spencer]

A **certain American businessman** had ability, good sense, and high character. For years he had floundered from one sanitarium to another. He had consulted the best known American psychiatrists. Then he had gone to Europe, placing himself in the care of a celebrated physician (the psychiatrist, **Dr. Jung**) who prescribed for him. Though experience had made him skeptical, he finished his treatment with unusual confidence. His physical and mental condition were unusually good.

90

Above all, he believed he had acquired such a profound knowledge of the inner workings of his mind and its hidden springs that relapse was unthinkable. Nevertheless, he was drunk in a short time. More baffling still, he could give himself no satisfactory explanation for his fall.

So he returned to this doctor, whom he admired, and asked him point-blank why he could not recover. He wished above all things to regain self-control. He seemed quite rational and well-balanced with respect to other problems. Yet **he had no control whatever over alcohol. Why was this?**

He begged the doctor to tell him the whole truth, and he got it. In the doctor's judgment he was utterly hopeless; he could never regain his position in society and he would have to place himself under lock and key or hire a bodyguard if he expected to live long. That was a great physician's opinion.

But this man still lives, and is a free man. He does not need a bodyguard nor is he confined. He can go anywhere on this earth where other free men may go without disaster, provided he remains willing to maintain a certain simple attitude.

Some or our alcoholic readers may think they can do without spiritual help. Let us tell you the rest of the conversation our friend had with his doctor.

The doctor said: "You have the mind of a chronic alcoholic. I have never seen one single case recover, where that state of mind existed to the extent that it does in you." Our friend felt as though the gates of hell had closed on him with a clang.

He said to the doctor, Is there no exception? "Yes," replied the doctor, "there is. Exceptions to cases such as yours have been occurring since early times. Here and there, once in a while, alcoholics have had what are called **vital spiritual experiences**. To me **these occurrences are phenomena**. They appear to be in the nature of huge **emotional displacements and rearrangements**.

Ideas, emotions, and attitudes which were once the guiding forces

91

of the lives of these men are suddenly cast to one side, and a completely **new set of conceptions and motives begin to dominate them**. In fact, I have been trying to produce some such emotional rearrangement within you. With many individuals the methods which I employed are successful, but I have never been successful with an alcoholic of your description." [see Appendix II—Spiritual Experience]

Upon hearing this, our friend was somewhat relieved, for he reflected that, after all, he was a good church member. This hope, however, was destroyed by the doctor's telling him that **while his religious convictions were very good, in his case they did not spell the necessary vital spiritual experience**.

Here was the terrible dilemma in which our friend found himself when he had the extraordinary experience, which as we have already told you, made him a free man.

> After being teased along, we finally learn the solution for our alcoholism: we pick up a kit of A.A. spiritual tools and have a vital spiritual experience, or a spiritual awakening, or a spiritual experience.

> We're told by Dr. Carl Jung that this vital experience is a phenomenon which involves an emotional rearrangement and a new set of concepts and motives to replace our old ones, much like the phenomena described by Drs. William Silkworth in "The Doctor's Opinion" and William James in "Appendix II—Spiritual Experience."

> But most of us remain confused on how we can become truly free. Steps 1, 2 and 3 provide the faith that Steps 4 through 12 will result in that vital experience necessary for our recovery.

Roland Hazard

The man Dr. Jung treated was Roland Hazard, who many consider to be the first link in the chain which lead to the formation of Alcoholics Anonymous.

Roland Hazard was a wealthy American textile businessman

from a prominent Rhode Island family who was involved in politics and founded of a number of well-known companies.

While in his mid-forties, Rowland was treated in 1926 by the psychiatrist Dr. Carl Jung in Zurich, Switzerland. He was a patient of Dr. Jung's for about a year, sobered up and shortly returned to drinking. Treated a second time by Dr. Jung, Rowland was told that there was no medical or psychological hope for an alcoholic of his type; his only hope was having a vital spiritual or religious experience. In short, he needed to undergo a genuine religious conversion experience.

Rowland was further treated in the early 1930s by Courtenay Baylor, who was a recovering alcoholic and proponent of the Emmanuel Movement, which used group therapy, relaxation techniques and autosuggestion as a treatment for alcoholism.

Rowland ultimately found sobriety through the spiritual practices of the Oxford Group, which sought a return to First Century Christianity with its members leading a spiritual life under God's Guidance.

In August 1934, Rowland was at his home in Shaftsbury, Vermont, 15 miles south of Manchester. It was during this stay in Shaftsbury that he learned through two other Oxford Groupers of Ebby Thacher's possible six month sentence to Windsor Prison for repeated public intoxication.

The two other Oxford Groupers were Sheppard Cornell and Cebra Graves, whose father was the judge before whom Ebby was to appear. In Bennington, Vermont, Rowland and Cebra intervened at the hearing and asked that Ebby be bound over to Rowland rather than going to jail. The judge granted their request. Ebby subsequently sobered up for a few years, joined the Oxford Group, and in November of 1934 passed their message to Bill Wilson.

Roland is thought to have relapsed in 1936, and the extent and duration of his sobriety after that is unknown. He never joined A.A., but remained an Oxford Grouper until his sudden cardiac death in 1945. Ebby relapsed intermittently for the rest of his life, and never became permanently sober.

We, in our turn, **sought the same escape with all the desperation of drowning men**. What seemed at first a flimsy reed, has proved to be the **loving and powerful hand of God**. A **new life** has been given us or, if you prefer, "**a design for living**" that really works.

The distinguished American psychologist, William James, in his book *Varieties of Religious Experience*, **indicates a multitude of ways in which men have discovered God**. We have no desire to convince anyone that there is only one way by which faith can be acquired. If what we have learned and felt and seen means anything at all, it means that **all of us**, whatever our race, creed, or color **are the children of a living Creator with whom we may form a relationship** upon simple and understandable terms as soon as we are willing and honest enough to try. Those having religious affiliations will find here nothing disturbing to their beliefs or ceremonies. There is no friction among us over such matters.

We think it no concern of ours what religious bodies our members identify themselves with as individuals. This should be an entirely personal affair which each one decides for himself in the light of past associations, or his present choice. **Not all of us join religious bodies, but most of us favor such memberships**.

We finally receive "the reveal" of the solution for our alcoholism at the end of this chapter, and the solution is God. This conclusion was based on Bill W.'s personal and historical white light, hot flash religious conversion experience he had in Towns Hospital, and the supportive writings of Carl Jung and William James.

When Bill assigned the vital spiritual experience required for sobriety as the hand of God, it caused confusion among the A.A. members of that time, who felt they would never get sober without having a religious conversion experience similar to Bill's.

After the Big Book was published, Bill added the "Appendix II—Spiritual Experience" in an effort to introduce the term spiritual awakening and distinguish between sudden and slow spiritual experiences.

A *sudden* personality change sufficient to bring about recovery from alcoholism is a religious spiritual *experience* which Bill called God-consciousness. A slower change in one's attitudes and actions sufficient to bring about recovery from alcoholism is a spiritual *awakening*, which Bill also implies is a religious event. In both cases we change, sometimes quickly, sometimes slowly.

On a personal level, because Bill identified an educational spiritual awakening as coming from "an unsuspected inner resource which they presently identify with their own conception of a Power greater than themselves," I think of a spiritual *awakening* as a *secular* educational process, not a slow religious event. I think of a spiritual *experience* as a sudden religious conversion. Although the results may be the same, in my mind the origin of the power to produce those results is not.

In the following chapter, there appears an explanation of alcoholism, as we understand it, then a chapter addressed to the agnostic. Many who once were in this class are now among our members. Surprisingly enough, we find such convictions no great obstacle to a spiritual experience.

Further on, **clear-cut directions are given showing how we recovered**. These are followed by three dozen personal experiences.

Each individual, in the **personal stories**, describes in his own language and from his own point of view **the way he established his relationship with God**. These give a fair cross section of our membership and a clear-cut idea of what has actually happened in their lives.

We hope no one will consider these self-revealing accounts in bad taste. Our hope is that many alcoholic men and women, desperately in need, will see these pages, and we believe that it is only by fully disclosing ourselves and our problems that they will be persuaded to say, "**Yes, I am one of them too; I must have this thing.**"

It was by reconnecting with the childhood God of Bill's upbringing that he was able to recover, and he included testimony from dozens of other alcoholics who had found or rediscovered their god in the personal stories in the back of the Big Book.

To the newcomer, the unequivocal message in the chapter "We Agnostics" is that God is required for recovery, no matter what we call God. We can say "God of our understanding," but it's still God we need. We can say "Higher Power," but that higher power should be God.

Those of us who have not chosen God to be our Higher Power, or any power in our lives, will be disappointed, but the Big Book provides a sloppy way out for secular atheists, agnostics, free-thinkers, humanists and anyone else who has a philosophy of life that, without theism or other supernatural beliefs, affirms our ability and responsibility to lead ethical lives of personal fulfillment that aspire to the greater good.

I've found in A.A. instead of struggling to convince myself to believe in God, I can turn to my existing moral values and use those to guide, direct and motivate me toward physical and emotional sobriety.

When I speak of God *inside* of A.A., I use the A.A. language so that others can relate to my recovery program. I state that my God in A.A., as an atheist, reflects the moral values embedded in the 12 Step spiritual principles, not an entity from the Bible. My God is not a "thing," but an ideology, and my conception of God has worked very well for me.

My experience has shown me many in A.A. are confused and offended if a member states they do not believe in God.

They mistakenly believe God is required for sobriety, when this is not true. The Big Book states only that God is *preferred* for sobriety, but not required, although many in A.A. don't believe it, which is unfortunate.

I make every effort in A.A. meetings not to come across as the "angry atheist," since alcoholic atheists like myself need to learn how to practice our code of love and tolerance, even when other members of our Christian-based Fellowship don't.

When I speak of God *outside* of A.A., I say I'm an atheist, and most normal people understand that being an atheist does not mean I have no spiritual values or moral compass.

My thirteen years of experience in A.A. has shown me:

1) I was able to get sober without relapse, and I am able to stay sober with a set of spiritual beliefs and moral values I can connect with and use in my new life—that has nothing to do with God—and you can too.

2) The purpose of the historical Big Book and 12 Steps is to lead us into a new life, not to mandate what type of religious power is required to get us there.

Chapter 3

MORE ABOUT ALCOHOLISM

Most of us have been unwilling to admit we were real alcoholics. No person likes to think he is **bodily and mentally different** from his fellows. Therefore, it is not surprising that our drinking careers have been characterized by **countless vain attempts to prove we could drink like other people**. The idea that somehow, **someday he will control and enjoy his drinking is the great obsession of every abnormal drinker**. The persistence of this **illusion** is astonishing. **Many pursue it into the gates of insanity or death**.

> No truer words were spoken for the alcoholic than those above. We yearn to embrace the fantasy that if we don't drink for some magical period of time, somehow we'll be rewarded by being transported back to a point in time when we were able to control our drinking.

> In this chapter we have four Step One related stories of folks just like us who have convinced themselves that one day they will be able to drink like gentlemen.

> The *Man of Thirty* believes decades of abstinence qualifies him to drink again. A restless, irritable, angry and resentful *Jim the Car Salesman* deludes himself that a splash of milk in whiskey will protect him from pending intoxication. The persistent *Jay-walker* demonstrates the true meaning of insanity— unsoundness of mind. And *Fred the Accountant* willingly and happily becomes seduced by the thought of having a few cocktails at dinner.

> *Did you have the great obsession? -- p. 30*

We learned that **we had to fully concede to our innermost selves that we were alcoholics. This is the <u>First Step</u> in recovery. The delusion that we are like other people, or presently may be, has to be smashed**.

Step 1: We admitted that we were powerless over alcohol—that our lives had become unmanageable.

We alcoholics are not like other people. We are not unique, but we constitute the eight percent of the population who have known genetic and environmental reasons that predispose us to addictions and compulsions of all types, including alcoholism.

We can't control our genetic makeup, and we're unable to control how we were raised as children. Some of us survived without becoming addicts, and are grateful for it. Those of us who failed to escape our addictive destiny must realize there is nothing we can do at this point other than learn how to live with our misfortune.

Step One is admitting who and what we are, and accepting that there is no turning back.

We alcoholics are men and women who have lost the ability to control our drinking. We know that **no real alcoholic ever recovers control**. All of us felt at times that we were regaining control, but such intervals—usually brief—were inevitably followed by still less control, which led in time to **pitiful and incomprehensible demoralization**. We are convinced to a man that alcoholics of our type are in the grip of a **progressive illness**. Over any considerable period **we get worse, never better**.

We are like men who have lost their legs; they never grow new ones. Neither does there appear to be any kind of treatment which will make alcoholics of our kind like other men. **We have tried every imaginable remedy**. In some instances there has been brief recovery, followed always by a still worse relapse. Physicians who are familiar with alcoholism agree **there is no such thing a making a normal drinker out of an alcoholic**. Science may one day accomplish this, but it hasn't done so yet.

Despite all we can say, many who are real alcoholics are not going to believe they are in that class. By every form of self-deception and experimentation, they will try to **prove themselves exceptions** to the rule, therefore nonalcoholic. If anyone who is showing inability to control his drinking can do the right-about-face and **drink like a gentleman**, our hats are off to him. Heaven knows, we have tried hard enough and long enough to drink like other people!

Here are some of the methods we have tried: Drinking beer only, limiting the number of drinks, never drinking alone, never drinking in the morning, drinking only at home, never having it in the house, never drinking during business hours, drinking only at parties, switching from scotch to brandy, drinking only natural wines, agreeing to resign if ever drunk on the job, taking a trip, not taking a trip, swearing off forever (with and without a solemn oath), taking more physical exercise, reading inspirational books, going to health farms and sanitariums, accepting voluntary commitment to asylums —we could increase the list ad infinitum.

We do not like to pronounce any individual as alcoholic, but **you can quickly diagnose yourself.** Step over to the nearest barroom and **try some controlled drinking**. Try to drink and stop abruptly. Try it more than once. It will not take long for you to decide, if you are honest with yourself about it. It may be worth a bad case of jitters if you get a full knowledge of your condition.

Though there is no way of proving it, we believe that early in our drinking careers most of us could have stopped drinking. But the difficulty is that **few alcoholics have enough desire to stop while there is yet time**. We have heard of a few instances where people, who showed definite signs of alcoholism, were able to stop for a long period because of an overpowering desire to do so. Here is one.

> We squirm, twist and writhe to convince ourselves we have not progressed past that point of no return marking our transition from hard drinker into alcoholism. With all our might and will, we clutch the fleeting and fragile delusion that we are still clinging to the rotting branch of sobriety on the side of the cliff, which in reality has already been ripped from its roots. We don't need to test ourselves with any further controlled experiments to confirm our true condition.

In our hearts we know that once we admit we have the illness of alcoholism, we will be forced into a totally different world. Our fear of that unknown realm is a powerful motivator to remain secure in our denial. It takes courage to admit the truth, but it gets easier the more beaten down we become.

We will do anything not to admit that we have lost our legs which will never grow back, or that we have already transitioned from a cucumber into a pickle.

This is the first part of Step One—we are powerless over alcohol. Our ability to deny that fact that everyone else near to us knows is true is remarkable. If we took a lie detector test claiming we weren't alcoholic, we would pass the test with flying colors.

A **man of thirty** was doing a great deal of **spree drinking**. He was very nervous in the morning after these bouts and quieted himself with more liquor. He was ambitious to succeed in business, but saw that he would get nowhere if he drank at all. Once he started, he had no control whatever. He made up his mind that **until he** had been successful in business and **had retired, he would not touch another drop**. An exceptional man, **he remained bone dry for twenty-five years** and retired at the age of fifty-five, after a successful and happy business career.

Then he **fell victim to a belief** which practically every alcoholic has **that his long period of sobriety and self-discipline had qualified him to drink as other men**. Out came his carpet slippers and a bottle. In two months he was in a hospital, puzzled and humiliated. He **tried to regulate his drinking** for a little while, making several trips to the hospital meantime. Then, gathering all his forces, he **attempted to stop altogether and found he could not**. Every means of solving his problem which money could buy was at his disposal. **Every attempt failed**. Though a robust man at retirement, he went to pieces quickly and **was dead within four years**.

This case contains a powerful lesson. Most of us have believed that if we remained sober for a long stretch, we could thereafter drink normally. But here is a man who at fifty-five years found he was just where he had left off at thirty. We have seen the truth demonstrated again and again: "**Once an alcoholic, always an alcoholic**." Commencing to drink after a period of sobriety, we are in a short time as bad as ever. If we are planning to stop drinking, there must be **no reservation** of any kind, **nor any lurking notion that someday we will be immune to alcohol**.

Our man of thirty believed his twenty-five year martyrdom of abstinence entitled him to drink again. He deserved to drink because he had acted as a good soldier in his business and community for two and a half decades. Once he started drinking, neither money nor self-will could overcome his illness. Our baffling malady never forgets that we will always be allergic to alcohol.

A.A.'s Step One supports this axiom. Step One doesn't say we're *temporarily* powerless over alcohol; we have a lifetime condition.

The man of thirty story was probably adapted from the chapter "First Steps" in the book *The Common Sense of Drinking,* written in 1934 by the alcoholic Richard Peabody, who attained sobriety for a brief time through the Emmanuel Movement, but died drunk at age 44.

Has your writing listed those things you attempted to do to control your use of alcohol? -- p. 33

Did you have a reservation of any kind or lurking notion that you will someday be immune to alcohol? -- p. 33

Can you identify with the mental states that precede a relapse into drinking?

Young people may be encouraged by this man's experience to think that they can stop, as he did, on their own will power. We doubt if many of them can do it, because **none will really want to stop**, and hardly one of them, because of the **peculiar mental twist** already acquired, will find he can win out. Several of our crowd, men of thirty or less, had been drinking only a few years, but they found themselves as helpless as those who had been drinking twenty years.

To be gravely affected, one does not necessarily have to drink a long time nor take the quantities some of us have. This is particularly true of women. Potential **female alcoholics often turn into the real thing and are gone beyond recall in a few years**.

Social and medical research studies have identified some differences between male and female alcoholics:

Prevalence: Alcoholism is more common among men (8%) than women (5%).

Age of the first drink: An estimated 40% of all persons of either sex who start drinking before age fifteen will be diagnosed as being alcohol dependent at some point in their lives.

Relapse: Ninety percent of alcoholics relapse at least once. Male alcoholics typically relapse when they are in social-drinking situations and A.A. can help them stay sober by inducing them to spend time with nondrinking friends and helping them cope when they do find themselves with friends who are drinking. Female alcoholics, on the other hand, are more likely to drink alone and when feeling sad, depressed or anxious, and A.A. is less effective in helping them handle such situations.

Risk: Women are more at risk for developing a drinking problem later in life, and are at greater risk for alcohol-related health problems as they get older due their physiology. Younger women (age 18 to 34) have higher rates of drinking-related problems than older women do, but the rates of alcohol dependence are greater among middle-aged women (age 35 to 49). Women are less likely than men to take risks during periods of excessive drinking, lessening their risk of injury or death. It is still unclear if the rates of death (all-cause mortality) are higher or lower in alcoholic men vs. women.

Physical: Alcohol related diseases tend to develop more quickly in women than in men, and the physical consequences of chronic, heavy drinking are accelerated in women. For example, a man may be a heavy drinker for 20 to 30 years and have moderate problems, while a woman can be a heavy drinker for only five years and show severe problems.

Women typically have less body mass and less water content in their bodies than men. Body water diffuses alcohol content as it's digested, which means women have a higher concentration of alcohol in their blood stream when they drink. This not only causes women to become more impaired from drinking, but exposes their brains and other organs to more alcohol before it's broken down.

Impact on the Brain: Excessive drinking may result in short term memory loss and brain shrinkage. Women are more vulnerable than men to the brain damaging effects of excess alcohol use, and the damage tends to appear after shorter periods of excessive drinking for women than for men.

Mental Health: Women are less likely than men to commit suicide or have legal problems, but they have more issues with their mental and physical health, drug use, and family and social life. More women than men have partners who also have an alcohol problem.

Genetics & Environment: Alcohol dependence is a complex genetic disease, with many variants spread across many genes contributing to the risk of addiction. Genetics and epigenetics is responsible for about half of the risk for alcohol dependency, with social environmental factors responsible for the rest. In twin studies, identical twins are more likely than fraternal twins to have similar rates of alcohol dependence, alcohol abuse, and heavy alcohol consumption.

A.A. Membership: Women make up about one-third of all A.A. members.

A.A. Effectiveness: A.A. helps both men and women stay sober by providing sober social networks and boosting confidence in coping with high-risk social situations. Both men and women participate equally in A.A., and benefit equally from their participation. However, the more deeply involved any alcoholic becomes in the A.A. Fellowship (has a sponsor, sponsors others, attends meetings frequently, reads A.A. literature and does service work), the higher the odds they will attain long term sobriety, regardless of their sex.

A.A. Success: A.A. has never been demonstrated to be more effective than other cognitive based abstinence programs for long term sobriety, and many high-risk alcohol abusers stop drinking forever completely on their own. Reliable studies of lifetime abstinence after participating in A.A. are nonexistent, and the results of clinical studies are fraught with procedural weaknesses. Abstinence rates for A.A. from 3% to 75% have been reported, but the general consensus is that a 5% to 8% lifetime abstinence rate is a more accurate expectation.

Certain drinkers, who would be greatly insulted if called **alcoholics, are astonished at their inability to stop**. We, who are familiar with the symptoms, see large numbers of potential alcoholics among young people everywhere. But try and get them to see it! As we look back, we feel we had gone on drinking many years beyond the point where we could quit on our will power. If anyone questions whether he has entered this dangerous area, **let him try leaving liquor alone for one year. If he is a real alcoholic and very far advanced, there is scant chance of success**. In the early days of our drinking we occasionally remained sober for a year or more, becoming serious drinkers again later. Though you may be able to stop for a considerable period, you may yet be a potential alcoholic. We think few, to whom this book will appeal, can stay dry anything like a year. Some will be drunk the day after making their resolutions; most of them within a few weeks.

For those who are unable to drink moderately **the question is how to stop altogether**. We are **assuming, of course, that the reader**

desires to stop. Whether such a person can quit upon a nonspiritual basis depends upon the extent to which he has already lost the power to choose whether he will drink or not. Many of us felt that we had plenty of character. There was a tremendous urge to cease forever. Yet we found it impossible. This is **the baffling feature of alcoholism as we know it—this utter inability to leave it alone, no matter how great the necessity or the wish**.

How then shall we help our readers determine, to their own satisfaction, whether they are one of us?

The experiment of quitting for a period of time will be helpful, but we think we can render an even greater service to alcoholic sufferers and perhaps to the medical fraternity. So **we shall describe some of the mental states that precede a relapse into drinking**, for obviously **this is the crux of the problem**.

What are the common mental states that precede a relapse?

Two simple warnings repeated in the rooms of A.A. are to beware when we get restless, irritable and discontented, or when we're Hungry, Angry, Lonely or Tired (H-A-L-T).

Relapse Warning Signs

No one is ever suddenly struck drunk. We start ruminating about drinking long before we take that first drink. We relapse emotionally and mentally before we do physically. This is the danger zone, and when it is critical to take preventative action to avoid a relapse.

The desire to relapse can happen suddenly and is usually brought on by triggers—an event, interaction or relationship that causes an alcoholic to justify drinking again. Triggers generally fall into one of three categories: emotional, mental or environmental. They are often based off old routines or memories, so they differ for each person.

Emotional relapse starts with symptoms such as rising stress levels, anxiety, frustration, fear, anger, boredom, loneliness, guilt and depression. Other symptoms include becoming secretive, intolerance, defensiveness, mood swings, isolation, poor sleeping and eating habits, and annoyance having to attend A.A. meetings or therapy sessions.

Mental relapse includes thinking about relapse, reminiscing about the people and places associated with our past life, glamorizing our past drinking, deluding ourself that we'll be able to control just one drink, and even planning our relapse.

Environmental: spending time with people we drank with, driving by or going into our old drinking haunts: bars, clubs, liquor stores; the loss of a friend or loved one, conflict with others, change in marital status, health problems, being emotionally or physically abused, social pressure, financial problems, work or job related problems, seeing and smelling alcoholic beverages, going to a place where alcohol is served, and being around people who are actively drinking.

Depression is a powerful relapse trigger. Symptoms include hopelessness, apathy, anxiety, irritability, dwindling energy, fluctuating appetite, feelings of worthlessness, problems concentrating, changing sleep patterns and a general lack of interest in things. These all lead to a consuming bad attitude, so why not drink?

Preventing Relapse

1) *Use a Lifeline*: Call someone now—anyone. Whether it is our sponsor, friend, or family member, talking our urges through with another person can help in determining why we want to drink and why we shouldn't.

2) *Pause when agitated*: make yourself wait thirty minutes before impulsively acting on an urge to drink. After a half-hour, wait an hour and reevaluate your obsession and your reasoning behind it. Time can help clarify your mind.

3) *Think, Think, Think*: about what will happen after we take that first drink. Likely it wouldn't stop there and we'll eventually find ourself at the same bottom we previously hit, if not a deeper one. Thinking about our actions and their consequences can curb our desire to imbibe.

4) *One day at a time*: focus on staying sober for just today, or just this hour or just this minute. Then repeat.

We know we can't control what other people say or do, and we can't always control the circumstances that come our way. The best thing we can do is be as prepared as possible. Some ways to do that include knowing our triggers, having a strong and accessible sponsor and support group to help us when confronted with our triggers, and help us to be alert to the warning signs.

SAMHSA's National Helpline – 1-800-662-4357

The Substance Abuse & Mental Health Service Administration (SAMHSA) National Helpline is a free, confidential, 24/7, 365-day-a-year treatment referral and information service for individuals and families facing mental and/or substance use disorders. Help available in both English and Spanish.

What sort of thinking dominates an alcoholic who repeats time after time the desperate experiment of the first drink? Friends who have reasoned with him after a spree which has brought him to the point of divorce or bankruptcy are mystified when he walks directly into a saloon. Why does he? Of what is he thinking?

My problem, like so many of my fellow alcoholics, was that I always believed the next time would be different. I believed it as honestly and deeply as I ever believed anything. I was absolutely convinced that if I just tried harder to control my drinking, I would be successful. I could not comprehend why I could not stop drinking whenever I wanted to; it made no sense to me. Even knowing that I was an alcoholic did not smash my delusion.

I was totally baffled. I never denied that whenever I took that first drink I ended up drunk every time; I simply was wholly convinced in my magic magnifying mind that tomorrow would be different. I was unable to accept Step One for decades.

Do you understand that these mental states are the crux of the problem? -- p. 35

Our first example is a friend we shall call **Jim**. This man has a charming wife and family. He **inherited a lucrative automobile agency**. He had a commendable World War record. He is a good salesman. Everybody likes him. He is an intelligent man, normal so far as we can see, except for a **nervous disposition**. He did no drinking until he was thirty-five. In a few years he became so violent when intoxicated that he had to be committed. On leaving the asylum **he came into contact with us**.

We told him what we knew of alcoholism and the answer we had found. He made a beginning. His family was re-assembled, and he **began to work as a salesman for the business he had lost through drinking**. All went well for a time, but **he failed to enlarge his spiritual life**. To his consternation, he found himself drunk half a dozen times in rapid succession. On each of these occasions we worked with him, reviewing carefully what had happened. He **agreed he was a real alcoholic** and in a serious condition. He knew he faced another trip to the asylum if he kept on. Moreover, he would lose his family for whom he had a deep affection.

> What does it mean when it says Jim "failed to enlarge his spiritual life?" One suspects that although he acknowledged he was a real alcoholic, he could not accept the suggestions of Steps Two and Three and the rest of the steps. When he drank again, it reflected his failure to accept Step One.

Yet **he got drunk again**. We asked him to tell us exactly how it happened. This is his story: "I came to work on Tuesday morning. I remember I **felt irritated** that I had to be a salesman for a concern I once owned. I **had a few words with the brass**, but nothing serious.

Then I decided to drive to the country and see one of my prospects for a car. On the way I **felt hungry** so I stopped at a roadside place where they have a bar. I had no intention of drinking. I just thought I would get a sandwich. I also had the notion that I might find a customer for a car at this place, which was familiar for I had been going to it for years. I had eaten there many times during the months I was sober. I sat down at a table and ordered a sandwich and a glass of milk. Still no thought of drinking. I ordered another sandwich and decided to have another glass of milk.

> The A.A. acronym, H-A-L-T, or Hungry, Angry, Lonely and Tired, is a clear warning sign of impending relapse. Jim was angry and resentful he had been demoted to being an employee of the business he once owned. He drove off into the countryside alone. He was hungry and probably tired from a long drive. It's no surprise he ended up drinking.

Suddenly the thought crossed my mind that **if I were to put an ounce of whiskey in my milk it couldn't hurt me** on a full stomach. I ordered a whiskey and poured it into the milk. I **vaguely sensed I was not being too smart**, but felt reassured as I was taking the whiskey on a full stomach.

The experiment went so well that I ordered another whiskey and poured it into more milk. That didn't seem to bother me so I tried another.

Thus started one more journey to the asylum for Jim. Here was the threat of commitment, the loss of family and position, to say nothing of that intense mental and physical suffering which drinking always caused him.

He had much knowledge about himself as an alcoholic. Yet **all reasons for not drinking were easily pushed aside** in favor of the foolish idea that he could take whiskey if only he mixed it with milk!

Whatever the precise definition of the word may be, we call this plain **insanity**. How can such a lack of proportion, of the ability to think straight, be called anything else?

You may think this an extreme case. To us it is not far-fetched, for this kind of thinking has been characteristic of every single one of us. We have sometimes reflected more than Jim did upon the consequences. But there was always the **curious mental phenomenon** that parallel with our sound reasoning there inevitably ran some **insanely trivial excuse for taking the first drink. Our sound reasoning failed to hold us in check**. The insane idea won out. Next day we would ask ourselves, in all earnestness and sincerity, how it could have happened. In some circumstances we have gone out deliberately to get drunk, feeling ourselves justified by nervousness, anger, worry, depression, jealousy or the like. But even in this type of beginning we are obliged to admit that our **justification for a spree was insanely insufficient** in the light of what always happened. We now see that when we began to drink deliberately, instead of casually, there was little serious or effective thought during the period of premeditation of what the terrific consequences might be.

No person who has spent any time in A.A. and has read the Big Book can forget the insanity of Jim the car salesman who thought milk might work as an antidote to whiskey. Jim knew what the consequences of his drinking would be, but it was not enough to prevent him from drinking.

We laugh about this story today because we can all relate to the delusion that if we mix alcohol with something magical, or drink on a full stomach, or don't mix beer and hard liquor, we will end up feeling mellow but won't get drunk.

I assumed when I put whiskey in my Christmas eggnog, made with milk and cream, I would be able to drink more without getting drunk. Before I went out for a night of heavy drinking, I would fill my stomach with bread, certain it would absorb most of the alcohol so I could drink more.

Later on, I decided to perform an experiment in controlled alcohol consumption. I decided to drink one ounce of whiskey every hour, and measure my alcohol level with a breathalyzer.

111

My goal in drinking was not to get drunk, but just to feel relaxed and carefree. I was sure if I could determine the minimum amount of whiskey I needed each hour just to feel mellow, then I could control my drinking and not get drunk.

The idiocy of this line of thinking reflected my peculiar mental twist. When I started the experiment, all I did was end up getting drunk because I had to drink more than one ounce an hour to suppress the craving which had kicked in after taking that first drink. My experiment was as stupid as those of all four examples in this chapter, and our outcomes were the same. Although I didn't appreciate it at the time, my silly experiment again demonstrated my powerlessness over alcohol—Step One. Knowing the inevitable consequences of the first drink could never prevent me from taking that drink.

The milk in the whiskey man was Ralph F., who is said to have gotten sober on June 6, 1938. His home town was Darien, Connecticut, and his Big Book story was titled "Another Prodigal Story." He started the first A.A. group in Darien, and at the time he wrote his story there were four in that group. He also may have worked in the pressroom at A.A.'s second International Convention in St. Louis in July of 1955.

Our behavior is as absurd and incomprehensible with respect to the first drink as that of an individual with a passion, say, for **jay-walking**. He **gets a thrill out of skipping in front of fast-moving vehicles**. He enjoys himself for a few years in spite of friendly warnings. Up to this point you would label him as a foolish chap having queer ideas of fun. Luck then deserts him and **he is slightly injured several times in succession**. You would expect him, if he were normal, to cut it out. Presently he is hit again and this time has a fractured skull. Within a week after leaving the hospital a fast-moving trolley car breaks his arm. He tells you he has decided to stop jay-walking for good, but in a few weeks he breaks both legs.

On **through the years this conduct continues**, accompanied by his continual promises to be careful or to keep off the streets altogether. Finally, he can no longer work, his wife gets a divorce and he is held up to ridicule. He **tries every known means to get the jay-walking idea out of his head**. He shuts himself up in an asylum, hoping to mend his ways. But the day he comes out he races in front of a fire engine, which breaks his back. **Such a man would be crazy, wouldn't he?**

You may think our illustration is too ridiculous. But is it? We, who have been through the wringer, have to admit **if we substituted alcoholism for jay-walking, the illustration would fit exactly**. However intelligent we may have been in other respects, **where alcohol has been involved, we have been strangely insane**. It's strong language—but isn't it true?

Some of you are thinking: "Yes, what you tell is true, but it doesn't fully apply. We admit we have some of these symptoms, but we have not gone to the extremes you fellows did, nor are we likely to, for we understand ourselves so well after what you have told us that such things cannot happen again. We have not lost everything in life through drinking and we certainly do not intend to. Thanks for the information."

That may be true of certain nonalcoholic people who, though drinking foolishly and heavily at the present time, are able to stop or moderate, because their brains and bodies have not been damaged as ours were. But **the actual or potential alcoholic, with hardly any exception, will be absolutely unable to stop drinking on the basis of self-knowledge.**

This is a point we wish to emphasize and re-emphasize, to smash home upon our alcoholic readers as it has been revealed to us out of bitter experience.

> The jay-walker holds a special place in our hearts. We love the jay-walker because like us, he is powerless over his crazy compulsion. We can all visualize him repeatedly running out in front of traffic like a fool.

We know he will be injured, and the odds that he will be killed increase every time he ventures out. But he keeps on doing it, despite the danger and his progressive injuries. He knows he will get hurt, yet keeps tempting fate. What alcoholic can't relate to that?

I knew I couldn't drink without getting drunk, but I kept taking that first drink despite adverse personal consequences which progressively got worse. I always believed that knowledge was power, but concerning alcohol, it wasn't.

Do you understand why an actual or potential alcoholic will be absolutely unable to stop drinking on the basis of self-knowledge? -- p. 39

Let us take another illustration. **Fred** is a partner in a well-known **accounting firm**. His income is good, he has a fine home, is happily married and the father of promising children of college age. He has so attractive a personality that he makes friends with everyone. If ever there was a **successful businessman**, it is Fred. To all appearance he is a stable, well balanced individual. Yet, **he is alcoholic**.

We first saw Fred about a year ago in a hospital where he had gone to recover from a bad case of jitters. It was his first experience of this kind, and he was much ashamed of it. Far from admitting he was an alcoholic , he told himself he came to the hospital to rest his nerves. The doctor intimated strongly that he might be worse than he realized. For a few days he was depressed about his condition.

He made up his mind to quit drinking altogether. It never occurred to him that perhaps he could not do so, in spite of his character and standing. **Fred would not believe himself an alcoholic**, **much less accept a spiritual remedy for his problem**. We told him what we knew about alcoholism. He was interested and **conceded that he had some of the symptoms**, but he was a long way from admitting that he could do nothing about it himself. He was positive that this humiliating experience, plus the knowledge he had acquired, would keep him sober the rest of his life. **Self-knowledge would fix it**.

We heard no more of Fred for a while. One day we were told that he was back in the hospital. This time he was quite shaky. He soon indicated he was anxious to see us. The story he told is most instructive, for here was a chap absolutely convinced he had to stop drinking, who had no excuse for drinking, who exhibited splendid judgment and determination in all his other concerns, yet was flat on his back nevertheless.

Let him tell you about it: "I was much impressed with what you fellows said about alcoholism, and I frankly did not believe it would be possible for me to drink again. I rather appreciated your ideas about the **subtle insanity which precedes the first drink**, but I was **confident it could not happen** to me **after what I had learned**. I reasoned I was not so far advanced as most of you fellows, that I had been usually successful in licking my other personal problems, and that I would therefore be successful where you men failed. I felt I had every right to be self-confident, that it would be **only a matter of exercising my will power and keeping on guard**.

In this frame of mind, I went about my business and for a time all was well. I had no trouble refusing drinks, and began to wonder if I had not been making too hard work of a simple matter. One day I went to Washington to present some accounting evidence to a government bureau. I had been out of town before during this particular dry spell, so there was nothing new about that. Physically, I felt fine. Neither did I have any pressing problems or worries. My business came off well. I was pleased and knew my partners would be too. **It was the end of a perfect day**, **not a cloud on the horizon**. I went to my hotel and leisurely dressed for dinner.

As I crossed the threshold of the dining room, the thought came to mind that **it would be nice to have a couple of cocktails with dinner**. That was all. Nothing more.

I ordered a cocktail and my meal. Then I ordered another cocktail. After dinner I decided to take a walk. When I returned to the hotel it struck me a highball would be fine before going to bed, so I stepped into the bar and had one.

I remember having several more that night and plenty next morning. I have a **shadowy recollection** of being in a airplane bound for New York, and of finding a friendly taxicab driver at the landing field instead of my wife. The driver escorted me for several days. I **know little of where I went or what I said and did**. Then came the hospital with the unbearable mental and physical suffering.

As soon as I regained my ability to think, I went carefully over that evening in Washington.

Not only had I been off guard, **I had made no fight whatever against the first drink**. This time **I had not thought of the consequences at all**. I had commenced to drink as carelessly as though the cocktails were ginger ale. I now remembered what my alcoholic friends had told me, how they prophesied that **if I had an alcoholic mind, the time and place would come—I would drink again**. They had said that though I did raise a defense, it would one day give way before some trivial reason for having a drink. Well, just that did happen and more, for what I had learned of alcoholism did not occur to me at all. I knew from that moment that I had an alcoholic mind. I saw that **will power and self-knowledge would not help in those strange mental blank spots**. I had never been able to understand people who said that a problem had them hopelessly defeated. I knew then. It was the crushing blow.

Two of the **members of Alcoholics Anonymous came to see me**. They grinned, which I didn't like so much, and then **asked me if I thought myself alcoholic and if I were really licked this time**. I had to concede both propositions. They piled on me heaps of evidence to the effect that an alcoholic mentality, such as I had exhibited in Washington, was a hopeless condition. They cited cases out of their own experience by the dozen. **This process snuffed out the last flicker of conviction that I could do the job myself**.

Then **they outlined the spiritual answer and program of action** which a hundred of them had followed successfully. Though I had been only a nominal churchman, their proposals were not, intellectually, hard to swallow.

But the **program of action**, though entirely sensible, **was pretty drastic**. It meant **I would have to throw several lifelong conceptions out of the window**. That was not easy. But the moment I made up my mind to go through with the process, I had the curious feeling that my alcoholic condition was relieved, as in fact it proved to be.

Quite as important was the discovery that **spiritual principles would solve all my problems**. I have since been brought into a way of living infinitely more satisfying and, I hope, more useful than the life I lived before. **My old manner of life was by no means a bad one, but I would not exchange its best moments for the worst I have now**. I would not go back to it even if I could."

Fred's story speaks for itself. We hope it strikes home to thousands like him. He had felt only the first nip of the wringer. Most alcoholics have to be pretty badly mangled before they really commence to solve their problems.

> Some of us found the obsession to drink more intense when everything in our life was going well, rather than when things were falling apart. We drank when times were good, and when they weren't good. We drank when we were happy and when we were sad. We drank when we got a job promotion or when we were fired. It didn't matter; we drank for any reason under the sun.
>
> The thought that there might be a spiritual answer and program of action which could help us was both a relief and a burden. We were relieved because it offered us a glimmer of hope that perhaps there was a way out of our alcoholic nightmare. But we were frightened because we did not know exactly what this new program of action would require of us.
>
> It's the choice between the devil we know and the devil we don't. Should we stay safe in our predictable misery, or venture out into an unknown land with the hope life might be better for us wherever we end up?

117

Fred the accountant was Harry Brick from New York City. He became sober in June, 1938, and was the author of the Big Book story "A Different Slant." In January, 1939, Harry was elected Board Chair of the Alcoholic Foundation, but had to be removed after he returned to drinking in December of that same year. Harry later sued A.A. for money he loaned them to print the big book.

Many doctors and psychiatrists agree with our conclusions. One of these men, staff member of a world-renowned hospital,* recently made this statement to some of us: "What you say about the general hopelessness of the average alcoholics' plight is, in my opinion, correct. As to two of you men, whose stories I have heard, there is no doubt in my mind that you were 100% hopeless, apart from divine help. Had you offered yourselves as patients at this hospital, I would not have taken you, if I had been able to avoid it. People like you are too heartbreaking. Though not a religious person, **I have profound respect for the spiritual approach** in such cases as yours. For most cases, **there is virtually no other solution.**"

> * The doctor who was a staff member at a world-renowned hospital was Dr. Percy Pollick, a psychiatrist at Bellevue Hospital in New York City.

Once more: The alcoholic at certain times has no effective mental defense against the first drink. Except in a few cases, neither he nor any other human being can provide such a defense. **His defense must come from a Higher Power**.

> The paragraph above is **Step Two**: *Came to believe that a Power greater than ourselves could restore us to sanity.*

> The entire chapter of "More About Alcoholism" presents testimony that our human will-power alone is insufficient to stop us from drinking *after* we take that first drink.

> Each of the four alcoholics discussed refused to accept a spiritual solution for their alcoholism.

They knew they were alcoholic, but couldn't let go of their conviction that just trying harder would fix their problem. If they kept hammering that square peg with all their might into that round hole, it would get in there eventually.

What is suggested is that *before* we take that first drink, self-will alone won't keep us from taking the drink. Because we have an insane, unsound alcoholic mind full of peculiar mental twists, our human will must be supplemented with a spiritual will or power of some type to keep us from taking that first drink.

In other words, on our own we don't have the power not to take that first drink. With the help of a spiritual power that we can connect with and employ, we will be able to resist that first drink, which we know always leads us to another. We need an additional mental boost to not take that first drink.

We discover as we read through the Big Book that there are many types and definitions of the spiritual motivational power we can create, identify and use to augment our own will power to stay away from that first drink.

Most sober alcoholics in A.A. identify their higher spiritual power as God, but I do not. No god ever got or kept me sober.

However, after I stopped drinking my brain function began to heal and improve so that I could adopt a different outlook on life. I attended A.A. meetings daily, found a sponsor, completed my 12 Step work including all my amends, began sponsoring other men and became involved in regular community A.A. service work.

Those actions resulted in a personality change such that my self-will and a bit of daily spiritual motivational power has been sufficient to keep me away from a drink continuously since my first A.A. meeting in 2006.

Note the doctor's reaction to alcoholism and the solution on page 43.

HOMEWORK

SESSION ONE

STEP 1

Preface, Forewords, Dr.'s Opinion, Bill's Story, There Is A Solution, More About Alcoholism

Pages 1 – 43

WRITE down your reactions to the readings as to how they apply to you and your illness, incorporating as much as possible of the considerations into your work. Think about:

1) Any reservations you may have that in fact, you are powerless over alcohol.

2) How the writings apply to your life.

3) How you are powerless over alcohol and begin to consider what you can truly "manage" in your life.

4) Have you listed those things you attempted to do to control your use of alcohol?

5) Did you have a reservation of any kind or lurking notion that you will someday be immune to alcohol?

SESSION TWO

STEPS 2 & 3

We Agnostics, How It Works

Pages 44 - 64

STEP 2 -- _Came to believe that a power greater than ourselves could restore us to sanity._

STEP 3 -- _Made a decision to turn our will and our lives over to the care of God as we understood Him._

READ "We Agnostics" & "How It Works" (Chapters 4 & 5, p.44-64), and "Appendix II—Spiritual Experience" (p.567)

WRITE down your reactions to the readings as to how they apply to you and your illness, incorporating as much as possible of the considerations into your work. Think about how the writings apply to your life.

1) Write in your notebook what you can believe about a Power greater than yourself.
2) Write on another page what you cannot believe about God.
3) As you go forward from this point, it is those things which you believe or which fit into your conception of God which you will be using and you can be comforted in knowing that "Our own conception, however inadequate, was sufficient to make the approach and to effect a contact with Him" – p.46

CONSIDERATIONS – We Agnostics, How It Works & Appendix II—Spiritual Experience (Step 3 – p.44-64)

1) Do you accept the fact that you have only two alternatives if you are an alcoholic – 1) an alcoholic death or 2) to live life on a spiritual basis?
2) Have you lacked power to manage life? – p.45
3) Note that "The main object of this book is to enable you to find a Power greater than yourself which will solve your problem." – p.45

4) Have you had honest doubts and prejudices about "God?" – p.45
5) What will he / she / it look like?
6) What will it be like when you find Him / Her / It?
7) Where did you get these ideas?
8) Had you abandoned the idea of God entirely? – p.45
9) Are you <u>willing</u> to lay aside your previous beliefs or prejudices and express a willingness to believe in a Power greater than yourself?
10) What is your concept of God? – p.46
11) Do you now believe or are you even willing to believe that there is a Power greater than yourself? – p.47
12) Do you recognize that when you can say "yes" to this question that you are "on the way" – p.47
13) Note the book once again refers you to <u>Appendix II</u> – p.47
14) What is it that Appendix II says that is indispensable?
15) Have you been open-minded or have you been obstinate, sensitive and unreasonably prejudiced about discussions about God?
16) What reservations do you have when you have completed this chapter?
17) Have you been biased and unreasonably prejudiced about the realm of the spirit? – p.51
18) Did your ideas work?
19) Will the God idea work? – p.52
20) Do you believe that "When we drew near to Him He disclosed Himself to us"? – p.57
21) Do you question whether you are <u>capable</u> of being honest with yourself?
22) Note the state of mind you are asked to have when you start the Steps: <u>Honesty, Fearlessness, Thoroughness, and a Willingness to go to any length</u> – p.58
23) What do <u>Half Measures</u> avail us? – p.59
24) Are you convinced that a life run on self-will can hardly be a success? – p.60
25) Can you see the effects of self-centeredness in your life?
26) How have you been self-centered? List examples in your notebook and discuss them with the group.
27) Did you know that you could not reduce self-centeredness much by wishing or trying on your own power? – p.62

a) Fearlessly face and answer the proposition that "Either God is everything or he is nothing?"
b) God either is or he isn't?
c) What is your choice to be?

Remember what it said on p.28, "If what we have learned and felt and seen means anything at all, it means that all of us, whatever our race, creed, or color are the children of a living Creator with whom we may form a relationship upon simple and understandable terms as soon as we are willing and honest enough to try."

- Are you willing to take this step? -- STEP THREE
- Many groups at this point commit to one another that they are going to take this step and they recite the Third Step Prayer together as set forth on p.63.

THIRD STEP PRAYER

God, I offer myself to Thee—to build with me and to do with me as Thou wilt. Relieve me of the bondage of self, that I may better do Thy will. Take away my difficulties, that victory over them may bear witness to those I would help of Thy Power, Thy Love, and Thy Way of life. May I do Thy will always! p.63.

Chapter 4

WE AGNOSTICS, HOW IT WORKS

Pages 44 – 64

WE AGNOSTICS

I once heard an agnostic A.A. member say: "If you believe it was God's will that got you sober, then you must believe it was God's will that kept you drunk most of your life. You can't say God is responsible for your sobriety and deny he wasn't responsible for your alcoholism."

If God is already your Higher Power of choice, there is little reason to read this chapter, and you can ignore the comments below, which are directed to those who have difficulty with the "God stuff" in A.A.

If God is *not* your Higher Power, the subtext of these fourteen chapter pages states that God needs to become your power of choice to stay sober and recover. In saying "Choose your own conception of God," the Big Book is still endorsing God as the alcoholic's Higher Power for sobriety, and nothing else.

I liken this to being asked to "Choose the footwear you want on your feet" (slippers, sneakers, loafers, boots, flip-flops, dress, etc) vs. "Choose the Nike footwear you want on your feet" (Air Max, Air Jordan, Cortez, etc).

In one case I'm asked to choose the *type* of shoe I want; in the other case I'm asked to choose the *style* of shoe I want within a single brand. In "We Agnostics," God is the type of shoe best for A.A. members, but we get to select whatever style of God we want. So in effect, we have no real choice for our Higher Power.

To make matters worse in "We Agnostics," Bill goes to great length to confuse the reader when discussing the religious vs.

the spiritual by introducing, mixing, twisting and intermingling the terms faith, Higher Power, God, God of our understanding and many other traditional expressions for God.

This chapter's cluttered chaos is of little help for any alcoholic who struggles with all the "God stuff" in the Big Book. The chapter simply offers up a celebration of the religious intercourse reflected in the six God Steps of 2, 3, 5, 6, 7 and 11, which holds little difficulty for Christian alcoholics that believe in God.

For those that have not chosen God as their Higher Power, this chapter can be challenging, confusing, confounding, depressing and disappointing.

As one who does not choose God as his Higher Power, in my comments I try to be fair and inclusive to alcoholics of all faiths, religions and those with no religion. As long as we know *we* aren't God, my experience has shown that anyone can get sober and find a new design for living in A.A., regardless of their belief or lack of belief in God.

WE AGNOSTICS

In the preceding chapters you have learned something of alcoholism. We hope we have made clear the **distinction between the alcoholic and the non-alcoholic. If, when you honestly want to, you find you cannot quit entirely, or if when drinking, you have little control over the amount you take, you are probably alcoholic. If that be the case, you may be suffering from an illness which only a spiritual experience will conquer.**

To one who feels he is an **atheist or agnostic** such an experience seems impossible, but to continue as he is means disaster, especially if he is an alcoholic of the hopeless variety. **To be doomed to an alcoholic death or to live on a spiritual basis are not always easy alternatives to face.**

How many times have we heard in the rooms of A.A. folks say

they don't know if they are alcoholic? If in doubt, the first paragraph of this chapter contains the best Yes / No test for alcoholism there is by asking us two simple questions:

1) Can I stop drinking *forever*?

2) Can I control the amount of alcohol I drink once I start drinking, *every single time* I take a drink?

If we answer "No" to either question, we are alcoholic. It's that simple. We are at Step One.

After we determine and admit we are alcoholic, we are faced with two additional Yes / No options: die, or start living life on a spiritual basis, as stated in Steps Two and Three.

Most of us had to seriously consider what would be the best of those two alternatives for us. We ask ourselves: "Would dying be the better choice? I'm not sure, I need to think about it a little longer." That's an example of our alcoholic mind in full flight from reality.

In the second paragraph, Bill implies that if one is atheist or agnostic, one cannot have a spiritual experience, which in Appendix II Bill refers to as a God-conscious religious experience, and is therefore doomed to die an alcoholic death.

Do not believe a word of it. Alcoholic atheists and agnostics around the world have gotten sober and found a joyous new way of life living on a non-religious, God-free, spiritual basis.

Do you accept the fact that you have only two alternatives if you are an alcoholic – 1) an alcoholic death or 2) to live a life on a spiritual basis?

But it isn't so difficult. About half our original fellowship were of exactly that type. At first some of us tried to avoid the issue, hoping against hope we were not true alcoholics. But **after a while we had to face the fact that we must find a spiritual basis of life or else**. Perhaps it is going to be that way with you. But cheer up, something like **half of us thought we were atheists or agnostics. Our experience shows that you need not be disconcerted**.

> If we are atheist or agnostic, what does Bill W. mean by saying half of us "thought" we were atheist or agnostic? That implies that down deep we really aren't atheist or agnostic; we just mistakenly think we are. That is a ridiculous statement.
>
> The huge problem with this chapter is definitional. During some parts of the chapter, Bill identifies being spiritual as believing in God. In other parts, he implies being spiritual means one does not believe in God. The same applies when Bill uses the term Higher Power. One moment it refers to God, in the next it doesn't. He can't have it both ways.
>
> As I read this chapter, I had to translate Wilson's text and sub-text into something that made sense to me. Right or wrong, I choose to define the terms "Higher Power" and "spirituality" as *secular*, or non-theistic, meaning "not God."
>
> So if I am spiritual, I don't believe in God. If I am religious, I believe in God, since God is Christian.

If a mere code of morals or a better philosophy of life were sufficient to overcome alcoholism, many of us would have recovered long ago. But we found that such codes and philosophies did not save us, no matter how much we tried. We could wish to be moral, we could wish to be philosophically comforted, in fact, we could will these things with all our might, but the needed power wasn't there. **Our human resources, as marshalled by the will, were not sufficient; they failed utterly**.

Lack of power, that was our dilemma. We had to find a power by which we could live, and it had to be a Power greater than ourselves. Obviously. But where and how were we to find this Power?

Well, **that's exactly what this book is about. Its main object is to enable you to find a Power greater than yourself which will solve your problem.**

127

We have already been presented with the premise that we will never be able to overcome our alcoholic addiction by ourselves, because we do not have enough power on our own to do so. Our human will power alone is insufficient.

Step Two says we need the additional aid of some type of power above and beyond ourselves to propel us into sobriety and a new way of life.

It's like starting with a single stage rocket to get us into Earth's orbit. We find that single engine rocket won't do the job; we need the additional power of a second booster rocket to be successful. What kind of booster rocket we choose to use is up to us.

We are told that whatever power we find will solve our problem. What problem? How to stop drinking? How to pay off the mortgage? How to get our spouse and family back? How to be happy?

At this point we don't know for certain what problem Bill is referring to, but later on we discover the root of "our problem" is selfishness and self-centeredness, and the 12 Steps can set us free from those two shortcomings.

That means **we have written a book** which we believe to be **spiritual as well as moral**. And it means, of course, that **we are going to talk about God**. Here **difficulty arises with agnostics**. Many times we talk to a new man and watch his hope rise as we discuss his alcoholic problems and explain our fellowship. But **his face falls when we speak of spiritual matters, especially when we mention God**, for we have re-opened a subject which our man thought he had neatly evaded or entirely ignored.

We know how he feels. We have shared his honest doubt and prejudice. **Some of us have been violently anti-religious**. To others, the word God brought up a particular idea of Him with which someone had tried to impress them during childhood. Perhaps we rejected this particular conception because it seemed inadequate.

128

With that rejection **we imagined we had abandoned the God idea entirely**. We were bothered with the thought that **faith** and dependence upon a **Power beyond ourselves** was somewhat weak, even cowardly.

We looked upon this world of warring individuals, warring theological systems, and inexplicable calamity, with deep skepticism. We looked askance at many individuals who claimed to be godly. How could a Supreme Being have anything to do with it all? And who could comprehend a Supreme Being anyhow? Yet, in other moments, we found ourselves thinking, when enchanted by a starlit night, "Who, then, make all this?" There was a feeling of awe and wonder, but it was fleeting and soon lost.

> The above paragraphs are an early example of Bill mixing and equating the terms spiritual, God, Higher Power and faith. Those terms do not mean the same thing in most alcoholics' minds.
>
> We need to get our definitions straight:
>
> The average person considers God religious. A spiritual Higher Power is something that is not God, and therefore not religious; it is secular in nature.
>
> Faith can be a belief in something either religious, such as God, or secular, such as some other type of non-God power.

Yes, we of agnostic temperament have had these thoughts and experiences. Let us make haste to reassure you. We found that **as soon as we were able to lay aside prejudice and express even a willingness to believe in a Power greater than ourselves, we commenced to get results**, even though it was impossible for any of us to fully define or comprehend **that Power, _which is God_**.

> In the above paragraph Bill states point-blank that the needed power for sobriety in A.A. is God. He assumes that because God became his personal Higher Power, it must become everyone's Higher Power. Therefore, God equals Higher Power. This is a grave supposition; inaccurate at best and arrogant at worst.

On the one hand, our book is trying to keep the door open for those of us that do not believe in God by suggesting we find some other power greater than we are to help us. On the other hand, our book states that the only higher power that can help us is God, or a God of our understanding, so we better figure out a way to accept that fact.

For alcoholics who easily believe in God, this chapter presents little difficulty or challenge. For those who struggle with some or all of the God concept, this chapter is remains frustrating since the terms God, Higher Power, spiritual and God of our understanding are continuously intertwined, jumbled and often at odds in their implication and meaning.

We cannot change the way this chapter was historically written, but we can absorb and appreciate the overriding message that whether we believe in God or not, we can get sober. God is not a requirement for sobriety, despite what Bill Wilson says.

Much to our relief, we discovered we did not need to consider another's conception of God. Our own conception, however inadequate, was sufficient to make the approach and to effect a contact with Him.

As soon as we admitted the possible existence of a Creative Intelligence, a Spirit of the Universe underlying the totality of things, **we began to be possessed of a new sense of power and direction, provided we took other simple steps.** We found that **God does not make too hard terms with those who seek Him.** To us, **the Realm of Spirit is broad, roomy, all inclusive**; never exclusive or forbidding to those who earnestly seek. It is open, we believe, to all men.

Bill W. clearly states on page 46, in no uncertain terms, that the Higher Power of choice for alcoholics must be God: "that Power, which is God." God is the Higher Power we all need to believe in, because that was the Higher Power Bill Wilson believed in. His dogma has wounded A.A., and driven many from the rooms that cannot believe in God.

To those folks we suggest ignoring Bill's damaging discourse on God and Higher Power, and use your own secular or spiritual beliefs to aid your recovery, whatever those beliefs may be.

Have you lacked power to manage your life? – p.45

Note that the main object of this book is to enable you to find a Power greater than yourself which will solve your problem. – p. 45

Have you had honest doubts and prejudices about God? – p.45

What will He / She / It look like? What will it be like when you find Him / Her / It? Where did you get these ideas?

Had you abandoned the idea of God entirely? – p.45

Are you willing to lay aside your previous beliefs or prejudices and express a willingness to believe in a Power greater than yourself?

What is your concept of God? – p.46

When, therefore, we speak to you of God, we mean your own conception of God. This applies, too, to other spiritual expressions which you find in this book. **Do not let any prejudice you may have against spiritual terms deter you from honestly asking yourself what they mean to you**. At the start, this was all we needed to commence spiritual growth, to affect our first conscious relation with God as we understood Him. Afterward, we found ourselves accepting many things which then seemed entirely out of reach. That was growth, but if we wished to grow we had to begin somewhere. So we used our own conception, however limited it was.

> When I came into A.A. I had to learn a totally different language—the language of A.A. The most confusing aspect for me centered on how alcoholics in the Fellowship used the terms God and Higher Power.
>
> I discovered that Christians, who made up the vast majority of A.A. members, used the terms interchangeably. Non-Christians

131

and those that did not believe in God used the terms God and Higher Power to mean two different things. One was theistic, the other was not.

Since members of A.A. had different definitions and conceptions of God and Higher Power, it made for a very bewildering introduction to A.A. because not everyone was on the same page.

Since God was never my Higher Power of choice, my sponsor suggested I replace in my mind all the references to God in the Big Book with whatever I thought of as my own spiritual power.

Unfortunately, my spirituality had no name. My higher power was not some *entity*, but a set of moral values which I could see reflected and embodied in the 12 Step principles.

So I ended up naming my higher power, for A.A. purposes, the Principles Of the Twelve Steps. I did not replace God with the acronym "P-O-T-S," although I thought about doing so, just to have a bit of fun in discussion meetings.

When I discuss God and Higher Power in the rooms today, I emphasize that I needed and found an intangible, non-human motivational power in addition to the human power of the Fellowship that I could use and connect with to help me stay sober. They are the 12 Step principles.

We needed to ask ourselves but one short question. **"Do I now believe, or am I even willing to believe, that there is a Power greater than myself?"** As soon as a man can say that he does believe, or is willing to believe, we emphatically assure him that he is on his way. It has been repeatedly proven among us that upon this simple cornerstone a wonderfully effective spiritual structure can be built. [Please be sure to **read Appendix II** on Spiritual Experience]

Having declared that God is the Higher Power needed for sobriety in A.A., in the above paragraphs Bill reassures us that we can choose our own conception of God. He says God is required for spiritual growth, and again identifies God the power we need going forward.

For the atheist or agnostic, it appears all roads in A.A. lead to God. Bill W.'s use of the terms Higher Power, spiritual and God of our understanding, all refer to the God of the Christian religion.

This makes sense, because the Big Book is a historical document which reflects Bill Wilson's personal experience. He experienced a white light, hot flash religious conversion experience in Towns Hospital on December 14, 1934 which made him a true believer in God.

The initial drafts of the Big Book were extremely religious in tone and substance. Without the intervention of the early pioneers Hank Parkhurst and Jim Burwell, who added "of our understanding" to Steps Three and Eleven, and removed "on our knees" from Step Seven, many who considered joining A.A. would have been repelled, having concluded it was just another religious sect rather than a non-religious, spiritual program.

Luckily for us, the addition of "Appendix II—Spiritual Experience" to the Big Book at the time of its second printing in 1941, helped clarify the true intent of the A.A. program and its approach.

Appendix II says that the *personality change* sufficient to bring about recovery from alcoholism has manifested itself among us in many different forms. A small number of us had, like Bill W., a sudden religious conversion "spiritual experience" leading to an instantaneous "God-consciousness."

But most of us experienced a slow "spiritual awakening," which was a gradual change over time in our attitudes and actions. This is called an "educational variety" transformation, and is considered by many to imply a more secular than religious transition.

The bottom line is that any alcoholic capable of honestly facing his problems in the light of his experience can recover, provided he does not close his mind to all spiritual principles.

What are those spiritual principles, one might ask? Many of us believe that they are the moral values embedded in the principles of the 12 Steps.

Do you now believe or are you even willing to believe that there is a Power greater than yourself? – p.47

Do you recognize that when you can say "yes" to this question that you are "on the way" – p.47

Note the book once again refers you to Appendix II – p.47

What is it that Appendix II says that is indispensable?

Have you been open-minded or have you been obstinate, sensitive and unreasonably prejudiced about discussions about God?

What reservations do you have when you have completed this chapter?

APPENDIX II—SPIRITUAL EXPERIENCE

The terms **"spiritual experience"** and **"spiritual awakening"** are used many times in this book which, upon careful reading, shows that **the personality change sufficient to bring about recovery from alcoholism has manifested itself among us in many different forms**.

Yet it is true that our first printing gave many readers the impression that these **personality changes, or religious experiences**, must be in the nature of sudden and spectacular upheavals. Happily for everyone, this conclusion is erroneous.

In the first few chapters a number of sudden revolutionary changes are described. Though it was not our intention to create such an impression, many alcoholics have nevertheless concluded that in order to recover they must acquire an immediate and overwhelming **"God-consciousness"** followed at once by a vast change in feeling and outlook.

Among our rapidly growing membership of thousands of alcoholics such transformations, though frequent, are by no means the rule. **Most of our experiences are** what the psychologist William James calls **the "educational variety"** because they develop slowly over a period of time.

Quite often friends of the newcomer are aware of the difference long before he is himself. He finally realizes that **he has undergone a profound alteration in his reaction to life**; that such a change could hardly have been brought about by himself alone. What often takes place in a few months could hardly be accomplished by years of self-discipline. With few exceptions our members find that they have **tapped an unsuspected inner resource** which they presently identify with their own conception **of a Power greater than themselves**.

Most of us think this awareness of a **Power greater than ourselves is the essence of spiritual experience. Our more religious members call it** "God-consciousness."

Most emphatically we wish to say that any alcoholic capable of honestly facing his problems in the light of our experience can recover, provided he does not close his mind to all spiritual principles. He can only be defeated by an attitude of intolerance or belligerent denial.

We find that no one need have difficulty with the spirituality of the program. **Willingness, honesty and open mindedness are the essentials of recovery**. But these are indispensable.

There is a principle which is a bar against all information, which is proof against all arguments and which cannot fail to keep a man in everlasting ignorance—that principle is contempt prior to investigation. [Herbert Spencer]

> Despite Bill W. equating a spiritual experience and a spiritual awakening as both coming from God, one quickly and one slowly, I've found it much more useful to speak of a spiritual experience as coming from God, and a spiritual awakening as

135

coming from some type of spiritual, *non-theistic* source of our own belief.

A.A. members may well disagree with this distinction, but my experience has shown me this approach has worked extremely well for my own sobriety, and when I take an atheist or agnostic through the 12 Steps.

That was great news to us, for we had assumed **we could not make use of spiritual principles unless we accepted many things on faith** which seemed difficult to believe. When people presented us with spiritual approaches, how frequently did we all say, "I wish I had what that man has. I'm sure it would work if I could only believe as he believes. But I cannot accept as surely true the many articles of faith which are so plain to him." So it was comforting to learn that we could commence at a simpler level.

Besides a seeming inability to accept much on faith, we often found ourselves handicapped by obstinacy, sensitiveness, and unreasoning prejudice. Many of us have been so touchy that even casual reference to spiritual things make us bristle with antagonism. This sort of thinking had to be abandoned. Though some of us resisted, we found no great difficulty in casting aside such feelings.

Faced with alcoholic destruction, we soon became as open minded on spiritual matters as we had tried to be on other questions. In this respect **alcohol was a great persuader. It finally beat us into a state of reasonableness**. Sometimes this was a tedious process; we hope no one else will be prejudiced for as long as some of us were.

The **reader may still ask why he should believe in a Power greater than himself**. We think there are good reasons. Let us have a look at some of them.

At this point in the chapter, Bill W. introduces the term "faith." He then begins to link faith with spirituality *and* a belief in a Higher Power, which Bill defines as God. Once again, these

136

analogies can be very confusing, incorrectly suggesting that if one does not believe in God, one has no faith in anything.

The word faith, although often used in a religious context, simply means "a complete trust or confidence in someone or something." For example, we have faith that the sun will rise every morning, or that if we jump off a stool gravity will always take us to the floor.

The practical individual of today is a stickler for facts and results. Nevertheless, the twentieth century readily accepts theories of all kinds, provided they are firmly grounded in fact. We have numerous theories, for example, about **electricity**. Everybody believes them without a murmur of doubt. Why this ready acceptance? Simply because it is impossible to explain what we see, feel, direct, and use, without a reasonable assumption as a starting point.

Everybody nowadays, believes in scores of assumptions for which there is good evidence, but no perfect visual proof. And does not science demonstrate that visual proof is the weakest proof? It is being constantly revealed, as mankind studies the material world, that outward appearances are not inward reality at all. To illustrate:

The prosaic **steel girder** is a mass of electrons whirling around each other at incredible speed. These tiny bodies are governed by precise laws, and these laws hold true throughout the material world. Science tells us so. We have no reason to doubt it. When, however, the perfectly **logical assumption is suggested that underneath the material world and life as we see it, there is an All Powerful, Guiding, Creative Intelligence**, right there our perverse streak comes to the surface and we laboriously set out to convince ourselves it isn't so. We read wordy books and indulge in windy arguments, **thinking we believe this universe needs no God** to explain it. Were our contentions true, **it would follow that life originated out of nothing, means nothing, and proceeds nowhere**.

Instead of regarding ourselves as intelligent agents, spearheads of God's ever advancing Creation, **we agnostics and atheists chose**

to believe that our human intelligence was the last word, the alpha and the omega, the beginning and end of all. **Rather vain of us, wasn't it?**

We, who have traveled this dubious path, beg you to **lay aside prejudice**, even against organized religion. We have learned that whatever the human frailties of various faiths may be, those faiths have given purpose and direction to millions. **People of faith have a logical idea of what life is all about**. Actually, we used to have no reasonable conception whatever. We used to amuse ourselves by cynically dissecting spiritual beliefs and practices when we might have observed that many spiritually-minded persons of all races, colors, and creeds were demonstrating a degree of stability, happiness and usefulness which we should have sought ourselves.

> Bill draws a false equivalency when he uses our ignorance of how electricity works or what makes up a steel girder as evidence that God exists. He further erroneously states that atheists and agnostics believe only in themselves, and deny any spiritual energy in the universe. On the other hand, faithful folks, Wilson states, know all about life, whereas the unfaithful don't.
>
> There is no reason for any alcoholic to become trapped in this chapter's discrimination and inconsistencies, as long as we remember *we are not God*, and that we do need some type of non-human, inspirational force or power that we can relate to and connect with to help us maintain sobriety and help us in our new life.
>
> I've seen visual proof in A.A. that atheists, agnostics and those that do not believe in God can get and stay sober. They have found a new, delightful design for living that works very well for them and those around them. They have found some type of non-human, spiritual aid to motivate, guide and direct them in their new life.
>
> *They are the living proof that anyone can get sober without God.*

Instead, we looked at the human defects of these people, and sometimes used their shortcomings as a basis of wholesale condemnation. We talked of intolerance, while we were intolerant ourselves. We missed the reality and the beauty of the forest because we were diverted by the ugliness of some its trees. **We never gave the spiritual side of life a fair hearing**.

In our **personal stories** you will **find a wide variation in the way each teller approaches and conceives of the Power which is greater than himself**. Whether we agree with a particular approach or conception seems to make little difference. Experience has taught us that these are matters about which, for our purpose, we need not be worried. They are questions for each individual to settle for himself.

On one proposition, however, these men and women are strikingly agreed. **Every one of them has gained access to, and believe in, a Power greater than himself. This Power has in each case accomplished the miraculous, the humanly impossible**. As a celebrated American statesman put it, "Let's look at the record."

> Bill returns to referring to the God of his understanding as his spiritual Higher Power. He seems to imply that this power, and this power alone, is responsible for the miracle of sobriety. If this is the case, some might sarcastically ask why one would need to bother with working the 12 Steps to acquire a spiritual awakening or experience which drives a change in our attitudes and actions leading to our new design for living.
>
> Some of our more religious newcomers in A.A. believe that God or the church *alone* has the power to keep them sober. Neither does, and Bill makes this clear in "Working With Others" on page 93 when he says that faith alone is insufficient for sobriety; to be vital it must be accompanied by self-sacrifice and unselfish, constructive action.

Here are thousands of men and women, worldly indeed. They flatly declare that **since they have come to believe in a Power greater than themselves, to take a certain attitude toward that Power, and to do certain simple things, there has been a revolutionary**

change in their way of living and thinking. In the face of collapse and despair, in the face of the total failure of their human resources, they found that a new power, peace, happiness, and sense of direction flowed into them. This happened soon after they whole-heartedly met a few simple requirements. Once confused and baffled by the seeming futility of existence, they show the underlying reasons why they were making heavy going of life. Leaving aside the drink question, they tell why living was so unsatisfactory. They show how the change came over them.

When many hundreds of people are able to say that the consciousness of the Presence of God is today the most important fact of their lives, they present a powerful reason why one should have faith.

At this point any alcoholic reader who is having difficulty with this chapter because of its focus on God as A.A.'s Higher Power of choice in sobriety, and the statement that God is the most important thing in our lives, may find it helpful to stop analyzing each paragraph and detach a bit.

As an atheist, when I struggled with all the God language in "We Agnostics," my sponsor suggested I ignore Bill's intermixing of the terms God, Higher Power, religion and spirituality. I could, as the Buddhists do in A.A., simply replace the word "God" with "Good," or some other term that made sense to me.

He also suggested that I take the time and make the effort to more fully identify and define a power other than myself that could help me in sobriety. This power, he said, would need to be one that I could emotionally connect with and be able to use to help guide, direct and motivate me in my new life.

He also said that one's higher power did not need to be a "thing" or an "entity." It could be a force, or energy, or a set of principles, or anything else that would help me in my sobriety. It could even be a door-knob, if that worked for me.

So I got out pen and paper and wrote down what my Higher

Power, or spiritual power, would look like to me, as best I could. What traits would that power have? How would I describe that power to someone in A.A.?

When I showed my work to my sponser, he simply pointed at the page and said "Good, that's your Higher Power, now start using it."

The only thing I had written down were some of the moral values related to the 12 Step principles, such as honesty, optimism, courage, integrity, willingness, humility, love, tolerance, kindness, forgiveness, perseverance, spiritual awareness and service to others.

Those intangible *values* of the 12 Step principles are the spiritual drivers that help me with my new design for living. In the rooms of A.A., I call them my God, my Higher Power, and my spiritual power.

This world of ours has made more material progress in the last century than in all the millenniums which went before. Almost everyone knows the reason. Students of ancient history tell us that the intellect of men in those days was equal to the best of today. Yet in ancient times, material progress was painfully slow. The spirit of modern scientific inquiry, research and invention was almost unknown. In the realm of the material, men's minds were fettered by superstition, tradition, and all sort of fixed ideas.

Some of the contemporaries of Columbus thought a round earth preposterous. Others came near putting Galileo to death for his astronomical heresies.

We asked ourselves this: **Are not some of us just as biased and unreasonable about the realm of the spirit as were the ancients about the realm of the material?**

Our job in A.A. is not to try to answer age old questions of theology and philosophy; there is no point to it. At the end of the day, what we believe is what we believe, regardless of

141

scientific or religious theory. What we believe in, or don't believe in, in no way implies that we are prejudiced against anyone else's beliefs, even when they don't agree with ours.

Have you been biased and unreasonably prejudiced about the realm of the spirit? – p.51

Did your ideas work?

Even in the present century, American newspapers were afraid to print an account of the Wright brothers' first successful flight at Kitty Hawk. Had not all efforts at flight failed before? Did not Professor Langley's flying machine go to the bottom of the Potomac River? Was it not true that the best mathematical minds had proved man could never fly? Had not people said God had reserved this privilege to the birds? Only thirty years later the conquest of the air was almost an old story and airplane travel was in full swing.

But in most fields our generation has witnessed complete liberation in thinking. Show any longshoreman a Sunday supplement describing a proposal to explore the moon by means of a rocket and he will say, "I bet they do it—maybe not so long either." Is not our age characterized by the ease with which we discard old ideas for new, by the complete readiness with which we throw away the theory or gadget which does not work for something new which does?

We had to ask ourselves why we shouldn't apply to our human problems this same **readiness to change our point of view**. We were having trouble with personal relationships, we couldn't control our emotional natures, we were prey to misery and depression, we couldn't make a living, we had a feeling of uselessness, we were full of fear, we were unhappy, we couldn't seem to be of real help to other people—was not a basic solution of these bedevilments more important than whether we should see newsreels of lunar flight? Of course it was.

When we saw others solve their problems by a simple reliance upon the Spirit of the Universe, we had to stop doubting the power of God. Our ideas did not work. But the God idea did.

Bill is correct. Our original ideas on how to control our drinking didn't work, but it's not an either / or solution, as Bill suggests.

God can work for those that believe in him even though there is no guarantee, but many in A.A. are able to stay sober and solve their problems just as easily without believing in God and without his help.

One classic example was Jim Burwell, an avid atheist, who was one of the first New Yorker pioneers who joined A.A. on June 15, 1938 and remained sober for the rest of his life until he died in 1974 from hip surgery complications.

Will the God idea work? – p.52

The Wright brothers' almost childish faith that they could build a machine which would fly was the main-spring of their accomplishment. Without that, nothing could have happened. **We agnostics and atheists were sticking to the idea that self-sufficiency would solve our problems. When others showed us that "God-sufficiency" worked with them, we began to feel like those who had insisted the Wrights would never fly**.

Just because atheists and agnostics do not believe in God does not automatically mean that they believe self-sufficiency is sufficient to solve all their problems. This is a false assumption. Most atheists use spiritual principles and powers to help them. They do not take on life alone any more than Christians do.

Logic is great stuff. We like it. We still like it. It is not by chance we were given the power to reason, to examine the evidence of our sense, and to draw conclusions. That is one of man's magnificent attributes. We agnostically inclined would not feel satisfied with a proposal which does not lend itself to reasonable approach and interpretation. Hence **we are at pains to tell why we think our present faith is reasonable, why we think it more sane and logical to believe than not to believe**, why we say our former thinking was soft and mushy when we threw up our hands in doubt and said, "**We don't know**."

Agnostic means "without knowledge." An agnostic is a person who holds a middle ground between atheism and theism. Agnostics believe that the existence of God is a definite possibility, but it is not within the realm of one's knowledge. It is irrelevant if agnosticism is reasonable, sane or logical. Agnostics in A.A. have no need to defend their uncertainty, and do not dismiss the religious beliefs of others.

Some argue that since no one really knows if God exists, it would be smarter to believe in God than not, because if there is a God we are saved. If there isn't a God, we've lost nothing. It's called "covering our bases," and exemplifies a profoundly dishonest, selfish and self-centered approach to life.

I prefer the insightful suggestion from the Roman Emperor and philosopher Marcus Aurelius who lived nineteen centuries ago. He said: "Live a good life. If there are gods and they are just, then they will not care how devout you have been, but will welcome you based on the virtues you have lived by.

If there are gods, but unjust, then you should not want to worship them.

If there are no gods, then you will be gone, but will have lived a noble life that will live on in the memories of your loved ones."

When we became alcoholics, crushed by a self-imposed crises we could not postpone or evade, **we had to fearlessly face the proposition that either God is everything or else He is nothing. God either is or He isn't. What was our choice to be?**

Bill presents the struggling alcoholic with the classic Hobson's choice: the single and only solution of God, followed by a misleading either / or choice.

This is wrong, and is damaging to A.A. as a whole, because Wilson's inflexible, assertive, authoritarian, dogmatic proposal discourages many non-theistic members from sticking with A.A.

God is everything to those that believe in God, but is nothing to those that don't believe in God. It is no different than saying that the supreme beings Allah or Zeus are everything to those that believe in them, and nothing to those that believe in God.

Who is A.A. to say what is the true and only God or Higher Power, or that God even exists?

Arrived at this point, we were **squarely confronted with the question of faith**. We couldn't duck the issue. Some of us had already walked far over the **Bridge of Reason** toward the **desired shore of faith**. The outlines and the promise of the New Land had brought luster to tired eyes and fresh courage to flagging spirits. Friendly hands had stretched out in welcome. We were grateful that Reason had brought us so far. But somehow, we couldn't quite step ashore. **Perhaps we had been leaning too heavily on reason** that last mile and we did not like to lose our support.

That was natural, but let us think a little more closely. Without knowing it, **had we not been brought to where we stood by a certain kind of faith?** For **did we not believe in our own reasoning?** Did we not have confidence in our ability to think? What was that but a sort of faith? Yes, we had been faithful, abjectly faithful to the God of Reason. So, in one way or another, we discovered that faith had been involved all the time!

We found, too, that **we had been worshippers**. What a state of mental goose-flesh that used to bring on! **Had we not variously worshipped people, sentiment, things, money, and ourselves?** And then, with a better motive, had we not worshipfully beheld the sunset, the sea, or a flower? Who of us had not loved something or somebody? How much did these feelings, these loves, these worships, have to do with pure reason? Little or nothing, we saw at last. Were not these things the tissue out of which our lives were constructed? Did not these feelings, after all, determine the course of our existence? **It was impossible to say we had no capacity for faith, or love, or worship**. In one form or another we had been living by faith and little else.

145

Imagine life without faith! Were nothing left but pure reason, it wouldn't be life. But **we believed in life**—of course we did. We could not prove life in the sense that you can prove a straight line is the shortest distance between two points, yet, there it was. **Could we still say the whole thing was nothing but a mass of electrons, created out of nothing, meaning nothing, whirling on to a destiny of nothingness? Of course we couldn't**. The electrons themselves seemed more intelligent than that. At least, so the chemist said. Hence, **we saw that reason isn't everything**. Neither is reason, as most of us use it, entirely dependable, though it emanate from our best minds. What about people who proved that man could never fly?

Yet we had been seeing another kind of flight, a **spiritual liberation** from this world, people who rose above their problems. They said **God made these things possible**, and we only smiled. We had seen spiritual release, but liked to tell ourselves it wasn't true.

> In the above paragraphs, Bill again mixes and intermingles the terms God, faith, life, worship, spiritual and reason. He suggests that since we all believe in life and love, we all have faith, and faith requires the belief in God. So if we believe in life and love, we automatically must believe in God. This is another deceptive and fallacious proposal which does no service to the struggling alcoholic in A.A.

> As for the source of life, just because one does not believe in God does not mean one understands how life was created, how it will end, and why we exist. The origins of our universe and existential reasoning have nothing to do with maintaining our sobriety and finding a new way of living in A.A.

Actually we were fooling ourselves, for **deep down in every man, woman, and child, is the fundamental idea of God**. It may be obscured by calamity, by pomp, by worship of other things, but in some form or other it is there. For **faith in a Power greater than ourselves, and miraculous demonstrations of that power in human lives, are facts as old as man himself**.

We finally saw that **faith in some kind of God was a part of our make-up**, just as much as the feeling we have for a friend. Sometimes we had to search fearlessly, but **He was there**. He was as much a fact as we were. **We found the Great Reality deep down within us**. In the last analysis it is only there that He may be found. It was so with us.

We can only clear the ground a bit. If our testimony helps sweep away prejudice, enables you to think honestly, encourages you to search diligently within yourself, then, **if you wish, you can join us on the Broad Highway**. With this attitude you cannot fail. the consciousness of your belief is sure to come to you.

> For many in A.A., the fundamental idea of God is not deep down in any of us. Neither is God the Great Reality for all of us. The truth is that something spiritual, mystical or religious may well be our Great Reality, but that doesn't mean it's God.

> We can have faith in some force or power beyond ourselves, but again, that does not mean that power is God. It might be Allah, or one of the hundreds of Hindu gods, or the no-god of the atheist Buddhists. It might be a set of moral principles or values, or it might simply be trying to live life by the Golden Rule—treating others the way we wish to be treated.

> Atheists, agnostics, non-believers, those that believe in other gods, and those that have no religious beliefs are welcome to join all of the A.A. Fellowship on the Broad Highway to sobriety. A.A. must remain fully inclusive, never exclusive, despite the extreme religious bias in "We Agnostics."

In this book you will read the experience of a **man who thought he was an atheist**. His story is so interesting that some of it should be told now. His change of heart was dramatic, convincing, and moving.

Our friend was a minister's son. He attended church school, where he became rebellious at what he thought an overdose of religious education. For years thereafter he was dogged by trouble and frustration. Business failure, insanity, fatal illness, suicide—these calamities in his immediate family embittered and depressed him.

147

Post-war disillusionment, ever more serious alcoholism, impending mental and physical collapse, brought him to the point of self-destruction.

One night, when confined in a hospital, he was approached by an alcoholic who had known a spiritual experience. Our friend's gorge rose as he bitterly cried out: "**If there is a God, He certainly hasn't done anything for me!**"

But later, alone in his room, he asked himself this question: "**Is it possible that all the religious people I have known are wrong?**" While pondering the answer he felt as though he lived in hell. Then, like a thunderbolt, a great thought came. It crowded out all else: "**Who are you to say there is no God?**"

This man recounts that **he tumbled out of bed to his knees**. In a few seconds **he was overwhelmed by a conviction of the Presence of God**. It poured over and through him with the certainty and majesty of a great tide at flood. The barriers he had built through the years were swept away. He **stood in the Presence of Infinite Power and Love**. He had stepped from bridge to shore. For the first time, he **lived in conscious companionship with his Creator**.

Thus was our friend's cornerstone fixed in place. No later vicissitude has shaken it. **His alcoholic problem was taken away**. That very night, years ago, it disappeared. Save for a few brief moments of temptation the thought of drink has never returned; and at such times a great revulsion has risen up in him. Seemingly he could not drink even if he would. **God had restored his sanity**.

> Like Bill Wilson's hot flash episode while hospitalized, the man who thought he was an atheist had a sudden religious conversion experience and his alcoholic obsession was immediately removed.
>
> Many interpret this religious conversion story not only as an attempt to coerce atheists and non-believers into Wilson's Christian based beliefs, but to suggest that only God can restore us to sanity and sobriety.

Although Bill W. probably had the best of intentions, his example of one person's experience damages A.A. by suggesting it is wrong to have secular beliefs. This attitude makes A.A. dogmatic and rigid, and worst of all, it deters many newcomers from staying with the A.A. program because of its insistence on believing in God.

Clinical studies based on interviews with rehabilitation facility patients have indicated that almost two-thirds of the alcoholics who started A.A. left A.A., *never* to return. Most of them left because of A.A.'s religious emphasis. The remaining third who left did return to A.A. at some point, and hopefully the others got sober elsewhere.

The Christian minister's son who said "Who are you to say there is no God?" was John Henry Fitzhugh Mayo, nicknamed "Fitz." He was the third A.A. member in New York who got sober while at Towns Hospital in the winter of 1935. He authored the big book story "Our Southern Friend," and remained sober until he died of cancer in 1943.

What is this but a miracle of healing? Yet its elements are simple. Circumstances made him willing to believe. He humbly offered himself to his Maker—then he knew.

Even so has **God restored us all to our right minds**. To this man, the revelation was sudden. Some of us grow into it more slowly. But He has come to all who have honestly sought Him.

When we drew near to Him He disclosed Himself to us.

This chapter is always a lively topic in Big Book Step Study groups because of the variety of members' beliefs and opinions. The only common thread I have experienced is that we can't get sober completely on our own and that we can't pray our way into sobriety, otherwise we wouldn't be in A.A.

We need two things for sobriety:

1) We need to be around folks just like us who have attained

sobriety and think like we do; that is the power of our Fellowship, *and*

2) We need to learn to connect, use and rely on whatever non-human spiritual or religious beliefs, force or principles we have to help us grow and prosper in our new, strange, sober life.

How we define and use our spiritual or religious power is up to us, and should never be dictated, ridiculed or dismissed by anyone in A.A.

Our *Kit of Spiritual Tools* for recovery has two pieces:

1) Fellowship – sponsor, sponsees, meetings, Home Group, service work, and 2) Design for Living – the Big Book and 12 Steps

Spirituality = Humility + Responsibility

Spirituality = Humility (Faith) + Responsibility (Action)

Spirituality = Humility (Steps 1,2,3) + Responsibility (Steps 4 to 12)

Step 1 is chaos, Step 2 is conviction, Step 3 is commitment and Steps 4 through 12 reflect our human conversion into a new life.

Do you believe that "When we drew near to Him He disclosed Himself to us?" – p.57

HOMEWORK

SESSION TWO

STEPS 2 & 3

We Agnostics, How It Works

Pages 44 - 64

<u>STEP 2</u> -- *Came to believe that a power greater than ourselves could restore us to sanity.*

<u>STEP 3</u> -- *Made a decision to turn our will and our lives over to the care of God as we understood Him.*

<u>WRITE</u> down your reactions to the readings as to <u>how they apply to you and your illness</u>, incorporating as much as possible of the considerations into your work. Think about how the writings apply to your life.

1) Write in your notebook what you <u>can</u> believe about a Power greater than yourself.

2) Write on another page what you <u>cannot</u> believe about God.

3) As you go forward from this point, it is those things which you believe or which fit into your conception of God which you will be using and you can be comforted in knowing that "Our own conception, however inadequate, was sufficient to make the approach and to effect a contact with Him." – <u>p.46</u>

SESSION THREE

STEP 4 - Resentments

How It Works

Pages 58 - 67

STEP 4 -- *Made a searching and fearless moral inventory of ourselves.*

INTRODUCTION

We come here with a huge load of stored up shame, guilt, and unresolved pain to be let go of. Step 4 helps us lay bare the conflicts of the past so that we are no longer at their mercy.

Step 4 gives us the means to find out who we are, and what we are not. It is about finding our assets as well as our defects of character. We discover that our problems began long before we took our first drink. We may have felt isolated and afraid, and it was our desire to change the way we felt that led to our drinking.

We have a disease. We are not responsible for being an alcoholic, any more than a diabetic is responsible for being diabetic. But now that we know we are an alcoholic, we are responsible for our recovery. There are no longer excuses because we realize we must live the Steps daily or we will die spiritually, emotionally and physically. We are working on practices - things we do - that we will use every day of our lives to move us from being restless, irritable and discontented toward keeping us sober and having serenity and peace of mind.

Do Step 4 as best you reasonably can, and that is more than good enough. Watch out for paralysis from fear or perfectionism. Remember, it's *your* Inventory, not someone else's.

BEFORE THE MEETING

1) READ the chapter "How It Works" (Chapter 5, p.64-71) and Step Four in the *Twelve Steps & Twelve Traditions*.
2) WRITE your "Grudge List" (Resentments of People, Institutions and Principles (p.64).

152

3) Complete Columnar Work on Grudge List.

4) List your Faults, or character defects (shortcomings; Seven Deadly Sins).

5) Write your Grudge List, one list at a time from top to bottom. Put down all the people, places, things, principles or institutions who you resent (feel bad about; are angry towards; harbor ill will towards, etc.) on a list.

6) Then make a brief note about how you *"were hurt or threatened"* (p.65), or where you had expectations of others, or others had expectations of you – where you were *sore* or were *"burned up"* (p.65).

DURING THE MEETING

Discuss any problems you are having. Exchange examples with one another.

PROMPT: before making a Grudge list, make a list of all people who "owe you something" – this gets to the issue of entitlement and will essentially be your resentment list.

Why work a Grudge List?

Resentments build us up to a drink. If we drink, we die. If we get rid of resentments, we are able to live life fully and be free of anger.

GRUDGE LIST EXAMPLE

PEOPLE

Spouse – always nags me
Employer – never satisfied with my work
Neighbor – always snooping, etc.

PRINCIPLES

having to pay tax – I don't make enough to have to pay so much tax...
"you reap what you sow" – I never got a break in life...
"your problems are of your own making" – it's not my fault I drink so much...

INSTITUTIONS

IRS – they won't leave me alone

Courts – if I could afford a good lawyer I wouldn't have all these problems

Creditors – they don't understand I don't have a job and can't make regular payments, *etc.*

COLUMNAR WORK

Transfer top 10 – 25 resentments from Grudge list to column format. Make four Headings:

NAME (I'm resentful at)

CAUSE (Why I'm angry)

AFFECTS MY (What part of self)

MY PART (My Faults – where was I to blame?)

<u>NAME</u>: one of the names from your Grudge List

<u>CAUSE</u>: write a few words which describe each specific instance which caused you to feel bad about this person, institution or principle. This is an important part of the exercise. Be specific. Rather than write that "He lied," write "He told me he would pay me back and he didn't."

<u>AFFECTS MY</u>: list how each incident affected you. Often, the incident affects our self-esteem, security, pocketbook, ambition, or personal relationships / sex and created fear and worry.

THIRD COLUMN DEFINITIONS

Self-esteem - How I think of myself.

Security - General sense of emotional well-being.

Pocketbook - Basic desire for money, property and possessions.

Personal Relations - Our relations with other people.

Sex Relations - Basic drive for sexual intimacy.

Selfish, self-centered, egotistical - "It's all about me!"

Pride - How I think others view me.

Ambitions - Our goals, plans and designs for the future. Ambition deals with the things that we want. In examining our ambitions we notice that we have the following types:

a) Emotional ambitions - Our ambitions for Emotional Security. Our "feelings."

b) Material ambitions - Our ambitions for "Our pocketbook." Our ambitions towards physical and financial well-being.

c) Social ambitions - Our "place or position in the herd." Our ambitions of how others view us. Our ambitions towards what people think about us.

d) Sexual ambitions - Our ambitions for sex relations.

MY PART: leave *BLANK* for now.

NAME	CAUSE	AFFECTS MY	MY PART / MY ROLE / FAULTS
MY MOTHER	Trying to control my feelings & actions. I say "I feel hungry," she says "You're not hungry."	Self-esteem; pride; personal relationship	
MY FATHER	Abandoned me as a child.	Self-esteem; personal relationship	

Make your Character Defect / Faults lists. If possible, order incidents and examples by age. Provide a short narrative describing examples of your faults. Be brief but specific. This is the self-analysis in which you will identify in the MY PART column your role in your resentments – where you were at fault (Grudge List). By doing this exercise, you will be relieved of the difficulty of forgiveness, and will set you free from that which you resent.

MY PART examples of common FAULTS	GRUDGE LIST examples of common INSTITUTIONS	GRUDGE LIST examples of common PRINCIPLES
Anger or Temper	Authority	God-Deity / Satan
Jealousy or Envy	Marriage	Certain Races
Pride or Vanity	Church	Religion
Selfish	Religion	Society
Frustration	Legal	Justice
Impatience	Government	Bible
Greed	Education System	Golden Rule
Gluttony or over-indulgence	Hospitals	Heaven / Hell
Lust or excessive sexual appetite	DMV	Certain Lifestyles
	Post Office	Life After Death
Sloth or laziness	Correctional System	Sin / Original Sin
Dishonesty	Welfare	Retribution
Theft or Fraud	IRS / Taxes	Adultery
Vandalism	Health/Mental Health System	Ten Commandments
Violence		"Love, honor, obey"
Cheating		"Can't be too thin"
Lying		"Don't put off until tomorrow..."
Criticism		"What goes around comes around"
Self – Pity		
Prejudice		
Intolerance		

Complete the Columnar Work. Fill in the <u>MY PART</u> column for each grudge or resentment, drawing on your Faults list.

List for each incident –

a) Where have I been at fault, to blame or doing wrong – selfish, dishonest, self-seeking or frightened?

b) What was the real issue?

c) What was the result – retaliation, fighting back, running away? Did it help? Can you forgive?

NAME	CAUSE	AFFECTS MY	MY PART / MY ROLE / FAULTS
MY MOTHER	Trying to control my feelings & actions. I say "I feel hungry," she says "You're not hungry."	Self-esteem; pride; personal relationship	Responded in anger; resisted but often yielded; did not help. Real issue was my lack of adequate self-esteem. I can forgive. She did the best she could at the time.
MY FATHER	Abandoned me as a child.	Self-esteem; personal relationship	Responded in anger. Ran away from home. Refused to visit him after the divorce. Real issue was continued anger at him. Have not forgiven him.

Chapter 5

HOW IT WORKS

Pages 58 – 67

Rarely have we seen a person fail who has thoroughly followed our path. Those who do not recover are people who cannot or will not completely give themselves to this simple program, usually men and women who are **constitutionally incapable of being honest with themselves**. There are **such unfortunates**. They **are not at fault**; they seem to have been born that way. They are naturally incapable of grasping and developing a manner of living which demands rigorous honesty. **Their chances are less than average**. There are those, too, who **suffer from grave emotional and mental disorders**, but many of them do recover if they have the capacity to be honest.

The title of this chapter is "How It Works," not "Why It Works," and is a hint of what is in store for us. The "It" is the program of A.A., which are the 12 Steps.

If we are able to be honest with ourselves, and with others, we have a chance. The only exception would be if we are so severely mentally ill that we cannot be honest with ourselves. Those very rare individuals are either sociopaths, who are people that lack a conscience and don't know the difference between right and wrong, or psychopaths, who have similar, but more dangerous symptoms than sociopaths.

Clinically, a sociopath is a person with antisocial personality disorder. Characteristics include repeated legal violations, pervasive lying and deception, physical aggressiveness, reckless disregard for the safety of self or others, consistent irresponsibility in work and family environments, and lack of remorse.

Psychopaths have a more severe form of sociopathy with

158

more symptoms, including lack of empathy, lack of deep emotional attachments, narcissism, superficial charm, dishonesty, manipulation and reckless risk-taking. Over ninety percent of psychopaths end up in the criminal justice system.

For clinicians to diagnosis someone as either a sociopath or psychopath, the individual in question must display the above characteristics *after* having been free of the influence of withdrawal, alcohol, drugs or other medications for a significant period of time, since those items can alter thinking and behavior in ways that can lead to a mistaken mental health diagnosis.

Since less than five percent of the population fits into these two categories, almost no alcoholic can legitimately use the excuse they are too mentally ill to be honest, or too ill to recover in the A.A. program.

Do you question whether you are capable of being honest with yourself?

Our stories disclose in a general way what we used to be like, what happened, and what we are like now. If you have decided you want what we have and are willing to go to any length to get it—then you are ready to take certain steps.

The paragraph above is an excellent, practical reminder for those in A.A. who are asked to share their story at a speaker meeting. It is the only time where it is appropriate to share a condensed part of one's drunk-a-log in order to qualify oneself as a real alcoholic. We are also reminded to share our story in a general way, and do not need to get into specifics and technical details.

Experienced speakers often divide their hourly A.A. talk into thirds: 1) what we were like during our drinking days, 2) how we found a way out through A.A., and 3) how the A.A. program transformed us into the person we are today.

The paragraph also reminds us that sobriety is not a free ride.

It requires going to any length, which means we have some work in front of us to do.

At some of these we balked. We thought we could find an easier, softer way. But we could not. With all the earnestness at our command, we beg of you to **be fearless and thorough from the very start. Some of us have tried to hold on to our old ideas and the result was nil until we let go absolutely.**

Most of us assume if we make some effort, or any effort at any task we attempt, some level of result will follow. If we make a little effort, we'll receive a little benefit. More effort equals more benefit, and if we go all-in, we will likely be successful.

In A.A., and in working the 12 Steps, unless we are fully committed and all-in, we receive *nothing*. We are presented with an all-or-none proposal. We can't just wade into the swimming pool up to our neck; we must jump in the deep end and completely submerse ourself.

Note the state of mind you are asked to have when you start the Steps – Honesty, Fearlessness, Thoroughness and a Willingness to go to any length. – pg. 58

Remember that we deal with **alcohol—cunning, baffling, powerful!** Without help it is too much for us. But **there is One who has all power—that One is God. May you find Him now!**

Another reminder that God is the one and only preferred Higher Power for A.A. members. We hear in the rooms some members share their vision of the solution to their alcoholic illness in religious terms: Alcohol is the evil Devil Lucifer—cunning, baffling and powerful, fighting with an all-powerful God. It's a battle of Titans, and only those that stand with God can get sober.

If these imaginary battle scenes work for Christians, more power to them. However, they do not work for all alcoholics. A more balanced message might be that if we are in fit spiritual condition, we have a good foundation to stay sober.

It is the responsibility of each alcoholic to define for themselves what it means to them to be in a fit spiritual condition.

Half measures availed us nothing. We stood at the **turning point**. We asked His protection and care with complete abandon.

As we embark on our 12 Step work knowing we must go all-in, and that decision is critical, we are reminded of standing at that frightening jumping off place described in the chapter "A Vision For You" when we know in our hearts we are alcoholic: "He cannot picture life without alcohol. Some day he will be unable to imagine life either with alcohol or without it... He will be at the jumping-off place. He will wish for the end." (Big Book, p.152)

We've reached that terrifying fork in the road. Which way do we go? Do we choose not drinking and a new life, or do we choose jails, institutions and death? We have a real life and death decision to make.

What do Half Measures avail us? – pg. 59

Here are the steps we took, which are suggested as a program of recovery:

1 - We admitted we were powerless over alcohol—that our lives had become unmanageable.

2 - Came to believe that a Power greater than ourselves could restore us to sanity.

3 - Made a decision to turn our will and our lives over to the care of God *as we understood him.*

4 - Made a searching and fearless moral inventory of ourselves.

5 - Admitted to God, to ourselves, and to another human being the exact nature of our wrongs.

6 - Were entirely ready to have God remove all these defects of character.

7 - Humbly asked Him to remove our shortcomings.

8 - Made a list of all persons we had harmed, and became willing to make amends to them all.

9 - Made direct amends to such people wherever possible, except when to do so would injure them or others.

10 - Continued to take personal inventory and when we were wrong promptly admitted it.

11 - Sought through prayer and meditation to improve our conscious contact with God *as we understood him*, praying only for knowledge of His will for us and the power to carry that out.

12 - Having had a spiritual awakening as the result of these steps, we tried to carry this message to alcoholics, and to practice these principles in all our affairs.

Many of us exclaimed, "**What an order! I can't go through with it.**" **Do not be discouraged**. No one among us has been able to maintain anything like perfect adherence to these principles. We are not saints. The point is, that **we are willing to grow along spiritual lines**. The **principles** we have set down **are guides to progress**. We claim **spiritual progress rather than spiritual perfection**.

> In Step 12, the steps are described as a set of principles, or guides to progress, although the actual principle each step represents is not stated anywhere in the Big Book. Those principles are spiritual in nature, meaning they are not physically tangible, and can guide and direct us into a new way of living.

> As we grow inside and outside of A.A., we may seek perfection in our new attitudes and actions, but as long as we are moving forward, neither backsliding or standing still, that is a good beginning. Let's not give up!

The 12 Step page in the back of this book has a list of common step principles.

Our description of the alcoholic, the chapter to the agnostic, and our personal adventures before *and after* make clear three pertinent ideas:

(a) That we were alcoholic and could not manage our own lives.

(b) That probably no human power could have relieved our alcoholism.

(c) That God could and would if He were sought.

A.A. oldtimers nickname these the "ABCs," which re-state the themes of the first three steps.

Being convinced, we were at **Step Three**, which is that **we decided to turn our will and our life over to God as we understood Him**. Just what do we mean by that, and just what do we do?

Being convinced of what? We are convinced of the truth of the first two steps. We can't stop drinking, our life is a mess, and we need some type of non-human power in addition to our own and that of the Fellowship to help us recover.

Step Three decides and defines for us what power we need for sobriety—that power is God.

The first requirement is that we be convinced that **any life run on self-will can hardly be a success**. On that basis we are almost always in collision with something or somebody, even though our motives are good.

We want what we want when we want it, and if we try hard enough, we know we'll get it. We are determined to control our life, and the lives of those around us in order to get our own way.

Most people try to live by self-propulsion. Each person is like **an actor who wants to run the whole show**; is forever trying to arrange the lights, the ballet, the scenery and the rest of the players in his own way.

If his arrangements would only stay put, **if only people would do as he wished, the show would be great**. Everybody, including himself, would be pleased. Life would be wonderful. In trying to make these arrangements our actor may sometimes be quite virtuous. He may be kind, considerate, patient, generous; even modest and self-sacrificing. On the other hand, he may be mean, egotistical, selfish and dishonest. But, as with most humans, he is more likely to have varied traits.

> Controlling the world and the individuals in it is a lot of work. It requires us to be many things to many people, so that we can manipulate them into doing what we want. We learn to become dishonest actors, donning a different mask and role depending on which person we face and which situation arises.

What usually happens? The show doesn't come off very well. He begins to think life doesn't treat him right. He decides to exert himself more. **He becomes, on the next occasion, still more demanding or gracious**, as the case may be. Still the play does not suit him. Admitting he may be somewhat at fault, he is sure that other people are more to blame. He becomes angry, indignant, self-pitying. What is his basic trouble? Is he not really a self-seeker even when trying to be kind? Is he not a victim of the delusion that he can wrest satisfaction and happiness out of this world if he only manages well? Is it not evident to all the rest of the players that these are the things he wants? And **do not his actions make each of them wish to retaliate**, snatching all they can get out of the show? Is he not, even in his best moments, a producer of confusion rather than harmony?

> Despite our best efforts, whether our motives are good or not, we will never be able to bend the world to our will. With every failure we redouble our efforts, trying ever harder, stomping on the toes of our targets, who then retaliate and withdraw.

> Yet we always fail. And when we fail we naturally become angry and resentful. We play the victim, and playing the victim leads to self-pity and resentments over not getting our way. It all starts with our dishonesty trying to manipulate others into doing what we want.

Our actor is self-centered—ego-centric, as people like to call it nowadays. He is like the retired business man who lolls in the Florida sunshine in the winter complaining of the sad state of the nation; the minister who sighs over the sins of the twentieth century; politicians and reformers who are sure all would be Utopia if the rest of the world would only behave; the outlaw safe cracker who thinks society has wronged him; and the alcoholic who has lost all and is locked up. **Whatever our protestations, are not most of us concerned with ourselves, our resentments, or our self-pity?**

Selfishness—self-centeredness! That, we think, is the root of our troubles. Driven by a hundred forms of fear, self-delusion, self-seeking, and self-pity, we step on the toes of our fellows and they retaliate. Sometimes they hurt us, seemingly without provocation, but we invariably find that at some time in the past we have made decisions based on self which later placed us in a position to be hurt.

> We discover that selfishness and self-centeredness is really the root of our troubles. This is our real problem, not alcohol, and is the problem referred to in "We Agnostics" (p.45) which states "That's exactly what this book is about. Its main object is to enable you to find a Power greater than yourself which will solve your problem."
>
> The reasons we are so selfish and self-centered can be uncovered and discovered during our inventory work of Steps Four and Ten, and can be discarded as we change our way of thinking and acting.

So **our troubles, we think, are basically of our own making**. They **arise out of ourselves, and the alcoholic is an extreme example of self-will run riot**, though he usually doesn't think so. Above everything, **we alcoholics must be rid of this selfishness**. We must, or it kills us! God makes that possible. And there often seems no way of entirely getting rid of self without His aid. Many of us had moral and philosophical convictions galore, but we could not live up to them even though we would have liked to.

165

Neither could we reduce our self-centeredness much by wishing or trying on our own power. We had to have God's help.

> The analogy of an alcoholic being a stage actor, chugging along by self-propulsion toward an ego-driven end, is a superb demonstration of the consequences of a life powered totally by selfishness and self-centeredness.
>
> It is impossible to ever be completely rid of our egoism, but it can be tempered by making a conscious effort to change our attitudes and actions. Motivation for doing so can flow from God, from the Fellowship, or from any type of non-human spiritual force or power we can connect with.
>
> Note that selfishness means "I want what you have;" self-centeredness means "the world revolves around me." They are two different, but complimentary personality traits.
>
> *Are you convinced that a life run on self-will can hardly be a success? – p.60*
>
> *Can you see the effects of self-centeredness in your life?*
>
> *How have you been self-centered? List examples in your notebook and discuss them with the group.*
>
> *Did you know that you could not reduce self-centeredness much by wishing or trying on your own power? – p.62*

This is the how and the why of it. First of all, **we had to quit playing God. It didn't work**. Next, we decided that hereafter in this drama of life, **God was going to be our Director**. He is the Principal; we are His agents. He is the Father, and we are His children. Most Good ideas are simple, and **this concept was the keystone of the new and triumphant arch through which we passed to freedom**.

When we sincerely took such a position, all sorts of remarkable things followed. **We had a new Employer**. Being all powerful, He provided what we needed, if we kept close to Him and performed His work well. Established on such a footing we became less and less interested in ourselves, our little plans and designs. More and more **we became interested in seeing what we could contribute to life**. As we felt new power flow in, as we enjoyed peace of mind, as we discovered we could face life successfully, as we became conscious of His presence, **we began to lose our fear of today, tomorrow or the hereafter. We were reborn**.

> In Step Two we yield to the fact that we aren't powerful enough to manage our life without some type of non-human, spiritual or religious help. Our book recommends that a fatherly God is the power we need to provide sanity and serenity as we are reborn into our new life.

> Whether or not we choose God as our Higher Power is up to us. We can choose whatever motivating and directing force we wish, including that of the Fellowship, and should never allow ourselves to be intimidated by those who have chosen God and believe God is the only power that can help alcoholics.

> God is only one employer among many, so we can select any one that best fits our needs.

We were now at <u>Step Three</u>. Many of us said to our Maker, as we understood him:

"God, I offer myself to Thee—to build with me and to do with me as Thou wilt. Relieve me of the bondage of self, that I may better do Thy will. Take away my difficulties, that victory over them may bear witness to those I would help of Thy Power, Thy Love, and Thy Way of life. May I do Thy will always!"

A more secular prayer might be:

I am grateful for the gifts I have received, am receiving, and will receive. Relieve me of the bondage of self, that I may become less selfish and self-centered. Lessen my fears and shortcomings, that I may better serve others. Let me live my life with love and tolerance. I ask only for the knowledge and power to do the next right thing right. And I am thankful for another day of sobriety.

167

We thought well before taking this step making sure we were ready; that we could at last abandon ourselves utterly to Him.

So many in A.A. revere the Christian Third Step Prayer because they have chosen God to be their Higher Power. For those who do not use God as their Higher Power, the simple phrase "Relieve me of the bondage of self" can be a quick reminder that an alcoholic life lived entirely in selfishness and self-centeredness is a recipe for failure.

The A.A. prayer I personally find most useful is the Serenity Prayer, although I omit the first word "God" to make it secular because I direct the prayer to no one: "Grant me the serenity to accept the things I cannot change, the courage to change the things I can, and the wisdom to know the difference." When I get irritable and restless during the day, I simply say "Relieve me of the bondage of self."

When we try to carry the message to other alcoholics in A.A. we are carrying A.A.'s message, not God's message. We carry the message forged by the experience of the members of the A.A. Fellowship. If some of us think that message comes from God, so be it, but I found the message in the Fellowship.

We need to remember that A.A. is not a religion, or a religious program, so we must be vigilant how we describe and pass on A.A.'s message.

A.A.'s message is that anyone can recovery from their hopeless state of mind and body and find a new life if they participate in the fellowship and work the 12 Step program.

We found it very desirable to **take this spiritual step with an understanding person**, such as our wife, best friend, or spiritual adviser. But it is better to meet God alone than with one who might misunderstand. The wording was, of course, quite optional so long as we expressed the idea, voicing it without reservation. This was only a beginning, though if honestly and humbly made, an effect, sometimes a very great one, was felt at once.

Some newcomers in A.A. may wish to repeat the Third Step Prayer with another person, but there is no requirement to do so. Taking and making pledges is not part of A.A. or recovery, as Bill W. alluded to in his story: "There was that proffered temperance pledge I never signed" (Big Book, p.10).

Step Three states "Made a decision to turn our will and our lives over to the care of God *as we understood him.*" For non-Christians, this step simply suggests that we ask for spiritual help. Since we are in A.A., we have already asked for the human help of the fellowship. Now we can ask for additional spiritual or religious help if we choose. That request does not need to be directed to any entity, nor does it need to have a name.

When I hit my bottom in my alcoholic life I did not say "God help me." I said to myself, "I've got to get help." When I say "Relieve me of the bondage of self" during my morning meditation, the request is not directed to God or to any thing or entity. It is simply a ritual request reminding me to try to be less selfish and self-centered during the day.

Next we launched out on a course of vigorous action, the first step of which is a personal housecleaning, which many of us had never attempted. Though our decision was a vital and crucial step, it could have little permanent effect unless at once followed by a strenuous effort to face, and to be rid of, the things in ourselves which had been blocking us. **Our liquor was but a symptom**. So **we had to get down to causes and conditions**.

Our vital and crucial decision was when we took Step Three. The things that had been blocking us from God or from our fellows, or from whatever spiritual force, power, or new life we believed in, were selfishness, dishonesty, resentment and fear. These four manifestations of our shortcomings are common to all alcoholics, and prevent us from living in happy harmony with ourself and our fellows.

Liquor was our solution for our pain; it was not our problem.

169

Getting down to causes and conditions means we need to examine our life before we can change our life.

Therefore, we started upon a personal inventory. This was **Step Four**. A business which takes no regular inventory usually goes broke. Taking commercial inventory is a fact-finding and a fact-facing process. It is an effort to discover the truth about the stock-in-trade. One object is to disclose damaged or unsalable goods, to get rid of them promptly and without regret. If the owner of the business is to be successful, he cannot fool himself about values.

We did exactly the same thing with our lives. We took stock honestly. First, we searched out the flaws in our make-up which caused our failure. Being convinced that **self**, manifested in various ways, **was what had defeated us, we considered its common manifestations**.

I came into A.A. because the booze no longer worked and I was suicidal. I knew of no way out of my obsession to drink and mangled existence. All I wanted was relief; relief of that constant committee blaring in my head twenty-four hours a day, relief of the guilt I had over my past behavior, relief of my fear of what might happen tomorrow and relief of the hopelessness I felt in my alcoholic despair.

Every oldtimer I met in A.A. told me I would *never* be free until I completed the 12 Step work. They were adamant on this point. They suggested that the sooner I started my step work, the sooner I would get relief, and wasn't that really what I wanted all along?

Step Four is the first step that requires any real work. The first three steps are little more than mental gamesmanship to get me fired up about putting pen to paper in Step Four, where relief begins. Identifying my role in my misery was crucial to my recovery. If I don't deal with my thinking, I'll go back to drinking.

Resentment is the "number one" offender. It destroys more alcoholics than anything else. From **it stem all forms of spiritual**

disease, for we have been not only mentally and physically ill, **we have been spiritually sick**. When the spiritual malady is overcome, we straighten out mentally and physically. **In dealing with resentments, we set them on paper. We listed people, institutions or principles with whom we were angry**. We asked ourselves **why we were angry**. In most cases it was found that our self-esteem, our pocketbooks, our ambitions, our personal relationships, (including sex) were hurt or threatened. So we were sore. We were "burned up."

On our **grudge list** we set opposite each name our injuries. **Was it our self-esteem, our security, our ambitions, our personal or sex relations, which had been interfered with?**

We were usually as definite as this example:

I'M RESENTFUL AT:

Mr. Brown

THE CAUSE & AFFECTS MY:

His attention to my wife (sex relations, self-esteem-fear). Told my wife of my mistress (sex relations, self-esteem-fear). Brown may get my job at the office (security, self-esteem-fear).

Mrs. Jones

THE CAUSE & AFFECTS MY:

She's a nut—she snubbed me. She committed her husband for drinking. He's my friend. She's a gossip (personal relationship, self-esteem-fear).

My Employer

THE CAUSE & AFFECTS MY:

Unreasonable, unjust, overbearing. Threatened to fire me for drinking and padding my expense account (security, self-esteem-fear).

My Wife

Misunderstands and nags. Likes Brown. Wants house put in her name (pride, personal sex relations, security-fear).

I was totally confused over the three column grudge list example in the Big Book and the inventory instructions, especially the "Affects my" column, and knew nothing about the "fourth column," or "My part; my role."

My sponsor explained the columns and stressed that it was *column three that will get me drunk*, not column four. Column three defines the threats and attacks on my personal well-being and manhood. Column four simply reminds me I'm a selfish son-of-a-bitch, which I already knew.

He said if I wanted serenity in an alcohol free life, I had to become comfortable in my own skin, and run my life on humility and gratitude rather than fearing what others thought of me and my real and imagined inadequacies.

My sponsor also warned me never to put myself or God on my resentment list for the following reasons:

Putting one's self on any resentment list was the height of arrogance, egoism, selfishness and self-centeredness, he said. Although we are instructed to "List people… with whom we were angry," carrying a grudge against one's self made no sense. If I was upset over my anger, sadness, depression, guilt or shame for my past behavior, it's called remorse and regret, and completing my 12 Step work will take care of it.

My sponsor said that resenting God made no sense since God was not a person. Besides, what had God ever done to me that I could resent him for? My alcoholism was not God's fault. My failure to believe in him, or not reach out to him, or blame him for my woes was not his fault. God had never harmed me in any way that I should now resent Him. The idea was ridiculous, so leave God off my resentment list.

Perhaps what I really resented was some aspect of the institutions of religion, the Bible or the church, or the principles of a God-like deity, such as Original Sin or the Ten Commandments, which are legitimate items for any grudge list.

THIRD COLUMN DEFINITIONS

Self-esteem - How I think of myself.

Security - General sense of emotional well-being.

Pocketbook – The basic desire for money, property and possessions.

Personal Relations - Our relations with other people.

Sex Relations - Basic drive for sexual intimacy.

Selfish, self-centered, egotistical - "It's all about me!"

Pride - How I think others view me.

Ambitions - Our goals, plans and designs for the future. Ambition deals with the things that we want. In examining our ambitions we notice that we have the following types:

a) Emotional ambitions - our ambitions for emotional security. Our "feelings."

b) Material ambitions - Our ambitions for "our pocketbook." Our ambitions towards physical and financial well-being.

c) Social ambitions - Our "place or position in the herd." Our ambitions of how others view us. Our ambitions towards what people think about us.

d) Sexual ambitions - Our ambitions for sex relations.

For column three, what part of self is affected, Bill W. said that: "We want to find exactly how, when, and where our natural desires have warped us. We wish to look squarely at the unhappiness this has caused others and ourselves.

By discovering what our emotional deformities are, we can move toward their correction. Without a willing and persistent effort to do this, there can be little sobriety or contentment for us. Without a searching and fearless moral inventory, most of us have found that the faith which really works in daily living is still out of reach." (12 & 12, p.43)

Column three embodies my character defects, a precursor to Steps 6 and 7. This is where I focus my daily efforts. With the help of the Step 10 daily inventory, I try to reduce my shortcomings and improve my relationships with those around me.

We went back through our lives. Nothing counted but **thoroughness and honesty**. When we were finished we considered it carefully. The first thing apparent was that this world and its people were often quite wrong. To conclude that others were wrong was as far as most of us ever got. The usual outcome was that people continued to wrong us and we stayed sore. Sometimes it was remorse and then we were sore at ourselves. But the more we fought and tried to have our own way, the worse matters got. As in war, the victor only seemed to win. Our moments of triumph were short-lived.

It is plain that a life which includes deep resentment leads only to futility and unhappiness. To the precise extent that we permit these, do we squander the hours that might have been worthwhile. But with the alcoholic, whose hope is the maintenance and growth of a spiritual experience, **this business of resentment is infinitely grave. We found that it is fatal**. For when harboring such feeling we shut ourselves off from the **sunlight of the Spirit**. The insanity of alcohol returns and we drink again. And with us, **to drink is to die**.

The short paragraph above uses the words *grave, fatal* and *die* to describe the outcome of unresolved resentments. These are powerful words, well worth taking seriously, and emphasize the necessity to address and eliminate all our resentments.

If we were to live, we had to be free of anger. The grouch and the

brainstorm were not for us. They may be the dubious luxury of normal men, but for alcoholics these things are **poison**.

We turned back to the list, for it held the key to the future. We were prepared to look at it from an entirely different angle. **We began to see that the world and its people really dominated us**. In that state, the wrong-doing of others, fancied or real, had power to actually kill. How could we escape? **We saw that these resentments must be mastered, but how?** We could not wish them away any more than alcohol.

This was our course: **We realized that the people who wronged us were perhaps spiritually sick**.

Though we did not like their symptoms and the way these disturbed us, **they, like ourselves, were sick too**. We asked God to help us show them the same tolerance, pity, and patience that we would cheerfully grant a sick friend. When a person offended we said to ourselves, "**This is a sick man. How can I be helpful to him? God save me from being angry. Thy will be done.**"

We avoid retaliation or argument. We wouldn't treat sick people that way. If we do, we destroy our chance of being helpful. We cannot be helpful to all people, but at least God will show us how to take a kindly and tolerant view of each and every one.

> Most of us in our alcoholism live our lives in anger. We are constantly angry about one thing or another. If we can't think of something specific to be angry about, which is rare, we make something up. Anger gets our juices flowing, and floods dopamine into our brain reward center so we can actually get a buzz off our outrage.
>
> Over time our prolonged anger, especially over a specific person or event, hardens into a resentment. It is like a loaf of bread, which is made up of a soft, pliable batter in the beginning, but once repeatedly baked in the oven of wrath, it becomes rock hard and almost impossible to crack open.

We put the embittered loaf on our shelf, and get started on making another one.

When this happens we naturally blame the other person for our own anger, which in turn makes us more angry. This vicious cycle continues and we drink to make it all go away.

Over time, when we could no longer resolve our anger, we knew we had to change our approach and resolve our past or we would destroy ourselves.

Referring to our list again. Putting out of our minds the wrongs others had done, **we resolutely looked for our own mistakes. Where had we been selfish, dishonest, self-seeking and frightened?** Though a situation had not been entirely our fault, we tried to disregard the other person involved entirely. **Where were we to blame?** The inventory was ours, not the other man's. **When we saw our faults we listed them.**

We placed them before us in black and white. **We admitted our wrongs honestly and were willing to set these matters straight.**

Experience has shown that taking the opposite approach to dealing with our resentments works, as strange as that sounds.

Instead of looking at the faults of those we resent, we look at our own faults in the situation or relationship. Where had *we* been selfish, dishonest, self-seeking and frightened? No matter how much the other person was at fault, we *always* had some part, however small. If we think we had no part, we should talk with our sponsor or others in the fellowship for an objective opinion.

When we admit we had some role in the situation, we must become willing to repair any damage we caused as best we can. We understand that the other person may be suffering too, with their own imperfections and shortcomings. They are just as human, vulnerable and emotionally sick as we are, so why not try to be helpful rather than vengeful?

Suddenly, a lose-lose situation can become win-win.

Our job is not to change the other person, but to change ourselves. Forgiveness, amends if needed, humility, empathy and gratitude go a long way in removing our resentments. When our resentments dissipate, we are much less likely to drink.

HOMEWORK

SESSION THREE

STEP 4 - Resentments

How It Works

Pages 58 – 67

STEP 4 -- *Made a searching and fearless moral inventory of ourselves.*

Do Step 4 as best you reasonably can, and that is more than good enough. Watch out for paralysis from fear or perfectionism. Remember, it's *your* Inventory, not someone else's.

1) WRITE your "Grudge List" (Resentments of People, Institutions and Principles (p.64).

2) Complete Columnar Work on Grudge List.

3) List your Faults, or character defects (shortcomings; Seven Deadly Sins).

4) Write your Grudge List, one list at a time top to bottom. Put down all the people, places, things, principles or institutions who you resent (feel bad about; are angry towards; harbor ill will towards, etc.) on a list.

5) Then list a brief note about how you "*were hurt or threatened*" (p.65), or where you had expectations of others, or others had expectations of you – where you were sore or were "*burned up*" (p.65).

PROMPT: before making a Grudge list, make a list of all people who "owe you something" – this gets to the issue of entitlement and will essentially be your resentment list.

SESSION FOUR

STEP 4 – Fear & Sex

How It Works

Pages 67 – 71

STEP 4 -- *Made a searching and fearless moral inventory of ourselves.*

BEFORE THE MEETING

READ from the last paragraph on p.68 of the Big Book (SEX Relationships) through the end of Chapter Five.

WRITE a list of the FEARS you have experienced throughout your life.

1) Go back to your analysis of your resentments to identify some of these fears.
2) With regard to each of these fears, write a short paragraph answering these questions:
a) When did this fear occur?
b) Why do I have this fear?
c) Did you feel you could handle the situation as you saw it?
d) If you could not handle the situation, who should you rely on?
3) After completing the FEAR list work, read page 68 in the Big Book, which gives us the solution to Fear. We *"ask Him to remove our fear and direct our attention to what He would have us be."*

WRITE a list of names of persons (SEX Relationships) we were involved in, and describe how or why they ended. Describe where we had been selfish, dishonest or inconsiderate. Who did we hurt? Did we unjustifiably arouse jealousy, suspicion or bitterness? Where were we at fault, and what should have been done instead? (p.69)

- Crushes, Steadies, Wives or Partners, Other

DURING THE MEETING

Discuss any problems you are having; exchange examples with one another.

179

Chapter 5

HOW IT WORKS

Pages 67 – 71

Notice that the word "**fear**" is bracketed alongside the difficulties with Mr. Brown, Mrs. Jones, the employer, and the wife. This short word somehow touches about every aspect of our lives. **It was an evil and corroding thread; the fabric of our existence was shot through with it**. It set in motion trains of circumstances which brought us misfortune we felt we didn't deserve. But did not we, ourselves, set the ball rolling? Sometimes **we think fear ought to be classed with stealing. It seems to cause more trouble**.

> Alcoholism is a fear-based disease. Who among us can argue that fear is not an evil and corroding thread that constantly winds through our lives? We constantly live in fear, although we are loathe to admit it.
>
> When we wake up in the morning having no memory of yesterday's drinking, we fear what we did in our blackout. Before retiring we fear what dangers and disaster tomorrow will bring. During the day we fear how our secrets will be revealed as we nip from the bottle we hid in our bathroom.
>
> Most of us deny we have any fear, but are usually able to admit we worry a lot. Once we realize that worry is the same thing as fear, we can begin to address our fears.

We reviewed our fears thoroughly. We put them on paper, even though we had no resentment in connection with them. **We asked ourselves why we had them. Wasn't it because self-reliance failed us?** Self-reliance was good as far as it went, but it didn't go far enough. Some of us once had great self-confidence, but it didn't fully solve the fear problem, or any other. When it made us cocky, it was worse.

Perhaps **there is a better way**—we think so. For we are now on a different basis; the basis of **trusting and relying upon God**. We trust infinite God rather than our finite selves. We are in the world to play the role He assigns. Just to the extent that we do as we think He would have us, and humbly rely on Him, does **He enable us to match calamity with serenity**.

We **never apologize to anyone for depending upon our Creator**. We can laugh at those who think spirituality the way of weakness. Paradoxically, it is the way of strength. The verdict of the ages is that **faith means courage**. All men of faith have courage. They trust their God. We never apologize for God. Instead we let Him demonstrate, through us, what He can do. **We ask Him to remove our fear and direct our attention to what He would have us be**. At once, we commence to outgrow fear.

Fear is an extraordinarily powerful emotion, and should never be underestimated. It is more destructive than resentment, because emotional fear has the power to stop us dead in our tracks, freezing us in the moment and preventing us from living in that moment. Fear wipes out the present of the present; our ability to live in the here and now which is the only joy we can ever have in life.

As with our character defects, our book suggests we ask God, or whatever force or power we believe in, to remove our fear. Done sincerely, honestly and with humility, there is nothing wrong with asking for religious or spiritual help, even if it seems pointless.

On a practical level, we are taught to try to live in this day, suggested by our "One day at a time" motto. Living one day at a time allows us to ask ourselves exactly what do I have to fear in this day, right now, at this very moment?

Yesterday's fears have passed since we're in today. Tomorrow's fear may still be lurking out there, but why waste time worrying about them today?

We can worry about them when they come due. So all we're left with are today's fears.

We can ask ourself: Can I do anything beyond asking for my fear to be removed in order to lessen my fear right now? Is my fear real, or is it just a fabrication of my magic magnifying mind? Should I speak with my sponsor or another person about my fear, knowing that a fear shared is a fear halved? Should I turn my thoughts to something I can do to help another person, in order to keep the focus off me and my fear? Can I accept that my fear may never completely disappear, but it can be lessened if I confront it, instead of running from it?

An oldtimer once told me "Since fear is in your mind, you can never outrun fear. Run toward it instead. Embrace it, and it will lose it's power." He was right.

Now about sex. Many of us **needed an overhauling** there. But above all, we tried to be sensible on this question. It's so easy to get way off the track. Here we find human opinions running to extremes—absurd extremes, perhaps. One set of voices cry that sex is a lust of our lower nature, a base necessity of procreation. Then we have the voices who cry for sex and more sex; who bewail the institution of marriage; who think that most of the troubles of the race are traceable to sex causes. They think we do not have enough of it, or that it isn't the right kind. They see its significance everywhere. One school would allow man no flavor for his fare and the other would have us all on a straight pepper diet. We want to stay out of this controversy. We do not want to be the arbiter of anyone's sex conduct. **We all have sex problems**. We'd hardly be human if we didn't. **What can we do about them?**

We reviewed our own conduct over the years past. **Where had we been selfish, dishonest, or inconsiderate? Whom had we hurt? Did we unjustifiably arouse jealousy, suspicion or bitterness? Where were we at fault, what should we have done instead?** We got this all down on paper and looked at it.

In this way **we tried to shape a sane and sound ideal for our**

182

future sex life. We subjected **each relation to this test—was it selfish or not? We asked God to mold our ideals and help us to live up to them.** We remembered always that our sex powers were God-given and therefore good, neither to be used lightly or selfishly nor to be despised and loathed.

Whatever our ideal turns out to be, we must be willing to grow toward it. **We must be willing to make amends where we have done harm, provided that we do not bring about still more harm in so doing.** In other words, **we treat sex as we would any other problem**. In meditation, we ask God what we should do about each specific matter. The right answer will come, if we want it.

> The beauty of the Step Four sex inventory is that we can use this inventory for *all* our personal relationships; we treat sex as we would any other relationship problem.
>
> For example, I have an unhealthy relationship with my step-father. I have some long smoldering resentments against him that I've identified and I have a role in. I don't like being around him because we share nothing in common, and have nothing to discuss when we are together. If I apply the sex relationship questions to this relationship, I ask myself:
>
> 1) Where had I been selfish, dishonest, or inconsiderate?
>
> 2) Who did I hurt, or how was I hurtful to him?
>
> 3) Did I arouse jealousy, suspicion or bitterness?
>
> 4) Where was I at fault, and what should I have done instead?
>
> 5) Had I been selfish in the relationship?
>
> We cannot change our old relationships, but we can examine our past behavior in detail to determine what part of our behavior we need to change going forward. After identifying our shortcomings related to how we behaved, we write down what we should have done in the situation. By doing so, we set a template for our future behavior in similar situations.

Of course we are always selfish, dishonest and inconsiderate in our relationships, for we are the actor trying to run the show. The damage we cause may require making some amends, but we should always review any amends we are considering with our sponsor *before* proceeding, because we do not want to harm anyone in the process.

God may inspire us, but he will not change our future sex or relationship behavior—only we can do that.

God alone can judge our sex situation. Counsel with persons is often desirable, but we let God be the final judge. We realize that some people are as fanatical about sex as others are loose. **We avoid hysterical thinking or advice**.

Suppose we fall short of the chosen ideal and stumble? Does this mean we are going to get drunk? Some people tell us so. But this is only a half-truth. It depends on us and on our motives. **If we are sorry for what we have done**, and have the honest desire to let God take us to better things, **we believe we will be forgiven** and will have learned our lesson. If we are not sorry, and our conduct continues to harm others, we are quite sure to drink. We are not theorizing. These are facts out of our experience.

To sum up about sex: We earnestly **pray for the right ideal, for guidance in each questionable situation, for sanity, and for the strength to do the right thing**. If sex is very troublesome, **we throw ourselves the harder into helping others**. We think of their needs and work for them. **This takes us out of ourselves**. It quiets the imperious urge, when to yield would mean heartache.

We all know the difference between right and wrong, whether it involves our behavior in a sexual or non-sexual relationship. We know how to do the next right thing right. Asking for strength and guidance to behave in ways that we would want others to behave toward us can help us stay on the right track. Working with others always takes us out of ourself, and is a very effective solution for almost any situation we are struggling with.

If we have been thorough about our personal inventory, we have written down a lot. We have **listed and analyzed our resentments**. We have begun to comprehend their futility and their fatality. We have commenced to see their terrible destructiveness. We have **begun to learn tolerance, patience and good will toward all men, even our enemies, for we look on them as sick people**. We have listed the people we have hurt by our conduct, and **are willing to straighten out the past if we can**.

In this book you read again and again that faith did for us what we could not do for ourselves. We hope you are convinced now that **God can remove whatever self-will has blocked you off from Him**. If you have already made a decision, and an inventory of your grosser handicaps, you have made a good beginning. That being so you have swallowed and digested some big chunks of truth about yourself.

> Most of us find if we do as honest and thorough an inventory as we can, we begin to get relief from the guilt, shame and low self-esteem we carry related to our past behavior. The religious among us may feel closer to God as well.
>
> When I was trying to identify my character defects, my sponsor suggested I start with the universally recognized seven deadly sins. An easy mnemonic to remember them is P-E-W-G-A-L-S (i.e. gals sitting in a church pew): P – Pride (selfishness), E – Envy, W – Wrath, G – Gluttony, A – Avarice (greed), L – Lust (craving; sexual or non-sexual), and S – Sloth (physical or emotional).
>
> The *manifestations* of my character defects, or how I express my defects in my daily life are demonstrated through my selfishness, dishonesty, resentment and fear.
>
> My defects and their manifestations are also connected to my column three inventory emotions which are interfered with: self-esteem, security, ambition and relationships.
>
> For example, my co-worker was promoted instead of me. I feel I deserved the promotion more than she did. Whether I really

185

did deserve the promotion is irrelevant; I can't change the way I feel.

My *character defects* are pride (I deserved the promotion because I think I'm a better worker than she is), envy (I'm jealous that she got a better position than I have now), greed (I want the extra money a promotion would bring), and wrath (down deep I'm mad I didn't get the position).

The *manifestations* of those defects are selfishness (I want her job), dishonesty (truthfully, I suspect I'm not as good a worker as she is, and I may not deserve a promotion), resentment (I hate that she got the job), and fear (how will I ever get ahead in this company?; maybe they are going to fire me).

In my third column, all this *affects* my self-esteem (fear), ambition, security and personal relationships (with both my co-worker and my family and friends because I'm mad and resentful).

HOMEWORK

SESSION FOUR

STEP 4 – Fear & Sex

How It Works

Pages 67 – 71

STEP 4 -- *Made a searching and fearless moral inventory of ourselves.*

WRITE a list of the FEARS you have experienced throughout your life.

1) Go back to your analysis of your resentments to identify some of these fears.

2) With regard to each of these fears, write a short paragraph answering these questions:

a) When did this fear occur?

b) Why do I have this fear?

c) Did you feel you could handle the situation as you saw it?

d) If you could not handle the situation, who should you rely on?

3) After completing the FEAR list work, read page 68 in the Big Book, which gives us the solution to Fear. We *"ask Him to remove our fear and direct our attention to what He would have us be."*

WRITE a list of names of persons (SEX Relationships) we were involved in, and describe how or why they ended. Describe where we had been selfish, dishonest or inconsiderate. Who did we hurt? Did we unjustifiably arouse jealousy, suspicion or bitterness? Where were we at fault, and what should have been done instead? (p.69)

- Crushes, Steadies, Wives or Partners, Other

187

SESSION FIVE

STEPS 5, 6, 7

Into Action

Pages 72 - 76

STEP 5 -- *Admitted to God, to ourselves and to another human being the exact nature of our wrongs.*

STEP 6 -- *Were entirely ready to have God remove all these defects of character.*

STEP 7 -- *Humbly asked Him to remove our shortcomings.*

READ Into Action (Chapter Six - p.72-76)

WRITE down your reactions to the readings as to how they apply to you and your illness.

BEFORE THE MEETING

Find someone to take your Fifth Step with, and SET A SPECIFIC DATE for taking it with that person.

DURING THE MEETING

1) Discuss the Step 5 process of Chapter Six.
2) Are there reservations about doing the Fifth Step and if so, what are they?
3) TAKE YOUR FIFTH STEP BEFORE THE NEXT MEETING!
Follow your Fifth Step with Steps 6 and 7 as outlined in the Big Book.

STEP 6

"*I...became willing*" (Bill's Story, p.13). Step 6 is about NOT doing what you want to do. What are you willing to give up? Are you ready for change?"

We become willing to give up our bondage of self-absorption.

We are of the conviction that we are powerless over our addiction to alcohol, and that our lives are unmanageable. When we try to manage life, life becomes unmanageable. Our compulsive physical cravings, our emotional obsessions and our spiritual void lead us to be restless, irritable, and discontented. These all motivate us to react to life events with selfishness, dishonesty, self-seeking, and fear.

We are worn out.

We are dishonest when we do not see the reality of what is unfolding before us in true perspective and proportion. We are selfish and self-seeking in that our own self-centered desire, disinterest, or disgust are the criteria by which we judge and react to life. [12 & 12, p.92 - 93]

We are fearful as we anticipate the sense of loss that will happen if we do not get what we desire, or lose what we have, or we are found out for who we are and what we have done. [12 & 12, p.76]

We are exhausted. And we drink.

Or we act and think as though we have been drinking, on an emotional dry bender. Now we are exhausted with our way, we are worn out by our habitual choices; we are sick and tired of the consequences of doing things our way.

Our way *did not work.* (We Agnostics, p.52)

In Step 6, when these things become objectionable to us, we are ready to give them up. This is a gift of desperation. When we could not spot or note our thought-habits and behaviors, we could not get rid of them. Today, when we can see and name them, we can renounce them, turn them over and change.

STEP 7

...to have my new found Friend take them away, root and branch. (Bill's Story, p.13)

Step 7 is about DOING what you do not want to do. What are you going to do instead? Will you ask for help to make these changes?"

189

We may think of a shortcoming as <u>falling short of our potential</u>. In Step 7 we are going to practice new things in our lives, and a *personality change sufficient to bring about recovery*, a conversion, begins to take place. (Appendix II, <u>p.567</u>)

We are asking for help and strength from the power that we discover within us, through the discipline of the practice of working this program as understood by Alcoholics Anonymous. While we cannot - nor should not - deny our instincts, we are asking the higher power of our understanding to remove that habitual and insatiable demand for the satisfaction of our instincts beyond our true needs.

The effort, or the act of working this Step, is in the asking. We are asking for help to have wisdom and clarity, to be made strong. How we go about asking – through prayer, through meditation or other spiritual practices, or by thinking it over – is up to us. We are not going to ask just once, we will ask again and again throughout our lifetime until in a moment of grace we find strength to go on without drinking or using.

We need spiritual strength to go forth into the world and take those actions that are consistent with, and even demanded by, the understanding we have from our quiet time alone with our higher power. We take refuge in and cooperate with this inner knowing in the process of letting go, of opening ourselves to change. We have come to see that we are a part of, rather than apart from, this universal family. This true perspective of humility gives us peace of mind. [12 & 12, <u>p.70</u>]

BIG BOOK TEXT FOR STEPS 5, 6 & 7

Chapter 6

INTO ACTION

Pages 72 - 76

Having made our personal inventory, what shall we do about it? We have been **trying to get a new attitude, a new relationship with our Creator, and to discover the obstacles in our path**. We have **admitted certain defects**; we have ascertained in a rough way what the trouble is; we have put our finger on the weak times in our personal inventory. **Now these are about to be cast out**. This **requires action on our part**, which, when completed, will mean that **we have admitted to God, to ourselves, and to another human being, the exact nature of our defects.** This brings us to the **Fifth Step** in the program of recovery mentioned in the preceding chapter.

> *Step 5: Admitted to God, to ourselves, and to another human being the exact nature of our wrongs.*

This is perhaps **difficult—especially discussing our defects with another person**. We think we have done well enough in admitting these things to ourselves.

There is doubt about that. In actual practice, **we usually find a solitary self-appraisal insufficient**. Many of us thought it necessary to go much further. We will be more reconciled to discussing ourselves with another person when we see good reasons why we should do so. The best reason first: **If we skip this vital step, we may not overcome drinking**. Time after time newcomers have tried to keep to themselves certain facts about their lives. Trying to avoid this humbling experience, they have turned to easier methods. Almost invariably they got drunk. Having persevered with the rest of the program, **they wondered why they fell.** We think **the reason is that they never completed their housecleaning**. They took inventory all right, but **hung on to some of the worst items in stock**. They only thought they had lost their egoism and fear; they only thought they had humbled themselves. But they had not learned enough of humility, fearlessness and honesty, in the sense we find it necessary, until they told someone else all their **life story**.

Once we have completed a thorough and honest inventory, little benefit is received until we share it with another human being. This is the occasion for telling our life story. If we tell all of our story, and not just the parts we feel safe disclosing, we will get relief from our hopeless state of mind and body.

For some reason confession face-to-face with another human being is cleansing. If our Step Five partner is an experienced A.A. member who has done the steps himself, there is little reason to be hesitant or frightened in discussing our defects with him. No doubt our partner was just as full of fear and defects as we are when they did their Fifth Step, but were able to face and overcome their trepidation.

More than most people, **the alcoholic leads a double life**. **He is very much the actor**. To the outer world he presents his **stage character**. This is the one he likes his fellows to see. He wants to enjoy a certain reputation, but knows in his heart he doesn't deserve it.

The inconsistency is made worse by the things he does on his sprees. Coming to his senses, he is revolted at certain episodes he vaguely remembers. These memories are a nightmare. He trembles to think someone might have observed him. As far as he can, he pushes these memories far inside himself. He hopes they will never see the light of day. He is under constant fear and tension—that makes for more drinking.

Psychologists are inclined to agree with us. We have spent thousands of dollars for examinations. We know but few instances where we have given these doctors a fair break. We have seldom told them the whole truth nor have we followed their advice. Unwilling to be honest with these sympathetic men, we were honest with no one else. Small wonder many in the medical profession have a low opinion of alcoholics and their chance for recovery!

We must be entirely honest with somebody if we expect to live long or happily in this world. Rightly and naturally, **we think well before we choose the person or persons with whom to take this intimate and confidential step**. Those of us belonging to a religious denomination which requires confession must, and of course, will want to go to the properly appointed authority whose duty it is to receive it. Though we have no religious conception, we may still do well to talk with someone ordained by an established **religion**. We often find such a person quick to see and understand our problem. Of course, we sometimes encounter people who do not understand alcoholics.

If we cannot or would rather not do this, we search our acquaintance for a close-mouthed, understanding **friend**. Perhaps our **doctor or psychologist** will be the person. It may be one of our own **family**, but we cannot disclose anything to our wives or our parents which will hurt them and make them unhappy. We have no right to save our own skin at another person's expense. Such parts of our story we tell to someone who will understand, yet be unaffected. **The rule is we must be hard on ourself, but always considerate of others**.

Notwithstanding the great necessity for discussing ourselves with someone, it may be one is so situated that there is no suitable person available. If that is so, **this step may be postponed, only, however, if we hold ourselves in complete readiness to go through with it at the first opportunity**. We say this because we are very anxious that we talk to the right person. It is important that he be able to keep a confidence; that he fully understand and approve what we are driving at; that he will not try to change our plan. But **we must not use this as a mere excuse to postpone**.

> Three pages in the Big Book are given to describe why it is so important for us to share our fourth step inventory with another human being. We must be able to totally trust the person we choose with this intimate task. Most A.A. members choose their sponsor, but someone knowledgeable and experienced with the A.A. 12 Step process and Step Five may be an option.

It seems foolhardy to choose a family member or friend for obvious reasons; they are too close to us and have too much personal history with us. It is unlikely they can remain objective and nonjudgmental, and our confession may endanger any future relationship.

Taking Step Five with a professional, whether that be a physician, psychologist, counselor or priest, is an option only if that professional has in-depth familiarity and experience with A.A. and the Step work process. Why? Because the fifth step process is not a one-sided regurgitation or recitation of our inventory. It is a discussion. It is a conversation; a verbal back and forth between oneself and the person who is listening to us. That person should ideally have extensive experience with A.A. and the 12 Steps, even though they may not be alcoholic.

When we decide who is to hear our story, we waste no time. We have a written inventory and we are prepared for a long talk. We explain to our partner what we are about to do and why we have to do it. He should realize that we are engaged upon a life-and-death errand. Most people approached in this way will be glad to help; they will be honored by our confidence.

We pocket our pride and go to it, illuminating every twist of character, every dark cranny of the past. Once we have taken this step, **withholding nothing,** we are delighted. **We can look the world in the eye.** We can be alone at perfect peace and ease. Our fears fall from us. We begin to feel the nearness of our Creator. We may have had certain spiritual beliefs, but now we begin to have a spiritual experience. The feeling that the drink problem has disappeared will often come strongly. We feel **we are on the Broad Highway, walking hand in hand with the Spirit of the Universe.**

Returning home we find a place where we can be quiet for an hour, carefully **reviewing what we have done.** We thank God from the bottom of our heart that we know Him better. Taking this book down from our shelf **we turn to the page which contains the twelve steps.**

Carefully reading the first five proposals **we ask if we have omitted anything**, for we are building an arch through which we shall walk a free man at last. Is our work solid so far? Are the stones properly in place? Have we skimped on the cement put into the foundation? Have we tried to make mortar without sand?

Once we decide who we want to hear our Fifth Step, here are a few suggestions well worth following:

1) Complete this step as soon as possible. Seek no reason for delay or procrastination, unless truly legitimate.

2) Go all-in. Jump in the pool, don't wade in. Don't lie, don't withhold the whole truth, don't skimp, don't obfuscate, don't apologize.

3) Tell *all* of your story, no matter how long it takes. If several sessions are required, so be it.

4) Never skip taking that hour after completing this step to review your work and determine if you left anything out. If you need to add something that was forgotten, immediately contact the person that heard your Fifth Step and share it with them.

If we can answer to our satisfaction, we then look at **Step Six**. We have emphasized willingness as being indispensable. **Are we now ready to let God remove from us all the things which we have admitted are objectionable?** Can He now take them all—every one? If we still cling to something we will not let go, **we ask God to help us be willing**.

Step 6: Were entirely ready to have God remove all these defects of character.

Our shortcomings reflect an imbalance in our character traits, and we try to rectify that imbalance by changing the way we think and act.

Our defects of character block our recovery. We can attain little emotional sobriety if we are consumed by our faults and flaws. Knowing that our imperfections will never completely go away

195

does not prevent us from taking action to lessen them.

Being entirely ready means just what it says. Once again we're asked to be all-in. We're not ready for only the defects we don't like to be removed, we're ready for *all* of them to be removed.

Note that Step Six does *not* say that God *will* remove all our defects; it asks us if we are *ready* for him to remove them. This is a critical distinction. Step Six is about being open to change. We become willing to change, just as we did in all the previous steps.

Will God literally remove all our defects at some point? It's unlikely, since he didn't put them there in the first place, and has never removed them before. If we expect our defects to be tempered, we are going to have to do the work of change. Asking for fellowship help and spiritual guidance during this process is a wise suggestion, since up to this point we have failed running our life on self-will alone.

When ready, we say something like this: "My Creator, I am now willing that you should have all of me, good and bad. **I pray that you now remove from me every single defect of character which stands in the way of my usefulness to you and my fellows**. Grant me strength, as I go out from here, to do your bidding. Amen." We have then completed **Step Seven**.

Step 7: Humbly asked Him to remove our shortcomings.

The fifty-six word Seventh Step Prayer is a call for aid from God to remove our character defects. It is nothing more than a petition, or request for help, and we all need help.

Of course no one is able to change our behavior other than ourselves. We can ask God, or anyone else, for the motivation and strength to change, but we must take the action and do the work ourselves.

It's all about inspiration and focus. Saying a daily prayer, regardless of what the prayer is about, motivates and reminds us to continue to live our new life as best we can.

Prayer can be our catalyst for change. We can call prayer whatever we want; it is the asking that matters.

Each day during my morning meditation I ask no one specifically or by name for my defects to be removed. I'm not trying to send a telegram to God in heaven or out into the void of our universe. I just ask.

I know good and well in my head and heart that lessening my shortcomings, which I identified in my Step Four inventory, is solely my responsibility. Reflection on my deficiencies each day simply reminds me to take concrete action to be less selfish and self-centered, and to try to think of someone else and do something for them. It's not that hard.

In the Big Book and the *Twelve Steps & Twelve Traditions* there are four clearly identified God-based prayers: the Third Step prayer, the Seventh Step prayer, the Eleventh Step prayer of St. Francis and the Serenity Prayer.

Since prayer and its derivatives are mentioned sixty-six times in the Big Book and in the *Twelve Steps & Twelve Traditions*, some of our more enthusiastic, religiously inclined A.A. members have composed multiple prayers out of those references, including prayers for each of the 12 Steps.

Even Dr. Silkworth endorsed prayer: "I earnestly advise every alcoholic to read this book through, and though perhaps he came to scoff, he may remain to pray." William D. Silkworth, M.D. (Big Book, p.xxxii)

Third Step Prayer

[Pg. 63] God, I offer myself to Thee – to build with me and do with me as Thou wilt. Relieve me of the bondage of self, that I may better do Thy will. Take away my difficulties, that victory over them may bear witness to those I would help of Thy Power, Thy Love and Thy Way of Life. May I do Thy will always!

Fourth Step Prayers

[Pg. 67] RESENTMENT – We asked God to help us show them the same tolerance, pity, and patience that we would cheerfully grant a sick friend. When a person offended we said to ourselves, "This is a sick man. How can I be helpful to him? God save me from being angry. Thy will be done."

[Pg. 68] FEAR – We ask Him to remove our fear and direct our attention to what He would have us be.

[Pg. 69] SEX – We asked God to mold our ideals and help us live up to them.

[Pg. 69] SEX – In meditation, we ask God what we do about each specific matter.

[Pg. 70] SEX – To sum up about sex: We pray for the right ideal, for guidance in each questionable situation, for sanity and for strength to do the right thing.

Fifth Step Prayers

[Pg. 75] We thank God from the bottom of our heart that we know Him better.

Sixth Step Prayer

[Pg. 76] If we still cling to something we will not let go, we ask God to help us be willing.

Seventh Step Prayer

[Pg. 76] My Creator, I am now willing that You should have all of me, good and bad. I pray that You now remove from me every single defect of character which stands in the way of my usefulness to you and my fellows. Grant me strength, as I go out from here, to do Your bidding. Amen

Eighth Step Prayer

[Pg. 76] If we haven't the will to do this, we ask until it comes.

Ninth Step Prayers

[Pg. 79] LEGAL MATTERS – We ask that we be given strength and direction to do the right thing, no matter what the personal consequences might be.

[Pg. 80] OTHERS EFFECTED – If we have obtained permission, have consulted with others, asked God to help and the drastic step is indicated, we must not shrink.

[Pg. 82] INFIDELITY – Each might pray about it, having the other one's happiness uppermost in mind.

[Pg. 83] FAMILY – So we clean house with the family, asking each morning in meditation that our Creator show us the way of patience, tolerance, kindliness and love.

Tenth Step Prayers

[Pg. 84] Continue to watch for selfishness, dishonesty, resentment and fear. When these crop up, we ask God at once to remove them.

[Pg. 85] Every day is a day when we must carry the vision of God's will into all our activities. "How can I best serve Thee–Thy will (not mine) be done."

Eleventh Step Prayers

[Pg. 86] NIGHT - After mediation on the day just completed, "We ask God's forgiveness and inquire what corrective measures should be taken."

[Pg. 86] MORNING - Before we begin our day, "We ask God to direct our thinking, especially asking that it be divorced from self-pity, dishonest or self-seeking motives."

[Pg. 86] MORNING - In thinking about our day, "We ask God for inspiration, an intuitive thought or decision."

[Pg. 87] MORNING - We usually conclude the period of

mediation with a prayer that we be shown all through the day what our next step is to be, that we be given whatever we need to take care of such problems. We especially ask for freedom from self-will, and are careful to make no requests for ourselves only. We may ask for ourselves, however, if others will be helped. We are careful never to pray for our own selfish ends.

[Pg. 87–88] ALL DAY - As we go through the day we pause, when agitated or doubtful, and ask for the right thought or action. We constantly remind ourselves we are no longer running the show, humbly saying to ourselves many times each day "Thy will be done."

[12 & 12, Pg. 99] Lord, make me a channel of thy peace--that where there is hatred, I may bring love--that where there is wrong, I may bring the spirit of forgiveness--that where there is discord, I may bring harmony--that where there is error, I may bring truth--that where there is doubt, I may bring faith--that where there is despair, I may bring hope--that where there are shadows, I may bring light--that where there is sadness, I may bring joy. Lord, grant that I may seek rather to comfort than to be comforted--to understand, than to be understood--to love, than to be loved. For it is by self-forgetting that one finds. It is by forgiving that one is forgiven. It is by dying that one awakens to Eternal Life. Amen.

Twelfth Step Prayers

[Pg. 102] Your job now is to be at the place where you may be of maximum helpfulness to others, so never hesitate to go anywhere if you can be helpful. You should not hesitate to visit the most sordid spot on earth on such an errand. Keep on the firing line of life with these motives and God will keep you unharmed.

[Pg. 164] Ask Him in your morning meditation what you can do each day for the man who is still sick. The answers will come if your own house is in order.

Serenity Prayer

[12 & 12, Pg. 41] In all times of emotional disturbance or indecision, we can pause, ask for quiet, and in the stillness simply say: "God grant me the serenity to accept the things I cannot change, courage to change the things I can, and wisdom to know the difference. Thy will, not mine, be done."

Serenity Prayer - long version

God grant me the serenity to accept the things I cannot change; courage to change the things I can; and wisdom to know the difference. Living one day at a time; enjoying one moment at a time; accepting hardships as the pathway to peace; taking, as He did, this sinful world as it is, not as I would have it; trusting that He will make all things right if I surrender to His Will; so that I may be reasonably happy in this life and supremely happy with Him forever and ever in the next. Amen.

http://silkworth.net/pages/aa/prayer.php

http://district17pa-aa.org/big-book-prayers/

HOMEWORK

SESSION FIVE

STEPS 5, 6, 7

Into Action

Pages 72 - 76

STEP 5 -- *Admitted to God, to ourselves and to another human being the exact nature of our wrongs.*

STEP 6 -- *Were entirely ready to have God remove all these defects of character.*

STEP 7 -- *Humbly asked Him to remove our shortcomings.*

WRITE down your reactions to the readings as to how they apply to you and your illness.

Find someone to take your Fifth Step with, and SET A SPECIFIC DATE for taking it with that person.

TAKE YOUR FIFTH STEP BEFORE THE NEXT MEETING!

Follow your Fifth Step with Steps 6 and 7 as outlined in the Big Book.

DURING THE MEETING

1) Discuss the Step 5 process of Chapter Six.

2) Are there reservations about doing the Fifth Step and if so, what are they?

SESSION SIX

STEPS 8, 9

Into Action

Pages 76 - 84

STEP 8 -- *Made a list of all persons we had harmed, and became willing to make amends to them all.*

STEP 9 -- *Made direct amends to such people wherever possible, except when to do so would injure them or others.*

READ

Read Steps 8 and 9 on p.76 - 84 of the Big Book.

Read Steps 8 and 9 in the Twelve Steps & Twelve Traditions.

WRITE

Make a list of all people you have harmed (refer to your Step 4 Inventory sheets).

Amend: State not simply "I am sorry," but add "What can I do to make it up to you?"

Sponsor: Be sure to review every amend you are planning to make with your sponsor before you make the amend.

NAME	SPECIFIC AMEND	NOTES
John	Three years ago, while drunk at work I stole construction materials from the warehouse for my own use.	I now have a different job. Amend needs to be in person and cash payment made for stolen items.

Amends often involve Friends, Family, Employers, Creditors and the Deceased.

CONSIDERATIONS

1) Do you have any misgivings about these steps? p.76

203

2) Do you feel different about going to some of these people?

3) What is your real purpose? – p.77

4) Is timing important in this step?

5) Can you approach people on your Eighth Step list in a helpful and forgiving spirit? – p.77; also see p.66 & 67

6) Do you recognize that nothing worthwhile can be accomplished until you clean your side of the street? – p.78

7) Is it important that you be praised for your Ninth Step efforts? – p.78

8) Have you discussed with your sponsor any criminal offenses you may have committed and which may still be open? If not, you should do so. – p.79

9) Do you understand how your Ninth Step may harm other people? – p.79

10) Have you studied your domestic troubles and the harm that may have been caused in these areas?

11) Do you understand the importance of not causing further harm by creating jealousy and resentment in a "tell all" session? – p.81

12) What does the author mean when he says the spiritual life is not a theory, we have to live it? – p.83

13) Do you see that in taking the Ninth Step you should be sensible, tactful, considerate and humble without being servile or scraping? – p.83

14) Are you experiencing the Promises set forth on p.83 & 84?

BIG BOOK TEXT FOR STEPS 8 & 9

Chapter 6

INTO ACTION

Pages 76 - 84

Now we need more action, without which we find that "Faith without works is dead." Let's look at **Steps Eight and Nine**.

Step 8 -- *Made a list of all persons we had harmed, and became willing to make amends to them all.*

Step 9 -- *Made direct amends to such people wherever possible, except when to do so would injure them or others.*

We have a **list of all persons we have harmed** and to whom **we are willing to make amends**. We made it when we took inventory. We subjected ourselves to a drastic self-appraisal. Now we go out to our fellows **and repair the damage done in the past**. We attempt to sweep away the debris which has accumulated out of our effort to live on self-will and run the show ourselves. If we haven't the will to do this, we ask until it comes.

An amend means two things: to make "a mend," and "to mend my ways." We make "a mend" for past behavior by admitting we were wrong and offering to make things right if we can. We "mend our ways" in the future by trying to avoid the types of behavior which caused us to have to make our amends in the first place.

Our two-part Step Eight is very clear. We list everyone we can remember that we have harmed in our past. Then we become willing to make amends to all of them.

At first glance this seems an impossible task and an unreasonable request. How on earth are we going to remember everyone in our lifetime that we might have harmed? And what about those that we harmed that we can't remember, probably because we were in a blackout?

Even if we could remember everyone, how could we possibly locate all of them in order to apologize? This assignment seems overwhelming. And what does "harmed" really mean anyway?

My sponsor told me not to panic. No one expects us to remember everyone we harmed, and not all of those we harmed require an amend. And over time we may remember folks we harmed that we don't remember right now, and we can deal with an amend a later date if needed.

My earliest memory of a harm I did was when I was five years old. A neighborhood kid blindsided me and punched me in the stomach. I know I had harmed him in some way I can no longer remember and deserved the attack, since I used to pick on him mercilessly all the time. He will go on my amends list, but there is no reason to try to track him down after sixty years to make an amend unless I am still consumed with guilt and shame over the incident.

It is very unwise to attempt Steps Eight and Nine without guidance from a sponsor. My sponsor suggested I make my amends list chronologically.

He said to think about people who I believe still owe me something, or had done *me* wrong. Think about them by *age group*: pre-school, elementary school, high school, college, and so on.

Think about people in my life connected to *common life events*: childhood, education, dating, marriages, partnerships and jobs.

Think about people by *category*: family, friends, neighbors, or business associates.

Step Eight just says to make a list. Once we have the list we can then decide if we are *willing* to make amends to all of them, even if we can't or don't *need* to make amends to all of them. If we are willing, we can choose which folks on our list we actually need to contact.

My sponsor suggested I carry with me at all times a pen and pad, so that if I was out and about and suddenly thought of someone I should put on my amends list, I could do so right away so I wouldn't forget. This approach worked out well for me, and within a few days I had a long list of people I had harmed. I was not certain I was willing to make amends to all of them, but I could decide that later with my sponsor's help.

To avoid sloth and procrastination, I was advised to set a calendar deadline to complete all my amends. I set mine at six months because I had to do some travelling for some of my amends. I circled the six month date on the calendar, and began counting down the days.

My sponsor and I also discussed the difference between "harms" and "bad behavior." A harm is a specific emotional or physical injury done to someone. Bad behavior is a pattern of behavior which is injurious and unwelcome. Amends may be made for both types, especially if one cannot remember specific harmful events, but know they treated someone poorly.

For example, I made an amend to one of my wife's relatives that I had not specifically harmed, but toward whom I had always behaved in a sarcastic, nasty and dismissive manner, which I know hurt her feelings. My amend was for the general way I had behaved, which I described, not for any specific event or injury.

Dr. Bob made his amends shortly after getting sober: "One morning he took the bull by the horns and set out to tell those he feared what his trouble had been. He found himself surprisingly well received, and learned that many knew of his drinking. Stepping into his car, he made the rounds of people he had hurt. He trembled as he went about, for this might mean ruin, particularly to a person in his line of business. At midnight he came home exhausted, but very happy. He has not had a drink since. As we shall see, he now means a great deal to his community, and the major liabilities of thirty years of hard drinking have been repaired in four." (A Vision For You, p.156)

Note that Bill W. committed to doing Steps Eight and Nine while he was in Towns Hospital: "At the hospital I was separated from alcohol for the last time... We made a list of people I had hurt or toward whom I felt resentment. I expressed my entire willingness to approach these individuals, admitting my wrong. Never was I to be critical of them. I was to right all such matters to the utmost of my ability." (Bill's Story, p.13)

Of interest is Bill W.'s later experience with Steps Eight and Nine. In "Bill's Story" he does not reveal if he actually made his amends as he promised. He obviously made living amends through his lifetime work with other alcoholics, but did he actually make specific amends to those he had harmed in his past?

I can find nothing of significance of Wilson writing about his *personal experience* doing his *own* amends documented anywhere in the Big Book, *Twelve Steps and Twelve Traditions, The Language of the Heart, A.A. Comes of Age* or in *Dr. Bob and the Good Oldtimers.*

Do you have any misgivings about these steps? – p.76 Do you feel different about going to some of these people?

Remember **it was agreed at the beginning we would go to any lengths for victory over alcohol**. Probably there are still some misgivings. As we look over the list of business acquaintances and friends we have hurt, we may feel diffident about going to some of them on a spiritual basis. Let us be reassured. To some people we need not, and probably should not emphasize the spiritual feature on our first approach.

We might prejudice them. **At the moment we are trying to put our lives in order**. But this is not an end in itself. **Our real purpose is to fit ourselves to be of maximum service to God and the people about us**. It is seldom wise to approach an individual, who still smarts from our injustice to him, and announce that we have gone religious. In the prize ring, this would be called leading with the chin.

Why lay ourselves open to being branded fanatics or religious bores? We may kill a future opportunity to carry a beneficial message. But **our man is sure to be impressed with a sincere desire to set right the wrong**. He is going to be more interested in a demonstration of good will than in our talk of spiritual discoveries.

We don't use this as an excuse for shying away from the subject of God. When it will serve any good purpose, we are willing to announce our convictions with tact and common sense.

> Our book says that we complete our amends in order to fit ourselves to be of maximum service to God and the people about us. Fit ourselves means to become the right size or shape for someone or something, and in this case it is a spiritual reference. We must become *emotionally* sober enough not only to make all our amends, but to be willing to help other people.
>
> We have the option during our amend to discuss the reasons why we are making the amend, and how A.A. has helped us in our recovery process. This is an often an extremely bad idea, unless we are asked directly.
>
> Almost no one cares or wants to hear *why* we are making our amend, and they certainly don't want to hear anything about religion or our spiritual conversion experiences. We are meeting with the individual to apologize for past wrongs and offering to set things right if we can—that's it.
>
> *What is your real purpose? – p.77 Is timing important in this step?*

The **question of how to approach the man we hated will arise**. It may be he has done us more harm than we have done him and, though we may have acquired a better attitude toward him, we are still not too keen about admitting our faults. Nevertheless, **with a person we dislike, we take the bit in our teeth**. It is harder to go to an enemy than to a friend, but we find it much more beneficial to us. **We go to him in a helpful and forgiving spirit, confessing our former ill feeling and expressing our regret**.

It is always more difficult to meet with a person we dislike than one we like, regardless of the reasons, some of which may be real and some imaginary. Who knows what really happened in situations long past? Who was really right or wrong at the time? We remember the events one way; our man remembers it another way. None of this matters.

Our *only* job is to make our amend for harms *we* have done. We are not there to discuss or argue. In a way, we are there to get in and get out by saying something like: "Remember that time I got mad at you and tried to run you over with my car when I was drunk? I just wanted to tell you that was wrong of me. Is there anything I can do to make it right?" And then be quiet; say no more.

You have presented your amend in less than thirty seconds. Should your man want to have further discussion after responding, that's up to you. Regardless of what happens after you have made your amend, you have fulfilled your obligation.

Whether or not the person you harmed forgives you is irrelevant. But must you forgive the person you harmed?

Since forgiveness technically means to stop feeling angry or resentful toward someone for an offense, flaw, or mistake, and since we know resentment is our number one offender, it may be wise to let go of any anger or resentment we carry.

Forgiveness does not mean we must believe that what someone did to us was acceptable, or that we must renew our friendship, or that things between us will go back to the way they were. Forgiveness means we let our *anger* go, not our impressions or memory of the event.

Can you approach people on your Eighth Step list in a helpful and forgiving spirit? – p.77; also see p.66 and 67.

Under no condition do we criticize such a person or argue.

Simply tell him that we will never get over drinking until we have done our utmost to straighten out the past. **We are there to sweep off our side of the street**, realizing that nothing worthwhile can be accomplished until we do so, never trying to tell him what he should do. **His faults are not discussed. We stick to our own.** If our manner is calm, frank, and open, we will be gratified with the result.

The reason for making amends is not to take the inventory of the other person. We simply state our regret, offer to make our wrong right by that person if possible, and move on. There is absolutely no necessity to discuss A.A. and why we are making the amend unless asked.

Do you recognize that nothing worthwhile can be accomplished until you clean your side of the street? – p.78.

In nine cases out of ten the unexpected happens. Sometimes the man we are calling upon admits his own fault, so feuds of years' standing melt away in an hour. Rarely do we fail to make satisfactory progress. Our former enemies sometimes praise what we are doing and wish us well. Occasionally, they will offer assistance. **It should not matter, however, if someone does throw us out of his office. We have made our demonstration, done our part. It's water over the dam**.

Most alcoholics' biggest fear is how their amend will be received, and it is impossible to know beforehand, even when it involves our family or closest friends. Therefore, some advance planning may be helpful.

My sponsor suggested I divide my amends into three categories: 1) those I am emotionally willing to do right now, 2) those I need to reflect upon but know I'll have the courage to do them shortly, and 3) those I never want to do.

Start with the easiest group first, which usually consists of family members and current close friends. Hopefully our efforts will be welcome, and few harsh words will be spoken. By the time we reach the last group, the ones we don't want to ever do and fear we will be thrown out of their office or house, we may have more courage to face the unknown based on our recent amends experience.

Most alcoholics who have gone through the amends process share that their mental prediction of how each person would respond to the amend was rarely what they expected. Some of the easy ones turned out not to be so easy, and some of the ones they feared the most were received without rancor or reprisal.

Is it important that you be praised for your Ninth Step efforts? – p.78.

Most alcoholics **owe money**. We **do not dodge our creditors**. Telling them what we are trying to do, we make no bones about our drinking; they usually know it anyway, whether we think so or not. Nor are we afraid of disclosing our alcoholism on the theory it may cause financial harm. Approached in this way, the most ruthless creditor will sometimes surprise us. Arranging the best deal we can we let these people know we are sorry. Our drinking has made us slow to pay. **We must lose our fear of creditors** no matter how far we have to go, for we are liable to drink if we are afraid to face them.

> Put yourself in your creditor's shoes. Would you rather be dealing with a deadbeat, irresponsible drunk trying to avoid paying you, or would you rather work with a sound and sober person to create a fair and rational re-payment plan?

Perhaps we have committed a **criminal offense** which might land us in jail if it were known to the authorities. We may be short in our accounts and unable to make good. We have already admitted this in confidence to another person, but we are sure we would be imprisoned or lose our job if it were known. Maybe it's only a petty offense such as padding the expense account. Most of us have done that sort of thing.

> The intimate sharing that occurs during Step Five between two alcoholics is not a legally protected conversation, unlike conversations between a lawyer and client, or priest and

penitent. This means that if a sponsee states he was the one who robbed the West Side Bank last July, the sponsor can be forced to divulge that confession in a courtroom.

One way we might deal with this difficulty is to tell our sponsee *before* starting Step Five if he or she committed a crime, they should speak of it only in vague and general terms because the law can force you to divulge their discussion of any criminal activity in court.

A sponsee might then decide to ask hypothetically, "If someone had committed a certain crime in the past, what type of reparation might be most appropriate?" Each sponsor and sponsee must use their own judgment in this complex legal area.

Have you discussed with your sponsor any criminal offenses you may have committed and which may still be open? If not, you should do so. – p.79.

Do you understand how your Ninth Step may harm other people? – p.79.

Maybe we are divorced, and have remarried but haven't kept up the alimony to number one. She is indignant about it, and has a warrant out for our arrest. That's a common form of trouble too.

Although these reparations take innumerable forms, there are some **general principles** which we find guiding. Reminding ourselves that **we have decided to go to any lengths** to find a spiritual experience, **we ask that we be given strength and direction to do the right thing, no matter what the personal consequences may be**. We may lose our position or reputation or face jail, but we are willing. We have to be. **We must not shrink at anything**.

Usually, however, other people are involved. Therefore, **we are not to be the hasty and foolish martyr who would needlessly sacrifice others to save himself** from the alcoholic pit. A man we know had remarried. Because of resentment and drinking, he had not paid alimony to his first wife. She was furious. She went to court and got an order for his arrest. He had commenced our way of life, had secured a position, and was getting his head above water. It would have been impressive heroics if he had walked up to the Judge and said, "Here I am."

We thought he ought to be willing to do that if necessary, but if he were in jail he could provide nothing for either family. We suggested he write his first wife admitting his faults and asking forgiveness. He did, and also sent a small amount of money. He told her what he would try to do in the future. He said he was perfectly willing to go to jail if she insisted. Of course she did not, and the whole situation has long since been adjusted.

Before taking drastic action which might implicate other people we secure their consent. If we have obtained permission, have consulted with others, asked God to help and the drastic step is indicated we must not shrink.

This brings to mind a story about one of our friends. While drinking, **he accepted a sum of money from a bitterly-hated business rival**, giving him no receipt for it. He subsequently denied having received the money and **used the incident as a basis for discrediting the man**. He thus **used his own wrong-doing as a means of destroying the reputation of another**. In fact, his rival was ruined.

He felt that he had done a wrong he could not possibly make right. If he opened that old affair, he was afraid it would destroy the reputation of his partner, disgrace his family and take away his means of livelihood. What right had he to involve those dependent upon him? How could he possibly make a public statement exonerating his rival?

After consulting with his wife and partner he came to the conclusion that it was better to take those risks than to stand before his Creator guilty of such ruinous slander. He saw that he had to place the outcome in God's hands or he would soon start drinking again, and all would be lost anyhow. He attended church for the first time in many years. After the sermon, he quietly got up and made an explanation. His action met wide-spread approval, and today he is one of the most trusted citizens of his town. This all happened years ago.

> "He accepted a sum of money from a bitterly-hated business rival." This anecdote is thought to have originated within the Oxford Group. (Big Book, p.80)

The chances are that we have **domestic troubles**. Perhaps we are **mixed up with women** in a fashion we wouldn't care to have advertised. We doubt if, in this respect, alcoholics are fundamentally much worse than other people. But **drinking does complicate sex relations in the home**. After a few years with an alcoholic, **a wife gets worn out, resentful and uncommunicative**. How could she be anything else? The husband begins to feel lonely, sorry for himself. He commences to look around in the night clubs, or their equivalent, for something besides liquor. Perhaps he is having a secret and exciting **affair** with "the girl who understands." In fairness we must say that she may understand, but what are we going to do about a thing like that? A man so involved often feels very remorseful at times, especially if he is married to a loyal and courageous girl who has literally gone through hell for him.

Whatever the situation, we usually have to do something about it. If we are sure our wife does not know, **should we tell her? Not always, we think**. If she knows **in a general way** that we have been wild, should we tell her in detail? Undoubtedly **we should admit our fault**. She may insist on knowing all the particulars. She will want to know who the woman is and where she is. We feel we ought to say to her that **we have no right to involve another person. We are sorry for what we have done and, God willing, it shall not be repeated**. More than that we cannot do; we have no right to go further. Though there may be justifiable exceptions, and though we wish to lay down no rule of any sort, we have often found this the best course to take.

Our design for living is not a one-way street. It is as good for the wife as for the husband. If we can forget, so can she. It is better, however, that one does not needlessly name a person upon whom she can vent jealousy.

215

Perhaps there are some cases where the utmost frankness is demanded. No outsider can appraise such an intimate situation. It may be that both will decide that the way of good sense and loving kindness is to **let bygones be bygones**. Each might pray about it, having the other one's happiness uppermost in mind. Keep it always in sight that we are dealing with that most terrible human emotion—jealousy. Good general-ship may decide that the problem be attacked on the flank rather than risk a face-to-face combat.

> Adultery is not uncommon with alcoholics. Disclosing names, dates and details of our affairs is rarely a wise decision, except when there may be medical risk to others from any sexually transmitted diseases we knowingly acquired.
>
> God will not prevent us from repeating our marriage deceit and betrayal, but we can avoid it by never doing it again. If our marriage or relationship is so severely damaged, despite our best efforts to mend it, that we are driven to seek other partners for sex or companionship, it's probably time to get divorced or leave the relationship.
>
> *Have you studied your domestic troubles and the harm that may have been caused in these areas? – p.80.*
>
> *Do you understand the importance of not causing further harm by creating jealousy and resentment in a "tell all" session? – p.81.*

If we have no such complication, there is plenty we should do at home. **Sometimes we hear an alcoholic say that the only thing he needs to do is to keep sober**. Certainly he must keep sober, for there will be no home if he doesn't. **But he is yet a long way from making good to the wife or parents whom for years he has so shockingly treated**. Passing all understanding is the patience mothers and wives have had with alcoholics. Had this not been so, many of us would have no homes today, and would perhaps be dead.

The alcoholic is like a tornado roaring his way through the lives of others. Hearts are broken. Sweet relationships are dead. Affections have been uprooted.

Selfish and inconsiderate habits have kept the home in turmoil. **We feel a man is unthinking when he says that sobriety is enough**. He is like the farmer who came up out of his cyclone cellar to find his home ruined. To his wife, he remarked, "Don't see anything the matter here, Ma. Ain't it grand the wind stopped blowin?"

> If an alcoholic is capable only of making amends and not drinking, they have failed to attain full sobriety. We seek true emotional sobriety, which involves living a lifestyle which is not ruled by our moods. We learn to confront and cope with all the temptations and negative feelings we suppressed when abusing drugs or alcohol. We learn to live in the present moment, whatever it holds for us. We learn to form deep, unselfish, personal bonds with others.

Yes, **there is a long period of reconstruction ahead. We must take the lead. A remorseful mumbling that we are sorry won't fill the bill at all**. We ought to **sit down with the family and frankly analyze the past** as we now see it, being very **careful not to criticize them**. Their defects may be glaring, but the chances are that our own actions are partly responsible. So **we clean house with the family**, asking each morning in meditation that our Creator **show us the way of patience, tolerance, kindliness and love.**

The spiritual life is not a theory. We have to live it. Unless one's family expresses a desire to live upon spiritual principles we think we ought not to urge them. We should not talk incessantly to them about spiritual matters. They will change in time. **Our behavior will convince them more than our words**. We must remember that ten or twenty years of drunkenness would make a skeptic out of anyone.

> We must take the lead in rebuilding relationships, both at home and in the community. We made the mess; it's our job to clean it up. In our discussions with family and friends, there are many ways that we can find out if there is any way we can right our past wrongs in addition to remaining sober.

> Going forward, we make our best effort to live by the 12 Step

spiritual principles, which include love, patience, tolerance, and kindness. Our purpose is never to decide or dictate how others should live their lives.

What does the author mean when he says the spiritual life is not a theory, we have to live it? – p.83.

There may be **some wrongs we can never fully right**. We don't worry about them if we can honestly say to ourselves that we would right them if we could. Some people cannot be seen—we send them an honest **letter**. And there may be a **valid reason for postponement** in some cases. But **we don't delay if it can be avoided**. We should **be sensible, tactful, considerate and humble without being servile or scraping**. As God's people we stand on our feet; we don't crawl before anyone.

Experience has shown that the longer we delay our amends without a valid reason, the more likely it is that we will get drunk. Postponement and procrastination are deadly because the passing of time causes our guilt and shame over the harms we have caused others to keep growing and eventually devour us.

Writing a letter to someone we have harmed may be appropriate if we cannot make a direct amend, for whatever reason. Whether or not the person receiving the letter responds to us is irrelevant; we have completed our part and need take no further action. It is always wise to review the text of our letter with our sponsor before mailing.

We may also wish to write a letter to people we are unable to contact. They may be persons who have died, who refuse to meet with us face-to-face, who we cannot locate, or where it is impractical to meet with them for whatever reason. Our act of writing the letter is enough. Our sponsor may wish to review our letter, even though we are not going to mail it.

Do you see that in taking the Ninth Step you should be sensible,

tactful, considerate and humble without being servile or scraping?
– p.83.

If we are painstaking about this phase of our development, we will be amazed before we are half way through. We are going to know a new freedom and a new happiness. We will not regret the past nor wish to shut the door on it. We will comprehend the word serenity and we will know peace. No matter how far down the scale we have gone, we will see how our experience can benefit others. That feeling of uselessness and self-pity will disappear. We will lose interest in selfish things and gain interest in our fellows. Self-seeking will slip away. Our whole attitude and outlook upon life will change. Fear of people and of economic insecurity will leave us. We will intuitively know how to handle situations which used to baffle us. We will suddenly realize that **God is doing for us what we could not do for ourselves**.

Are these extravagant promises? We think not. They are being fulfilled among us—sometimes quickly, sometimes slowly. They will always materialize if we work for them.

A.A. members are quick to recognize that there are twelve Ninth Step promises. The number twelve seems to hold a degree of symbolism for us.

Many of us have received a few of the promises before reaching Steps Eight and Nine, and some of us never receive all of the promises. We know that nothing and no one can promise us anything, not even God. What we can say with certainty is expressed in the first sentence: "If we are painstaking about this phase of our development, we will be amazed before we are half way through." That is our only guarantee.

All of us have been astonished at the changes that have taken place in our life after we became sober and embarked on our 12 Step work because we have undergone a change in our attitudes and actions in life.

Is God doing for us what we cannot do for ourselves? Who knows?

We might reflect on the fact that we were not struck sober; we had to work for our physical and emotional sobriety. Even if we had a sudden spiritual experience, which is quite rare in A.A., we became deeply engaged with the Fellowship and completed the 12 Step program. We pray and mediate daily. We have created a higher power, or higher force, or higher set of principles we can draw on. We work the A.A. program principles all day, every day, to the best of our ability. We do our part, and reap the rewards of our efforts.

Are you experiencing the Promises set forth on pgs.83 and 84?

HOMEWORK

SESSION SIX

STEPS 8, 9

Into Action

Pages 76 - 84

STEP 8 -- *Made a list of all persons we had harmed, and became willing to make amends to them all.*

STEP 9 -- *Made direct amends to such people wherever possible, except when to do so would injure them or others.*

WRITE

Make a list of all people you have harmed (refer to your Step 4 Inventory sheets).

Amend: State not simply "I am sorry" but add "what can I do to make it up to you?"

Sponsor: Be sure to review every amend you are planning to make with your sponsor <u>before</u> you make the amend.

Amends often involve Friends, Family, Employers, Creditors and the Deceased.

SESSION SEVEN

STEPS 10 & 11

Into Action

Pages 84 - 88

STEP 10 -- *Continued to take personal inventory and when we were wrong, promptly admitted it.*

STEP 11 -- *Sought though prayer and meditation to improve our conscious contact with God as we understood Him, praying only for knowledge of His will for us and the power to carry that out.*

Continue making your Amends where appropriate.

READ

Read Steps 10 and 11 on p.84 - 88 (Chapter 6 – "Into Action") of the Big Book.

Read Steps 10 and 11 in the Twelve Steps & Twelve Traditions.

WRITE down your reactions to the readings as to how they apply to you and your illness, incorporating as much as possible of the considerations into your work. Think about:

CONSIDERATIONS

1) What are the specific instructions outlined for taking Step Ten?
2) What do we watch for? – p.84
3) Note that "By this time sanity will have been returned – we will seldom be interested in liquor" – p.84
4) Is this the sanity referred to in Step Two?
5) What is the proper use of will power? – p.85
6) What is a suggestion for taking the Eleventh Step on a daily basis?
7) Do you follow the procedure outlined on p.86–87 regarding your daily morning meditations and the way you proceed through the day?
8) Has your attitude about a Power greater than yourself changed since you studied the chapter "We Agnostics?"
9) Do you believe "It Works – It Really Does!"

Chapter 6

INTO ACTION

Pages 84 - 88

This thought brings us to **Step Ten**, which suggests we continue to take personal inventory and continue to set right any new mistakes as we go along.

> *Step 10* -- *Continued to take personal inventory and when we were wrong, promptly admitted it.*

We vigorously commenced this way of living as we cleaned up the past. We have entered the world of the Spirit. Our next function is to grow in understanding and effectiveness. This is not an overnight matter. It should **continue for our lifetime.** Continue to **watch for selfishness, dishonesty, resentment, and fear.** When these crop up, we ask God at once to remove them. We discuss them with someone immediately and make amends quickly if we have harmed anyone. Then we resolutely turn our thoughts to someone we can help. Love and tolerance of others is our code.

For alcoholics, even in sobriety, little time will pass without an attack of selfishness, dishonesty, resentment or fear. What do we do when that happens and we can't reach for our bottle?

It is suggested that we *immediately* do four things:

1) Ask that those feelings be removed.

2) Speak with someone, even if it is not our sponsor or someone in A.A.

3) Make an amend, if that is contributing to our distress.

4) Think about someone we can help to get us out of our all-consuming selfishness and self-centeredness, with the implication that action should follow our thoughts.

The first suggestion is spiritual in nature; we ask for help from God, our Higher Power or our spiritual values or principles for aid to move us into a more loving and tolerant mood. The remaining three suggestions are action steps.

Our response when these thoughts occur should be immediate, not delayed. We can think of it as putting our hand on a hot stove. We know we will get burned if our hand stays there very long, so we remove it *immediately*, just as we know our emotional and physical sobriety will be threatened if we flounder around in selfishness, dishonesty, resentment, or fear for very long.

If we get little relief after completing the four suggestions—*repeat them*. If we become desperate, we can write out a formal inventory, write down our gratitude list, go to a meeting, speak with our sponsor again, and continue sharing our emotional anxiety with other alcoholics in our support group.

And **we have ceased fighting anything or anyone—even alcohol**. For by this time **sanity will have returned**. We will seldom be interested in liquor. **If tempted, we recoil from it as from a hot flame. We react sanely and normally**, and we will find that this has happened automatically. We will see that our new attitude toward liquor has been given us without any thought or effort on our part. It just comes! That is the miracle of it. We are not fighting it, neither are we avoiding temptation. We feel as though we had been placed in a position of neutrality—safe and protected. We have not even sworn off. Instead, **the problem has been removed**. It does not exist for us. **We are neither cocky nor are we afraid**. That is our experience. That is how we react **so long as we keep in fit spiritual condition**.

By this point in our step work our constant obsession to drink should have been removed, and the squirrel-cage committee in our head should have slowed down. If not, do not be discouraged, but continue the step work and making a daily effort, as directed by our Big Book, to do the things which help us remain in a fit spiritual condition.

224

What keeps us in a fit spiritual condition? Prayer, meditation, daily inventory, an attitude of gratitude, service work, deep connection with the Fellowship through our sponsor and meetings, reading the Big Book and leaning on our home group or support group.

Above all, we don't drink or drug, no matter what happens.

It is easy to let up on the spiritual program of action and rest on our laurels. We are headed for trouble if we do, for **alcohol is a subtle foe. We are not cured of alcoholism**. What we really have is **a daily reprieve contingent on the maintenance of our spiritual condition**. Every day is a day when we must carry the vision of God's will into all of our activities. "How can I best serve Thee—Thy will (not mine) be done." These are thoughts which must go with us constantly. We can exercise our will power along this line all we wish. It is the proper use of the will.

Much has already been said about receiving strength, inspiration, and direction from Him who has all knowledge and power. If we have carefully followed directions, we have begun to sense the flow of His Spirit into us. To some extent **we have become God-conscious**. We have begun to develop this **vital sixth sense**. But **we must go further and that means more action**.

> What is a "vital sixth sense?" Humans have five senses: sight, hearing, touch, taste and smell. In A.A. it is hoped that as we undergo a spiritual awakening or psychic change, we will develop a vital sixth sense, or a "God consciousness," which is the goal of Step Eleven. That God consciousness is thought to evolve from our spiritual experience or spiritual awakening, which is our personality change sufficient to bring about recovery.
>
> One must remember that the purpose of sobriety is not to find God, but to find a new design for living, which does not require God. If any A.A. member finds sobriety through God as their Higher Power, we can celebrate.

However, many alcoholics are able to find the same peace, serenity and new life without God, or any vital sixth sense.

We are also reminded that it takes work to stay physically sober, and that it takes a lot more work to stay emotionally sober. Nothing comes automatically. Our daily gift of sobriety is based on not picking up a drink of course, but it is also based on our effort to maintain a fit spiritual condition.

Notice that our daily reprieve does not depend on the *status* of our spiritual condition; it depends on the *maintenance* of our spiritual state of mind. Our inspiration and ability to maintain our spiritual condition may come from God, our Higher Power, or whatever spiritual force, beliefs or values we have chosen to connect with in life.

We must never become complacent in our recovery. Experience has shown that many who forgo their daily spiritual maintenance routine end up drinking.

Our hubris usually starts with omitting our daily spiritual routine, which usually involves some amount of prayer and meditation. Then we being skipping meetings, just a few in the beginning, then more as time goes on. Next comes a reduction in our service work. We resign from service committees and stop participating in home group activities. Then we stop calling and meeting with other alcoholics. We begin to ignore our sponsees, refuse to take on new ones, and may even suggest that our sponsees get another sponsor because we have "too many other obligations."

After a while we stop our daily spiritual routine completely. We no longer attend any A.A. meetings. We stop all communication with our sponsor and sponsees. We forgo any service work. We begin to believe we can rely on ourselves to stay sober, and don't need to waste any more time with A.A.

Like the Man of Thirty in "More About Alcoholism" (Big Book, p.32), we soon find ourselves drinking after a period of abstinence, certain we will be able to control our drinking this time. After we take those first drinks, our craving returns and we end up just where we started before ever coming into A.A.

The lucky ones will eventually return to A.A. The unlucky ones will end up in jails, institutions or the morgue.

What are the specific instructions outlined for taking Step Ten?

What do we watch for? – p.84.

Note that by this time sanity will have been returned – we will seldom be interested in liquor. – p.84.

Is this the sanity referred to in Step Two?

What is the proper use of will power? – p.85.

Step Eleven suggests **prayer and meditation**. We shouldn't be shy on this matter of prayer. Better men than we are using it constantly. **It works, if we have the proper attitude and work at it**. It would be easy to be vague about this matter. Yet, we believe we can make some definite and valuable suggestions.

Step 11: Sought though prayer and meditation to improve our conscious contact with God as we understood Him, praying only for knowledge of His will for us and the power to carry that out.

Out of necessity I was forced to re-visit Step Eleven. I had been sober in A.A. for a few years, had completed all my 12 Steps and was active in service work. I basically ignored prayer and meditation because I thought I didn't need it since I didn't believe in God, and because I thought meditation was for old hippies.

My problem was that I had not developed a routine, daily spiritual ritual to keep me grounded in sobriety. All I did was say "Relieve me of the bondage of self" when I woke up, and "Thanks for keeping me sober" before retiring. That was a start, but over time I found it insufficient to keep me in that spiritual place I needed throughout the day.

227

One of my sponsees told me all he could do in the beginning was to perform prayer and meditation one day a week. He called it "spiritual Wednesdays." Then he progressed to two days a week—adding "spiritual Saturdays." In time he learned the benefit and necessity of "spiritual Every Day" of the week.

When we retire at night, we constructively review our day. Were we resentful, selfish, dishonest or afraid? Do we owe an apology? Have we kept something to ourselves which should be discussed with another person at once? Were we kind and loving toward all? What could we have done better? Were we thinking of ourselves most of the time? Or were we thinking of what we could do for others, of what we could pack into the stream of life? But we must be careful not to drift into worry, remorse or morbid reflection, for that would diminish our usefulness to others. After making our review we ask God's forgiveness and inquire what corrective measures should be taken.

I wrote down the above seven questions and put them on my bedside table to ask myself before turning off the lights. Over time my answers were always that I could have done better during the day, and that I was rarely kind and loving to everyone because of my innate selfishness. None of my answers varied much from the persistent character defects I had identified in Step Four.

Rather than drifting toward the pity-pot, I asked myself if there was anything I needed to do tomorrow to correct my shortcomings of today. If so, I wrote it down to remind myself the next morning.

I asked for no forgiveness, because I didn't need to be forgiven for being human and making mistakes. What I did need to do was to make a conscious effort not to repeat those mistakes.

I have not memorized those seven questions. If I'm travelling, or not in my own bed and don't have my list with me, or if I'm just in a hurry or have a bad attitude, I simply ask myself, "Where did I mess up today?"

228

On awakening let us think about the twenty-four hours ahead. We consider our plans for the day. Before we begin, we ask God to direct our thinking, especially **asking that it be divorced from self-pity, dishonest or self-seeking *motives*.** Under these conditions we can employ our mental faculties with assurance, for after all God gave us brains to use. Our thought-life will be placed on a much higher plane when our thinking is cleared of wrong motives.

We all make future plans, and most of us have a day calendar on our phone or at our desk. Step Eleven is not about planning our doctor appointments, shopping trips, picking up our children from school, job or customer meetings, or romantic dates. It is about planning our attitude and actions.

Despite all of our obligations, some welcome and others not, what is our attitude going to be as we carry out our duties? Will we go forth in anger and resentment for commitments we have reluctantly made? Will we be trying to manipulate folks during certain engagements? Will we be cursing under our breath at having to attend that office meeting? Will we try to put down a co-worker behind their back because they deserve it? Will we lie to our new customer in order to make the sale?

Whatever our plans, are they honorable in motive? To answer that question, I use the Oxford Group's Four Absolutes as a qualification test: honesty, unselfishness, love and purity. If my motive is honest and pure of heart, and flows from love and unselfishness, then I'm probably in good shape.

If we remind ourselves upon awakening to spend the next twenty-four hours with the best possible attitude we can muster, following the spiritual principles of our program, trying to do the next right thing right and accept that the world is not out there to do our bidding, odds are we will enjoy a much better day, regardless of what the day may bring.

In thinking about our day **we may face indecision**. We may not be able to determine which course to take.

Here we ask God for inspiration, an intuitive thought or a decision. We relax and take it easy. We don't struggle. We are often surprised how the right answers come after we have tried this for a while.

What used to be the hunch or the occasional inspiration gradually becomes a working part of the mind. Being still inexperienced and having just made conscious contact with God, it is not probable that we are going to be inspired at all times. We might pay for this presumption in all sorts of absurd actions and ideas. Nevertheless, we find that our thinking will, as time passes, be more and more on the plane of inspiration. We come to rely upon it.

> When we face indecision it is suggested that we relax and ask for inspiration to help us make a decision. This is good advice, but A.A. offers us additional options beyond prayer. We have a sponsor we can speak with, and a home group or support group who knows us well who we can confide in. We may have other non-A.A. folks we can consult, or even professional help may be indicated. Now that we are sober and living a more loving, giving and spiritual life, we have no shortage of people inside and outside the fellowship who can help us, if we are willing to ask for help.

We usually **conclude the period of meditation with a prayer** that we be shown all through the day what our next step is to be, that we be given whatever we need to take care of such problems. We ask especially for freedom from self-will, and are careful to make no request for ourselves only. We may ask for ourselves, however, if others will be helped. We are careful never to pray for our own selfish ends. Many of us have wasted a lot of time doing that and it doesn't work. You can easily see why.

> For those of us who have used prayer all our lives, we may want to re-assess how we pray. Prayer is nothing more than a petition, or a request for something. That request may be directed to God, to our Higher Power, to something or someone else, or to no one or nothing in particular.

The purpose of prayer is not to get what we are requesting. We pray to consciously remind ourselves that we are not running the show and that we are not God. We are really speaking to our better self in order to remind ourself that we have chosen to live our life based on the moral values embedded in the spiritual 12 Step principles, regardless of what happens each day.

Our requests direct us where to focus our energy and effort in life. If we suspect we will be facing a difficult situation tomorrow, we can ask that love and tolerance remain our code. If we are concerned about a sick friend, we can ask that they be given strength and peace of mind to deal with their illness, which may motivate us to give them a call to check on them. We can pray that we will continue to use our spiritual principles to guide and direct our life, because those principles have helped us in the past and will help us in the future.

If circumstances warrant, **we ask our wives or friends to join us** in morning meditation. If we belong to a religious denomination which requires a definite morning devotion, we attend to that also. If not members of religious bodies, we sometimes **select and memorize a few set prayers which emphasize the principles** we have been discussing. There are many helpful books also. Suggestions about these may be obtained from one's priest, minister, or rabbi. Be quick to see where religious people are right. Make use of what they offer.

Experience suggests it really doesn't matter *how* we pray, as long as we *do it.* There is no right or wrong way to pray, if done sincerely. Each of us in A.A. prays differently, and no one in A.A., including our sponsor, should tell us how to pray. If we need guidance in prayer, Step Eleven in the *Twelve Steps and Twelve Traditions* offers suggestions, and there are endless other avenues available for support.

Asking others to join us in daily prayer seemed ridiculous to me until one of my sponsees told me that asking his wife to join him in his morning meditation helped save his marriage, because it provided a daily set time for the two of them to have an intimate conversation after saying their prayers.

As we go through the day we pause when agitated or doubtful, and ask for the right thought or action.

We constantly **remind ourselves we are no longer running the show**, humbly saying to ourselves many times each day "Thy will be done." We are then in much less danger of excitement, fear, anger, worry, self-pity, or foolish decisions. We become much more efficient. We do not tire so easily, for we are not burning up energy foolishly as we did when we were trying to arrange life to suit ourselves.

It works—it really does.

We **alcoholics are undisciplined**. So **we let God discipline us** in the simple way we have just outlined.

But this is not all. There is **action and more action. Faith without works is dead**. The next chapter is entirely devoted to Step Twelve.

We alcoholics need daily structure, ritual and discipline in our lives. While drinking, we lived a life of anger, fear, selfishness and self-centeredness which turned us into a mound of willful indifference, irresponsibility and uselessness.

Prayer and meditation introduces us to a practical humility which we can use to better our life and the lives of those around us. We now have a solution for our incessant restlessness, irritability and discontentedness, aggravated by our doubts and indecisions. We ask for spiritual help through prayer and receive fellowship help through meetings and interactions with other alcoholics.

As for our relationship with God, Bill W. provided a stern warning to us when he wrote about believing we had a pipeline to God: "I am a firm believer in both guidance and prayer. But I am fully aware, and humble enough, I hope, to see there may be nothing infallible about my guidance. The minute I figure I have got a perfectly clear pipeline to God, I have become egotistical enough to get into real trouble. Nobody can cause more needless grief than a power-driver who thinks he has got it straight from God." (As Bill Sees It, Letter, 1950)

Several years ago I met a church going newcomer who said he had a sudden conversion experience after joining A.A. In no time he became convinced that every selfish and self-centered thought he had came straight from God. He was certain that whatever he thought or did was blessed by the Holy Spirit, regardless of how reckless or ridiculous. Needless to say, he ended up drinking again.

What is a suggestion for taking the Eleventh Step on a daily basis? p.86

Do you follow the procedure outlined on pgs. 86 to 88 regarding your daily morning meditations and the way you proceed through the day?

Has your attitude about a Power greater than yourself changed since you studied the chapter "We Agnostics?"

Do you believe: It works – it really does?

HOMEWORK

SESSION SEVEN

STEPS 10 & 11

Into Action

Pages 84 - 88

STEP 10 -- _Continued to take personal inventory and when we were wrong, promptly admitted it._

STEP 11 -- _Sought though prayer and meditation to improve our conscious contact with God as we understood Him, praying only for knowledge of His will for us and the power to carry that out._

WRITE down your reactions to the readings as to <u>how they apply to you and your illness</u>, incorporating as much as possible of the considerations into your work.

Continue making your Amends where appropriate.

STEP 12

Working With Others

Pages 89 – 103

STEP 12 -- *Having had a spiritual awakening as the result of these steps, we tried to carry this message to alcoholics and to practice these principles in all our affairs.*

READ

Read Chapter Seven – "Working with Others" (p.89–103)

Read Step 12 in the Twelve Steps & Twelve Traditions

WRITE down your reactions to the readings as to how they apply to you and your illness, incorporating as much as possible of the considerations into your work. Think about:

CONSIDERATIONS

1) "Having had a spiritual awakening as a result of these steps."
2) Can you again see the "entire psychic change" mentioned by Dr. Silkworth working in your life?
3) What are the step-by-step requirements for a Twelfth Step? Have you ever tried this? Share you experience with the group.
4) In cases where the alcoholic has not responded, have you worked with his family?
5) Did you offer them your way of life and what results did you have in that situation?
6) Do you believe that you should *"Burn the idea into the consciousness of every man that he can get well regardless of anyone. The only condition is that he trust in God and clean house*? p.98.
7) Is this the basis of the statement that this is a "selfish program?"
8) What are the principles we are to practice in all our affairs?
9) Why does Bill say "all our affairs?"
10) What does this mean to you?

235

11) How can you apply the Twelve Steps outside the meeting rooms? Do you do it?

11) What are some of your daily practices in life to maintain sobriety and to grow spiritually?

BIG BOOK TEXT FOR STEP 12

Chapter 7

WORKING WITH OTHERS

Pages 89 – 103

At the end of "Into Action" and as an introduction to "Working With Others," Bill W. said that *"Faith without works is dead."*

This quote comes from James 2:14-26 in the King James version of the Bible: "What doth it profit, my brethren, though a man say he hath faith, and have not works? Can faith save him? If a brother or sister be naked, and destitute of daily food, and one of you say unto them, depart in peace, be ye warmed and filled; notwithstanding ye give them not those things which are needful to the body; what doth it profit? Even so *faith, if it hath not works, is dead*, being alone.

Yea, a man may say, Thou hast faith, and I have works: shew me thy faith without thy works, and I will shew thee my faith by my works. Thou believest that there is one God; thou doest well: the devils also believe, and tremble. But wilt thou know, O vain man, that *faith without works is dead?*

Was not Abraham our father justified by works, when he had offered Isaac his son upon the altar? Seest thou how faith wrought with his works, and by works was faith made perfect? And the scripture was fulfilled which saith, Abraham believed God, and it was imputed unto him for righteousness, and he was called the Friend of God. *Ye see then how that by works a man is justified, and not by faith only.*

Likewise also was not Rahab the harlot justified by works, when she had received the messengers, and had sent them out another way? For as the body without the spirit is dead, so *faith without works is dead* also."

Dr. Bob was an example that faith alone, or good works alone, will not keep us sober. As a physician, Dr. Bob spent his medical career helping his patients, but he did not stay sober. Nor did the years Dr. Bob spent in church and as a member of the Christian based Oxford Group keep him sober. In varying degrees he had faith and he had works as he tended to his patients, but he never worked with other alcoholics by the methods described in A.A.

For us, all the faith in the world will not get us sober, and good works alone will not get us sober. As Bill states further on in this chapter, "Faith must be accompanied by self-sacrifice and unselfish, constructive action." (Big Book, p.93)

WORKING WITH OTHERS

Practical experience shows that nothing will so much insure immunity from drinking as intensive work with other alcoholics. It works when other activities fail. This is our **twelfth suggestion**: **Carry this message to other alcoholics!** You can help when no one else can. You can secure their confidence when others fail. Remember they are very ill.

Step 12 -- *Having had a spiritual awakening as* **the result** *of these steps, we tried to carry this message to alcoholics and to practice these principles in all our affairs.*

Life will take on new meaning. To watch people recover, to see them help others, to watch loneliness vanish, to see a fellowship grow up about you, to have a host of friends—this is an experience you must not miss. We know you will not want to miss it. Frequent contact with newcomers and with each other is the bright spot of our lives.

Our book resolutely declares that *nothing* will so much insure immunity from drinking as *intensive work* with other alcoholics. It works when other activities *fail.*

This means that when *all* other activities fail as we try to stay sober, the intensive work of sponsoring another alcoholic and working with him on the 12 Step program will save us.

This fact was well demonstrated by Dr. Bob, who had a daily

obsession to drink for almost three years, and stayed sober *only* because he worked with other alcoholics: "Unlike most of our crowd, I did not get over my craving for liquor much during the first two and one-half years of abstinence. It was almost always with me." (Dr. Bob's Nightmare, Big Book, p.181)

There is little in our new life that can surpass the joy of watching another alcoholic heal. It is a win-win for both parties, keeping us grateful, sober and serene.

Having had a spiritual awakening as a result of these steps. Can you again see the entire psychic change mentioned by Dr. Silkworth working in your life?

Perhaps you are not acquainted with any drinkers who want to recover. You can easily find some by asking a few doctors, ministers, priests or hospitals. They will be only too glad to assist you. Don't start out as an evangelist or reformer. Unfortunately a lot of prejudice exists. You will be handicapped if you arouse it. Ministers and doctors are competent and you can learn much from them if you wish, but it happens that **because of your own drinking experience you can be uniquely useful to other alcoholics**. So **cooperate; never criticize**. **To be helpful is our only aim**.

In Bill Wilson's early years there were no formal A.A. meetings or Big Book. No alcoholics gathered in one place regularly for sobriety, but they did gather together to drink, which is where Bill unsuccessfully sought them out. Today, we can find ample alcoholics to work with at A.A. meetings, and because we are sober alcoholics, we have some authority in the message of hope and recovery that we carry.

When you discover a prospect for Alcoholics Anonymous, find out all you can about him. **If he does not want to stop drinking, don't waste time trying to persuade him**. You may spoil a later opportunity. This advice is given for his family also. They should be patient, realizing they are dealing with a sick person.

Alcoholics end up in A.A. for many reasons. Some have an

honest desire to stop drinking. Others don't know where else to go when the drink stops working or they are suicidal. Some come because of threats from spouses or family members, and the courts force many into our rooms.

It doesn't matter why a person is in A.A. It may take time for them to accept Step One, and we can't make anyone want to stop drinking for good. Until they do, we can set an example of how we got sober, found and maintain our new life, and how much better it is than our old way of living.

If there is any indication that he wants to stop, have a good talk with the person most interested in him—usually his wife. Get an idea of his behavior, his problems, his background, the seriousness of his condition, and his religious leanings. You need this information to put yourself in his place, to see how you would like him to approach you if the tables were turned.

Back in 1935 when Bill W. started A.A., speaking with family members of alcoholics was only natural, since families were an active part of the alcoholics' recovery process. Since most of the alcoholics at that time were men, it was the wives who were consulted.

Inquiring about the alcoholic's religious leanings may have been made for two reasons. The first was to determine if they believed in God, since A.A. is a God-based program. The second reason was because A.A. was comprised predominately of Protestants who were also Oxford Group members before A.A. left the group in 1937 (New York) and 1939 (Akron).

Since the Oxford Group was multi-denominational and used members' guidance to interpret God's guidance, the Catholic Church forbade Catholics to join the group. They felt the Oxford Group was putting Catholics under ecclesiastical jurisdiction separate from the Pope, and were also upset when the Oxfords solicited member donations, which was seen as trying to take funds which would have otherwise been donated to the Catholic Church.

In New York City in early 1937, leaders of the Oxford Group at the Calvary Mission ordered alcoholics staying there not to attend "drunks only" meetings at Bill W.'s Clinton Street home. The Wilson's were labelled as "not maximum," which was an Oxford term for those believed to be lagging in their devotion to Oxford Group principles.

In late 1939, Akron, Ohio members of the "alcoholic squad" withdrew from the Oxford Group and began holding A.A. meetings at Dr. Bob's house.

In early A.A., many of the wives came with their husbands to Oxford Group meetings, and later to A.A. meetings, where they passed the time by meeting separately with the other wives to chat, commiserate and support each other. This practice led to the formation of Al-Anon by Lois Wilson and her friend Anne B., who was the wife of an alcoholic, in May, 1951.

Al-Anon's core purpose today is helping families and friends of alcoholics find hope and encouragement to live joyful, serene lives. Today's Al-Anon Family Groups is a spiritually based organization that helps the families and friends of alcoholics connect and support each other through meetings, information, and shared experiences.

Sometimes it is wise to wait till he goes on a binge. The family may object to this, but unless he is in a dangerous physical condition, it is better to risk it. **Don't deal with him when he is very drunk**, unless he is ugly and the family needs your help. **Wait for the end of the spree, or at least for a lucid interval**. Then let his family or a friend **ask him if he wants to quit for good and if he would go to any extreme to do so**. If he says yes, then his attention should be drawn to you as a person who has recovered. You should be described to him as one of a fellowship who, as part of their own recovery, try to help others and who will be glad to talk to him if he cares to see you.

If he does not want to see you, **never force yourself upon him**. Neither should the family hysterically plead with him to do anything, nor should they tell him much about you. They should wait for the end of his next drinking bout. You might place this book where he can see it in the interval. Here no specific rule can be given. The family must decide these things. But urge them not to be over-anxious, for that might spoil matters.

Usually the family should not try to tell your story. When possible, **avoid meeting a man through his family**. Approach through a doctor or an institution is a better bet. If your man needs hospitalization, he should have it, but not forcibly unless he is violent. Let the doctor, if he will, tell him he has something in the way of a solution.

When your man is better, the doctor might suggest a visit from you. Though you have talked with the family, leave them out of the first discussion. Under these conditions your prospect will see he is under no pressure. He will feel he can deal with you without being nagged by his family. Call on him while he is still jittery. He may be more receptive when depressed.

See your man alone, if possible. At first engage in general conversation. After a while, turn the talk to some phase of drinking. Tell him enough about your drinking habits, symptoms, and experiences to encourage him to speak of himself. If he wishes to talk, let him do so. You will thus get a better idea of how you ought to proceed. If he is not communicative, give him a sketch of your drinking career up to the time you quit. But say nothing, for the moment, of how that was accomplished. If he is in a serious mood dwell on the troubles liquor has caused you, being **careful not to moralize or lecture**. If his mood is light, tell him humorous stories of your escapades. Get him to tell some of his.

When he sees you know all about the drinking game, **commence to describe yourself as an alcoholic**.

Tell him how baffled you were, how you finally learned that you were sick. Give him an account of the struggles you made to stop. **Show him the mental twist which leads to the first drink** of a spree. We suggest you do this as we have done it in the chapter on alcoholism.

If he is alcoholic, he will understand you at once. He will match your mental inconsistencies with some of his own.

The chapter "Working With Others" is an excellent instruction section on how to do a twelfth-step call and how to sponsor an alcoholic. Today's suggestions are similar to those of 1935:

1) Determine if the newcomer wants to stop drinking. Since he is physically and mentally sick with alcoholism, he may not tell the truth, or know the truth. Even if he just wants to want to stop drinking, it's a start.

2) Don't meet with him when he is drunk, since his mind is mush. Wait until he sobers up a bit so he can keep his eyes open and comprehend some of your message.

3) It is usually much more effective and safer if two or three alcoholics see the prospect together, rather than seeing the man alone.

4) A.A. is based on attraction, so don't talk down to the alcoholic by moralizing, lecturing and evangelizing.

5) Tell him you're a hopeless alcoholic because you could not stop drinking *for good*, and were never able to control your drinking *every time* you drank, due to your fatal mental obsession and physical allergy which is the hallmark of our medical illness.

If you are satisfied that he is a real alcoholic, begin to **dwell on the hopeless feature** of the malady. **Show him**, from your own experience, **how the queer mental condition surrounding that first drink prevents normal functioning of the will power**. Don't, at this stage, refer to this book, unless he has seen it and wishes to discuss it. And **be careful not to brand him as an alcoholic. Let him draw his own conclusion**. If he sticks to the idea that he can still control his drinking, tell him that possibly he can—if he is not too alcoholic. But insist that if he is severely afflicted, **there may be little chance he can recover by himself**.

Continue to **speak of alcoholism as an illness, a fatal malady**. Talk about the conditions of body and mind which accompany it. Keep his attention focused mainly on **your personal experience**. Explain that many are doomed who never realize their predicament. Doctors are rightly loath to tell alcoholic patients the whole story unless it will serve some good purpose.

> In "There Is A Solution" (Big Book, p.21) we are introduced to the real alcoholic: "He may start off as a moderate drinker; he may or may not become a continuous hard drinker; but at some stage of his drinking career he begins to lose all control of his liquor consumption, once he starts to drink."

> It rarely requires a lengthy discussion for one alcoholic to recognize another alcoholic. We don't label others as alcoholics, but they will quickly figure it out on their own. Because of our enthusiasm to help the newcomer, it may be difficult not to analyze their situation and give advice, but if we simply stick to sharing our own experience with alcoholism the new man will not feel threatened, and will hopefully continue to listen to us.

> The only reason I stayed in A.A. was hearing numerous other alcoholics share about the hopelessness of our illness and our total inability to recover solely on our own. I could relate to their stories, and was desperate to find out how they got better.

But you may **talk to him about the hopelessness of alcoholism because you offer a solution**. You will soon have your friend admitting he has many, if not all, of the traits of the alcoholic. If his own doctor is willing to tell him that he is alcoholic, so much the better. Even though your protégé may not have entirely admitted his condition, he has become very curious to know how you got well. Let him ask you that question, if he will. **Tell him exactly what happened to you. Stress the spiritual feature freely**. If the man be agnostic or atheist, make it emphatic that **he does not have to agree with your conception of God**. He can choose any conception he likes, provided it makes sense to him.

244

The main thing is that he be willing to believe in a power greater than himself and that he live by spiritual principles.

This is the cornerstone of A.A.: *The main thing is that he be willing to believe in a power greater than himself and that he live by spiritual principles.*

When I finally accepted the fact that after the alcohol stopped working for me I still couldn't stop drinking when I really wanted to, I knew I needed some type of help. I tried, but couldn't do it on my own. I assumed joining A.A. would provide me with the human help of the Fellowship, which it did.

Living by the spiritual principles of the 12 Steps seemed fairly simple, since I had always strived to be a decent person, knew right from wrong, and had a good moral character. I assumed that sobriety would not remove my desire or ability to live with honesty and integrity.

What I did not realize was that I would also need some type of non-human help, or power greater than myself, in addition to the help from my A.A. fellows. This was a confusing proposition.

Our Big Book suggests I use God as that power greater than myself to help me, but since I could never connect with God, that didn't work for me. I couldn't force myself to believe in something I never believed in.

Over time in A.A. I realized that I could use anything I wanted as my spiritual guide, and it didn't have to be "my own conception of *God*." Instead, it became my own conception of my non-human spiritual beliefs, which most of us have in one form or another, whether we are religious or secular beings. My spiritual beliefs in A.A. are the A.A. principles.

Today, I live by the phrase: "*The main thing is that he be willing to live by the power of the spiritual principles.*" That's what works for me. I use the moral values embedded in the 12 Step principles as my "Higher Power" in A.A. The principles *are* my higher power, and that is how I live my life today.

When dealing with such a person, you had better use everyday language to describe spiritual principles. There is no use arousing any prejudice he may have against certain theological terms and conceptions about which he may already be confused. Don't raise such issues, no matter what your own convictions are.

Your prospect may belong to a religious denomination. His religious education and training may be far superior to yours. In that case he is going to wonder how you can add anything to what he already knows. But **he will be curious to learn why his own convictions have not worked and why yours seem to work so well**.

When I speak with another alcoholic, especially during a twelfth-step call, I tell him exactly what happened to me in my illness.

I was hopeless, helpless, suicidal and saw no way out. The drink had stopped working, and the consequences of my illness were beginning to pile up with loss of job, wife, family and friends. Legal and financial troubles were on the horizon. A.A. offered me a solution for all my problems. A.A. didn't teach me how to not-drink, but how to live a fulfilling, sober life in the real world.

Unlike the recommendation in our book, I rarely discuss the spiritual aspect of A.A. because experience has taught me that introducing God, Higher Power or spirituality with a fresh new man who is not even in A.A. yet can be a recipe for disaster.

Like myself when I was in my cups, I know of no alcoholic who wants to hear that God or some Higher Power will fix their problem. Certainly if the prospect asks about God, or the spirituality of A.A., I will share my experience, but I never bring it up on my own; it's way too early.

The main message I carry is that I was unable to get better without help, and that help is available in A.A. if he wants it.

He may be an example of the truth that faith alone is insufficient. **To be vital, faith must be accompanied by self-sacrifice and unselfish, constructive action**. Let him see that you are not there to instruct him in religion. Admit that he probably knows more about it than you do, but call to his attention the fact that **however deep his faith and knowledge, he could not have applied it or he would not drink**. Perhaps your story will help him see where he has failed to practice the very precepts he knows so well. We represent no particular faith or denomination. We are dealing only with general principles common to most denominations.

> This is one of the most critical paragraphs in the Big Book because it reminds us that faith and God *alone* will not get us sober. No church alone will get us sober, as Dr. Bob's experience demonstrated. The self-sacrifice and unselfish, constructive action required of us is to pass the A.A. message of hope and recovery to another *alcoholic*.

> Some in A.A. think of self-sacrifice as Steps 1 through 3, where we relinquish our belief that we alone can control our alcoholism and don't need any help, and think of unselfish, constructive action as Steps 4 through 12.

Outline the program of action, explaining how you **made a self-appraisal**, how you **straightened out your past** and why you are now endeavoring to be helpful to him. It is important for him to realize that **your attempt to pass this on to him plays a vital part in your recovery**. Actually, **he may be helping you more than you are helping him**. Make it plain he is under no obligation to you, that **you hope only that he will try to help other alcoholics when he escapes his own difficulties**. Suggest how important it is that he place the welfare of other people ahead of his own.

Make it clear that he is not under pressure, that he needn't see you again if he doesn't want to. You should not be offended if he wants to call it off, for he has helped you more than you have helped him.

If your talk has been sane, quiet and full of human understanding, you have perhaps made a friend. Maybe you have disturbed him about the question of alcoholism. This is all to the good. **The more hopeless he feels, the better**. He will be more likely to follow your suggestions.

Your candidate may give reasons why he need not follow all of the program. He may rebel at the thought of a drastic housecleaning which requires discussion with other people. Do not contradict such views. Tell him you once felt as he does, but you doubt whether you would have made much progress had you not taken action. **On your first visit tell him about the Fellowship of Alcoholics Anonymous**. If he shows interest, **lend him your copy of this book**.

> In today's world, unlike the 1930s, almost everyone is somewhat familiar with A.A., or at least knows it exists.
>
> Many suggest to the new prospect that he attend a few A.A. meetings where he can remain quiet and anonymous if he chooses, and begin to learn about the A.A. fellowship and 12 Step program. After speaking with a newcomer, I always give the person a copy of our local A.A. meeting directory, although it is available on-line. If they are destitute, I'll give them a copy of the Big Book. I share with him which meetings I attend should he want to speak further in person, and provide my phone number as well. After that, it is up to that person to take the next step.

Unless your friend wants to talk further about himself, **do not wear out your welcome**. Give him a chance to think it over. If you do stay, let him steer the conversation in any direction he likes. Sometimes a new man is anxious to proceed at once, and you may be tempted to let him do so. This is sometimes a mistake. If he has trouble later, he is likely to say you rushed him. **You will be most successful with alcoholics if you do not exhibit any passion for crusade or reform**. Never talk down to an alcoholic from any moral or spiritual hilltop; simply **lay out the kit of spiritual tools for his inspection**. Show him how they worked with you. Offer him friendship and fellowship. Tell him that if he wants to get well you will do anything to help.

If he is not interested in your solution, if he expects you to act only as a banker for his financial difficulties or a nurse for his sprees, you may have to drop him until he changes his mind. This he may do after he gets hurt some more.

In this part of the chapter of "Working With Others," we start to learn how to sponsor someone.

Sponsorship is like holding a baby in your arms while he's throwing up on you; you love the baby but hate the mess he makes.

Although it is not written in the Big Book, men sponsor men and women sponsor women for obvious reasons. Sex and romance was not a huge issue in the early years of A.A. since almost all the members were men, unlike today where one-third of A.A. members are women.

If you are working with a man who is willing to stop drinking for good and start on his path to recovery, your kit of spiritual tools consists of two things:

1) the *A.A. Fellowship* – sponsor, sponsee, Home Group, meetings, support group and service work.

2) the *Design for Living* – the Big Book and 12 Steps.

If he is sincerely interested and wants to see you again**, ask him to read this book** in the interval. After doing that, he must decide for himself whether he wants to go on. He **should not be pushed or prodded** by you, his wife, or his friends. If he is to find God, the desire must come from within.

If he thinks he can do the job in some other way, or prefers some other spiritual approach, encourage him to follow his own conscience. We have no monopoly on God; we merely have an approach that worked with us. But point out that we alcoholics have much in common and that you would like, in any case, to be friendly. Let it go at that.

Do not be discouraged if your prospect does not respond at once.

Search out another alcoholic and try again. You are sure to find someone desperate enough to accept with eagerness what you offer. **We find it a waste of time to keep chasing a man who cannot or will not work with you**. If you leave such a person alone, he may soon become convinced that he cannot recover by himself.

To spend too much time on any one situation is to deny some other alcoholic an opportunity to live and be happy. One of our Fellowship failed entirely with his first half dozen prospects. He often says that if he had continued to work on them, he might have deprived many others, who have since recovered, of their chance.

> Once we start to sponsor someone, or offer to take them through the 12 Steps, there are many approaches we can use. However, with experience as our teacher and input from our sponsor, we will discover a method that works best for us. We can't beat anyone into sobriety, so if he is not yet ready to work the program, it's time to move on to someone who is.
>
> What I say to folks who are unable to do the work involved in the 12 Steps is that I need to work with willing alcoholics to stay sober myself. Since it seems they aren't ready to do the work, I'm glad to speak with them at any time about A.A. and recovery, and if and when they become willing to embark on the 12 Step work they can let me know.

Suppose now you are making your **second visit to a man**. He has read this volume and says **he is prepared to go through with the Twelve Steps of the program of recovery**. Having had the experience yourself, you can give him much practical advice. **Let him know you are available** if he wishes to make a decision and tell his story, but do not insist upon it if he prefers to consult someone else.

He may be broke and homeless. If he is, you might try to help him about getting a **job**, or give him a little **financial assistance**. But you should not deprive your family or creditors of money they should have. Perhaps you will want to take the man into your **home** for a few days. But be sure you use discretion.

Be certain he will be welcomed by your family, and that **he is not trying to impose upon you for money, connections, or shelter**. Permit that and you only harm him. You will be making it possible for him to be insincere. You may be aiding in his destruction rather than his recovery.

> We all naturally want to do as much as we can for the still suffering alcoholic, but they must travel their own path. We carry the message, not the alcoholic.

> Most of us never provide a job for the newcomer, because they are usually unreliable, irresponsible and often relapse. Giving or loaning money to an alcoholic should be treated as a charity gift, because we will rarely be repaid. Only once have I heard of an alcoholic taking another alcoholic into their home, and that involved a family relative. The results were disastrous.

> Referring alcoholics to social service workers or rehabilitation facilities is commonly done, but in the long run the alcoholic will need to find their own way in recovery, just as they did while they were drinking.

Never avoid these responsibilities, but be sure you are doing the right thing if you assume them. **Helping others is the foundation stone of your recovery**. A kindly act once in a while isn't enough. **You have to act the Good Samaritan every day**, if need be. It may mean the loss of many nights' sleep, great interference with your pleasures, interruptions to your business. It may mean sharing your money and your home, counseling frantic wives and relatives, innumerable trips to police courts, sanitariums, hospitals, jails and asylums. Your telephone may jangle at any time of the day or night.

Your wife may sometimes say she is neglected. A drunk may smash the furniture in your home, or burn a mattress. You may have to fight with him if he is violent. Sometimes you will have to call a doctor and administer sedatives under his direction. Another time you may have to send for the police or an ambulance. Occasionally you will have to meet such conditions.

Accepting the responsibility of sponsorship entails substantial obligations and burdens, and should never be undertaken lightly. Remember the alcoholic is a very sick man, just as we were when we came into A.A. Experience, common sense, patience, tolerance, empathy, frequent consultation with our sponsor, and being able to set firm physical and personal boundaries is needed when working with any alcoholic.

We seldom allow an alcoholic to live in our homes for long at a time. It is not good for him, and it sometimes creates serious complications in a family.

Though an alcoholic does not respond, there is no reason why you should neglect his family. You should continue to be friendly to them. The family should be offered your way of life. Should they accept and practice spiritual principles, there is a much better chance that the head of the family will recover. And even though he continues to drink, the family will find life more bearable.

> Despite what it says in our Big Book, it is not our job as a recovered alcoholic to work with any alcoholic's family other than at a level of basic courtesy, especially because what we say and do with our sponsee is confidential. Nor is it our job to offer the alcoholic's family our way of life.

> Al-Anon Family Groups is available for the families of alcoholics, and its use should be encouraged. Al-Anon's 12 Step program mirror's A.A.'s 12 Step program, and the Al-Anon fellowship is an invaluable resource for the family and friends of alcoholics.

For the type of alcoholic who is able and willing to get well, little charity, in the ordinary sense of the word, is needed or wanted. The **men who cry for money and shelter** before conquering alcohol, **are on the wrong track**. Yet we do go to great extremes to provide each other with these very things, when such action is warranted. This may seem inconsistent, but we think it is not.

It is not the matter of giving that is in question, but **when and how to give**. That often makes the difference between failure and success.

The minute we **put our work on a service plane**, the alcoholic **commences to rely upon our assistance rather than upon God**. He clamors for this or that, claiming he cannot master alcohol until his material needs are cared for. Nonsense. Some of us have taken very hard knocks to learn this truth: **Job or no job—wife or no wife—we simply do not stop drinking so long as we place dependence upon other people ahead of dependence on God.**

Burn this idea into the consciousness of every man that **he can get well regardless of anyone. The only condition is that he trust in God and clean house**.

> If God is the alcoholic's spiritual Higher Power, they will do well to rely on God during their life journey. We all need to rely on some intangible power, or force, or set of moral principles of our own understanding to heal.
>
> But we also need to rely on the human fellowship of A.A., and most importantly, we need to do the all 12 Step program work required for sobriety. No one can make us sober other than ourself—neither God or the Fellowship.
>
> In this chapter, the suggestions for an alcoholic to begin his recovery journey are to:
>
> 1) Work all the 12 Steps of A.A. with a sponsor.
>
> 2) Deeply engage and participate with the A.A. Fellowship.
>
> 3) Enlarge our spiritual condition through the daily ritual of prayer and meditation of our own creation.
>
> 4) Try to carry the message of hope and recovery we have received through sponsorship and regular A.A. service work.
>
> *Do you believe that you should burn the idea into the consciousness of every man that he can get well regardless of anyone? The only condition is that he trust in God and clean house? – p.98 Is this the basis of the statement that this is a "selfish program?"*

Now, **the domestic problem**: There may be **divorce, separation, or just strained relations**. When your prospect has made such reparation as he can to his family, and has thoroughly explained to them the new principles by which he is living, **he should proceed to put those principles into action at home**. That is, if he is lucky enough to have a home. Though his family be at fault in many respects, he should not be concerned about that.

He should **concentrate on his own spiritual demonstration. Argument and fault-finding are to be avoided** like the plague. In many homes this is a difficult thing to do, but it must be done if any results are to be expected. If persisted in for a few months, the effect on a man's family is sure to be great. The most incompatible people discover they have a basis upon which they can meet. Little by little the family may see their own defects and admit them. These can then be discussed in an atmosphere of helpfulness and friendliness.

After they have seen tangible results, the family will perhaps want to go along. These things will come to pass naturally and in good time provided, however, **the alcoholic continues to demonstrate that he can be sober, considerate, and helpful, regardless of what anyone says or does**. Of course, we all fall much below this standard many times. But we must try to repair the damage immediately lest we pay the penalty by a spree.

Once again, our book suggests we ignore the behavior of others and focus on demonstrating our own progress in recovery. Especially in family life, playing the victim, blaming others for our own faults or trying to force family members to adopt the A.A. way of life is a recipe for failure.

Despite the uncertainty, confusion, chaos and sorrow around us, if we persist in practicing the 12 Step principles to the best of our ability at all times, we will likely stay sober. We can rarely fully repair the damage we caused by our past behavior, and that should never be our sole goal.

If there be divorce or separation, there should be no undue

haste for the couple to get together. The man should be sure of his recovery. The wife should fully understand his new way of life. If their old relationship is to be resumed it must be on a better basis, since the former did not work. This means a new attitude and spirit all around. **Sometimes it is to the best interests of all concerned that a couple remain apart**. Obviously, no rule can be laid down. Let the alcoholic continue his program day by day. When the time for living together has come, it will be apparent to both parties.

Let no alcoholic say he cannot recover unless he has his family back. This just isn't so. In some cases the wife will never come back for one reason or another. Remind the prospect that his recovery is not dependent upon people. It is dependent upon his relationship with God. **We have seen men get well whose families have not returned at all. We have seen others slip when the family came back too soon**.

Both you and the new man must walk day by day in the path of spiritual progress. If you persist, remarkable things will happen. When we look back, we realize that the things which came to us when **we put ourselves in God's hands** were better than anything we could have planned. **Follow the dictates of a Higher Power** and you will presently live in a new and wonderful world, no matter what your present circumstances!

When working with a man and his family, you should take care not to participate in their quarrels. You may spoil your chance of being helpful if you do. But **urge upon a man's family that he has been a very sick person and should be treated accordingly**. You should warn against arousing resentment or jealousy. You should point out that **his defects of character are not going to disappear overnight**. Show them that he has entered upon a period of growth. Ask them to remember, when they are impatient, the blessed fact of his sobriety.

If you have been successful in solving your own domestic problems, tell the newcomer's family how that was accomplished. In this way you can set them on the right track without becoming critical of them.

The story of how you and your wife settled your difficulties is worth any amount of criticism.

No one can or should attempt to solve another's domestic problems, especially their relationship difficulties. It's none of our business, and we should not be working with any alcoholic's family with the goal of resolving their domestic issues.

In addition to the fellowships of A.A. and Al-Anon, there are ample medical, marriage and mental health counselors available who have far more expertise than the average alcoholic in addressing a wide variety of domestic concerns. We should encourage our alcoholic newcomer and their family to avail themselves of such aid whenever needed.

In cases where the alcoholic has not responded, have you worked with his family? Did you offer them your way of life and what results did you have in this situation?

Assuming we are spiritually fit, we can do all sorts of things alcoholics are not supposed to do. People have said we must not go where liquor is served; we must not have it in our homes; we must shun friends who drink; we must avoid moving pictures which show drinking scenes; we must not go into bars; our friends must hide their bottles if we go to their houses; we mustn't think or be reminded about alcohol at all. Our experience shows that this is not necessarily so.

What does spiritually fit actually mean, and how do we know if we are spiritually fit? Does it imply what gives us meaning and purpose in life are not material goods, but spiritual growth?

Are we spiritually fit if we spend our day striving to practice the moral values embedded in the A.A. Twelve Step principles or in the Bible's Ten Commandments if we are Christian?

If we practice daily inventory, prayer and meditation, are we spiritually fit?

If we perform daily service work with other alcoholics are we spiritually fit?

If we live by the Golden Rule with honesty, unselfish motives and actions, compassion, humility, empathy and kindness, are we spiritually fit?

If we are trustworthy, reliable, kind, responsible and caring, are we fit?

If we are comfortable in our own skin, and live in the here and now of each moment of each day as best we can, are we fit?

If we are able to sustain loving, high quality relationships with our family and the people about us, are we fit?

Should we be the judge of our own spiritual fitness, or should we rely on others to judge us? After all, the best way to determine how another alcoholic is doing is not to ask him, but to ask his family.

We meet these conditions every day. An alcoholic who cannot meet them still has an alcoholic mind; there is something the matter with his spiritual status. His only chance for sobriety would be someplace like the Greenland Ice Cap, and even there an Eskimo might turn up with a bottle of scotch and ruin everything! Ask any woman who has sent her husband to distant places on the theory he would escape the alcohol problem.

In our belief **any scheme of combating alcoholism which proposes to shield the sick man from temptation is doomed to failure**. If the alcoholic tries to shield himself he may succeed for a time, but usually winds up with a bigger explosion than ever. We have tried these methods. These attempts to do the impossible have always failed.

So our rule is not to avoid a place where there is drinking, if we have a legitimate reason for being there. That includes bars, nightclubs, dances, receptions, weddings, even plain ordinary whoopee parties. To a person who has had experience with an alcoholic, this may seem like tempting Providence, but it isn't. You will note that we made and important qualification.

Therefore, **ask yourself** on each occasion, "**Have I any good social, business, or personal reason for going to this place?** Or am I expecting to steal a little vicarious pleasure from the atmosphere of such places?" If you answer these questions satisfactorily, you need have no apprehension. Go or stay away, whichever seems best. **But be sure you are on solid spiritual ground before you start and that your *motive* in going is thoroughly good. Do not think of what you will get out of the occasion.**

Think of what you can bring to it. But if you are shaky, you had better work with another alcoholic instead!

> After we've completed our 12 Step work and have some time under our belt in sobriety, we will slowly begin to return to society at large. Our need for isolation has diminished, our obsession to drink has hopefully disappeared, and at some point we will be invited to places where alcohol is available.
>
> Whether it be for lunch at a restaurant-bar with co-workers, a niece's wedding reception with lots of champagne, a surprise birthday party for a friend, or an executive business dinner where we hope to impress our boss, we will come face-to-face with a decision: Do we go or not?
>
> Carefully deliberating our decision is prudent. Taking some quiet time to reflect honestly on our *motives* in attending is paramount. Do we really need to be there, regardless of whether we want to or not? Do we hope to reminisce about our old drinking days by watching others drink with impunity? Do we wish to play the martyr and invoke self-pity from others because we can no longer drink?
>
> How long must I stay at the event, and can I get away early if I need to? Do I feel spiritually fit and confident I can deal with any temptation which may arise?
>
> Many alcoholics consult with their sponsor before attending an event, and some set up check-in times to call their sponsor while they are at the event.

Being able to take along a solid, sober alcoholic friend to the event is ideal, if that is possible.

We must remember that no one can force us to attend any occasion if we feel uncomfortable, uneasy or unfit. Declining invitations is difficult, especially if it involves business obligations, but it is better than the alternative—drinking and relapsing.

We do not need to justify to anyone why we decline an invitation. Saying, "Thank you for the invitation, but I'm unable to attend" is sufficient. Should the situation involve a mandatory work outing with our boss, a private and confidential discussion may be appropriate, and if necessary you can lie and say that you already have plans.

But the best solution when invited to mandatory events is to be honest and not avoid them. It is our responsibility, no one else's, to fit into society, and when I had to attend drinking functions I tripled my effort, working hard with my sponsor beforehand, to get myself into a fit spiritual condition, knowing I could always easily leave the event if I panicked or became unable to cope.

The more I thought about what I could bring to the party, rather than wallowing in fear of how tempted I might be, the easier it was to get through the occasion. As a matter of fact, I usually had the best time of my life at such festivities because I was sober and could have some fun for a change.

As a footnote, I have attended dozens of parties where alcohol was served, and I *never* had anyone ask me why I wasn't drinking, or why I didn't want a drink.

Remember that we have an illness, and like any other illness, we need to apply the proper remedy despite our fear of how others may judge us, or what the consequences may be.

Why set with a long face in places where there is drinking, sighing about the good old days. **If it is a happy occasion, try to increase**

259

the pleasure of those there; if a business occasion, go and attend to your business enthusiastically. If you are with a person who wants to eat in a bar, by all means go along. Let your friends know they are not to change their habits on your account. At a proper time and place explain to all your friends why alcohol disagrees with you. If you do this thoroughly, few people will ask you to drink. While you were drinking, you were withdrawing from life little by little. Now you are getting back into the social life of this world. **Don't start to withdraw again just because your friends drink liquor**.

Once we have made the decision to attend an event, we may be petrified, especially if we know we are going to be around people we don't know or have never met before. This is a normal reaction, whether an alcoholic or not. We all want to put on a good face and be accepted in whatever social situation we find ourselves.

If we try to replace our anxiety with an unselfish and grateful attitude, we will find our fears lessened.

We will be less self-conscious if we are grateful to have been invited and think more of what we can contribute to the event rather than what we can get out of it.

There is no need to explain to any attendee that we are alcoholic and are having a hard time. We make no excuses for our internal struggles, nor do we need to broadcast them in public. Not only is it no one's business, but they really don't care.

Since becoming sober I've attended multiple parties with people who didn't know me. An alcoholic beverage has always been offered, and I always respond, "No thanks, I'll grab a coke." *Never* has anyone pushed or interrogated me on why I don't want alcohol. If I was pushed, I'd simply say, "I don't drink." Remember that 30% of Americans have not drunk any alcohol in the past year, and 14% have never had a drink of alcohol in their life, so refusing a drink is not unusual.

Of course our close personal friends and family, who often knew all about our alcoholism long before we did, will find out about our abstinence and A.A. membership fairly quickly. This will make it easier to be around them where alcohol is served, and it is unlikely they will comment on our choice of beverage.

What about spur of the moment invitations to places where alcohol is served?

The same advice applies. If we know with complete certainty we are fit for travel, then why not go along? However, if there is even the slightest doubt in our mind, it is safest to politely decline the invitation by saying something like: "I'd love to join you, but I can't. Thanks for asking me." There is no need to explain or defend our decision.

Your job now is to be at the place where you may be of maximum helpfulness to others, so **never hesitate to go anywhere if you can be helpful**. You should not hesitate to visit the **most sordid spot on earth** on such an errand. Keep on the firing line of life with these motives and **God will keep you unharmed**.

When we discover another alcoholic in need, or are asked to help another alcoholic, we automatically want to respond "Yes, whatever you need," without knowing any details. This is a mistake. One might respond when asked for help, "I'd like to do whatever I can, but tell me more first."

We can then take our time to make a reasoned decision, and remember that we never have to give an immediate answer to any request. Use of common sense, consultation with others, including our sponsor, and timely reflection is a prudent approach.

If we are asked to go somewhere on a twelfth-step call, there is safety and experience in numbers. Rarely would we make such a call alone, because we don't know what we will be getting into when confronting an unknown, active alcoholic.

Both our physical and emotional safety can be threatened, and no encounter is worth that risk.

We may justifiably fear going into the unknown, even with other alcoholics, especially if we are a group of females. Inviting some trusted male alcoholics along is one option, or meeting at a daytime public location may be another option. If in doubt, don't go.

On the other hand, our fear may arise from our own perceived inadequacies. Maybe we won't do a good job. Perhaps we will be frightened travelling to more run-down areas of the city, fearing we may get lost going to places we've never been to before. Should we have a meeting in a potentially dangerous location in the evening? Should we go into housing projects where drug dealers live and ply their trade? Should we visit certain depressed ethnic or racial areas of our city?

I once went on an urgent twelfth step call alone and at dusk in a ghetto filled with roaming drug dealers trying to sell me their wares in front of the apartment of the man who requested help. That was stupid of me in many ways, especially going alone.

I should have known better, but felt young and invincible as a newly sober alcoholic. God would have not protected me from robbery, assault or injury had it occurred. I was just lucky, and never repeated my mistake.

Consultation with our sponsor and others can help us reach commonsense decisions about twelfth-step calls. Taking our sponsor along with us, especially if we are a newcomer, may be well advised

Many of us keep **liquor in our homes**. We often need it to carry green recruits through a severe hangover. Some of us still serve it to our friends provided they are not alcoholic. But some of us think we should not serve liquor to anyone. We never argue this question. We feel that each family, in the light of their own circumstances, ought to decide for themselves.

262

When I was married my non-alcoholic wife kept liquor in our home. A few times, when alone, I was tempted to take a sip, but I knew I would have no defense after I took that first drink, so I never yielded to that temptation.

Today I live alone, and do not keep liquor at home. I have no fear of doing so, it's just that most of my friends don't drink. I ask the ones that do drink to bring their own booze, and to take any leftovers back home with them when they leave. I've never had a problem with this approach.

We are careful never to show intolerance or hatred of drinking as an institution. Experience shows that such an attitude is not helpful to anyone. Every new alcoholic looks for this spirit among us and is immensely relieved when he finds we are not witch-burners. A spirit of intolerance might repel alcoholics whose lives could have been saved, had it not been for such stupidity. We would not even do the cause of temperate drinking any good, for not one drinker in a thousand likes to be told anything about alcohol by one who hates it.

Some day we hope that Alcoholics Anonymous will help the public to a better realization of the gravity of the alcoholic problem, but **we shall be of little use if our attitude is one of bitterness or hostility**. Drinkers will not stand for it.

After all, our problems were of our own making. Bottles were only a symbol. Besides, **we have stopped fighting anybody or anything**. We have to!

No one likes an angry, fanatical, crusading alcoholic. That type of behavior is unwelcomed by all, and accomplishes nothing. Alcohol was never the cause of our miserable life; it was our inability to live life on life's terms sober because we were full of selfishness and self-centeredness, and could not get our own way all the time.

Since Bill W. drank through thirteen years of failed Prohibition between 1920 and 1933, it is not surprising he included his thoughts on the dangers of institutional hatred of alcohol in the Big Book.

What are the step-by-step requirements for a Twelfth Step? Have you ever tried this?

What are the principles we are to practice in all our affairs? Why does Bill say "all our affairs?" What does this mean to you?

How can you apply the Twelve Steps outside the meeting rooms? Do you do it?

What are some of your daily practices in life to maintain sobriety and to grow spiritually?

STEP 12

Working With Others

Pages 89 – 103

STEP 12 -- *Having had a spiritual awakening as the result of these steps, we tried to carry this message to alcoholics and to practice these principles in all our affairs.*

WRITE down your reactions to the readings as to how they apply to you and your illness, incorporating as much as possible of the considerations into your work.

TAKING NEW OUR DESIGN FOR LIVING INTO THE REAL WORLD

(SPOUSES, FAMILY, EMPLOYERS)

Once we have completed the 12 Steps, we are challenged to practice the principles of the steps in all our affairs. This is our acid test, and is demonstrated by and through our relationships with our spouses or partners, our employers and employees, our family, our friends, and the people about us.

TO WIVES

Bill W. wrote this chapter after he had asked Anne Smith, Dr. Bob's wife, to do it but she refused. Bill's wife Lois wanted to write the chapter but not surprisingly, Bill would not let her, perhaps afraid of what she might write based on her knowledge of Bill's multiple adulterous affairs.

It is also rumored that Bill originally wanted to include a Big Book chapter written for wives in the hopes of increasing overall book sales.

This chapter does adequately describe the impact the alcoholic's drinking has on others, and alcoholics in recovery need to be reminded they are not the only ones affected by their drinking. We are also reminded that it is useless to try to solve another person's drinking problems for them, since this will never work and may cause resentment from the alcoholic who sees other people interfering with their problem.

In today's world, the "To Wives" chapter is awful. It is paternalistic, outdated and offers dreadful advice on spousal relationships. In fairness to Bill who wrote during the 1930s, it is understandable that he identified the male as the alcoholic husband, and the female as the non-alcoholic wife, since only a few women were A.A. members at the time.

Unions of same-sex marriage and homosexuality were criminally illegal, and the LGBTQ community didn't openly exist, so those aspects were not discussed. Nor was there any mention of the domestic violence risks to women.

Fetal alcohol syndrome was omitted because it was not discovered until 1973. It can cause brain damage to children born to mothers who drink alcohol during their pregnancy, and occurs in one in every thousand live births in the United States.

"To Wives" disappoints by shifting focus from the alcoholic and his problem with alcohol to the spouse and her problem with the alcoholic. The chapter appears to hold the sober wife responsible for her alcoholic husband's emotional sobriety after he has stopped drinking. The wife's role becomes one of submission and compliance with a set of ridiculous directives in order for her husband to recover.

The bottom line in this chapter is: If your husband drinks, it's mainly your fault because you have not behaved in a spiritual manner as instructed. This ludicrous proposition does a severe disservice not only to wives, women, and all spouses, but is not consistent with the A.A. program's emphasis on taking personal responsibility for treating our illness.

The chapter should be read, but most of the assumptions, conclusions and advice should be discounted, and be aware of the chapter's bias and limitations.

THE FAMILY AFTERWARD

This well written chapter is an effort to educate families of the alcoholic of the possible challenges and experiences they will encounter when their loved one transitions into sobriety.

Examples are given on what to expect when dealing with a newly sober family member, including what troubles may arise in the family and how one might deal with them.

Family members of addicts and alcoholics suffer terribly until the afflicted individual finally agrees to seek help. Parents, children, spouses, siblings and others all suffer their own pain as they watch a loved one struggle. Once the alcoholic is sober, the family dynamic will not immediately return to normal. Healing the open wounds left by alcoholism takes time and understanding on all sides.

TO EMPLOYERS

Hank Parkhurst, A.A. #2 in New York, wrote this chapter. He was both an employer and an employee. He had been a Standard Oil of New Jersey executive who lost his job because of his drinking. Afterwards, he created a small company called Honor Dealers, possibly as a way of getting back at Standard Oil. His company provided gas stations with the opportunity to buy gasoline, oil, and automobile parts on a cooperative basis.

This helpful chapter starts by recounting three tragic stories of former employees whose lives were lost due to alcoholism. Hank argues that their deaths might have been avoided if employers knew more about alcoholism the disease, and were willing to support alcoholic employees in a manner consistent with the Big Book recommendations.

Chapter 8

TO WIVES

* Written in 1939, when there were few women in A.A., this chapter assumes that the alcoholic in the home is likely to be the husband. But many of the suggestions given here may be adapted to help the person who lives with a woman alcoholic—whether she is still drinking or is recovering in A.A. A further source of help is noted on page 121. [Al-Anon Family Groups]

With few exceptions, our book thus far has spoken of men. But what we have said applies quite as much to women. Our activities on behalf of women who drink are on the increase. There is every evidence that women regain their health as readily as men if they try our suggestions.

The first woman to seek help from Alcoholics Anonymous was Lillian Kuestrardt from Akron, Ohio, nicknamed "*Lil,*" who got sober in 1935 but quickly relapsed. Lil eventually got sober outside of A.A.

In March, 1937, a little less than two years after A.A. was founded, *Florence Rankin* got sober and became the first woman to attain *some* length of sobriety in A.A. Due to Florence having been sober more than a year, "One Hundred Men" was discarded as the preferred name for the Big Book. She married an alcoholic, relapsed and committed suicide in 1943 at age 48. She was the author of the chapter "A Feminine Victory," in the first edition of the Big Book.

Sylvia Kauffmann was the first woman to achieve *long term* sobriety in A.A. She got sober in Chicago with the help of Earl Treat in September, 1939, and she remained sober for thirty-five years until her death in 1974. Her story was recounted in the Big Book as "The Keys of the Kingdom."

In April, 1939 her psychiatrist, Dr. Harry Tiebout, gave *Marty Mann* an early manuscript of the Big Book, and persuaded her to attend her first A.A. meeting at the home of Bill W. in New York. Despite several relapses during her first year and a half, Marty succeeded in becoming sober by 1940 and, apart from a brief relapse nearly twenty years later, remained sober until her death in 1980 at age 75. Her Big Book story was "Women Suffer Too."

Marty was instrumental in the founding of High Watch Farm in Kent, Connecticut in 1939, the world's first recovery center founded on the principles of Alcoholics Anonymous. She also helped start the Yale School of Alcohol Studies (now at Rutgers), and organized the National Committee for Education on Alcoholism (NCEA), now called the National Council on Alcoholism and Drug Dependence or NCADD.

Marty believed alcoholism ran in families and education about the medical nature of the disease was essential. Three ideas formed the basis of her message: 1) Alcoholism is a disease and the alcoholic a sick person, 2) The alcoholic can be helped and is worth helping, and 3) Alcoholism is a public health problem and therefore a public responsibility.

Today, there are more women in A.A. than in the early years, but men continue to make up the majority of members. In the 2014 A.A. Membership Survey, 62% of members were men and 38% were women. The average age of all members was 50, with only 12% aged under 30.

Early Women in AA:

https://aaagnostica.org/2013/04/14/marty-mann-and-the-early-women-of-aa/

But for every man who drinks others are involved—the wife who trembles in fear of the next debauch; the mother and father who see their son wasting away.

It took time and a return of sanity to for me to realize that my drinking affected others. I thought I was only harming myself when I drank, and had little appreciation how my behavior affected my wife, friends and family.

After I had been sober for several years, my Texas mother's best friend, a long time Al-Anon member, kindly explained to me that not only had my alcoholic behavior hurt my loving mother, but it had hurt my mother's best friends who cared about her. They hated seeing her in the pain which I caused, and felt her pain through my addiction.

Among us are wives, relatives and friends whose problem has been solved, as well as some who have not yet found a happy solution. **We want the wives of Alcoholics Anonymous to address the wives of men who drink too much. What they say will apply to nearly everyone bound by ties of blood or affection to an alcoholic**.

The result of this wish was the formation of the Al-Anon Family Groups in 1951 by Lois Wilson and Anne B. The two women had met in 1941 while accompanying their husbands to A.A. meetings. Al-Anon is a worldwide fellowship that offers a program of recovery for the families and friends of alcoholics, whether or not the alcoholic recognizes the existence of a drinking problem or seeks help.

Alateen, founded in 1957, is part of the Al-Anon fellowship designed to support the younger family and friends of alcoholics through their teenage years.

As wives of Alcoholics Anonymous, we would like you to feel that we understand as perhaps few can. We want to analyze mistakes we have made. We want to leave you with the feeling that **no situation is too difficult and no unhappiness too great to be overcome**.

We have traveled rocky roads, there is no mistake about that. We have had long rendezvous with **hurt pride, frustration, self-pity, misunderstanding and fear**.

These are not pleasant companions. We have **been driven to maudlin sympathy, to bitter resentment**. Some of us veered from extreme to extreme, ever hoping that one day our loved ones would be themselves once more.

Our loyalty and the desire that our husbands hold up their heads and be like other men have begotten all sorts of predicaments. We have been unselfish and self-sacrificing. We have told innumerable lies to protect our pride and our husbands' reputations. We have prayed, we have begged, we have been patient. We have struck out viciously. We have run away. We have been hysterical. We have been terror stricken. We have sought sympathy. We have had retaliatory love affairs with other men.

Our **homes have been battle grounds** many an evening. In the morning we have kissed and made up. Our friends have counseled chucking the men and we have done so with finality, only to be back in a little while hoping, always hoping. Our men have sworn great solemn oaths that they were through drinking forever. We have believed them when no one else could or would. Then, in days, weeks, or months, a fresh outburst.

We seldom had friends at our homes, never knowing how or when the men of the house would appear. We **could make few social engagements**. We **came to live almost alone**. When we were invited out, our husbands sneaked so many drinks that they spoiled the occasion. If, on the other hand, they took nothing, their self-pity made them killjoys.

There **was never financial security**. Positions were always in jeopardy or gone. An armored car could not have brought the pay envelopes home. The checking account melted like snow in June.

Sometimes **there were other women**. How heart-breaking was this discovery; how cruel to be told they understood our men as we did not!

The bill collectors, the sheriffs, the angry taxi drivers, the policemen, the bums, the pals, and even the ladies they sometimes brought home—our husbands thought we were so inhospitable. "Joykiller, nag, wet blanket"—that's what they said. Next day they would be themselves again and we would forgive and try to forget.

We have tried to hold the love of our children for their father. **We have told small tots that father was sick, which was much nearer the truth than we realized**. They struck the children, kicked out door panels, smashed treasured crockery, and ripped the keys out of pianos. In the midst of such pandemonium they may have rushed out threatening to live with the other woman forever. In desperation, we have even got tight ourselves—the drunk to end all drunks. The unexpected result was that our husbands seemed to like it.

Perhaps at this point **we got a divorce and took the children** home to father and mother. Then we were severely criticized by our husband's parents for desertion. Usually we did not leave. We stayed on and on. We finally **sought employment ourselves** as destitution faced us and our families.

We began to ask medical advice as the sprees got closer together. The alarming **physical and mental symptoms**, the deepening pall of **remorse, depression and inferiority** that settled down on our loved ones—these things terrified and distracted us. As animals on a treadmill, we have patiently and wearily climbed, falling back in exhaustion after each futile effort to reach solid ground. Most of us have entered the final stage with its commitment to health resorts, sanitariums, hospitals, and jails. Sometimes there were screaming delirium and insanity. Death was often near.

> I had three wives that suffered through my alcoholic behavior, which persisted whether I was drunk or not. My selfishness and self-centeredness permeated all aspects of those marriages. Seldom was I aware how much my selfish alcoholic behavior affected their lives, and even when I was, I didn't care. It was their job to put up with me, and if they had a problem with that they should blame themselves since they knew what I was like before they married me.
>
> I was never emotionally available for my first wife because I

273

loved my bottle more than I loved her. Alcohol and work always came first, and after a decade of neglect she finally had enough and we divorced.

Determined to rebuild my life and "cut back" on my drinking, I married my second wife. She died of cancer seven months after our wedding, and I lost all interest in sobriety or changing my life. I deserved to drink, and I did.

My third wife was my hard-drinking bar buddy, and we enjoyed each other's shortcomings for many years until I sobered up and joined A.A. I became a different person, no longer the man she had married, and we divorced two years later.

All of my wives suffered with my illness, although financial insecurity and adultery played no role. Proper amends were made, but I know the pain of our past persists in their lives.

Under these conditions we naturally make mistakes.

Some of them rose out of ignorance of alcoholism. Sometimes **we sensed dimly that we were dealing with sick men**. Had we fully understood the nature of the alcoholic illness, we might have behaved differently.

How could men who loved their wives and children be so unthinking, so callous, so cruel? There could be no love in such persons, we thought. And just as we were being convinced of their heartlessness, they would surprise us with fresh resolves and new attentions. For a while they would be their old sweet selves, only to dash the new structure of affection to pieces once more. **Asked why they commenced to drink again, they would reply with some silly excuse, or none. It was so baffling, so heartbreaking**. Could we have been so mistaken in the men we married? **When drinking, they were strangers**. Sometimes they were so inaccessible that it seemed as though a great wall had been built around them.

And even if they did not love their families, how could they be so blind about themselves? What had become of their judgment, their common sense, their will power? **Why could they not see that drink meant ruin to them?** Why was it, when these dangers were pointed out that they agreed, and then got drunk again immediately?

These are some of the questions which race through the mind of every woman who has an alcoholic husband. We hope this book has answered some of them. Perhaps your husband has been living in that strange world of alcoholism where everything is distorted and exaggerated. You can see that he really does love with his better self. Of course, there is such a thing as incompatibility, but in nearly every instance the alcoholic only seems to be unloving and inconsiderate; it is usually because he is warped and sickened that he says and does these appalling things. Today most of our men are better husbands and fathers than ever before.

Try not to condemn your alcoholic husband no matter what he says or does. He is just another very sick, unreasonable person. Treat him, when you can, as though he had pneumonia. When he angers you, **remember that he is very ill**.

As an only child of an alcoholic father, I witnessed how his alcoholism affected his wife, who was my mother. We were financially secure at the time, but my father was a serial adulterer and my mother knew it. He was an angry, violent drunk, and my mother and I lived in terror of his rages. We knew he was ill, but that didn't make life any easier.

No neighbors were allowed in our house due to my father's unpredictable behavior. Many a night my mother and I fled our home, seeking safety and shelter with friends after my father broke into a drunken rampage.

My mother lived in isolation and fear for as long as I can remember. It was apparent to me she was constantly jumpy, restless and depressed. She cried all the time. We didn't go out, rarely socialized, and seemed trapped in a cycle of despair.

No one discussed my father's alcoholism, and in the 1950s A.A. and Al-Anon were never a part of the picture.

Women with domestic troubles sought support and refuge through their own family, close friends and the church.

Divorce after eleven years of marriage brought relief, but becoming a self-supporting, single-parent family in the early 1960s was not easy for either one of us.

There is an important exception to the foregoing. We realize some men are thoroughly bad intentioned, that no amount of patience will make any difference. **An alcoholic of this temperament may be quick to use this chapter as a club over your head. Don't let him get away with it**. If you are positive he is one of this type you may feel you had better leave him. **Is it right to let him ruin your life and the lives of your children?** Especially when he has before him a way to stop his drinking and abuse if he really wants to pay the price.

The problem with which you struggle usually falls within one of four categories:

One: Your husband may be only a heavy drinker.

His drinking may be constant or it may be heavy only on certain occasions. Perhaps he spends too much money for liquor. It may be slowing him up mentally and physically, but he does not see it. Sometimes he is a source of embarrassment to you and his friends. He is positive he can handle his liquor, that it does him no harm, that drinking is necessary in his business. He would probably be insulted if he were called an alcoholic. This world is full of people like him. Some will moderate or stop altogether, and some will not. Of those who keep on, a good number will become true alcoholics after a while.

In "There Is A Solution" the heavy drinker reminds us of the moderate drinker: "If there is a good reason, the moderate drinker can give up liquor entirely. They can take it or leave it alone." (There Is A Solution, p.20)

Two: Your husband is showing lack of control, for he is unable to stay on the water wagon even when he wants to. He often gets entirely out of hand when drinking. He admits this is true, but is positive that he will do better. He has begun to try, with or without your cooperation, various means of moderating or staying dry. Maybe he is beginning to lose his friends. His business may suffer somewhat. He is worried at times, and is becoming aware that he cannot drink like other people. He sometimes drinks in the morning and through the day also, to hold his nervousness in check. He is remorseful after serious drinking bouts and tells you he wants to stop. But when he gets over the spree, he begins to think once more how he can drink moderately next time. We think this person is in danger. These are the **earmarks of a real alcoholic**. Perhaps he can still tend to business fairly well. He has by no means ruined everything. As we say among ourselves, **"He wants to stop."**

> Although there are no solid statistics, it is estimated that five to ten percent of drinkers progress from moderate drinking through hard drinking and into alcoholism.
>
> The hard drinker is always teetering on the brink of disaster. Sometimes it seems they are real alcoholics; other days we're not so certain.
>
> "There Is A Solution" describes the hard drinker: "Then we have a certain type of hard drinker. He may have the habit badly enough to gradually impair him physically and mentally. It may cause him to die a few years before his time. If a sufficiently strong reason—ill health, falling in love, change of environment, or the warning of a doctor—becomes operative, this man can also stop or moderate, although he may find it difficult and troublesome and may even need medical attention." (There Is A Solution, p.20)

Three: This husband has gone much further than husband number two. Though once like number two he became worse. His friends have slipped away, his home is a near-wreck and he cannot hold a position. Maybe the doctor has been called in, and the weary round of sanitariums and hospitals has begun. **He admits he cannot drink like other people, but does not see why. He clings to the notion that he will yet find a way to do so.**

He may have come to the point where **he desperately wants to stop but cannot**. His case presents additional questions which we shall try to answer for you. You can be quite hopeful of a situation like this.

Four: You may have a husband of whom you completely despair. He has been placed in one **institution** after another. He is **violent**, or appears definitely **insane** when drunk. Sometimes he drinks on the way home from the hospital. Perhaps he has had **delirium tremens**. Doctors may shake their heads and advise you to have him committed. Maybe you have already been obliged to put him away. This picture may not be as dark as it looks. Many of our husbands were just as far gone. Yet they got well.

> Our last two types of husbands are real alcoholics as described earlier: He may start off as a moderate drinker; he may or may not become a continuous hard drinker; but at some stage of his drinking career he begins to lose all control of his liquor consumption, once he starts to drink. (There Is A Solution, p.21).

> These types are doomed just as we were doomed. There was no turning back. We have already lost our legs.

Let's now go back to **number one**. Oddly enough, he is often difficult to deal with. He enjoys drinking. It stirs his imagination. His friends feel closer over a highball. Perhaps you enjoy drinking with him yourself when he doesn't go too far. You have passed happy evenings together chatting and drinking before your fire. Perhaps you both like parties which would be dull without liquor. We have enjoyed such evenings ourselves; we had a good time. We know all about liquor as a social lubricant. Some, but not all of us, think it has its advantages when reasonably used.

The first principle of success is that **you should never be angry**. Even though your husband becomes unbearable and you have to leave him temporarily, you should, if you can, go without rancor. Patience and good temper are most necessary.

Our next thought is that you should **never tell him what he must do** about his drinking. If he gets the idea that you are a nag or a killjoy,

278

your chance of accomplishing anything useful may be zero. He will use that as an excuse to drink more. He will tell you he is misunderstood. This may lead to lonely evenings for you. He may seek someone else to console him—not always another man.

Be determined that your husband's drinking is not going to spoil your relations with your children or your friends. They need your companionship and your help. **It is possible to have a full and useful life, though your husband continues to drink**. We know women who are unafraid, even happy under these conditions. **Do not set your heart on reforming your husband**. You may be unable to do so, no matter how hard you try.

We know these suggestions are sometimes difficult to follow, but you will save many a heartbreak if you can succeed in observing them. Your husband may come to appreciate your reasonableness and patience. This may lay the groundwork for a friendly talk about his alcoholic problem. Try to have him bring up the subject himself. **Be sure you are not critical** during such a discussion. Attempt instead, to put yourself in his place. Let him see that **you want to be helpful rather than critical**.

When a discussion does arise, you might **suggest he read this book** or at least the chapter on alcoholism. Tell him you have been worried, though perhaps needlessly. You think he ought to know the subject better, as everyone should have a clear understanding of the risk he takes if he drinks too much. Show him you have confidence in his power to stop or moderate. Say you do not want to be a wet blanket; that **you only want him to take care of his health**. Thus you may succeed in interesting him in alcoholism.

He probably has several alcoholics among his own acquaintances. You might suggest that you both take an interest in them. Drinkers like to help other drinkers. Your husband may be willing to talk to one of them.

If this kind of approach does not catch your husband's interest, it may be best to drop the subject, but after a friendly talk your husband will usually revive the topic himself. This may take patient waiting, but it will be worth it. Meanwhile **you might try to help the wife of another serious drinker**. If you act upon these principles, your husband may stop or moderate.

> Expecting a long-abused wife or spouse not to become angry, unreasonable or critical, or not give the alcoholic their opinion about their drinking, is unrealistic. A spouse's job is not to make their spouse comfortable with their disease. This encourages the alcoholic to play the victim, which does nothing to address the real issue.
>
> The spouse should waste no time trying to reform an ill person. They can be supportive by expressing their love for their spouse, and their willingness to support their spouse once they agree to treat their illness.
>
> When I was in my cups, my loving Texas mother, a long-time Al-Anon member, would always say to me: "Son, I love you and know you want to get better. You know where you can get help, and I'll be there with you when you do."
>
> In Al-Anon they call this detaching with love, and emotionally detaching is necessary to maintain the sanity and good health of those that love another alcoholic.

Suppose, however, that your husband fits the description of **number two**. The same principles which apply to husband number one should be practiced. But after his next binge, **ask him if he would really like to get over drinking for good**. Do not ask that he do it for you or anyone else. **Just would he like to?**

The chances are he would. **Show him your copy of this book** and tell him what you have found out about alcoholism. Show him that as alcoholics, the writers of the book understand. Tell him some of the interesting stories you have read. If you think he will be shy of a spiritual remedy, **ask him to look at the chapter on alcoholism**. Then perhaps he will be interested enough to continue.

If he is enthusiastic your cooperation will mean a great deal. **If he is lukewarm or thinks he is not an alcoholic**, we suggest you **leave him alone. Avoid urging him to follow our program. The seed has been planted** in his mind. He knows that thousands of men, much like himself, have recovered. But don't remind him of this after he has been drinking, for he may be angry. Sooner or later, you are likely to find him reading the book once more. Wait until repeated stumbling convinces him he must act, for **the more you hurry him the longer his recovery may be delayed**.

> No one can criticize a spouse or friend who shares the book *Alcoholics Anonymous* with another alcoholic. Although hard to believe, some alcoholics have entered A.A. on their own after reading the Big Book; they needed no other inducement.

If you have a **number three** husband, you may be in luck. **Being certain he wants to stop**, you can go to him with this volume as joyfully as though you had struck oil. He may not share your enthusiasm, but **he is practically sure to read the book** and he may go for the program at once. If he does not, you will probably not have long to wait. Again, **you should not crowd him**. Let him decide for himself. Cheerfully see him through more sprees. Talk about his condition or this book only when he raises the issue. In some cases it may be better to let someone outside the family present the book. They can urge action without arousing hostility. If your husband is otherwise a normal individual, your chances are good at this stage.

> We must remember when the Big Book was published in 1939, there were very few A.A. meetings nationally, and most of the information about A.A. was contained in the Big Book. Encouraging potential members to read the book made sense, and it remains an approach worth pursuing today.

You would suppose that men in the **fourth classification** would be quite hopeless, but that is not so. Many of Alcoholics Anonymous were like that. Everybody had given them up. Defeat seemed certain. Yet often such men had spectacular and powerful recoveries.

There are exceptions. **Some men have been so impaired by alcohol that they cannot stop**. Sometimes there are cases where alcoholism is complicated by other disorders. A good doctor or psychiatrist can tell you whether these complications are serious. In any event, try to have your husband read this book. His reaction may be one of enthusiasm. **If he is already committed to an institution**, but can convince you and your doctor that he means business, **give him a chance to try our method**, unless the doctor thinks his mental condition too abnormal or dangerous. We make this recommendation with some confidence. For years we have been working with alcoholics committed to institutions. Since this book was first published, A.A. has released thousands of alcoholics from asylums and hospitals of every kind. The majority have never returned. The power of God goes deep!

You may have the **reverse situation** on your hands. Perhaps you have a **husband who is at large**, but who should be committed. **Some men cannot or will not get over alcoholism**. **When they become too dangerous**, we think the kind thing to do is to **lock them up**, but of course a good doctor should always be consulted. The wives and children of such men suffer horribly, but not more than the men themselves.

> The first paragraph of "How It Works" says: "Those who do not recover are people who cannot or will not completely give themselves to this simple program, usually men and women who are constitutionally incapable of being honest with themselves... There are those, too, who suffer from grave emotional and mental disorders, but many of them do recover if they have the capacity to be honest."

> Those who cannot be honest with themselves and may have been institutionalized periodically include sociopaths and psychopaths. Research suggests that five percent of the general population fall into this category. Not all alcoholics carry these diagnoses, but if one is a sociopath or psychopath, there is a high probability they are also an addict or alcoholic, and their likelihood of permanent recovery is slight.

But sometimes you must start life anew. We know women who have done it. **If such women adopt a spiritual way of life their road will be smoother**.

If your husband is a drinker, **you probably worry over what other people are thinking** and you hate to meet your friends. You draw more and more into yourself and you think everyone is talking about conditions at your home. You avoid the subject of drinking, even with your own parents. You do not know what to tell your children. When your husband is bad, **you become a trembling recluse**, wishing the telephone had never been invented.

We find that **most of this embarrassment is unnecessary**. While you need not discuss your husband at length, you can quietly let your friends know the nature of his illness. But you must be on guard not to embarrass or harm your husband.

When you have carefully explained to such people that he is a sick person, you will have created a new atmosphere. Barriers which have sprung up between you and your friends will disappear with the growth of sympathetic understanding. You will no longer be self-conscious or feel that you must apologize as though your husband were a weak character. He may be anything but that. Your new courage, good nature and lack of self-consciousness will do wonders for you socially.

In this more enlightened age, there is little social shame admitting we have an alcoholic in the family. Our national crisis of drug addiction and alcoholism has been well publicized, and most people know someone, or knows someone who knows someone, with an addiction problem.

Today, there is an abundance of help and support available for the families and friends of people with alcoholism and addiction:

For family members of alcoholics: https://al-anon.org

For adult children of alcoholics: https://adultchildren.org

For family members of drug addicts: https://www.nar-anon.org

For family members of gamblers: https://gam-anon.org

For family members of sex addicts: https://www.sanon.org

The same principle applies in **dealing with the children**. Unless they actually need protection from their father, it is **best not to take sides in any argument he has with them while drinking**. Use your energies to promote a better understanding all around. Then that terrible tension which grips the home of every problem drinker will be lessened.

Frequently, you have felt obliged to tell your husband's employer and his friends that he was sick, when as a matter of fact he was tight. Avoid answering these inquiries as much as you can. Whenever possible, let your husband explain. **Your desire to protect him should not cause you to lie to people when they have a right to know where he is and what he is doing.**

Discuss this with him when he is sober and in good spirits. Ask him what you should do if he places you in such a position again. But be careful not to be resentful about the last time he did so.

There is **another paralyzing fear**. You may be **afraid your husband will lose his position**; you are thinking of the **disgrace and hard times** which will befall you and the children. This experience may come to you. Or you may already have had it several times. Should it happen again, regard it in a different light. Maybe it will prove a blessing! It may convince your husband he wants to stop drinking forever. And now you know that he can stop if he will! Time after time, this apparent calamity has been a boon to us, for it opened up a path which led to the discovery of God.

Even though we may be ashamed and embarrassed about our spouse's drinking, there is no reason to lie for them. They must suffer their own consequences, even when our heart yearns to rescue them and protect their reputation, and ours.

284

My alcoholic father remarried after my mother divorced him when I was eleven years old. My step-mother, or my Texas Mom as I like to call her, is a decades long-time member of Al-Anon.

A few years ago she told me a story about my father. One summer day he had left the house drunk early in the morning, and she didn't know where he had gone. Late in the afternoon she heard a knock on the door, and a neighbor pointed to my father who had passed out in the front yard by the street.

My mother thanked the neighbor and left him there, despite the neighbor's request for her to take him indoors. After my mother refused, the neighbor called the police, who arrived and offered to help carry him into the house. My mother declined their offer, and left him outside all night, as painful as it was for her.

This is how we detach with love from our alcoholic. We love them, but we don't rescue them. We let them suffer their own consequences of drinking, even when it may put them at risk of harm or injury. We do them no favor enabling their drinking.

We have elsewhere **remarked how much better life is when lived on a spiritual plane**. If God can solve the age-old riddle of alcoholism, He can solve your problems too. **We wives** found that, like everybody else, we **were afflicted with pride, self-pity, vanity and all the things which go to make up the self-centered person; and we were not above selfishness or dishonesty**. As our husbands began to apply spiritual principles in their lives, we began to see the desirability of doing so too.

At first, some of us did not believe we needed this help. We thought, on the whole, we were pretty good women, capable of being nicer if our husbands stopped drinking. But it was a silly idea that we were too good to need God. **Now we try to put spiritual principles to work in every department of our lives**. When we do that, we find it solves our problems too; the ensuing lack of fear, worry and hurt feelings is a wonderful thing. We urge you to try our program, for nothing will be so helpful to your husband as the radically changed attitude toward him which God will show you how to have. Go along with your husband if you possibly can.

If you and your husband find a solution for the pressing problem of drink you are, of course, going to very happy. But all problems will not be solved at once. Seed has started to sprout in a new soil, but growth has only begun. In spite of your new-found happiness, there will be ups and downs. Many of the old problems will still be with you. This is as it should be.

The faith and sincerity of both you and your husband will be put to the test. These workouts should be regarded as part of your education, for thus you will be learning to live. You will make mistakes, but if you are in earnest they will not drag you down. Instead, you will capitalize them. A better way of life will emerge when they are overcome.

> It is not our job as an alcoholic to take our non-alcoholic spouse's inventory and make recovery recommendations before we have our own lives in order. Pushing other people to live a spiritual life when we are unable to do so ourself is hypocrisy. Even after we attain sobriety, we are not tasked with running other people's lives; we don't run the show anymore.
>
> In reality, most of us constantly take everyone else's inventory in our head. We just can't help it. But we keep it in our head only for a moment; any longer and we'll probably become angry, develop a resentment and end up drinking.
>
> Nothing would make me happier if everyone lived a truly spiritual life, freed from the bondage of self and excess material desires. If we all followed the 12 Step principles, all of our lives would improve, and the world would become a better place.
>
> Unfortunately, I do not have that much power. It is neither my right, privilege or purpose in life to assume the mantle of Director of the Universe, inside the home or outside of it.

Some of the snags you will encounter are irritation, hurt feelings and resentments. Your husband will sometimes be unreasonable and you will want to criticize. Starting from a speck on the domestic horizon, great thunderclouds of dispute may gather. These family dissensions are very dangerous, especially to your husband. Often you must carry the burden of avoiding them or keeping them under control. Never forget that resentment is a deadly hazard to an alcoholic. We do not mean that you have to agree with you husband whenever there is an honest difference of opinion. Just be careful not to disagree in a resentful or critical spirit.

You and your husband will find that you can dispose of serious problems easier than you can the trivial ones. Next time you and he have a heated discussion, no matter what the subject, it should be the privilege of either to smile and say, "This is getting serious. I'm sorry I got disturbed. Let's talk about it later." If your husband is trying to live on a spiritual basis, he will also be doing everything in his power to avoid disagreement or contention.

Your husband knows he owes you more than sobriety. He wants to make good. Yet you must not expect too much. His ways of thinking and doing are the habits of years. Patience, tolerance, understanding and love are the watchwords. Show him these things in yourself and they will be reflected back to you from him. **Live and let live** is the rule. If you both show a willingness to remedy your own defects, there will be little need to criticize each other.

We women carry with us a picture of the ideal man, the sort of chap we would like our husbands to be. It is the most natural thing in the world, once his liquor problem is solved, to feel that he will now measure up to that cherished vision. The chances are he will not for, like yourself, he is just beginning his development. Be patient.

Another feeling we are very likely to entertain is one of resentment that love and loyalty could not cure our husbands of alcoholism. We do not like the thought that the contents of a book or the work of another alcoholic has accomplished in a few weeks that for which we struggled for years. At such moments we forget that **alcoholism is an illness over which we could not possibly have had any power**. Your husband will be the first to say it was your devotion and care which brought him to the point where he could have a spiritual experience. Without you he would have gone to pieces long ago. When resentful thoughts come, try to pause and count your blessings. After all, your family is reunited, alcohol is no longer a problem and you and your husband are working together toward an undreamed of future.

Still another difficulty is that **you may become jealous of the attention he bestows on other people, especially alcoholics**. You have been starving for his companionship, yet he spends long hours helping other men and their families. You feel he should now be yours. The fact is that **he should work with other people to maintain his own sobriety**. Sometimes he will be so interested that he becomes really neglectful. Your house is filled with strangers. You may not like some of them. He gets stirred up about their troubles, but not at all about yours. It will do little good if you point that out and urge more attention for yourself. We find it a real mistake to dampen his enthusiasm for alcoholic work. You should join in his efforts as much as you possibly can. We suggest that you direct some of your thought to the wives of his new alcoholic friends. They need the counsel and love of a woman who has gone through what you have.

It is probably true that you and your husband have been living too much alone, for **drinking many times isolates the wife of an alcoholic**. Therefore, you probably need fresh interests and a great cause to live for as much as your husband. If you cooperate, rather than complain, you will find that his excess enthusiasm will tone down. Both of you will awaken to a new sense of responsibility for others. You, as well as your husband, ought to **think of what you can put into life instead of how much you can take out**. Inevitably your lives will be fuller for doing so. You will lose the old life to find one much better.

Perhaps your husband will make a fair start on the new basis, but just as things are going beautifully he dismays you by coming home drunk. If you are satisfied he really wants to get over drinking, you need not be alarmed. Though it is infinitely better that he have no relapse at all, as has been true with many of our men, it is by no means a bad thing in some cases.

288

Your husband will see at once that he must redouble his spiritual activities if he expects to survive. You need not remind him of his spiritual deficiency—he will know of it. Cheer him up and ask him how you can be still more helpful.

The slightest sign of fear or intolerance may lessen your husband's chance of recovery. In a weak moment he may take your dislike of his high-stepping friends as one of those insanely trivial excuses to drink.

> Two accurate statements in the above paragraphs are that your spouse owes you more than sobriety and that drinking isolates the spouse of an alcoholic.

> Hopefully, as the alcoholic remains sober, learns how to practice some of the 12 Step principles of love, tolerance, kindness, patience, empathy and unselfishness, the spousal relationship will slowly improve. It may take years, but over time the suffering spouse may begin to trust their alcoholic partner and emerge from their protective bunker. If the alcoholic keeps the recovery focus on himself and not on his spouse or others, all his relationships usually improve.

We never, **never try to arrange a man's life so as to shield him from temptation**. The slightest disposition on your part to guide his appointment or his affairs so he will not be tempted will be noticed. Make him feel absolutely free to come and go as he likes. This is important. **If he gets drunk, don't blame yourself**. God has either removed your husband's liquor problem or He has not. If not, it had better be found out right away. Then you and your husband can get right down to fundamentals. **If a repetition is to be prevented, place the problem, along with everything else, in God's hands**.

> God may inspire spiritual growth, but God will not prevent an alcoholic from drinking or repair broken relationships. That job is solely in the alcoholic's hands.

> Despite the irrelevance of most of this chapter in the real world, the values we adopt as a result of our spiritual awakening during our 12 Step work allows us to practice the A.A. principles.

In doing so, we find that our life, and the lives of those around us, usually change for the better.

We realize that we have been giving you much direct advice. We may have seemed to lecture.

If that is so we are sorry, for we ourselves don't always care for people who lecture us. But what we have related is based upon experience, some of it painful. We had to learn these things the hard way. That is why we are anxious that you understand, and that you avoid these unnecessary difficulties.*

So to you out there—who may soon be with us—we say "Good luck and God bless you."

The fellowship of Al-Anon Family Groups was formed about thirteen years after this chapter was written. Though it is entirely separate from Alcoholics Anonymous, it uses the general principles of the A.A. program as a guide for husbands, wives, relatives, friends, and others close to alcoholics. The foregoing pages (though addressed only to wives) indicate the problems such people may face. Alateen, for teen-aged children of alcoholics, is a part of Al-Anon.

A final word on the chapter "To Wives."

Even if partners or spouses are able to reunite in sobriety, both parties should be sensitive to the early warning signs of a relationship in trouble.

The big four are: 1) attacking the person, not the behavior, 2) feeling or expressing contempt toward your spouse or partner, 3) always being on the defensive even if you don't realize it, and 4) stonewalling, shutting down or walking out.

Other signs of trouble in relationships:

Time Together

Your partner's familiar ways of acting now irritate you, or worse. Everything your partner does annoys you. Both of you are quick to find a fault and to pounce on it. You can do nothing right. You're passive aggressive toward one another. You find excuses to do things without your partner. You feel exhausted after spending time with each other, so you spend less time with each other. You are happier when your spouse is away from home for an afternoon, at a meeting, or away on a business trip. You feel indifferent to your spouse. Your spouse tries to isolate you from your family and friends. You feel lonely.

Communications

You can no longer communicate. Discussions have become impossible. You fight about the same thing over and over and over, especially about money. You don't fight fair, or you don't fight at all. You walk on eggshells and avoid physical and eye contact with your partner. Subtle and not-so-subtle verbal abuse has become habitual. Your partner isn't the person you turn to when you're stressed. You have nothing nice to say to one another. You stop talking altogether.

Trust

Trust has been broken and you're always suspicious. There's no honesty. You're keeping secrets. You don't talk with one another about your problems or feelings. You don't respect each other.

Intimacy

Sex and intimacy are non-existent. One or both of you have started to detach emotionally. You realize that there is emotional and / or physical abuse in your marriage or relationship. One or both of you have considered cheating or has cheated, in real life or online, either physically or emotionally.

Chapter 9

THE FAMILY AFTERWARD

Our women folk have suggested certain attitudes a wife may take with the husband who is recovering. Perhaps they created the impression that he is to be wrapped in cotton wool and placed on a pedestal. Successful readjustment means the opposite. **All members of the family should meet upon the common ground of tolerance, understanding and love**. **This involves a process of deflation**. The alcoholic, his wife, his children, his in-laws; each one is likely to have fixed ideas about the family's attitude towards himself or herself. Each is interested in having his or her wishes respected. We find **the more one member of the family demands that the others concede to him, the more resentful they become**. This makes for discord and unhappiness.

And why? Is it not because each wants to play the lead? Is not each trying to arrange the family show to his liking? Is he not unconsciously trying to see what he can take from the family life rather than give?

Cessation of drinking is but the first step away from a highly strained, abnormal condition. A doctor said to us, "**Years of living with an alcoholic is almost sure to make any wife or child neurotic. The entire family is, to some extent, ill.**" Let families realize, as they start their journey, that **all will not be fair weather**. Each in his turn may be footsore and may straggle.

There will be alluring shortcuts and bypaths down which they may wander and lose their way.

It's said that friends are God's way of apologizing for family, since we get to choose our friends, but not our family.

Even if we are estranged from certain family members, our alcoholism has sown a wide swath of destruction through all our family, and the ones closest to us have been the most severely affected. They may recover from the damage we inflicted upon them, or they may not.

Suppose we tell you some of the obstacles a family will meet; suppose we suggest how they may be avoided—even converted to good use for others. **The family of an alcoholic longs for the return of happiness and security**. They remember when father was romantic, thoughtful and successful. Today's life is measured against that of other years and, when it falls short, the family may be unhappy.

Family confidence in dad is rising high. The good old days will soon be back, they think. Sometimes they demand that dad bring them back instantly! God, they believe, almost owes this recompense on a long overdue account. But the head of the house has spent years in pulling down the structures of business, romance, friendship, health—these things are now ruined or damaged. **It will take time to clear away the wreck**. Though the old buildings will eventually be replaced by finer ones, **the new structures will take years to complete**.

We seldom appreciate that it took years for the alcoholic to progress into their full-blown disease. No one becomes a real alcoholic overnight. We heal from our disease in three areas: physical, mental and spiritual, but it takes time, and all those areas overlap to some degree.

If we are fortunate, most of our body physically heals from the toxic damage of alcohol within a few months. We may have sustained brain, liver, pancreas, heart or other organ damage, but often recover sufficient function over time.

We must also heal emotionally and spiritually. Two common conditions many of us must face and overcome in early sobriety are the Pink Cloud and the Post-Acute Withdrawal Syndrome.

Pink Cloud

Early in sobriety alcoholics often experience a temporary and transient "Pink Cloud," which is a pessimistic term used to describe a deceptive high-on-life feeling resulting from the return to sobriety and ability to express our emotions.

Being on a pink cloud causes us to become detached from reality as we become preoccupied with our good feelings and forget about the difficult journey in front of us. It is a defense mechanism which may cause us to ignore our pending familial, financial and legal issues awaiting resolution, as we forget or ignore the devastating damage our addictive behavior has had on others.

Our excessively positive outlook leads to overconfidence, and we lose sight of the crucial day-to-day self-monitoring that's so important for successful recovery. We may begin to skip our A.A. meetings or counseling sessions because we feel like we don't need support and have sobriety under control. We begin to feel grandiose in our sobriety and imagine we can still socialize with our old drinking friends or go to the bar without having to worry about wanting a drink. This is a recipe for relapse.

The negative consequences that come from living in the pink cloud are the feeling that addiction is not a problem, and that we deserve to be happy.

To help us stay on track during the pink cloud phase:

1) Attend our A.A. meetings every day, even if we feel confident that we don't need them.

2) Ask for help with any problems or issues in our life, even if they aren't directly related to our alcoholism.

3) If we went through rehabilitation treatment, fully engage in our aftercare plan.

4) Know the three stages of relapse—emotional, mental and physical—and stay mindful of our thoughts, actions and behaviors so that we can see the signs of relapse and seek help immediately.

5) Make healthy lifestyle choices, including eating nutritious food, getting enough sleep and exercising every day. These

can help us maintain equilibrium once the pink cloud dissipates.

Post-Acute Withdrawal Syndrome

Our brain is clearly damaged from years of drinking. Even after we stop drinking, 75% of alcoholics and 90% of drug addicts will experience some level of long term withdrawal symptoms, called the Post-Acute Withdrawal Syndrome (PAWS), which can seriously threaten our sobriety.

PAWS symptoms are a result of a persistent chemical brain dysfunction caused by the brain readjusting to the withdrawal of alcohol and drugs.

Recovery from PAWS usually takes between six months and four years. Symptoms often increase during times of anxiety, making stress management more difficult.

PAWS symptoms can include:

1) *Thinking and Memory*: an inability to think clearly, combined with problems with abstract thinking, short-term memory, concentration and reasoning.

2) *Stress sensitivity*: manifested by difficulty thinking clearly and trouble managing daily stress.

3) *Emotional overreaction or numbness*: manifested by reacting disproportionately to daily events with unpredictable mood swings, and becoming emotionally numb if emotionally overloaded.

4) *Sleep disturbances*: including nightmares, difficulty falling asleep or staying asleep, and general changes in our sleep patterns.

5) *Physical problems*: although unusual, physical symptoms may include intermittent dizziness, gait and balance problems, sluggish reflexes and impaired eye-hand coordination.

Personally, I experienced PAWS related thinking and memory problems, stress sensitivity and sleep disturbances for four long, miserable years after I got sober. It was an extremely frustrating and unpleasant condition, and just another reason for me to never to return to drinking.

Father knows he is to blame; it may take him many seasons of hard work to be restored financially, but he shouldn't be reproached. Perhaps he will never have much money again. But the wise family will admire him for what he is trying to be, rather than for what he is trying to get.

Now and then **the family will be plagued by specters from the past**, for the drinking career of almost every alcoholic has been marked by escapades, funny, humiliating, shameful or tragic. The first impulse will be to bury these skeletons in a dark closet and padlock the door. The family may be possessed by the idea that future happiness can be based only upon forgetfulness of the past. We think that such a view is self-centered and in direct conflict with the new way of living.

Henry Ford once made a wise remark to the effect that **experience is the thing of supreme value is life**. That is true only if one is willing to **turn the past to good account**. We grow by our willingness to face and rectify errors and convert them into assets. The alcoholic's past thus becomes the principal asset of the family and frequently it is almost the only one!

This painful past may be of infinite value to other families still struggling with their problem. We think each family which has been relieved owes something to those who have not, and when the occasion requires, each member of it should be only too willing to bring former mistakes, no matter how grievous, out of their hiding places. Showing others who suffer how we were given help is the very thing which makes life seem so worthwhile to us now. Cling to the thought that, in God's hands, **the dark past is the greatest possession you have—the key to life and happiness for others**.

With it you can avert death and misery for them.

Spoken or unspoken, each family member, including the alcoholic, holds in their mind the memories of past events. Those memories will be unintentionally distorted, so what actually happened, unless captured on video or by contemporaneous journaling, will never be fully recognized.

Despite that fact, whatever memory we have is our true memory, and this is how we respond to it today, despite knowing that our memory is deficient.

Factual details fade, but how we felt at the time usually doesn't, and our challenge in sobriety is if and how we can best use our past to our benefit and the benefit of others.

Mentally separating the past event from the emotions surrounding it may allow us to turn hard times into teachable moments.

For example, when my wife died when we were both 43 years old and just a few months after we had gotten married, I was devastated. My intense anger persisted even after I joined A.A., but I was finally able to substitute gratitude for the resentment over my belief that my wife had been unfairly taken from me.

Why not be grateful for the time we had together, however short, rather than letting years of hate destroy my life today? Honor her by being thankful for what we had, not outraged over what I have lost. This is a message worth sharing.

It is possible to dig up past misdeeds so they become a blight, a veritable plague. For example, **we know of situations in which the alcoholic or his wife have had love affairs**. In the first flush of spiritual experience they forgave each other and drew closer together. The miracle of reconciliation was at hand. Then, under one provocation or another, **the aggrieved one would unearth the old affair and angrily cast its ashes about**.

A few of us have had these growing pains and they hurt a great deal. Husbands and wives have sometimes been obliged to separate for a time until new perspective, new victory over hurt pride could be re-won. In most cases, the alcoholic survived this ordeal without relapse, but not always. So we think that unless some good and useful purpose is to be served, **past occurrences should not be discussed**.

> Using past events known to both spouses as a weapon in the current relationship is like throwing a boomerang. If we repeatedly throw it, one of those times it will return and smack us in the head, and we will have accomplished nothing.
>
> When reading this section, one cannot help but reflect on Bill W.'s multiple adulterous affairs after the Big Book was published, and wonder how honest he was about them.
>
> Of interest to Big Book history lovers, the sentence "We know of situations in which the alcoholic or his wife have had love affairs" is said to have referred to Eddie R., who was the first prospect approached by Bill W. and Dr. Bob in Akron, Ohio before they succeeded with Bill Dotson, A.A. number three, "The man in the bed" in 1935.
>
> Eddie came from a prominent Youngstown, Ohio family. He got sober in the Oxford Group and soon afterwards, his wife Ruth, a university professor, told him of an adulterous affair she had in the past. Eddie got drunk, but eventually sobered up in 1949 with the Youngstown Ohio group. He attended Dr. Bob's funeral the following year with about a year of sobriety. (Big Book, p.124)

We families of Alcoholics Anonymous keep few skeletons in the closet. Everyone knows about the others' alcoholic troubles. This is a condition which, in ordinary life, would produce untold grief; there might be scandalous **gossip**, laughter at the expense of other people, and a tendency to take advantage of intimate information. Among us, these are rare occurrences. We do talk about each other a great deal, but we almost invariably temper such talk by a spirit of love and tolerance.

Another principle we observe carefully is that **we do not relate intimate experiences of another person** unless we are sure he would approve. We find it better, when possible, to **stick to our own stories**. A man may criticize or laugh at himself and it will affect others favorably, but criticism or ridicule coming from another often produce the contrary effect. Members of a family should watch such matters carefully, for one careless, inconsiderate remark has been known to raise the very devil. **We alcoholics are sensitive people. It takes some of us a long time to outgrow that serious handicap**.

> Step Six in the *Twelve Steps and Twelve Traditions* (12 & 12, p.67) states that "Gossip barbed with our anger, a polite form of murder by character assassination, has its satisfactions for us, too. Here we are not trying to help those we criticize; we are trying to proclaim our own righteousness."
>
> Our twelfth tradition states that anonymity is the spiritual foundation of all our traditions, reminding us to place principles before personalities.
>
> Both these excerpts remind us there are times to keep our mouths shut, just as our grandmother did when she told us if we can't say something nice about someone, don't say anything at all. As much as we would like to, it is not our job in A.A. to take the inventory of our fellow members or anyone else in our world, whether they deserve it or not.

Many **alcoholics are enthusiasts**. They run to extremes. At the beginning of recovery a man will take, as a rule, one of two directions. He may either plunge into a frantic attempt to get on his feet in **business**, or he may be so enthralled by his **new life** that he **talks or thinks of little else**. In either case certain family problems will arise. With these we have had experience galore.

We think it dangerous if he rushes headlong at his **economic problem**. The family will be affected also, pleasantly at first, as they feel their money troubles are about to be solved, then not so pleasantly as they find themselves neglected.

Dad may be tired at night and preoccupied by day. He may take small interest in the children and may show irritation when reproved for his delinquencies. If not irritable, he may seem dull and boring, not gay and affectionate as the family would like him to be. Mother may complain of inattention. They are all disappointed, and often let him feel it. Beginning with such complaints, a barrier arises. He is straining every nerve to make up for lost time. He is **striving to recover fortune and reputation** and feels he is doing very well.

Sometimes **mother and children** don't think so. Having been neglected and misused in the past, they **think father owes them more than they are getting**. They want him to make a fuss over them. They expect him to give them the nice times they used to have before he drank so much, and to **show his contrition for what they suffered**. But dad doesn't give freely of himself. **Resentment grows**. He becomes still less communicative. Sometimes he explodes over a trifle. The family is mystified. They criticize, pointing out how he is falling down on his spiritual program.

This sort of thing can be avoided. Both father and the family are mistaken, though each side may have some justification. It is of little use to argue and only makes the impasse worse. The family must realize that **dad, though marvelously improved, is still convalescing**. They should be thankful he is sober and able to be of this world once more. Let them praise his progress. Let them remember that **his drinking wrought all kinds of damage that may take long to repair**. If they sense these things, they will not take so seriously his periods of crankiness, depression, or apathy, which will disappear when there is tolerance, love, and spiritual understanding.

The head of the house ought to remember that he is mainly to blame for what befell his home. He can scarcely square the account in his lifetime. But he must see the danger of over-concentration on financial success. Although **financial recovery** is on the way for many of us, we found **we could not place money first**. For us, **material well-being always followed spiritual progress; it never preceded**.

Since the home has suffered more than anything else, it is well that a man exert himself there. He is not likely to get far in any direction if he fails to show unselfishness and love under his own roof. We know there are difficult wives and families, but the man who is getting over alcoholism must remember he did much to make them so.

As each member of a resentful family begins to see his shortcomings and admits them to the others, he lays a basis for helpful discussion. These family talks will be constructive if they can be carried on without heated argument, self-pity, self-justification or resentful criticism. Little by little, mother and children will see they ask too much, and father will see he gives too little. **Giving, rather than getting, will become the guiding principle**.

> When Bill W. got sober in the 1930s, the husband was usually the sole breadwinner and the wife tended to the home and children. An alcoholic husband who didn't work forced the wife to work, and their family income was often insufficient to support the family. Once sober, it was no surprise the husband tried to make up for income lost during his time of unemployment, ignoring certain family needs.
>
> Since the home is where we spend most of our time and are nearest to those we love, it is our responsibility as newly sober adults to bring our A.A. principles into our home life. Staying sober and financial issues aside, developing and improving our relationship with our spouse and children should be our top priority. This takes time, effort, patience, kindness, empathy, understanding and a concerted daily effort on our part.
>
> Being as unselfish as we can will go a long way to repairing years of broken promises and the emotional damage we inflicted. Whether or not our spouse or family members adopt a more spiritual and tolerant attitude should not diminish or undermine our best efforts to repair the damage we inflicted on our household.

Assume on the other hand that father has, at the outset, a stirring

301

spiritual experience. Overnight, as it were, **he is a different man**. He **becomes a religious enthusiast**. He is unable to focus on anything else. As soon as his sobriety begins to be taken as a matter of course, the family may look at their strange new dad with apprehension, then with irritation. There is **talk about spiritual matters morning, noon and night**. He may demand that the family find God in a hurry, or exhibit amazing indifference to them and say he is above worldly considerations. He may tell mother, who has been religious all her life, that she doesn't know what it's all about, and that she had better get his brand of spirituality while there is yet time.

> No one wants to live with or listen to a religious alcoholic evangelist twenty-four hours a day who wants to covert everyone to their way of thinking and acting. It is better for us to quietly focus on improving our patience, love and tolerance of those around us, and refrain from giving religious, spiritual or other advice to our family members. They will find their own way in due time without our help, and how they live their life is none of our business anyway. .

When father takes this tack, the family may react unfavorably. They may be **jealous of a God who has stolen dad's affections**. While grateful that he drinks no more, **they may not like the idea that God has accomplished the miracle where they failed**. **They often forget father was beyond human aid**. They may not see why their love and devotion did not straighten him out. Dad is not so spiritual after all, they say. If he means to right his past wrongs, why all this concern for everyone in the world but his family? What about his talk that God will take care of them? They suspect father is a bit balmy!

He is not so unbalanced as they might think. Many of us have experienced dad's elation. We have indulged in **spiritual intoxication**. Like a gaunt prospector, belt drawn in over the ounce of food, our pick struck gold. Joy at our release from a lifetime of frustration knew no bounds. **Father feels he has struck something better than gold**. For a time he may try to hug the new treasure to himself. He may not see at once that he has barely scratched a limitless lode which will pay

302

dividends only if he mines it for the rest of his life and insists on giving away the entire product.

If the family cooperates, dad will soon see that he is suffering from a distortion of values. He will perceive that his spiritual growth is lopsided, that for an average man like himself, **a spiritual life which does not include his family obligations may not be so perfect after all**. If the family will appreciate that dad's current behavior is but a phase of his development, all will be well. In the midst of an understanding and sympathetic family, these vagaries of dad's spiritual infancy will quickly disappear.

The opposite may happen should the family condemn and criticize. Dad may feel that for years his drinking has placed him on the wrong side of every argument, but that **now he has become a superior person with God on his side**. If the family persists in criticism, this fallacy may take a still greater hold on father. Instead of treating the family as he should, he may retreat further into himself and feel he has spiritual justification for so doing.

Though the family does not fully agree with dad's spiritual activities, they should let him have his head.

Even if he displays a certain amount of neglect and irresponsibility towards the family, **it is well to let him go as far as he likes in helping other alcoholics**. During those first days of convalescence, **this will do more to insure his sobriety than anything else**. Though some of his manifestations are alarming and disagreeable, we think dad will be on a firmer foundation than the man who is placing business or professional success ahead of spiritual development. He will be less likely to drink again, and anything is preferable to that.

No one, including the family, is responsible for developing and maintaining the alcoholic's emotional sobriety. It is up to the alcoholic, and is not dependent on how the family treats them, or how anyone else treats them.

Learning how to develop and remain within our emotional

303

boundaries, especially involving family members, takes practice and time. The alcoholic can seek guidance from their sponsor, support group or any number of clinical professionals to assist them. Facing family conflict head on, with good intention and a wiliness to change and adapt as necessary to fluctuating family dynamics can work wonders for our home life.

Those of us who have spent much time in the world of spiritual make believe have eventually seen the childishness of it. This dream world has been replaced by a great sense of purpose, accompanied by a growing consciousness of the power of God in our lives. We have come to believe He would like us to **keep our heads in the clouds with Him, but that our feet ought to be firmly planted on earth**. That is where our fellow travelers are, and that is where our work must be done. These are the realities for us. We have found **nothing incompatible between a powerful spiritual experience and a life of sane and happy usefulness**.

One more suggestion: **Whether the family has spiritual convictions or not, they may do well to examine the principles by which the alcoholic member is trying to live**. They can hardly fail to approve these simple principles, though the head of the house still fails somewhat in practicing them. Nothing will help the man who is off on a spiritual tangent so much as the wife who adopts a sane spiritual program, making a better practical use of it.

There will be other profound changes in the household. Liquor incapacitated father for so many years that **mother became head of the house**. She met these responsibilities gallantly. By force of circumstances, **she was often obliged to treat father as a sick or wayward child**. Even when he wanted to assert himself he could not, for his drinking placed him constantly in the wrong. **Mother made all the plans and gave the directions**. When sober, father usually obeyed. Thus mother, through no fault of her own, became accustomed to wearing the family trousers. **Father, coming suddenly to life again, often begins to assert himself**. This means trouble, unless the family watches for these tendencies in each other and comes to a friendly agreement about them.

Shifting power dynamics within the family once a spouse becomes sober can be traumatic for all involved. There is no easy solution, nor is there a single solution.

All parties must be open, honest and willing to change and adapt. Once again, consult and assistance from one's sponsor or clinical professionals during these transition periods may be worthwhile in many cases.

Drinking isolates most homes from the outside world. Father may have laid aside for years all normal activities—clubs, civic duties, sports. When he renews interest in such things, a feeling of jealousy may arise. The family may feel they hold a mortgage on dad, so big that no equity should be left for outsiders. Instead of developing new channels of activity for themselves, **mother and children demand that he stay home and make up the deficiency**.

At the very beginning, **the couple ought to frankly face the fact that each will have to yield here and there** if the family is going to play an effective part in the new life. **Father will necessarily spend much time with other alcoholics, but this activity should be balanced**. New acquaintances who know nothing of alcoholism might be made and thoughtful considerations given their needs. The problems of the community might engage attention. Though the family has no religious connections, they may wish to make contact with or take membership in a religious body.

Alcoholics who have derided religious people will be helped by such contacts. Being possessed of a spiritual experience, the alcoholic will find he has much in common with these people, though he may differ with them on many matters. If he does not argue about religion, he will make new friends and is sure to find new avenues of usefulness and pleasure. He and his family can be a bright spot in such congregations. He may bring new hope and new courage to many a priest, minister, or rabbi, who gives his all to minister to our troubled world. We intend the foregoing as a helpful suggestion only.

So far as we are concerned, there is nothing obligatory about it. As non-denominational people, we cannot make up others' minds for them. Each individual should consult his own conscience.

> How, when and by what manner the alcoholic and his family re-integrate themselves into society is best left up to each family to decide on their own. Going slow may be a good start while tempering expectations. However, the alcoholic will need to work regularly with other alcoholics to maintain their own sobriety, so liberal family flexibility in this area should be encouraged.

We have been speaking to you of serious, sometimes tragic things. We have been dealing with alcohol in its worst aspect. **But we aren't a glum lot**. If newcomers could see no joy or fun in our existence, they wouldn't want it. **We absolutely insist on enjoying life**. We try not to indulge in cynicism over the state of the nations, nor do we carry the world's troubles on our shoulders. When we see a man sinking into the mire that is alcoholism, we give him first aid and place what we have at his disposal. For his sake, we do recount and almost relive the horrors of our past. But those of us who have tried to shoulder the entire burden and trouble of others find we are soon overcome by them.

So we think **cheerfulness and laughter make for usefulness**. Outsiders are sometimes shocked when we burst into merriment over a seemingly tragic experience out of the past. But why shouldn't we laugh? We have recovered, and have been given the power to help others.

Everybody knows that those in bad health, and those who seldom play, do not laugh much. So **let each family play together or separately as much as their circumstances warrant**. We are sure **God wants us to be happy, joyous, and free**. We cannot subscribe to the belief that his life is a vale of tears, though it once was just that for many of us. But it is clear that **we made our own misery**. God didn't do it. **Avoid then, the deliberate manufacture of misery**, but if trouble comes, cheerfully capitalize it as an opportunity to demonstrate His omnipotence.

As I approached the doorway to the room where I attended my first A.A. meeting, I was startled by the roar of camaraderie and laughter coming through the entrance. I wasn't certain what I would find behind that door, but those inside did not sound unhappy or glum.

I hated the sound of laughter because it had been so long since I laughed. Nothing to laugh about if you were in my shoes, I thought. I was in still shaky, miserable, hopeless and depressed. None of that was funny.

During my early days, I was amazed how jovial the crowd was whenever I attended an A.A. meeting. They just wouldn't stop laughing. What I didn't realize was that they were mostly laughing at themselves. Over time I began to appreciate their self-deprecating humor, and a few of them were truly witty and clever.

After a few dozen meetings I found myself joining in their laughter, and the relief was enormous. Just being able to laugh out loud was healing in ways I never appreciated.

For times when I am glum, I always get a chuckle when I remember our Rule 62: "Let's not take ourselves too seriously."

Now about health: A body badly burned by alcohol does not often recover overnight nor do twisted thinking and depression vanish in a twinkling. We are convinced that **a spiritual mode of living is a most powerful health restorative**. We, who have recovered from serious drinking, are miracles of mental health. But we have seen remarkable transformations in our bodies. Hardly one of our crowd now shows any mark of dissipation.

But this does not mean that we disregard human health measures. God has abundantly supplied this world with fine doctors, psychologists, and practitioners of various kinds. Do not hesitate to take your health problems to such persons. Most of them give freely of themselves, that their fellows may enjoy sound minds and bodies.

Try to remember that though God has wrought miracles among us, **we should never belittle a good doctor or psychiatrist**. Their services are often indispensable in treating a newcomer and in following his case afterward.

One of the many doctors who had the opportunity of reading this book in manuscript form told us that the use of **sweets** was often helpful, of course depending upon a doctor's advice. He thought all alcoholics should constantly have **chocolate** available for its quick energy value at times of fatigue. He added that occasionally in the night a vague craving arose which would be satisfied by **candy**. Many of us have noticed a tendency to eat sweets and have found this practice beneficial.

> My fear of being discovered and diagnosed as an alcoholic prevented me from visiting my primary care physician for many years. Besides, I always had to have a few drinks before going, and was afraid he might notice I was half-drunk at 10 am in the morning.

> For the two years before I became sober I had been having symptoms I knew were abnormal and should be investigated. Fear of my alcoholism surpassed my fear of what I suspected was cancer. Once sober, my fears were confirmed, and I remember my doctor repeatedly asking me "Why didn't you see me earlier? We could have cured you if you had."

> I periodically pass on this story to others in the hope that even if they are alcoholic, they should see their physician regularly and for anything abnormal they discover. Alcoholics have the same type of medical problems and health risks as everyone else, and even if our bodies are badly beaten, they are worth treating.

> As for sugar, my addiction for anything chocolate, including chocolate sweets, cakes and candy skyrocketed after I became sober, and I still struggle with excess weight, pre-diabetes and recurrent dental caries as a result. A 12 Step approach does help limit my intake, but I'll probably never reach total abstinence.

Interestingly, chocolate contains sugar, which releases brain opioids and dopamine; and caffeine and theobromine, both stimulants; and anandamide, which is an endogenous cannabinoid found in the brain. No wonder I love chocolate!

A word about sex relations. Alcohol is so sexually stimulating to some men that they have over-indulged. Couples are occasionally dismayed to find that when drinking is stopped the man tends to be impotent. Unless the reason is understood, there may be an emotional upset. Some of us had this experience, only to enjoy, in a few months, a finer intimacy than ever. There should be no hesitancy in consulting a doctor or psychologist if the condition persists. We do not know of many cases where this difficulty lasted long.

Three out of four chronic male alcoholics have significant erectile dysfunction, the severity of which is dependent on the amount they drink daily. Testosterone levels are reduced in chronic alcoholics. Long term symptoms of excessive drinking include decreased sexual desire, sexual aversion, difficulty in erection, difficulty in achieving orgasm and premature ejaculation. Most symptoms are reversible after two or three months of abstinence.

The alcoholic may find it hard to re-establish friendly relations with his children. Their young minds were impressionable while he was drinking. Without saying so, they may cordially hate him for what he has done to them and to their mother. The children are sometimes dominated by a pathetic hardness and cynicism. They cannot seem to forgive and forget. This may hang on for months, long after their mother has accepted dad's new way of living and thinking.

It took me twenty-five years to accept the fact that my alcoholic father did not hate me when I was a child even though he behaved as if he did, and that my abused mother did the best she could dealing with him, instead of divorcing him sooner and removing both of us from a caustic household.

Both of my parents were very sick individuals at the time, and remained so all their lives. My decades of anger and resentment against them for what I perceived they had done to me slowly gave way to sadness and grief after I entered A.A.

Alcoholism is truly an extended family disease, and it is estimated that one alcoholic negatively affects the lives of at least ten to fifteen family members and close friends.

It is estimated that between 25% to 35% of children in the U.S. under the age of 18 are exposed to alcohol abuse in the family at some point in time. Children of alcoholics are much more likely to be victims of trauma, to grow up to be addicts, to marry addicts, to have multiple chronic diseases, and to need psychological counseling. Those who grow up with an alcoholic parent are five times more likely to develop alcoholism during their own adult life.

Studies of adult children of alcoholics have identified similar personality traits among them:

1) They can only guess what normal behavior is.

2) Have difficulty following a project from beginning to end.

3) Lie when it would be just as easy to tell the truth.

4) Judge themselves without mercy.

5) Have difficulty having fun.

6) Take themselves very seriously.

7) Have difficulty with intimate relationships.

8) Overreact to changes over which they have no control.

9) Constantly seek approval and affirmation.

10) Usually feel that they are different from other people.

11) Are either super responsible or super irresponsible; there's no middle ground.

12) Are extremely loyal, even in the face of evidence that the loyalty is undeserved.

13) Are impulsive. They lock themselves into a course of action without giving serious consideration to alternative behaviors or possible consequences. This impulsively leads to confusion, self-loathing and loss of control over their environment. In addition, they spend an excessive amount of energy cleaning up the messes they make.

In time they will see that he is a new man and in their own way they will let him know it. When this happens, they can be invited to join in morning meditation and then they can take part in the daily discussion without rancor or bias. From that point on, progress will be rapid. Marvelous results often follow such a reunion.

Children of alcoholics are especially vulnerable to the long term damage caused by their alcoholic parents, and many do not overcome that damage for the remainder of their lives.

Population studies have suggested that as many as 140 million Americans (45% of U.S. population) have been exposed to some form of alcoholism or alcoholic behaviors in their family, and up to one-third of those people are children.

Children of alcoholics endure chronic and extreme levels of tension and stress as the result of growing up in a home where one or both parents struggle with alcoholism. And those who grow up with an alcoholic parent are five times more likely to develop alcoholism in their adult lives.

Very young children may exhibit symptoms of bed wetting, separation anxiety, frequent nightmares and crying or problems with becoming unusually upset. Older children of alcoholics exhibit symptoms of depression, apathy, excessive guilt, feelings of hopelessness and helplessness, rigidity, obsessiveness, an intense need for perfection, hoarding, isolation, social withdrawal and excessive self-consciousness.

They all live by the emotional code of: *"Don't talk, don't trust and don't feel."*

Many adult children of alcoholics develop some form of Post-Traumatic Stress Disorder (PTSD), which is often expressed as a hypervigilance of their surroundings and the acute monitoring of comments or actions of others. This behavior is a carry-over from growing up mentally on guard most of the time.

The clinical Adverse Childhood Experiences (ACE) studies have examined the relationship between a variety of known childhood risk factors for disease, disability and early mortality.

ACEs are strongly related to the development and prevalence of a wide range of health problems throughout a person's lifespan, including those associated with alcoholism and substance abuse.

ACE childhood event indicators include the presence or absence of physical, sexual or emotional abuse, physical or emotional neglect, intimate partner violence, mother treated violently, substance abuse within the household, household mental illness, parental separation or divorce, and an incarcerated household member.

The confluence of post-traumatic stress disorder and childhood traumatic experiences can lead to a high likelihood that a child will develop an addiction of some type as an adult.

My own ACE score was six out of ten. A score greater than four or more suggests a five-fold increase in the likelihood of developing alcoholism later in life. None of my adverse childhood events caused my alcoholism, but when those environmental factors unite with my strong familial genetic predisposition for alcoholism, my calculated risk of adult alcoholism was 70%.

Other research studies have suggested that early onset daily drinking, before age 14, carries a 50% lifetime risk of alcohol abuse, and anecdotal evidence suggests if a person starts drinking alone, every day by age 12, there is a 100% likelihood they will become an alcoholic as an adult.

The ACE test:

https://www.npr.org/sections/health-shots/2015/03/02/387007941/take-the-ace-quiz-and-learn-what-it-does-and-doesnt-mean

https://acestoohigh.com/got-your-ace-score/

https://www.cdc.gov/violenceprevention/childabuseandneglect/acestudy/index.html

Whether the family goes on a spiritual basis or not, the alcoholic member has to if he would recover. The others must be convinced of his new status beyond the shadow of a doubt. **Seeing is believing** to most families who have lived with a drinker.

Here is a case in point: One of our friends is a heavy smoker and coffee drinker. There was no doubt he over-indulged. Seeing this, and meaning to be helpful, his wife commenced to admonish him about it. He admitted he was overdoing these things, but frankly said that he was not ready to stop. His wife is one of those persons who really feels there is something rather sinful about these commodities, so she nagged, and her intolerance finally threw him into a fit of anger. He got drunk.

Of course our friend was wrong—dead wrong. He had to painfully admit that and mend his spiritual fences. Though he is now a most effective member of Alcoholics Anonymous, he still smokes and drinks coffee, but neither his wife nor anyone else stands in judgment. She sees she was wrong to make a burning issue out of such a matter when his more serious ailments were being rapidly cured.

Some alcoholics have additional addictions and compulsions, and may also have a mental illness requiring medical treatment. Common wisdom suggests the most important action for such folks is to stop drinking first. Treating their alcoholism is a top priority.

313

The "heavy smoker and coffee drinker" in the Big Book was Earl Treat from Chicago. His story is titled "He Sold Himself Short" in the second edition of the Big Book. Earl's date of sobriety was originally April 1937. He had a brief slip in July of 1937, after which he stayed sober until his death in 1962.

Earl grew up in a small town near Akron, Ohio, and lived with his parents until age 27 while he worked in Akron. In 1930, during the Depression, he moved to Chicago and began morning drinking. By 1932, he was going on two and three day binges. His wife became fed up and called his father to take him back to Akron. For the next five years he bounced back and forth between Chicago and Akron trying to sober up.

In January of 1937, his father told him about the A.A. group in Akron, where he was indoctrinated by eight or nine men, after which he was allowed to attend his first A.A. meeting, which was led by Bill Dotson (A.A. #3). He stayed in Akron for two or three weeks and spent time with Dr. Bob who took him through all the steps in one afternoon.

He returned to Chicago later in 1937 to start A.A. there. One day he got angry and drunk after his wife criticized his coffee drinking and smoking. When he slipped he realized that the alcoholic had to continue to take his own inventory every day if he wanted to stay sober in recovery.

Soon Dr. Dan Craske of Chicago began to refer prospects to Earl, and another doctor in Evanston referred a woman named Sylvia Kauffmann to him. She was the author of "The Keys of the Kingdom." Earl suggested she go back to Akron where she sobered up. Once sober, she was sent back to Chicago to help Earl with his A.A. work.

Also, it was Earl who suggested that Bill W. document the A.A. experience, resulting in Bill writing "Twelve Points to Assure Our Future," first published in the April 1946 *A.A. Grapevine*. These are now known as the long form of the Twelve Traditions.

Earl later urged Bill to condense them into the short form Twelve Traditions as we know them today.

We have three little **mottoes** which are apropos.

Here they are:

First Things First

Live and Let Live

Easy Does It

> Mottos are not slogans. The key difference between the two is that a motto is defined as a short sentence or phrase that expresses the principle or rule guiding the behavior of a particular person, whereas a slogan is defined as a group of words or a phrase that is easy to remember and is used by a group or business to attract attention; it is a marketing tool.

> Some feel that First Things First represents Wisdom, Live and Let Live represents Tolerance and Easy Does It represents Moderation.

Chapter 10

TO EMPLOYERS

Although this chapter is addressed to employers who are assumed to be non-alcoholic, it can apply equally to an employer who is a recovered alcoholic. As he did in the chapter "To Wives," Bill is not so subtly promoting the purchase of the Big Book to all business firms, hoping to increase sales.

The author of this Big Book chapter was Hank Parkhurst, the second A.A. member in New York, whose story was titled "The Unbeliever" in the first edition of the Big Book.

Hank was a salesman, an atheist, and a former Standard Oil of New Jersey executive who had lost his job because of his drinking. After getting fired he started a small business called Honor Dealers in Newark, New Jersey, which was a buying cooperative for gasoline, motor oil and automobile parts.

He and Jim Burwell, author of "The Vicious Cycle," lead the fight against excessive talk of God in the 12 Steps, which resulted in the compromise phrase "God as we understood Him" in Steps Three and Eleven.

Sadly, Hank returned to drinking in September 1939, five months after the Big Book was published, and died in 1954 from alcoholism at Glenwood Sanitarium in Trenton, New Jersey at the age of fifty-seven.

TO EMPLOYERS

Among many employers nowadays, we think of one member who has spent much of his life in the world of big business. He has hired and fired hundreds of men. He knows the alcoholic as the employer sees him. His present views ought to prove exceptionally useful to business men everywhere.

But let him tell you:

I was at one time assistant manager of a corporation department employing sixty-six hundred men. One day my secretary came in saying **Mr. B**. insisted on speaking with me. I told her to say that I was not interested. I had warned him several times that he had but one more chance. Not long afterward he had called me from Hartford on two successive days, so drunk he could hardly speak. I told him he was through—finally and forever.

My secretary returned to say that it was not Mr. B. on the phone; it was Mr. B.'s brother, and he wished to give me a message. I still expected a plea for clemency, but these words came through the receiver: "I just wanted to tell you Paul **jumped from a hotel window** in Hartford last Saturday. He left us a note saying you were the best boss he ever had, and that you were not to blame in any way."

Another time, as I opened a letter which lay on my desk, a newspaper clipping fell out. It was the **obituary** of one of the best salesmen I ever had. After two weeks of drinking, he had placed his toe on the trigger of a loaded shotgun—the barrel was in his mouth. I had discharged him for drinking six weeks before.

Still another experience: A woman's voice came faintly over long distance from Virginia. She wanted to know if her husband's company insurance was still in force. Four days before he had **hanged himself** in his woodshed. I had been obliged to discharge him for drinking, though he was brilliant, alert, and one of the best organizers I have ever known.

Here were three exceptional men lost to this world because I did not understand alcoholism as I do now. What irony—I became an alcoholic myself! And but for the intervention of an understanding person, I might have followed in their footsteps. My downfall cost the business community unknown thousands of dollars, for it takes real money to train a man for an executive position. This kind of waste goes on unabated. **We think the business fabric is shot through with a situation which might be helped by better understanding all around**.

Nearly **every modern employer feels a moral responsibility for the well-being of his help**, and he tries to meet these responsibilities. That he has not always done so for the alcoholic is easily understood. To him the alcoholic has often seemed a fool of the first magnitude.

Because of the employee's special ability, or of his own strong personal attachment to him, the employer has sometimes kept such a man at work long beyond a reasonable period. Some employers have tried every known remedy. In only a few instances has there been a lack of patience and tolerance. And we, who have imposed on the best of employers, can scarcely blame them if they have been short with us.

In the 1930s, probably due in part to the influence of A.A., employers began to create Employee Assistance Programs (EAPs), which were work-based support programs designed to assist employees in resolving personal problems that were adversely affecting the employee's performance.

EAPs offer assistance in many ways:

Direct Access: employees call the counselor's office directly.

Quick Response: the first counseling session occurs within a few days, and a crisis is dealt with immediately.

Professional: counselors have earned a master's or doctorate degree in psychology or counseling, and are experts in human behavior.

Confidentiality: the employer never knows who uses the service.

Off-Site: counseling takes place at the counselor's office.

Direct Treatment: additional referrals are made only when the employee requires another specialist or ongoing care.

Coverage: a 24/7 hot-line with offices located in towns and cities where employees are located.

EAPs deliver various benefits for employers, including lower medical costs, reduced employee turnover and absenteeism, and higher employee productivity.

Here, for instance, is a typical example: An officer of one of the largest banking institutions in America knows I no longer drink.

One day he told me about an **executive** of the same bank who, from his description, **was undoubtedly alcoholic**. This seemed to me like an opportunity to be helpful, so I spent two hours talking about alcoholism, the malady, and described the symptoms and results as well as I could. His comment was, "Very interesting. But I'm sure this man is done drinking. He has just returned from a three-months' leave of absence, has taken a cure, looks fine, and to clinch the matter, the board of directors told him this was his last chance."

> The executive of a bank who was undoubtedly alcoholic was Clarence Snyder from Cleveland, Ohio. He was an executive at the Cleveland City National Bank who became sober in A.A. on February 11, 1938 after visiting with Dr. Bob in Akron.
>
> Snyder returned to Cleveland later that year and started a number of A.A. groups. He was responsible for the tradition of sponsorship in A.A., wrote the first pamphlet on sponsorship in 1944, formed the first Central Office Committee in A.A., developed A.A.'s first newsletter called the "Bulletin to All Groups" that in 1942 was renamed the "Cleveland Central Bulletin," and initiated the practice of rotation of officers both within groups and the Central Office Committee. In July, 1950 he helped organize a convention in Cleveland celebrating A.A.'s fifteenth anniversary, which was attended by three thousand members, and was designated A.A.'s first International Convention.
>
> Clarence was instrumental in the establishment of A.A. groups for women and for African-Americans. He was part of the team that wrote the Big Book and facilitated the break between the religious Oxford Groups and A.A., which opened the way for Roman Catholic alcoholics to participate in A.A.

319

Clarence became very hostile toward Bill W. over anonymity issues. He opposed the A.A. Traditions and continued to use his full name in public. He led a small group to contest the creation of the General Service Conference and the New York General Service Office.

Snyder would have been considered one of the founders of A.A. along with Dr. Bob and Bill W. if it had not been for his abrasive personality, which led to a break in his relationship with Bill W.

His story was titled "The Home Brewmeister." He started the Cleveland A.A. group on May 18, 1939 at the Cleveland Heights home of Abby G., a patent attorney. This was A.A. Group #3, and Clarence claimed it was the first group to be called "Alcoholics Anonymous."

He attended John D. Rockefeller's A.A. dinner on February 8, 1940, remained active in A.A., and his A.A. work became increasingly Christian fundamentalist in nature. He died 46 years sober in March, 1984.

The only answer I could make was that if the man followed the usual pattern, he would go on a bigger bust than ever. I felt this was inevitable and wondered if the bank was doing the man an injustice. **Why not bring him into contact with some of our alcoholic crowd? He might have a chance**. I pointed out that I had had nothing to drink whatever for three years, and this in the face of difficulties that would have made nine out of ten men drink their heads off. Why not at least afford him an opportunity to hear my story? "Oh no," said my friend, "This chap is either through with liquor, or he is minus a job. If he has your will power and guts, he will make the grade."

I wanted to throw up my hands in discouragement, for I saw that I had failed to help my banker friend understand. He simply could not believe that his brother-executive suffered from a serious illness.

There was nothing to do but wait.

Presently the man did slip and was fired. Following his discharge, we contacted him. Without much ado, he accepted the principles and procedure that had helped us. He is undoubtedly on the road to recovery. To me, this incident illustrates lack of understanding as to what really ails the alcoholic, and lack of knowledge as to what part employers might profitably take in salvaging their sick employees.

If you desire to help it might be well to disregard your own drinking, or lack of it. Whether you are a hard drinker, a moderate drinker or a teetotaler, you may have some pretty strong opinions, perhaps prejudices. Those who drink moderately may be more annoyed with an alcoholic than a total abstainer would be. Drinking occasionally, and understanding your own reactions, it is possible for you to become quite sure of many things which, so far as the alcoholic is concerned, are not always so. As a moderate drinker, you can take your liquor or leave it alone. Whenever you want to, you control your drinking. Of an evening, you can go on a mild bender, get up in the morning, shake your head and go to business. To you, liquor is no real problem. You cannot see why it should be to anyone else, save the spineless and stupid.

When dealing with an alcoholic, there may be a natural annoyance that a man could be so weak, stupid and irresponsible. Even when you understand the malady better, you may feel this feeling rising.

> When we deal with newcomers, and especially those who have relapsed multiple times because they probably never got sober in the first place, love and tolerance can evaporate.

> It is very easy to become frustrated with those who claim to not understand the program, those who pretend they are constitutionally incapable of sobriety, or those who are simply too lazy to do the work required for recovery.

> Remembering our own mental and physical distress, rampant dishonesty and manifold delusions when we first came into A.A. might help us reclaim a more tolerant attitude. We were sick people, and need to give newcomers time for their brains

to heal enough to fully engage in the program. This may take a few weeks, months or even years in some extreme cases.

As long as we, as A.A. members, make it clear to those suffering that the door of A.A. will always be open to them whenever they are ready, is often the only thing we can do.

A **look at the alcoholic in your organization** is many times illuminating. Is he not usually brilliant, fast-thinking, imaginative and likeable? When sober, does he not work hard and have a knack of getting things done? If he had these qualities and did not drink would he be worth retaining? Should he have the same consideration as other ailing employees? **Is he worth salvaging?** If your decision is yes, whether the reason be humanitarian or business or both, then **the following suggestions may be helpful**.

Can you discard the feeling that you are dealing only with habit, with stubbornness, or a weak will? If this presents difficulty, re-reading chapters two and three, where the alcoholic sickness is discussed at length might be worthwhile. You, as a business man, want to know the necessities before considering the result. If you concede that your employee is ill, can he be forgiven for what he has done in the past? Can his past absurdities be forgotten? **Can it be appreciated that he has been a victim of crooked thinking, directly caused by the action of alcohol on his brain?**

I well remember the shock I received when a prominent doctor in Chicago told me of cases where pressure of the spinal fluid actually ruptured the brain. No wonder an alcoholic is strangely irrational. Who wouldn't be, with such a fevered brain? Normal drinkers are not so affected, nor can they understand the aberrations of the alcoholic.

The prominent doctor in Chicago was Dr. Dan Craske, who was mentioned in Earl Treat's story "He Sold Himself Short."

Your man has probably been trying to conceal a number of scrapes, perhaps pretty messy ones. They may be disgusting. You may be at a loss to understand how such a seemingly above-board chap could be so involved. But these **scrapes can generally be charged, no matter how bad, to the abnormal action of alcohol on his mind**. When drinking, or getting over a bout, an alcoholic, sometimes the model of honesty when normal, will do incredible things. Afterward, his revulsion will be terrible. Nearly always, these antics indicate nothing more than temporary conditions.

This is not to say that all alcoholics are honest and upright when not drinking. Of course that isn't so, and such people may often impose on you. Seeing your attempt to understand and help, some men will try to take advantage of your kindness. **If you are sure your man does not want to stop, he may as well be discharged**, the sooner the better. You are not doing him a favor by keeping him on. Firing such an individual may prove a blessing to him. It may be just the jolt he needs. I know, in my own particular case, that nothing my company could have done would have stopped me for, so long as I was able to hold my position, I could not possibly realize how serious my situation was. Had they fired me first, and had they then taken steps to see that I was presented with the solution contained in this book, I might have returned to them six months later, a well man.

An employer's decision to retain or fire an alcoholic is a difficult one. A large company may have to deal with employee unions even if they have an active Employee Assistance Program. It is always difficult to determine if the alcoholic is truly committed to recovery, or is just lying to save his job.

A smaller business, with only a few employees, has a more difficult time. Each employee is often critical to the business, and usually everyone in the company knows each other personally. Having to fire such an individual, especially if well liked and needed, may significantly disrupt the business and company morale.

But **there are many men who want to stop, and with them you can go far**. Your understanding treatment of their cases will pay dividends.

Perhaps you have such a man in mind. He wants to quit drinking

323

and you want to help him, even if it be only a matter of good business. You now know more about alcoholism. You can see that he is mentally and physically sick. You are willing to overlook his past performances. **Suppose an approach is made something like this**:

State that you know about his drinking, and that it must stop. You might say you appreciate his abilities, would like to keep him, but cannot if he continues to drink. A firm attitude at this point has helped many of us.

Next he can be assured that **you do not intend to lecture, moralize, or condemn**; that if this was done formerly, it was because of misunderstanding. If possible express a lack of hard feeling toward him. At this point, it might be well to **explain alcoholism, the illness**. Say that you believe he is a gravely-ill person, with this qualification— being perhaps fatally ill, **does he want to get well?** You ask, because many alcoholics, being warped and drugged, do not want to quit. But does he? **Will he take every necessary step, submit to anything to get well, to stop drinking forever?**

If he says yes, does he really mean it, or down inside does he think he is fooling you, and that after rest and treatment he will be able to get away with a few drinks now and then? We believe a man should be thoroughly probed on these points. **Be satisfied he is not deceiving himself or you**.

Whether you mention this book is a matter for your discretion. If he temporizes and still thinks he can ever drink again, even beer, he might as well be discharged after the next bender which, if an alcoholic, he is almost certain to have. He should understand that emphatically. **Either you are dealing with a man who can and will get well or you are not. If not, why waste time with him?** This may seem severe, but it is usually the best course.

After satisfying yourself that your man wants to recover and that he will go to any extreme to do so, **you may suggest a definite course of action**. For most alcoholics who are drinking, or who are just getting over a spree, a certain amount of **physical treatment** is desirable, even imperative. The matter of physical treatment should, of course, be referred to your own doctor. Whatever the method, its object is to thoroughly **clear mind and body of the effects of alcohol**. In competent hands, this seldom takes long nor is it very expensive. Your man will fare better if placed in such physical condition that he can think straight and no longer craves liquor.

If you propose such a procedure to him, it may be necessary to advance the cost of the treatment, but we believe it should be made plain that any expense will later be deducted from his pay. It is better for him to feel fully responsible.

If your man accepts your offer, it should be pointed out that **physical treatment is but a small part of the picture**. Though you are providing him with the best possible medical attention, he should understand that he must undergo a change of heart. **To get over drinking will require a transformation of thought and attitude**. We all had to **place recovery above everything**, for without recovery we would have lost both home and business.

Can you have every confidence in his ability to recover? While on the subject of confidence, can you adopt the attitude that so far as you are concerned this will be a strictly personal matter, that his alcoholic derelictions, the treatment about to be undertaken, will never be discussed without his consent? It might be well to have a long chat with him on his return.

To return to the subject matter of this book: It contains full suggestions by which the employee may solve his problem. To you, some of the ideas which it contains are novel. Perhaps you are not quite in sympathy with the approach we suggest. By no means do we offer it as the last word on this subject, but so far as we are concerned, it has worked with us. After all, are you not looking for results rather than methods? Whether your employee likes it or not, he will learn the grim truth about alcoholism. That won't hurt him a bit, even though he does not go for this remedy.

We suggest you **draw the book to the attention of the doctor who**

is to attend your patient during treatment. If the book is read the moment the patient is able, while acutely depressed, realization of his condition may come to him.

We **hope the doctor will tell the patient the truth about his condition**, whatever that happens to be. When the man is presented with this volume it is best that no one tell him he must abide by its suggestions. The man must decide for himself.

You are betting, or course, that your changed attitude plus the contents of this book will turn the trick. In some cases it will, and in others it may not. But we think that if you persevere, the percentage of successes will gratify you. As our work spreads and our numbers increase, we hope your employees may be put in personal contact with some of us. Meanwhile, **we are sure a great deal can be accomplished by the use of the book alone**.

On your employee's return, talk with him. Ask him if he thinks he has the answer. If he feels free to discuss his problems with you, if he knows you understand and will not be upset by anything he wishes to say, he will probably be off to a fast start.

In this connection, can you remain undisturbed if the man proceeds to tell you shocking things? He may, for example, reveal that he has padded his expense account or that he has planned to take your best customers away from you. In fact, he may say almost anything if he has accepted our solution which, as you know, demands rigorous honesty. Can you charge this off as you would a bad account and start fresh with him? If he owes you money you may wish to make terms.

If he speaks of his home situation, you can undoubtedly make helpful suggestions. Can he talk frankly with you so long as he does not bear business tales or criticize his associates? With this kind of employee such an attitude will command undying loyalty.

The greatest enemies of us alcoholics are resentment, jealousy, envy, frustration, and fear. Wherever men are gathered together in business there will be **rivalries** and, arising out of these, a certain amount of **office politics**.

Sometimes we alcoholics have an idea that people are trying to pull us down. Often this is not so at all. But **sometimes our drinking will be used politically**.

One instance comes to mind in which a malicious individual was always making friendly little jokes about an alcoholic's drinking exploits. In this way he was **slyly carrying tales**.

In another case, an alcoholic was sent to a hospital for treatment. Only a few knew of it at first but, within a short time, it was bill boarded throughout the entire company. Naturally this sort of thing decreased the man's chance of recovery. The employer can many times protect the victim from this kind of talk. The employer cannot play favorites, but he can always defend a man from needless provocation and unfair criticism.

As a class, **alcoholics are energetic people**. They work hard and they play hard. Your man should be on his mettle to make good. Being somewhat weakened, and faced with physical and mental readjustment to a life which knows no alcohol, he may overdo. You may have to curb his desire to work sixteen hours a day. You may need to encourage him to play once in a while. **He may wish to do a lot for other alcoholics** and something of the sort may come up during business hours. A reasonable amount of latitude will be helpful. **This work is necessary to maintain his sobriety**.

Despite the size or type of company, it is usually worthwhile to error on the side of hope and compassion and give the alcoholic at least one chance to recover and remain employed.

Remember that alcoholism is a disease, the alcoholic is an ill person, and alcoholics can be helped and are worth helping.

A general approach with the alcoholic employee might involve several steps:

1) Acquaint yourself with the characteristics and disease of alcoholism.

2) Be prepared to discount and forget your man's past, except

for financial debts owed.

3) Confidentially offer him medical treatment and cooperation, provided you think he wants to stop.

4) Suspend the alcoholic temporarily from his job and give him enough time to recover physically, which may require a short-term rehabilitation facility admission.

5) Consider giving him a copy of the Big Book.

6) Have a frank talk with him when he gets back from his treatment, assuring him of your full support, encouraging him to say anything he wishes about himself, and making it clear his past behavior will not be held against him.

7) Ask him if he is willing to place his recovery from alcoholism ahead of all else.

8) Don't let him overwork.

9) Protect him, when justified, from malicious gossip.

10) If, after you have given him a fair chance, he is still unable to stop drinking, let him go.

After your man has gone along without drinking for a few months, you may be able to make use of his services with other employees who are giving you the alcoholic run-around—provided, of course, they are willing to have a third party in the picture. **An alcoholic who has recovered, but holds a relatively unimportant job, can talk to a man with a better position**. Being on a radically different basis of life, he will never take advantage of the situation.

Your man may be trusted. Long experience with alcoholic excuses naturally arouses suspicion. When his wife next calls saying he is sick, you may jump to the conclusion he is drunk. If he is, and is still trying to recover, he will tell you about it even if it means the loss of his job. For **he knows he must be honest if he would live at all**. He will appreciate knowing you are not bothering your head about him, that you are not suspicious nor are you trying to run his life so he will be shielded from temptation to drink. **If he is conscientiously following the program of recovery he can go anywhere your business may call him**.

In case he does stumble, even once, you will have to decide whether to let him go. If you are sure he doesn't mean business, there is no doubt you should discharge him. If, on the contrary, you are sure he is doing his utmost, **you may wish to give him another chance**. But you should feel under no obligation to keep him on, for your obligation has been well discharged already.

There is another thing you might wish to do. If your organization is a large one, **your junior executives might be provided with this book**. You might let them know you have no quarrel with alcoholics of your organization. These juniors are often in a difficult position. Men under them are frequently their friends. So, for one reason or another, they cover these men, hoping matters will take a turn for the better. They often jeopardize their own positions by trying to help serious drinkers who should have been fired long ago, or else given an opportunity to get well.

After reading this book, **a junior executive can go to such a man and say approximately this**, "Look here, Ed. Do you want to stop drinking or not? You put me on the spot every time you get drunk. It isn't fair to me or the firm. I have been learning something about alcoholism. If you are an alcoholic, you are a mighty sick man. You act like one. The firm wants to help you get over it, and if you are interested, there is a way out. If you take it, your past will be forgotten and the fact that you went away for treatment will not be mentioned. But if you cannot or will not stop drinking, I think you ought to resign."

Your junior executive may not agree with the contents of our book. He need not, and often should not show it to his alcoholic prospect. But at least he will understand the problem and will no longer be misled by ordinary promises. He will be able to take a position with such a man which is eminently fair and square. He will have no further reason for covering up an alcoholic employee.

It boils right down to this: **No man should be fired just because he is alcoholic. If he wants to stop, he should be afforded a real chance. If he cannot or does not want to stop, he should be discharged.** The exceptions are few.

> The above paragraph contains good advice for dealing with any employed alcoholic. A.A.'s Tradition Three states that the only requirement for A.A. membership is a desire to stop drinking, and in A.A.'s first step we admit our powerlessness over alcohol and begin to accept our need for help. If an alcoholic employee can follow these two precepts, their employer may want to give them another chance.

We think this method of approach will accomplish several things. It will permit the rehabilitation of good men. At the same time you will feel no reluctance to rid yourself of those who cannot or will not stop. **Alcoholism may be causing your organization considerable damage in its waste of time, men and reputation.** We hope our suggestions will help you plug up this sometimes serious leak. We think we are sensible when we urge that you stop this waste and **give your worthwhile man a chance.**

The other day an approach was made to the vice president of a large industrial concern. He remarked: "I'm glad you fellows got over your drinking. But the policy of this company is not to interfere with the habits of our employees. If a man drinks so much that his job suffers, we fire him. I don't see how you can be of any help to us for, as you see, we don't have any alcoholic problem."

This same company spends millions for research every year. Their cost of production is figured to a fine decimal point. They have recreational facilities. There is company insurance. There is a real interest, both humanitarian and business, in the well-being of employees. But alcoholism well, they just don't believe they have it.

Perhaps this is a typical attitude. We, who have collectively seen a great deal of business life, at least from the alcoholic angle, had to smile at this gentleman's sincere opinion. **He might be shocked if**

he knew how much alcoholism is costing his organization a year. That company may harbor many actual or potential alcoholics. We believe that managers of large enterprises often have little idea how prevalent this problem is. Even if you feel your organization has no alcoholic problem, it may pay to take another look down the line. You may make some interesting discoveries.

Ten percent of deaths among working adults are alcohol-related, killing 88,000 people in the U.S. each year, which works out to 241 deaths every day, or one every six minutes.

Alcoholism is also a massive drain on the American economy, costing over $250 billion annually.

It is estimated that among full-time workers, 8% are alcohol abusers. The construction, food service and entertainment industries have the highest percentage of employees with alcohol abuse, reported at 12%.

Workplace costs are due to decreases in worker productivity (72%), health care expenses for treating problems caused by excessive drinking (11%), law enforcement and criminal justice expenses (10%) and losses from motor vehicle accidents related to excessive alcohol use (5%).

Specific employer expenses from workplace alcoholism are due to general absenteeism, increased sick leave, higher rates of tardiness, increased accidents and injuries, missed project and production deadlines, higher cost and use of worker's compensation and disability benefits, increased worker turnover and their replacement costs, diverted supervisory, managerial and coworker time, friction among workers, damage to a company's reputation, increased general liability and higher rates of theft and fraud.

Employers also have non-alcoholic employees who must care for alcoholics, often forced to take time off from work to take a loved one to the emergency room or tend to their sick alcoholic at home.

Of course, this chapter refers to alcoholics, sick people, deranged men. What our friend, the vice president, had in mind was the habitual or whoopee drinker. As to them, his policy is undoubtedly sound, but he did not distinguish between such people and the alcoholic.

It is not to be expected that an alcoholic employee will receive a disproportionate amount of time and attention. He should not be made a favorite. The right kind of man, the kind who recovers, will not want this sort of thing. He will not impose. Far from it. He will work like the devil and thank you to his dying day.

Today **I own a little company**. There are two alcoholic employees who produce as much as five normal salesmen. But why not? They have a new attitude, and they have been saved from a living death. I have enjoyed every moment spent in getting them straightened out.

Hank Parkhurst's little company with two alcoholic employees was the Honor Dealers Company, and the two employees were Bill Wilson and Jimmy Burwell, an atheist whose story is recorded in "The Vicious Cycle."

Henry "Hank" Parkhurst was born in Marion, Iowa on March 13, 1895. He was a Standard Oil of New Jersey executive before he got fired due to his drinking. In the fall of 1935, Hank got sober in Towns Hospital, becoming New York A.A. member #2.

The small company was formed in 1937 by Hank as a way of getting back at Standard Oil. Hank's plan was to provide gas stations with the opportunity to buy gasoline, oil, auto polish and automobile parts on a lower cost, cooperative basis.

An atheist, Hank lead the fight, helped by Jim Burwell, to add "God as we understood Him" to the 12 Steps. Hank and Jimmy B. wanted to leave God completely out of the Big Book and refer instead to the "spiritual nature" of the recovery the 12 Steps were designed to bring about.

332

Ruth Hock, A.A.'s first secretary, was hired by Honor Dealers when the company started. A lot of people dropped in to discuss their drinking problems when Bill visited, and little cooperative business was conducted there after April, 1938 when Bill started writing the Big Book full time and dictating it to Ruth.

Hank was infatuated with Ruth, and he wanted to get divorced and marry her. After questions arose over how he handled some of A.A.'s finances, Hank eventually closed the office, became estranged from Bill W., and returned to drinking in September, 1939.

After the Honor Dealers office closed, Bill and Ruth opened the office for the Alcoholic Foundation back in New York City.

During the 1940s, Hank travelled throughout the Midwest selling porcelain mugs and figurines. Some say Hank intermittently became involved in A.A., but after he died in Pennington, New Jersey in 1954, Lois Wilson ascribed his death to drinking, and others have said he was also on pills.

Despite Hank's return to drinking and the chaos in A.A. he caused, without Hank the Big Book might never have been completed. Of the Big Book, Ruth Hock said, "It wouldn't have been written without Bill, and it wouldn't have been published without Hank."

Chapter 11

A VISION FOR YOU

For most normal folks, drinking means conviviality, companionship and colorful imagination. It means release from care, boredom and worry. It is joyous intimacy with friends and a feeling that life is good. But **not so with us in those last days of heavy drinking**. The old pleasures were gone. They were but memories. **Never could we recapture the great moments of the past**. There was an insistent yearning to enjoy life as we once did and a heartbreaking obsession that some new miracle of control would enable us to do it. There was **always one more attempt—and one more failure**.

The less people tolerated us, the more we withdrew from society, from life itself. As **we became subjects of King Alcohol**, shivering **denizens of his mad realm**, the chilling vapor that is **loneliness settled down**. It thickened, ever becoming blacker. Some of us **sought out sordid places**, hoping to find understanding companionship and approval. Momentarily we did—**then would come oblivion and the awful awakening to face the hideous Four Horsemen—Terror, Bewilderment, Frustration, Despair**. Unhappy drinkers who read this page will understand!

> The Four Horsemen in the Bible's "Book of Revelation" symbolize the evils to come at the end of the world. A.A.'s four horsemen symbolize the depths of our drinking; when we are all-consumed by fear, confusion, anger and depression.
>
> As an alcoholic, my four horses are Selfishness (black), Dishonesty (yellow), Resentment (red) and Fear (pale). They are the manifestations of my character defects that I must confront every day. Those four stallions will always be with me, and I need to learn how to harness them as we travel on that Broad Highway to recovery.
>
> Admittedly, our four alcoholic mounts are far less sensational than the Four Horsemen of the Bible. Yet if we carefully

334

examine our lives, it becomes clear they're no less threatening to our life and well-being.

They may not overwhelm our senses nor signal the end of history. And yet, they are all—in their own way—harbingers of our own death if left unrecognized, unchecked or ignored.

BIBLE HISTORY

In the Bible's Book of Revelation, Jesus opens seven seals of judgment to begin the Tribulation period on earth. The first four seals he opens are the Four Horsemen, and each is released from heaven to usher in various judgments on the earth. While some catastrophic judgments are specific events, these are overarching judgments that will last for long periods throughout the Tribulation.

In Revelation, the apostle John describes a series of apocalyptic visions he experienced during his exile on the Isle of Patmos in the Aegean Sea. In one of these visions, he saw Four Horsemen, the first riding a white horse (Conquest), the second a red horse (War), the third a black horse (Famine), and the fourth riding a pale horse (Death).

The seventh seal is opened and represents the Day of the Lord, which is the time of Christ's intervention in this world to wrest control from Satan's dominion and from the rebellious human rulers under him, and to establish the Kingdom of God here on earth. So the first six seals are all preliminary destructive events that lead up to the Day of the Lord.

Book of Revelation 6:1-8

1. And I saw when the Lamb opened one of the seals, and I heard, as it were the noise of thunder, one of the four beasts saying, Come and see.

2. And I saw, and behold a white horse: and he that sat on him had a bow; and a crown was given unto him: and he went forth conquering, and to conquer.

3. And when he had opened the second seal, I heard the second beast say, Come and see.

4. And there went out another horse that was red: and power was given to him that sat thereon to take peace from the earth, and that they should kill one another, and there was given unto him a great sword.

5. And when he had opened the third seal, I heard the third beast say, Come and see. And I beheld, and lo a black horse; and he that sat on him had a pair of balances in his hand.

6. And I heard a voice in the midst of the four beasts say, "A measure of wheat for a penny, and three measures of barley for a penny; and see thou hurt not the oil and the wine."

7. And when he had opened the fourth seal, I heard the voice of the fourth beast say, Come and see.

8. And I looked, and behold a pale horse, and his name that sat on him was Death, and Hell followed with him. And power was given unto them over the fourth part of the earth, to kill with sword, and with hunger, and with death, and with the beasts of the earth.

Now and then a serious drinker, being dry at the moment says, "I don't miss it at all. Feel better. Work better. Having a better time." As ex-problem drinkers, we smile at such a sally. We know **our friend is like a boy whistling in the dark to keep up his spirits**.

He fools himself. Inwardly he would give anything to take half a dozen drinks and get away with them. He will presently try the old game again, for **he isn't happy about his sobriety. He cannot picture life without alcohol. Some day he will be unable to imagine life either with alcohol or without it. Then he will know loneliness such as few do. He will be at the jumping-off place. He will wish for the end**.

At some point, almost all alcoholics reach their jumping-off place. We skip along, nervously twitching our shoulders, whistling to hide our fear, pretending all is well after a few days of not drinking, despite the obsession roaring in our head which will drive us to drink again. We know in our hearts our time is up, in spite of our pathetic attempts to delude ourselves and others.

We are done. We pray to not wake up in the morning. We wonder how long it will take us to die if we leave our car engine running while we sit enclosed in a dark garage. We try to get up enough courage to throw a rope over a joist hook in the basement and hang ourselves. How fast must we drive our car into a freeway bridge abutment to ensure our death? How many sleeping pills or pain pills do I need to swallow for them to kill me? Do I have enough courage to stick the shotgun in my mouth and pull the trigger?

Is there no other way out?

We have shown how we got out from under. You say, "Yes, I'm willing. But am I to be consigned to a life where I shall be stupid, boring and glum, like some righteous people I see? **I know I must get along without liquor, but how can I? Have you a sufficient substitute?**"

Yes, there is a substitute and it is vastly more than that. **It is a fellowship in Alcoholics Anonymous**. There you will find release from care, boredom and worry. Your imagination will be fired. **Life will mean something at last**. The most satisfactory years of your existence lie ahead. Thus we find the fellowship, and so will you.

"How is that to come about?" you ask. "Where am I to find these people?"

You are going to meet these new friends in your own community. Near you, alcoholics are dying helplessly like people in a sinking ship. If you live in a large place, there are hundreds. High and low, rich and poor, these are future fellows of Alcoholics Anonymous. Among them you will make lifelong friends.

You will be bound to them with new and wonderful ties, for **you will escape disaster together and you will commence shoulder to shoulder your common journey**. Then you will know what it means to give of yourself that others may survive and rediscover life. You will learn the full meaning of "Love thy neighbor as thyself."

> And the second is like, namely this, Thou shalt love thy neighbor as thyself. There is none other commandment greater than this. [Mark 12:31 King James version]

It may seem incredible that **these men are to become happy, respected, and useful** once more. **How can they rise out of such misery, bad repute and hopelessness?** The practical answer is that **since these things have happened among us, they can happen with you**. Should you wish them above all else, and be willing to make use of our experience, we are sure they will come. The age of miracles is still with us. Our own recovery proves that!

Our hope is that when this chip of a book is launched on the world tide of alcoholism, defeated drinkers will seize upon it, to follow its suggestions. Many, we are sure, will rise to their feet and march on. They will approach still other sick ones and fellowships of Alcoholics Anonymous may spring up in each city and hamlet, havens for those who must find a way out.

> The chapter "A Vision For You" is the capstone of the recovery experience of Bill W. and other alcoholics in Big Book. In the first third of the book Bill tells us what he is going to tell us. In the middle of the book he tells us how alcoholics can recover, and in the final third of the book he tells us what he told us.

In the chapter "Working With Others" you gathered an idea of how we approach and aid others to health. Suppose now that through you several families have adopted this way of life. You will want to know more of how to proceed from that point. **Perhaps the best way of treating you to a glimpse of your future will be to describe the growth or the fellowship among us**.

Bill W. repeats and elaborates on his own story in this following section, which summarizes his narrative from "Bill's Story."

Here is a brief account:

Years ago, in 1935, one of our number [Bill W.] made a journey to a certain western city [Akron]. From a business standpoint, his trip came off badly. Had he been successful in his enterprise [a proxy fight to take over control of the National Rubber Machinery Co.], he would have been set on his feet financially which, at the time, seemed vitally important. But his venture wound up in a law suit and bogged down completely. The proceeding was shot through with much hard feeling and controversy.

Bitterly discouraged, he found himself in a strange place, discredited and almost broke. Still physically weak, and sober but a few months [five months], he saw that his predicament was dangerous. He wanted so much to talk with someone, but whom?

One dismal afternoon he paced a hotel lobby [Mayflower Hotel] wondering how his bill was to be paid. At the end of the room stood a glass covered directory of local churches. Down the lobby a door opened into an attractive bar. He could see the gay crowd inside. In there he would find companionship and release. Unless he took some drinks, he might not have the courage to scrape an acquaintance and would have a lonely weekend.

Of course he couldn't drink, but why not sit hopefully at a table, a bottle of ginger ale before him? After all, had he not been sober six months now? Perhaps he could handle, say, three drinks—no more! Fear gripped him. He was on thin ice. Again it was the old, insidious insanity—that first drink. With a shiver, he turned away and walked down the lobby to the church directory. Music and gay chatter still floated to him from the bar.

But what about his responsibilities—his family and the men who would die because they would not know how to get well, ah—yes, those other alcoholics?

339

Even though our Big Book says we should get and stay sober for ourselves and no one else, I found one of the most helpful tools I had after I stopped drinking and still had that raging obsession to drink was to think about how much I would let down my wife, family and close friends if I relapsed. I had also met a few alcoholics in A.A. that I cared for, and didn't want to let them down either.

I support newcomers using any mental means they can to prevent them from taking that deadly first drink. For some, it is safety through God, prayer and meditation. For others, it is fear of losing our spouse or family, fear of losing our job, fear of arrest or fear of incarceration by a drug court if we relapse.

Today, I do not think about drinking and have no fear of relapse. I stay sober for myself of course, but also for all those around me, with whom I have established wonderful new relationships that I want to retain. It is not fear that drives me sober today, but gratitude for having a new design for living, and a loving family and friends with whom to share my sober life.

There must be many such in this town. He would phone a clergyman. His sanity returned and he thanked God. Selecting a church at random from the directory, he stepped into a booth and lifted the receiver.

His call to the clergyman [Rev. Walter Tunks] led him presently to a certain resident of the town [Dr. Bob Smith], who, though formerly able and respected, was then nearing the nadir of alcoholic despair.

The Reverend Walter Tunks of the St. Paul Episcopal Church referred Bill W. to Norman Sheppard, who then referred him to Henrietta Sieberling, who was 47 years old and a member of the Oxford Group. Bill introduced himself as another member of the Oxford Group, and "a rum hound from New York." Henrietta met with Bill at her gatehouse, Stan Hywet Hall, on the Sieberling estate. She arranged a dinner meeting the next day with Dr. Bob and his wife Anne.

It was the usual situation; home in jeopardy, wife ill, children

340

distracted, bills in arrears and standing damaged. He had a desperate desire to stop, but saw no way out, for he had earnestly tried many avenues of escape. Painfully aware of being somehow abnormal, the man did not fully realize what it meant to be alcoholic.*

This refers to Bill's first visit with Dr. Bob. These men later became co-founders of A.A. Bill's story opens the text of this book; Dr. Bob's heads the Story Section.

When our friend related his experience, the man agreed that no amount of will power he might muster could stop his drinking for long. A spiritual experience, he conceded, was absolutely necessary, but the price seemed high upon the basis suggested. He told how he lived in constant worry about those who might find out about his alcoholism. He had, of course, the familiar alcoholic obsession that few knew of his drinking. Why, he argued, should he lose the remainder of his business, only to bring still more suffering to his family by foolishly admitting his plight to people from whom he made his livelihood? He would do anything, he said, but that.

Being intrigued, however, he invited our friend to his home [Bill W. moved to Dr. Bob's house at the request of his wife Anne]. Sometime later, and just as he thought he was getting control of his liquor situation, he went on a roaring bender [at an AMA convention in Atlantic City, NJ] For him, this was the spree that ended all sprees. He saw that he would have to face his problems squarely that God might give him mastery.

One morning he took the bull by the horns and set out to tell those he feared what his trouble had been. He found himself surprisingly well received, and learned that many knew of his drinking. Stepping into his car, he made the rounds of people he had hurt. He trembled as he went about, for this might mean ruin, particularly to a person in his line of business [colorectal surgeon].

At midnight he came home exhausted, but very happy. He has not had a drink since. As we shall see, he now means a great deal to his community, and the major liabilities of thirty years of hard

341

drinking have been repaired in four.

> The brilliance of Bill W. was that he learned the power of one alcoholic carrying a personal message of recovery to another alcoholic, which is called witnessing. Combined with performing a moral inventory, adopting God or a higher power of some type, and continued daily involvement in the Fellowship, we can not only find a new way of life but can do it without drinking or taking drugs to change the way we feel.

But life was not easy for the two friends. Plenty of difficulties presented themselves. Both saw that they must keep spiritually active. One day they called up the head nurse of a local hospital [Mrs. Hall, who was in charge of admissions at Akron City Hospital]. They explained their need and inquired if she had a first class alcoholic prospect.

She replied, "Yes, we've got a corker. He's just beaten up a couple of nurses. Goes off his head completely when he's drinking. But he's a grand chap when he's sober, though he's been in here eight times in the last six months. Understand he was once a well-known lawyer in town, but just now we've got him strapped down tight." *

This refers to Bill's and Dr. Bob's first visit to A.A. Number Three. See the Pioneer Section. This resulted in A.A.'s first group, at Akron, Ohio, in 1935.

Here was a prospect all right but, by the description, none too promising. The use of spiritual principles in such cases was not so well understood as it is now. But one of the friends [Dr. Bob] said, "Put him in a private room. We'll be down."

Two days later, a future fellow of Alcoholics Anonymous stared glassily at the strangers beside his bed. "Who are you fellows, and why this private room? I was always in a ward before."

Said one of the visitors, "We're giving you a treatment for alcoholism."

Hopelessness was written large on the man's face as he replied,

342

"Oh, but that's no use. Nothing would fix me. I'm a goner. The last three times, I got drunk on the way home from here. I'm afraid to go out the door. I can't understand it."

For an hour, the two friends told him about their drinking experiences. Over and over, he would say: "That's me. That's me. I drink like that."

The **man in the bed** was told of the acute poisoning from which he suffered, how it deteriorates the body of an alcoholic and warps his mind. There was much talk about the mental state preceding the first drink.

> The man in the bed was Bill Dotson, living in Kenmore, Ohio. He was a lawyer born in Carlisle County, KY located in the southwest corner of the state. He started drinking on his farm at age fifteen. After graduating from the University of Kentucky, he served in the Army during World War I. He took night classes at the Akron Law School and was admitted to the Ohio bar in 1926.

> His sobriety date was June 26, 1935, making him A.A member number three following Dr. Bob, and was the first person other than Bill W. and Dr. Bob to stay sober in A.A. without a slip. Bill never submitted his story for the first edition Big Book for unclear reasons, and he died in Cleveland at age 62 from a heart attack in September, 1954.

"Yes, that' me," said the sick man, "the very image. You fellows know your stuff all right, but I don't see what good it'll do. You fellows are somebody. I was once, but I'm a nobody now. From what you tell me, I know more than ever I can't stop." At this both the visitors burst into a laugh. Said the future Fellow Anonymous: "Damn little to laugh about that I can see."

The two friends spoke of their spiritual experience and told him about the course of action they carried out.

He interrupted: "I used to be strong for the church, but that won't fix it. I've prayed to God on hangover mornings and sworn that I'd never touch another drop but by nine o'clock I'd be boiled as an owl."

Next day found the prospect more receptive. He had been thinking it over. "Maybe you're right," he said. "God ought to be able to do anything." Then he added, "He sure didn't do much for me when I was trying to fight this booze racket alone."

On the third day the lawyer gave his life to the care and direction of his Creator, and said he was perfectly willing to do anything necessary. His wife came, scarcely daring to be hopeful, though she thought she saw something different about her husband already. He had begun to have a spiritual experience.

That afternoon he put on his clothes and walked from the hospital a free man. He entered a political campaign, making speeches, frequenting men's gathering places of all sorts, often staying up all night. He lost the race by only a narrow margin. But he had found God—and in finding God had found himself.

That was in June, 1935. He never drank again. He too, has become a respected and useful member of his community. He has helped other men recover, and is a power in the church from which he was long absent.

So, you see, **there were three alcoholics in that town, who now felt they had to give to others what they had found, or be sunk**. After several failures to find others, a **fourth** turned up. He came through an acquaintance who had heard the good news. He proved to be a **devil-may-care young fellow** whose parents could not make out whether he wanted to stop drinking or not.

They were deeply religious people, much shocked by their son's refusal to have anything to do with the church. He suffered horribly from his sprees, but it seemed as if nothing could be done for him. He consented, however, to go to the hospital, where he occupied the very room recently vacated by the lawyer.

He had three visitors [Bill W., Dr. Bob, Bill Dotson]. After a bit, he said, "The way you fellows put this spiritual stuff makes sense. I'm ready to do business. I guess the old folks were right after all." So one more was added to the Fellowship.

In Akron, A.A. number four, Ernie Galbraith, the "devil may care young chap," had enlisted for a one year tour in the Army when he was only fourteen. After getting out of the Army he went to Mexico where he worked for an oil company, then rode the range in Texas. He had been married twice and had a son. After returning to Akron he had trouble holding a job because of his drinking.

He married Dr. Bob's daughter Sue in 1941, against Bob's wishes. Sue liked Ernie, but he later turned out to be trouble and relapsed frequently. They were married 24 years and had two children, a son Mickey and daughter Bonna, before divorcing in 1965. Ernie remarried, achieving some periods of sobriety after 1946.

In 1969, Bonna shot herself, after first killing her six-year old daughter. She was twenty-three years old at the time of her death. Sue claims that Bonna was an alcoholic and was also using "diet pills."

Ernie died two years later in 1971, after which Sue married her childhood sweetheart, Ray Windows, who died in 1989.

Ernie's story, "The Seven Month Slip" was in the first edition of the Big Book. http://the12traditions.com/174/ernie-g-aa-4/

In Toledo, Ohio there was *another* Ernie G. named Ernie Gerig who got sober in 1939 in Akron. He helped start A.A. in Toledo in 1940, and was married to Ruth G.

http://silkworth.net/aagrowth/oh_Toledo_Ohio.html

Don't get these two Ernie G.'s mixed up.

All this time our friend of the hotel lobby incident remained in that town. He was there three months. He now returned home, leaving behind his first acquaintances, the lawyer and the devil-may-care chap. These men had found something brand new in life.

Though **they knew they must help other alcoholics if they would remain sober**, that motive became secondary. It was transcended by the happiness they found in giving themselves for others. They shared their homes, their slender resources, and gladly devoted their spare hours to fellow-sufferers. They were willing, by day or night, to place a new man in the hospital and visit him afterward. They grew in numbers. They experienced a few distressing failures, but in those cases they made an effort to bring the man's family into a spiritual way of living, thus relieving much worry and suffering.

A year and six months later these three had succeeded with seven more. Seeing much of each other, scarce an evening passed that someone's home did not shelter a little gathering of men and women, happy in their release, and constantly thinking how they might present their discovery to some newcomer. In addition to these casual get-togethers, it became customary to set apart one night a week for a meeting to be attended by anyone or everyone interested in a spiritual way of life. Aside from fellowship and sociability, the prime object was to provide a time and place where new people might bring their problems.

The "seven more" newcomers were probably:

1) Ernie Gailbraith - Akron, July 1935 (The Seven Month Slip); relapsed at seven months.

2) Hank Parkhurst - New York, September 1935 (The Unbeliever); relapsed in Sept 1939.

3) Phil Smith - Akron, September 1935.

4) John Henry "Fitz" Mayo - New York, October 1935 (Our Southern Friend).

5) Harold Grisinger - Akron, January 1936.

6) Walter Bray - Akron, February 1936 (The Back-Slider).

7) Joe Doeppler - Akron, April 1936 (The European Drinker).

Outsiders became interested. One man and his wife placed their large home at the disposal of this strangely assorted crowd. This couple has since become so fascinated that they have dedicated their home to the work. Many a distracted wife has visited this house to find loving and understanding companionship among women who knew her problem, to hear from the lips of their husbands what had happened to them, to be advised how her own wayward mate might be hospitalized and approached when next he stumbled.

> In the summer of 1935, alcoholics in Akron began meeting on Wednesday nights at an Oxford Group couple's house belonging to T. Henry and Clarace Williams at 876 Palisades Drive. The Williams' were not alcoholic.

> T. Henry was an engineer at the company where Bill W. unsuccessfully waged that proxy battle to gain control of tire-maker National Rubber Machinery in May of 1935. The company was founded in 1928 and located at 917 Swietzer Ave, Akron, Ohio. In 1942 they switched from making machinery for the rubber industry to machinery for the plastic industry.

> After the Akron alcoholics left the Oxford Group in October of 1939, they moved their meetings to Dr. Bob's house at 855 Ardmore Avenue until January 1940, when the meetings became so large they moved again to the King School at 805 Memorial Parkway, and were designated A.A. Group #1.

Many a man, yet dazed from his hospital experience, has stepped over the threshold of that home into freedom. Many an alcoholic who entered there came away with an answer. He succumbed to that gay crowd inside, who laughed at their own misfortunes and understood his. Impressed by those who visited him at the hospital, he capitulated entirely when, later, in an upper room of this house, he heard the story of some man whose experience closely tallied with his own. The expression on the faces of the women, that indefinable something in the eyes of the men, the stimulating and electric atmosphere of the place, conspired to let him know that here was haven at last.

Early A.A. meetings in Akron were very different than they are today. They were based on the Oxford Group Christian meeting format, which consisted of prayer, quiet time, and a reading from a Bible devotional. The leader would then give witness by telling about his or her past life and what God had done for them. Witnessing lasted about thirty minutes, then the leader would open the floor to those in attendance. Those present would raise their hands; the leader would call upon them, and then they too would give witness.

Once alcoholics left the Oxford Group in Akron, A.A. members were expected to show up every day, six days a week, at Dr. Bob's house in the morning for a short service led by Dr. Bob's wife Anne, based on a reading from the Southern Methodist meditational booklet called *The Upper Room*, together with coffee and discussion as to how everyone was getting along.

At least once a week alcoholics would also meet in the evening, when everyone would sit around in the kitchen or living room and talk about any problems they had and ask for help and suggestions.

An A.A. member could also drop by Dr. Bob's office at any time and talk with him one-on-one.

http://hindsfoot.org/aameet.pdf

The very practical approach to his problems, the absence of intolerance of any kind, the informality, the genuine democracy, the uncanny understanding which these people had were irresistible. He and his wife would leave elated by the thought of what they could now do for some stricken acquaintance and his family. They knew they had a host of new friends; it seemed they had known these strangers always. They had seen miracles, and one was to come to them. **They had visioned the Great Reality—their loving and All Powerful Creator**.

Now, this house will hardly accommodate its weekly visitors, for they number sixty or eighty as a rule. Alcoholics are being attracted from far and near. From surrounding towns, families drive long distances to be present. A community thirty miles away [Cleveland] has fifteen fellows of Alcoholics Anonymous. Being a large place, we think that someday its Fellowship will number many hundreds. [Written in 1939]

> Estimates of A.A. membership in 2017 were 2.1 million members in more than 120,000 A.A. groups, residing in 180 countries worldwide.

But life among Alcoholics Anonymous is more than attending gatherings and visiting hospitals. Cleaning up old scrapes, helping to settle family differences, explaining the disinherited son to his irate parents, lending money and securing jobs for each other, when justified—these are everyday occurrences. **No one is too discredited or has sunk too low to be welcomed cordially—if he means business**. Social distinctions, petty rivalries and jealousies —these are laughed out of countenance. Being wrecked in the same vessel, being restored and united under one God, with hearts and minds attuned to the welfare of others, the things which matter so much to some people no longer signify much to them. How could they?

> "Meaning business" technically means we have the desire to stop drinking, which is our third Tradition, and we are welcome in A.A.

> My experience has shown me that there are many reasons alcoholics come into our rooms and end up sober, and not all of them had any initial desire to stop drinking. Those folks were just looking for any way out of their alcoholic nightmare.

> Experience suggests most folks come into A.A. for one of two reasons: 1) The alcohol has stopped working. They drink and drink but can no longer get drunk. All the emotions they hate and fear remain, regardless of how much booze they pour on them. Blackouts are their only relief. 2) The consequences of their drinking have forced them into the rooms.

Consequences may arise from the courts who have ordered A.A. attendance in lieu of incarceration. They may come from employers as a condition of job retention, or they may come from spouses or family members who threaten to leave the alcoholic if they don't seek care.

Regardless of the reasons folks end in up in A.A., a certain number do get and stay sober. The reason anyone comes into A.A. doesn't matter; what matters is if are they willing to do the 12 Step work and become deeply engaged in the Fellowship and service work. If they are, they have a good chance of remaining sober and finding a new life.

Under only slightly different conditions, the same thing is taking place in many eastern cities. In one of these there is a well-known hospital for the treatment of alcoholic and drug addiction [Charles Towns Hospital, 293 Central Park West, New York City]. Six years ago one of our number was a patient there [Bill W.]. Many of us have felt, for the first time, the Presence and Power of God within its walls. We are greatly indebted to the doctor in attendance there [William Silkworth M.D.], for he, although it might prejudice his own work, has told us of his belief in ours.

Every few days this doctor suggests our approach to one of his patients. Understanding our work, he can do this with an eye to selecting those who are willing and able to recover on a spiritual basis. Many of us, former patients, go there to help. Then, in this eastern city [New York], there are informal meetings such as we have described to you, where you may now see scores of members. There are the same fast friendships, there is the same helpfulness to one another as you find among our western [Akron] friends. There is a good bit of travel between East and West and we foresee a great increase in this helpful interchange.

Some day we hope that every alcoholic who journeys will find a Fellowship of Alcoholics Anonymous at his destination. To some extent this is already true. Some of us are salesmen and go about.

Little clusters of twos and threes and fives of us have sprung up in other communities, through contact with our two larger centers. Those of us who travel drop in as often as we can. This practice enables us to lend a hand, at the same time avoiding certain alluring distractions of the road, about which any traveling man can inform you.

Thus we grow. And so can you, though you be but one man with this book in your hand. We believe and hope it contains all you will need to begin.

We know what you are thinking. You are saying to yourself: "I'm jittery and alone. I couldn't do that." But you can. You forget that **you have just now tapped a source of power much greater than yourself**. To duplicate, with such backing, what we have accomplished is only a matter of willingness, patience and labor.

We know of an A.A. member who was living in a large community [Hank Parkhurst from Montclair, New Jersey]. He had lived there but a few weeks when he found that the place probably contained more alcoholics per square mile than any city in the country. This was only a few days ago at this writing (1939). The authorities were much concerned. He got in touch with a prominent psychiatrist [Dr. Howard of Montclair, New Jersey] who had undertaken certain responsibilities for the mental health of the community. The doctor proved to be able and exceedingly anxious to adopt any workable method of handling the situation. So he inquired, what did our friend have on the ball?

Our friend proceeded to tell him. And with such good effect that the doctor agreed to a test among his patients and certain other alcoholics from a clinic which he attends. Arrangements were also made with the chief psychiatrist of a large public hospital to select still others from the stream of misery which flows through that institution [Dr. Russel E. Blaisdell of Rockland State Hospital near Orangeburg, New York. He attended the Rockefeller Dinner on February 8, 1940].

So our fellow worker will soon have friends galore. Some of them may sink and perhaps never get up, but if our experience is a criterion, more than half of those approached will become fellows of

Alcoholics Anonymous. When a few men in this city have found themselves, and have discovered the joy of helping others to face life again, there will be no stopping until everyone in that town has had his opportunity to recover—if he can and will.

Still you may say: "But I will not have the benefit of contact with you who wrote this book." We cannot be sure. God will determine that, so you must remember that your real reliance is always upon Him. He will show you how to create the fellowship you crave.

Our book is meant to be suggestive only. We realize we know only a little. God will constantly disclose more to you and to us. **Ask** Him in your morning meditation **what you can do each day for the man who is still sick. The answers will come, if your own house is in order. But obviously you cannot transmit something you haven't got**. See to it that your relationship with Him is right, and great events will come to pass for you and countless others. This is the **Great Fact** for us.

Abandon yourself to God as you understand God. Admit your faults to Him and to your fellows. Clear away the wreckage of your past. Give freely of what you find and join us. **We shall be with you** in the **Fellowship of the Spirit**, and you will surely meet some of us as you trudge the **Road of Happy Destiny**.

May God bless you and keep you—until then.

> The first 164 pages of the Big Book describes how Bill Wilson got sober through the Fellowship of A.A., God, and the 12 Step program. The Big Book is suggestive, since no one can force us to accept its tenants.
>
> Simply reading this book will do little to release us from our addiction; it will not result in recovery. The Great Fact is that we need to undergo some type of transformative spiritual experience or spiritual awakening, which is a change in our attitudes and actions sufficient enough to bring about our recovery from alcoholism. We must then carry the message to

other alcoholics that A.A. can help any alcoholic recover from our hopeless state of mind and body.

Bill W. experienced a religious transformation by being struck God-conscious. If Bill had done nothing else after his hot flash event in Towns Hospital in December of 1934, A.A. would not exist today. Bill may have remained sober for the rest of his life, but the rest of us would have been on our own.

Another Great Fact for A.A. is that Bill was the perfect example of suffering transmuted into a prescription for personal recovery. Bill transformed his personal experience into a step-by-step guide that any alcoholic can use to seek a new, sober way of life. He laid out a simple, but not easy, 12 Step program, supported by a Fellowship of similar sufferers, that can free us from the obsession to drink and start us down that Broad Highway to peace and serenity.

In Appendix II, Bill reassured us that even if we did not have a sudden, personal religious or spiritual experience as he did, we can still get better in A.A. We can undergo that slow spiritual awakening as our brains heal and we get honest with ourselves. Honesty results in a willingness to examine and clean up our past as best as we can, so we can put it behind us forever, except to use as an example of what we were like when we share our story with other alcoholics.

Making amends for yesterday's wrongs allows us to live in this day, without fear of what tomorrow may bring. The practice of a daily personal inventory keeps us anchored in the present. Prayer and meditation, however we define and use it, allows us to connect and employ whatever non-human, religious or spiritual motivating force we believe in to help guide us through life. Sharing what we have learned and experienced during recovery with our fellow sufferers keeps us from becoming bogged down in selfishness and self-centeredness, which is the root of all our troubles.

A.A. allows us to grasp the hand of those that reach out to us for help, and by doing so, we help ourselves and all those around us.

A.A. is no success story in the ordinary sense of the word. It is a story of suffering transmuted, under grace, into spiritual progress. [As Bill Sees It, Suffering Transmuted, p.35]

BIG BOOK STORIES

There have been four editions of the Big Book: 1939, 1955, 1976 and 2001. In the second half of the fourth edition of *Alcoholics Anonymous*, there are 388 pages containing forty-two personal stories of alcoholics who joined A.A. For each edition, some of the stories in the back were replaced, usually because the author later relapsed, or simply to add more contemporary narratives to the mix.

Most of the personal stories describe how the destitute alcoholic found A.A., and in doing so found God and sobriety. Those religious and spiritual eruptions are moving, but unfortunately, little is shared in the stories on the intense effort required for sobriety, which is the hands on labor required to fully complete the 12 Step program, become passionately integrated into the A.A. Fellowship, begin sponsoring other alcoholics, and preforming A.A. group service work.

Part I -- Pioneers of A.A.

Contains ten stories showing that sobriety can be lasting.

Doctor Bob's Nightmare. The co-founder of Alcoholics Anonymous. The birth of our Society dates from his first day of permanent sobriety, June 10, 1935.

1) Alcoholic Anonymous Number Three

Pioneer member of Akron's Group No. 1, the first A.A. group in the world. He kept the faith; therefore, he and countless others found a new life. Bill Dotson was the author, and was A.A. #3 in Akron.

2) Gratitude in Action

The story of Dave Bancroft, one of the founders of A.A. in Montreal, Quebec, Canada in 1944.

3) Women Suffer Too

Despite great opportunities, alcohol nearly ended her life. An early member, she spread the word among women in our pioneering period.

The author was Marty Mann, who founded the National Council on Alcoholism.

4) Our Southern Friend

Pioneer A.A. minister's son and Southern farmer, he asked, "Who am I to say there is no God?" The author was John Henry Fitzhugh (Fitz) Mayo, A.A. #3 in New York City.

5) The Vicious Cycle

How it finally broke a Southerner's obstinacy and destined this salesman to start A.A. in Philadelphia. The author was Jim Burwell, the New York atheist credited with the use of "God as we understood Him" in the 12 Steps. He founded groups in Philadelphia and Baltimore.

6) Jim's Story

This physician, one of the earliest members of A.A.'s first black group, tells of how freedom came as he worked among his people. The author was Dr. Jim Scott, who founded A.A.'s first African-American group in Washington, D.C. in 1940.

7) The Man Who Mastered Fear

He spent eighteen years running away, and then found he didn't have to run. So he started A.A. in Detroit. The author was Archie Trowbridge, founder of A.A. in Detroit.

8) He Sold Himself Short

But he found there was a Higher Power that had more faith in him than he had in himself. Thus, A.A. was born in Chicago. The author was Earl Treat, founder of A.A. in Chicago.

9) The Keys of the Kingdom

This worldly lady helped to develop A.A. in Chicago and thus passed her keys to many. The author was Sylvia Kauffmann, and she helped Earl Treat expand A.A. in Chicago.

Part II -- They Stopped In Time

Contains seventeen stories which may help us decide whether we are alcoholic and if A.A. is for us.

1) The Missing Link

He looked at everything as the cause of his unhappiness—except alcohol. Author unknown.

2) Fear of Fear

This lady was cautious. She decided she wouldn't let herself go in her drinking. And she would never, never take that morning drink! The author was Ceil Mansfield from New York City.

3) The Housewife Who Drank at Home

She hid her bottles in clothes hampers and dresser drawers. In A.A., she discovered she had lost nothing and had found everything. Author unknown.

4) Physician, Heal Thyself!

Psychiatrist and surgeon, he had lost his way until he realized that God, not he, was the Great Healer. Author unknown.

5) My Chance to Live

A.A. gave this teenager the tools to climb out of her dark abyss of despair. Author unknown.

6) Student of Life

Living at home with her parents, she tried using willpower to beat the obsession to drink. But it wasn't until she met another alcoholic and went to an A.A. meeting that sobriety took hold. Author unknown.

7) Crossing the River of Denial

She finally realized that when she enjoyed her drinking, she couldn't control it, and when she controlled it, she couldn't enjoy it. Author unknown.

8) Because I'm an Alcoholic

This drinker finally found the answer to her nagging question, "Why?" Author unknown.

9) It Might Have Been Worse

Alcohol was a looming cloud in this banker's bright sky. With rare foresight he realized it could become a tornado. The author was Chet Rude, who was an executive at a large Midwest bank.

10) Tightrope

Trying to navigate separate worlds was a lonely charade that ended when this gay alcoholic finally landed in A.A. Author unknown.

11) Flooded With Feeling

When a barrier to God collapsed, this self-described agnostic was at Step Three. Author unknown.

12) Winner Takes All

Legally blind but no longer alone, she found a way to stay sober, raise a family, and turn her life over to the care of God. Author unknown.

13) Me an Alcoholic?

Alcohol's wringer squeezed this author—but he escaped quite whole. Author unknown.

14) The Perpetual Quest

This lawyer tried psychiatrists, biofeedback, relaxation exercises, and a host of other techniques to control her drinking. She finally found a solution, uniquely tailored, in the Twelve Steps. Author unknown.

15) A Drunk, Like You

The more he listened at meetings, the more he came to know about his own drinking history. Author unknown.

16) Acceptance Was the Answer

The physician wasn't hooked, he thought—he just prescribed drugs medically indicated for his many ailments. Acceptance was his key to liberation. The author was Dr. Paul Ohliger from Laguna Niguel, California.

17) Window of Opportunity

This young alcoholic stepped out a second-story window and into A.A. Author unknown.

PART III -- They Lost Nearly All

Contains fifteen stories of those who believed their drinking was hopeless, but they found hope in A.A.

The fifteen stories in this group tell of alcoholism at its miserable worst. Many tried everything—hospitals, special treatments, sanitariums, asylums, and jails. Nothing worked. Loneliness, great physical and mental agony—these were the common lot. Most had taken shattering losses on nearly every front of life. Some went on trying to live with alcohol. Others wanted to die.

Alcoholism had respected nobody, neither rich nor poor, learned nor unlettered. All found themselves headed for the same destruction, and it seemed they could do nothing whatever to stop it.

Now sober for years, they tell us how they got well. They prove to almost anyone's satisfaction that it's never too late to try Alcoholics Anonymous.

1) My Bottle, My Resentments, and Me

From childhood trauma to skid row drunk, this hobo finally found a Higher Power, bringing sobriety and a long-lost family. Author unknown.

2) He Lived Only to Drink

I had been preached to, analyzed, cursed, and counseled, but no one had ever said, I identify with what's going on with you. It happened to me and this is what I did about it. Author unknown.

3) Safe Haven

This A.A. found that the process of discovering who he really was began with knowing who he didn't want to be. Author unknown.

4) Listening to the Wind

It took an angel to introduce this Native American woman to A.A. and recovery. Author unknown.

5) Twice Gifted

Diagnosed with cirrhosis, this sick alcoholic got sobriety—plus a lifesaving liver transplant. Author unknown.

6) Building a New Life

Hallucinating and restrained by sheriff's deputies and hospital staff, this once-happy family man received an unexpected gift from God—a firm foundation in sobriety that would hold up through good times and bad. Author unknown.

7) On the Move

Working the A.A. program showed this alcoholic how to get from geographics to gratitude. The author was Bob K. from Concord, California.

8) A Vision of Recovery

A feeble prayer forged a lasting connection with a Higher Power for this Micmac Indian [Mi'kmaq Indian Nation]. Author unknown.

9) Gutter Bravado

Alone and unemployable, he was given two options by the court, get help or go to jail, and his journey toward teachability began. Author unknown.

10) Empty on the Inside

She grew up around A.A. and had all the answers—except when it came to her own life. The author was Beth H. from Cincinnati, Ohio.

11) Grounded

Alcohol clipped this pilot's wings until sobriety and hard work brought him back to the sky. The author was Lyle Prouse from Conyers, Georgia.

12) Another Chance

Poor, black, totally ruled by alcohol, she felt shut away from any life worth living. But when she began a prison sentence, a door opened. The author was Bertha V. from Louisville, Kentucky.

13) A Late Start

It's been ten years since I retired, seven years since I joined A.A. Now I can truly say that I am a grateful alcoholic. Author unknown.

14) Freedom From Bondage

Young when she joined, this A.A. believes her serious drinking was the result of even deeper defects. She here tells how she was set free. The author was Wynn Corum from California.

15) A.A. Taught Him to Handle Sobriety

God willing, we may never again have to deal with drinking, but we have to deal with sobriety every day. The author was Bob P. from Connecticut.

As an alcoholic physician who practiced general internal medicine before I retired, I could easily relate to many aspects of Dr. Bob's story.

*Dr. **Robert Holbrooke Smith**, a co-founder of Alcoholics Anonymous. The birth of our Society dates from his first day of permanent sobriety, June 10, 1935. To 1950, the year of his death, he **carried the A.A. message to more than 5,000 alcoholic men and women**, and to all these he gave his medical services without thought of charge. In this prodigy of service, he was well assisted by **Sister Ignatia** at St. Thomas Hospital in Akron, Ohio, one of the greatest friends our Fellowship will ever know.*

The first thing that struck me when reading this introduction to Dr. Bob's story, originally titled "The Doctor's Nightmare," was that it was highly unlikely Dr. Bob personally met and worked one-on-one with 5,000 alcoholics over 15 years. If he did, it meant he counseled one brand new alcoholic every single day for the rest of his life, an unlikely scenario.

Common sense suggests that Dr. Bob oversaw and spoke with multiple groups of alcoholics who had been admitted at Akron City Hospital and St. Thomas Hospital, which may well have numbered in the thousands.

Dr. Bob would not have been able to spread the A.A. word as widely as he claims without the help of Sister Ignatia, who was previously a music teacher in the Cleveland school system before she joined the hospital ministry. At St. Thomas Hospital, she became the admissions officer, and on August 16, 1939, Dr. Bob persuaded her to officially admit their first alcoholic patient, Walter B., to St. Thomas.

June 10, 1935 is referred to as the founding date of A.A. since it was the date of Dr. Bob's last drink. However, American Medical Association records of the convention Dr. Bob attended indicated the convention started on June 10 of that year, so that the true date of Dr. Bob's last drink and the birth of A.A. was likely one week later, on June 17, 1935.

I was born in a small New England village of about seven thousand souls.

Dr. Bob was born on August 8, 1879 in St. Johnsbury, Vermont, which is 120 miles northeast of East Dorset, Vermont, the birthplace of A.A.'s other co-founder Bill Wilson, who was born on November 26, 1895.

The general **moral standard** was, as I recall it, far above the average. No beer or liquor was sold in the neighborhood, except at the State liquor agency where perhaps one might procure a pint if he could convince the agent that he really needed it. Without this proof the expectant purchaser would be forced to depart empty handed with none of what I later came to believe was the great panacea for all human ills. Men who had liquor shipped in from Boston or New York by express were looked upon with great distrust and disfavor by most of the good townspeople. The **town was well supplied with churches and schools** in which I pursued my early educational activities.

My father was a professional man of recognized ability [a judge] and **both my father and mother were most active in church affairs** [North St. Johnsbury Congregational Church]. Both father and mother were considerably above the average in intelligence.

Unfortunately for me **I was the only child**, which perhaps **engendered the selfishness** which played such an important part in bringing on my alcoholism.

From childhood through high school I was more or less **forced to go to church**, Sunday School and evening service, Monday night Christian Endeavor and sometimes to Wednesday evening prayer meeting. This had the effect of **making me resolve** that when I was free from parental domination, **I would never again darken the doors of a church**. This resolution I kept steadfastly for the next forty years, except when circumstances made it seem unwise to absent myself.

Like Dr. Bob, I was a selfish and self-centered only child forced by my parents to attend multiple church functions several times a week to augment their personal community and business standing. My parent's Episcopal church attendance had little to do with the love of God or religion; it was all about my father making corporate business contacts and my mother's social climbing fixation.

I hated having to dress up in a suit and tie to attend church, but I had no distaste for God, simply because I never, ever believed in God. Despite my best efforts, I could not force myself to believe in some imaginary friend that I couldn't connect with or comprehend.

Like Dr. Bob, I vowed never to return to church after I was able to leave home, and I've kept that promise to this day.

After high school [St. Johnsbury Academy, 1898] came four years in **one of the best colleges** in the country where drinking seemed to be a major extra-curricular activity [Dartmouth University, 1899 to 1902]. Almost everyone seemed to do it. I did it more and more, and had lots of fun without much grief, either physical or financial. I seemed to be able to snap back the next morning better than most of my fellow drinkers, who were cursed (or perhaps blessed) with a great deal of morning-after nausea. Never once in my life have I had a headache, which fact leads me to believe that I was an alcoholic almost from the start.

My whole life seemed to be centered around doing what I wanted to do, without regard for the rights, wishes, or privileges of anyone else; a state of mind which became more and more predominant as the years passed. I was graduated with "summa cum laude" in the eyes of the drinking fraternity, but not in the eyes of the Dean.

Like Dr. Bob, I was full of selfishness and self-centeredness. I wanted my own way all the time, and when I didn't get it I became angry and drank.

364

My first alcoholic blackout occurred while attending one of the best colleges in the country, the Ivy League University of Pennsylvania in Philadelphia. It happened during sophomore year, and it scared me sober since I knew if I continued my hard drinking I would never be able to achieve a high enough grade point average to get into medical school.

Fortunately, at that point in my drinking career, I was able to successfully cut back on my drinking enough to graduate with honors.

The next three years I spent in Boston, Chicago, and Montreal in the employ of a large manufacturing concern, selling railway supplies, gas engines of all sorts, and many other items of heavy hardware. During these years, I drank as much as my purse permitted, still without paying too great a penalty, although I was beginning to have morning "jitters" at times. I lost only a half day's work during these three years.

My next move was to take up the **study of medicine**, entering one of the largest universities in the country [University of Michigan, 1905 to 1907].

There I took up the business of drinking with much greater earnestness than I had previously shown. On account of my enormous capacity for beer, I was elected to membership in one of the drinking societies, and soon became one of the leading spirits. Many mornings I have gone to classes, and even though fully prepared, would turn and walk back to the fraternity house because of my jitters, not daring to enter the classroom for fear of making a scene should I be called on for recitation.

This went from bad to worse until sophomore spring when, after a prolonged period of drinking, I made up my mind that I could not complete my course, so I packed my grip and went South and spent a month on a large farm owned by a friend of mine. When I got the fog out of my brain, I decided that quitting school was very foolish and that I had better return and continue my work. When I reached school, I discovered the faculty had other ideas on the subject.

After much argument they allowed me to return and take my exams, all of which I passed creditably. But they were much disgusted and told me they would attempt to struggle along without my presence. After many painful discussions, **they finally gave me my credits** and I **migrated to another of the leading universities of the country** and entered as a Junior that Fall [Rush Medical University, where Dr. Bob graduated in 1910].

There my drinking became so much worse that the boys in the fraternity house where I lived felt forced to send for my father, who made a long journey in the vain endeavor to get me straightened around. This had little effect however, for I kept on drinking and used a great deal more hard liquor than in former years.

Coming up to final exams I went on a particularly strenuous spree. When I went in to write the examinations, my hand trembled so I could not hold a pencil. I passed in at least three absolutely blank books. I was, of course, soon on the carpet and the upshot was that I had to go back for two more quarters and remain absolutely dry, if I wished to graduate. This I did, and proved myself satisfactory to the faculty, both in deportment and scholastically.

I conducted myself so creditably that **I was able to secure a much coveted internship** in a western city [Akron, OH], where I spent two years. During these two years I was kept so busy that I hardly left the hospital at all. Consequently, I could not get into any trouble.

> Dr. Bob began drinking in his late teens and had progressed into full blown alcoholism by his early thirties. Bill W., on the other hand, began drinking at age 21 and was an alcoholic within seven years.
>
> Unlike Bill, given sufficient reason as a hard drinker, Dr. Bob was able to control his drinking until he completed his medical training.
>
> My story was the same. I remained a heavy, hard drinker, but drank only after all my scholastic work was done and never drank when I was on duty in medical training.

366

When those two years were up, I **opened an office downtown** [157 S. Main Street, Akron; practiced colorectal surgery]. Then I had some money, all the time in the world, and considerable stomach trouble. I soon discovered that **a couple of drinks would alleviate my gastric distress**, at least for a few hours at a time, so it was not at all difficult for me to **return to my former excessive indulgence**.

> When I entered private medical practice outside of Boston, Massachusetts, I drank fairly heavily after work to relieve the stress of the day and help me sleep at night. At no time did I drink before or during work, because I feared harming my patients if I did not remain clear-headed. My physical condition did not suffer, other than having a few minor hangovers from time to time.

By this time **I was beginning to pay very dearly physically** and, in hope of relief, voluntarily **incarcerated myself at least a dozen times in one of the local sanitariums** [Fair Oaks Villa, Cuyahoga Falls, Ohio]. I was **between Scylla and Charybdis** now, because if I did not drink my stomach tortured me, and if I did, my nerves did the same thing.

> All alcoholics know of the dilemma of not wanting to drink but having to drink. It's like being caught between a rock and a hard place, or caught between the devil and the deep blue sea. No matter which choice we make, we are in trouble.
>
> Scylla is the geographic name of a small finger of land on the Italian coast, which projects into the Strait of Messina, and sits opposite the Sicilian coast. In between is a treacherous whirlpool named Charybdis.
>
> In Homer's *The Odyssey*, when Ulysses sailed through this narrow passageway avoiding the danger of the whirlpool, Scylla, a female monster with twelve feet and six heads, managed to snatch and kill six of his sailors.

After three years of this, I wound up in the local hospital [People's Hospital] where they attempted to help me, but I would get my friends to smuggle me a quart, or I would steal the alcohol about the building, so that I got rapidly worse.

Finally my father had to send a doctor out from my home town who managed to get me back there some way and I was in bed about two months before I could venture out of the house. I stayed about town a couple of months more and **returned to resume my practice**. I think I must have been thoroughly **scared by what had happened**, or by the doctor, or probably both, so that **I did not touch a drink again until the country went dry**.

With the **passing of the Eighteenth Amendment** [Prohibition in 1919] I felt quite safe. I knew everyone would buy a few bottles, or cases, of liquor as their exchequers permitted, and it would soon be gone. Therefore it would make no great difference, even if I should do some drinking. At that time I was not aware of the almost unlimited supply the government made it possible for us doctors to obtain, neither had I any knowledge of the bootlegger who soon appeared on the horizon. **I drank with moderation at first, but it took me only a relatively short time to drift back into the old habits** which had wound up so disastrously before.

During the next few years, I developed **two distinct phobias**. One was the **fear of not sleeping**, and the other was the **fear of running out of liquor**. Not being a man of means, I knew that if I did not stay sober enough to earn money, I would run out of liquor. Most of the time, therefore, **I did not take the morning drink which I craved so badly, but instead would fill up on large doses of sedatives** to quiet the jitters, which distressed me terribly.

It is ironic that one often uses alcohol to stop alcohol's withdrawal side effects. If I stopped drinking at midnight I would often wake up with the shakes about three hours later as my blood alcohol levels fell. This required I ingest more alcohol, so at the end of the day I couldn't go more than a few hours without drinking some amount of liquor. Since liquor worked, I never needed to use sedatives or other drugs for my withdrawal symptoms.

Alcohol addiction was a cruel master, and by the time I had full blown alcoholism I had already stopped practicing medicine and taken on a medical consulting business unrelated to direct patient care. My fear of harming patients while drunk no longer existed, so I stayed employed as long as I could, eventually drinking around the clock, both at work and at home.

Of note, the most common sedative in use during the 1930s were the notoriously addictive barbiturates. Barbital was synthesized and introduced in 1903 under the brand name Veronal, and phenobarbital was introduced in 1912. Barbiturates were routinely and copiously prescribed by doctors to help people sleep, to treat their anxiety, to help control socially unruly people, and for many other psychiatric conditions.

Occasionally, I would yield to the morning craving, but if I did, it would be only a few hours before I would be quite unfit for work. This would lessen my chances of smuggling some home that evening, which in turn would mean a night of futile tossing around in bed followed by a morning of unbearable jitters. During the subsequent fifteen years **I had sense enough never to go to the hospital if I had been drinking**, and very seldom did I receive patients. I would sometimes hide out in one of the clubs of which I was a member, and had the habit at times of registering at a hotel under a fictitious name. But my friends usually found me and I would go home if they promised that I should not be scolded.

If my wife was planning to go out in the afternoon, I **would get a large supply of liquor and smuggle it home and hide it** in the coal bin, the clothes chute, over door jambs, over beams in the cellar and in cracks in the cellar tile. I also made use of old trunks and chests, the old can container, and even the ash container. The water tank on the toilet I never used, because that looked too easy. I found out later that my wife inspected it frequently.

I used to put eight or twelve ounce bottles of alcohol in a fur lined glove and toss it onto the back airing porch when winter days got dark enough. My bootlegger had hidden alcohol at the back steps where I could get it at my convenience. Sometimes I would bring it in my pockets, but they were inspected, and that became too risky. I used also to put it up in four ounce bottles and stick several in my stocking tops. This worked nicely until my wife and I went to see Wallace Beery in "Tugboat Annie," after which the pant-leg and stocking racket were out!

> I was married to three wives during my alcoholic days. All of them knew I drank to excess, so I had no need to hide my bottles. But I did try to hide how much I drank every day, so I would rarely drink in front of them.

> If we were both at home at the same time and it was happy hour time, I would nurse my drink with them, but when they left the room I would guzzle directly from one of the liquor bottles I kept in the pantry. I hoped they would not notice how frequently those bottles disappeared, but I suspect they did.

I will not take space to relate all my **hospital or sanitarium experiences**.

During all this time **we became more or less ostracized by our friends**. We **could not be invited out because I would surely get tight** and my wife dared not invite people in for the same reason. My **phobia for sleeplessness demanded that I get drunk every night**, but in order to get more liquor for the next night, I had to stay sober during the day, at least up to four o' clock. **This routine went on** with few interruptions **for seventeen years**. It was really a horrible nightmare, this earning money, getting liquor, smuggling it home, getting drunk, morning jitters, taking large doses of sedatives to make it possible for me to earn more money, and so on ad nauseam.

I used to promise my wife, my friends, and my children that I would drink no more—promises which seldom kept me sober even through the day, though I was very sincere when I made them.

> Like Dr. Bob, my social life evaporated because I was always drunk. I had to drink before going out to parties so I wouldn't

have to drink so much at the guest's home. Often I'd accidentally end up drunk by the time I arrived, and behaved in embarrassing ways, so I was rarely invited back.

The only friends I invited to my home were hard drinkers and alcoholics. As I became more isolated in my drinking, those invitations stopped. Ironically, several of my hard drinking friends became so concerned over my excessive consumption they suggested I needed to stop drinking and get help.

For the benefit of **those experimentally inclined**, I should mention the **so-called beer experiment**. When beer first came back, I thought that I was safe. I could drink all I wanted of that. It was harmless; nobody ever got drunk on beer. So I filled the cellar full, with the permission of my good wife. It was not long before I was drinking at least a case and a half a day. I put on thirty pounds weight in about two months, looked like a pig, and was uncomfortable from shortness of breath. It then occurred to me that after one was all smelled up with beer nobody could tell what had been drunk, so **I began to fortify my beer with straight alcohol**. Of course, **the result was very bad**, and that ended the beer experiment.

I, too, was experimentally inclined, but in a different way. I decided I would calculate how much alcohol I would need to drink every hour to maintain a modest, but acceptable blood alcohol level. I hated being drunk, but loved that soft, relaxing warmth a small but consistent amount of alcohol could provide.

Armed with a breathalyzer, I tried to correlate varying amounts of hourly alcohol intake against the way I was feeling and my calculated blood alcohol level. Needless to say, my experiment failed because as soon as I took that first drink, I could not regulate how much I drank afterwards.

Although I didn't know it at the time, this was the best evidence for the truth in Step One of my powerlessness over alcohol. Once I took that first drink, that uncontrollable alcoholic craving kicked in, and it was off to the races.

About the time of the beer experiment **I was thrown in with a crowd of people [Oxford Group] who attracted me** because of their seeming poise, health, and happiness. They spoke with great freedom from embarrassment which I could never do, and they seemed very much at ease on all occasions and appeared very healthy. More than these attributes, **they seemed to be happy**.

I was self-conscious and ill at ease most of the time, my health was at the breaking point, and I was thoroughly miserable. I sensed **they had something I did not have**, from which I might readily profit. I learned that **it was something of a spiritual nature**, which did not appeal to me very much, but I thought it could do no harm. I gave the matter much time and study for the next two and a half years, but still got tight every night nevertheless. I **read everything I could find**, and **talked to everyone** who I thought knew anything about it.

My good wife became deeply interested and it was her interest that sustained mine, though I at no time sensed that it might be an answer to my liquor problem. How my wife kept her faith and courage during all those years I'll never know, but she did. If she had not, I know I would have been dead a long time ago. For some reason, we alcoholics seem to have the gift of picking out the world's finest women. Why they should be subjected to the tortures we inflicted upon them, I cannot explain.

> Dr. Bob's description of how he felt among his Oxford Group friends was similar to how I felt when I first walked into the rooms of A.A. Those A.A. folks seems happy *and* sober. They spoke of spiritual matters, and I read up on A.A. and chatted with folks about the Fellowship to learn more.
>
> We must remember there was no A.A. when Dr. Bob originally sought relief from his drinking, and that the formal mission of the Oxford Group was not to help alcoholics. Dr. Bob simply was lucky he found a partial support group for his illness, even though he was unable to stop drinking while active with the Oxfords.

About this time **a lady [Henrietta Seiberling] called up my wife** one Saturday afternoon, **saying she wanted me to come over that evening to meet a friend of hers who might help me**. It was the day before Mother's Day and I had come home plastered, carrying a big potted plant which I set down on the table and forthwith went upstairs and passed out. The next day she called again. Wishing to be polite, though I felt very badly, I said, "**Let's make the call**," and extracted from my wife a promise that **we would not stay over fifteen minutes**.

We entered her house at exactly five o' clock and it was eleven fifteen when we left. I had a couple of shorter talks with this man [Bill W.] afterward, and **stopped drinking abruptly**. This dry spell lasted for about three weeks. Then I went to Atlantic City to attend several days' meeting of a National Society [American Medical Association] of which I was a member. I **drank all the Scotch they had on the train** and bought several quarts on my way to the hotel.

This was on Sunday. I got tight that night, stayed sober Monday till after the dinner and then proceeded to get tight again. I drank all I dared in the bar, and then went to my room to finish the job. Tuesday I started in the morning, getting well organized by noon. I did not want to disgrace myself, so **I then checked out**. I bought some more liquor on the way to the depot. I had to wait some time for the train. **I remember nothing from then on until I woke up at a friend's house** [Lilly, who was Dr Bob's receptionist in his medical practice in Cuyahoga Falls, Ohio], **in a town near home**. These good people notified my wife, who sent my newly-made friend over to get me. He came and got me home and to bed, gave me a few drinks that night, and one bottle of beer the next morning.

That was **June 10, 1935, and that was my last drink**. As I write nearly six years have passed.

The question which might naturally come into your mind would be: "**What did the man do or say that was different from what others had done or said?**" It must be remembered that I had read a great deal and talked to everyone who knew, or thought they knew, anything about the subject of alcoholism. **This man was a man who had experienced many years of frightful drinking**, who had had most all the drunkard's experience known to man, but **who had been cured by** the very means I had been trying to employ, that is to say, **the spiritual approach**. He gave me information about the subject of alcoholism which was undoubtedly helpful.

Of far more importance was the fact that he was the first living human with whom I had ever talked, who knew what he was talking about in regard to alcoholism from actual experience. In other words, **he talked my language**. He knew all the answers, and certainly not because he had picked them up in his reading.

> Despite Dr. Bob's overwhelming desire to stop drinking, his religious background, Bible knowledge, membership in the Oxford Group, stays in rehabilitation facilities, supportive spouse and multiple efforts to stop drinking, he could not.
>
> Then he met Bill W., the only man with whom he could relate and connect with on a personal, emotional and spiritual level concerning his alcoholism. Bill had found a solution, and because of their strong connection and trust, Dr. Bob found hope he could stop drinking for good and recover with Bill's support.
>
> During their initial six hour discussion, Bill made it clear to Dr. Bob that one alcoholic helping another was the key to success. Dr. Bob was keeping Bill sober just as much as Bill was helping Dr. Bob stay sober. This mutual redemption through mutual fellowship forms the unique foundation of A.A.

It is a most wonderful blessing to be relieved of the terrible curse with which I was afflicted. My health is good and I have regained my self-respect and the respect of my colleagues. My home life is ideal and my business is as good as can be expected in these uncertain times.

I spend a great deal of time passing on what I learned to others who want and need it badly. I do it for four reasons:

1. Sense of **duty**.

2. It is a **pleasure**.

3. Because in so doing I am **paying my debt** to the man who took time to pass it on to me.

4. Because every time I do it I take out a little more **insurance for myself against a possible slip**.

> We who have been blessed with recovery through the 12 Step program and the Fellowship of A.A. have the solemn responsibility to pass on our freely given gift. Trying to carry the message of hope and recovery to other alcoholics is not an option. We owe them, and we owe ourselves and those around us the maintenance of our own sobriety, so that we can continue to carry the A.A. message to others.

Unlike most of our crowd, I **did not get over my craving for liquor much during the first two and one-half years** of abstinence. **It was almost always with me**. But at no time have I been anywhere near yielding. I used to get terribly upset when I saw my friends drink and knew I could not, but I schooled myself to believe that though I once had the same privilege, I had abused it so frightfully that it was withdrawn. So it doesn't behoove me to squawk about it, for after all, nobody ever used to throw me down and pour any liquor down my throat.

> Working with other alcoholics was the only thing that kept Dr. Bob sober during the years he was forced to live with his relentless obsession to drink. Why it took so long for his obsession to dissipate is not known, but it did eventually leave him.

> My own obsession did not disappear until after I got a sponsor, completed all the work of the 12 Steps, attended A.A. meetings daily, became active in my Home Group, finished all my amends, developed a personal, secular prayer and meditation daily routine, began sponsoring other alcoholics and tried each day to practice the principles of the 12 Steps. Getting me up to speed in A.A. took place over six months or so.

I do not believe God removed my obsession to drink. My experience has shown me that by following the guidelines of our 12 Step program and doing the recovery work required, anyone's alcoholic obsession will ultimately fade away.

If you think you are an atheist, an agnostic, a skeptic, or have any other form of intellectual pride which keeps you from accepting what is in this book, **I feel sorry for you**. If you still think you are strong enough to beat the game alone, that is your affair. But if you really and truly want to quit drinking liquor for good and all, and sincerely feel that you must have some help, we know that **we have an answer for you**. It never fails if you go about it with one half the zeal you have been in the habit of showing when getting another drink.

Your Heavenly Father will never let you down!

> Just because an alcoholic is atheist or agnostic, it does not mean he or she cannot accept the tenants in the Big Book and recover. It does not mean they don't believe in a spiritual force or power of their own understanding which can help them into sobriety and a wonderful new way of living.
>
> Experience has shown us in A.A. that the power of God is *not* required for recovery, but the recognition that *we aren't God* is, since we're no longer in charge of the universe.
>
> The only two powers I have successfully used during my thirteen years of sobriety with no relapses, are:
>
> 1) The Spiritual Power of A.A.'s Design for Living:
>
> That power emanates from the Big Book and the moral values embedded in the 12 Step principles. I use the intangible and spiritual values of love, tolerance, kindness, forgiveness, willingness, courage, compassion, honesty, integrity and service to others to guide my actions. Daily reflection on these values and applying these principles maintains my spiritual condition.
>
> 2) The People Power of our Fellowship:

376

The human side of A.A. consists of attending meetings, having a sponsor and home group, sponsorship, and service work with other alcoholics.

Doing the next right thing right and treating others as I would like to be treated are my ultimate guidelines. Some call it God's will or the Golden Rule. I call it recovery.

Any and all of us can get sober in A.A., if we're willing to do the work, continue the work, and generously share what we've been so freely given with our fellow sufferers.

APPENDIX II — SPIRITUAL EXPERIENCE

I love all of the Big Book, and all of the Big Book text matters. However, if this appendix had not been added after the first publication of *Alcoholics Anonymous*, I would have fled A.A. as fast as I could after my first few meetings.

The A.A. fellowship in my large, sprawling metropolitan Bible Belt community is deeply religious, although our local members deny it. By religious, I mean that the core message I hear perpetually repeated in our rooms is that "God will get you sober." There is little discussion of any power other than God that can relieve our alcoholism. Attaining god-consciousness through a religious experience is the goal. Little attention is given to any mention of a non-religious Higher Power or any variety of spirituality which does not involve God.

Modest emphasis is devoted to the power of working all of the 12 Steps in sobriety. When the 12 Steps are discussed in my A.A. rooms, praying to God, improving our conscious contact with God, and turning our will and our lives over to God is the primary thrust.

Appendix II states that the personality change sufficient to bring about recovery from alcoholism has manifested itself among us in many different forms, and those forms are either a spiritual experience or a spiritual awakening.

Strictly speaking, in Appendix II a *spiritual experience* is described as a relatively sudden event, lasting only minutes or perhaps a few hours, while a *spiritual awakening* is described as a gradual transformation that can take days, weeks, months or even longer.

In his 1902 book, *The Varieties of Religious Experience*, Dr. William James, known as the Father of American Psychology, wrote that "The only cure for dipsomania [alcoholism] is religiomania." In Appendix II, he calls a spiritual awakening an experience of the "educational variety" because it occurs slowly. Both experiences lead to "that personality change sufficient to bring about recovery from alcoholism."

Although one suspects Bill W. attributed both the spiritual experience and the spiritual awakening as coming directly from God, he does muddy the water by describing a spiritual experience as a sudden "God-consciousness" event, and a spiritual awakening as resulting from "members... tapped an unsuspected inner resource which they presently identify with their own conception of a Power greater than themselves."

This distinction allowed me to simplify the implication and significance of Appendix II. Personally, I think of, and speak of, a spiritual experience as religious based event, and a spiritual awakening as a non-religious event.

My slow spiritual awakening came not from God, but from my completion of the 12 Steps and willingness to try to follow the spiritual principles embedded in those steps.

If my sponsee is religious and believes in God, there is no difficulty in going through the Big Book and 12 Steps with him and speaking of the spiritual experience which comes from God.

If my sponsee does *not* embrace God as his higher power, I can speak of a spiritual awakening, which is a slower, educational variety change which does not mandate a belief in God.

I have never met any alcoholic who did not undergo some degree and type of personality change after completing their 12 Step process, even if they relapsed later.

When I speak with atheists, agnostics and freethinkers in our fellowship, I suggest the source of our personality change, or a slow, educational variety spiritual awakening, can be attributed to simply doing the 12 Step work.

Not drinking, asking for spiritual guidance, completing our

moral inventory and sharing it with another, making all our amends, creating a daily spiritual meditation ritual, taking a daily personal inventory, and helping other alcoholics in service work results in, and qualifies for me, as a spiritual awakening.

APPENDIX II — SPIRITUAL EXPERIENCE

The terms "spiritual experience" and "spiritual awakening" are used many times in this book which, upon careful reading, shows that the personality change sufficient to bring about recovery from alcoholism has manifested itself among us in many different forms.

Yet it is true that our first printing gave many readers the impression that these personality changes, or religious experiences, must be in the nature of sudden and spectacular upheavals. Happily for everyone, this conclusion is erroneous.

In the first few chapters a number of sudden revolutionary changes are described. Though it was not our intention to create such an impression, many alcoholics have nevertheless concluded that in order to recover they must acquire an immediate and overwhelming "God-consciousness" followed at once by a vast change in feeling and outlook.

Among our rapidly growing membership of thousands of alcoholics such transformations, though frequent, are by no means the rule. Most of our experiences are what the psychologist William James calls the "educational variety" because they develop slowly over a period of time.

Quite often friends of the newcomer are aware of the difference long before he is himself. He finally realizes that he has undergone a profound alteration in his reaction to life; that such a change could hardly have been brought about by himself alone. What often takes place in a few months could hardly be accomplished by years of self-discipline. With few exceptions our members find that they have tapped an unsuspected inner resource which they presently identify with their own conception of a Power greater than themselves.

Most of us think this awareness of a Power greater than ourselves is the essence of spiritual experience. Our more religious members call it "God-consciousness."

Most emphatically we wish to say that any alcoholic capable of honestly facing his problems in the light of our experience can recover, provided he does not close his mind to all spiritual principles. He can only be defeated by an attitude of intolerance or belligerent denial.

We find that no one need have difficulty with the spirituality of the program. Willingness, honesty and open mindedness are the essentials of recovery. But these are indispensable.

There is a principle which is a bar against all information, which is proof against all arguments and which cannot fail to keep a man in everlasting ignorance—that principle is contempt prior to investigation. [Herbert Spencer]

> Before creating A.A. as a formal fellowship, Bill Wilson studied the history of past medical and religious societies and organizations which attempted to help the alcoholic.
>
> He understood that A.A. needed the support of both the medical profession and the church, especially the Catholic Church, to be successful. To that end, he consulted repeatedly with the medical and religious leaders of his day as he wrote the Big Book, ensuring they would not object to anything he had written.
>
> The first physician who recognized alcoholism as a medical illness was **Dr. Benjamin Rush** (1746-1813) of Philadelphia, who is often called the father of American psychiatry and the father of the American temperance movement.
>
> Rush wrote a 36-page paper titled "An Enquiry into the Effects of Ardent Spirits on the Human Body and Mind," which described chronic drunkenness as a "progressive and odious disease" and stated that total abstinence was the only effective treatment. In 1810 Rush promoted the creation of

"Sober Houses," where alcoholics could be confined and rehabilitated.

The **Washingtonians** started in 1840 and lasted until 1847. In the beginning the society favored moral persuasion to reform alcoholics through signing an abstinence pledge. Members included teetotalers and temperance advocates, but over time the membership evolved into large numbers of non-alcoholic temperance advocates, and their work shifted from reformation of the alcoholic to pursuing legal means to prohibit the sale of alcohol.

In 1906, the **Emmanuel Movement** used a psychologically-based approach to religious healing. The movement began as an outreach of the Emmanuel Church in Boston. In practice, the religious element was de-emphasized and the primary modalities were individual and group therapy. Episcopal priests Elwood Worcester and Samuel McComb established a clinic at the Boston church which lasted 23 years until 1929, and offered members both medical and psychological services. The movement did remain focused on the treatment of alcoholism.

In 1921, Frank Buchman was invited to visit Cambridge, England. His non-denominational First Century Christian Fellowship later became known as the **Oxford Group**, and received wide publicity during the 1920s and 1930s. Between 1935 and 1939, A.A. members attended Oxford Group meetings to help them treat their alcoholism.

Core Oxford Group principles consisted of the "Four Absolutes" of Honesty, Unselfishness, Purity and Love, thought to have originated from scripture from the Sermon on the Mount.

The Oxfords also advocated the "Five C's" of Confidence, Confession, Conviction, Conversion and Continuance, and the "Five Procedures" of 1) Give in to God, 2) Listen to God's direction, 3) Check for guidance, 4) Make Restitution for wrongs, and 5) Sharing for witness and confession.

Both Bill W. and Dr. Bob were Oxford Group members before forming A.A., and most of A.A. grew directly out of the Oxford Group and its principles. The Oxford Group still exists today, re-named "Initiatives of Change," with their headquarters in Caux, Switzerland.

THE MEDICAL VIEW ON A.A.

Since Dr. Silkworth's first endorsement of Alcoholics Anonymous, medical societies and physicians throughout the world have set their approval upon us. Following are excerpts from the comments of doctors present at the actual meeting of the Medical Society of the State of New York where a paper on A.A. was read:

Dr. Foster Kennedy, neurologist: "This organization of Alcoholics Anonymous calls on two of the greatest reservoirs of power known to man, religion and that instinct for association with one's fellows, the herd instinct. I think our profession must take appreciative cognizance of this great therapeutic weapon. If we do not do so, we shall stand convicted of emotional sterility and of having lost the faith that moves mountains, without which medicine can do little."

Dr. G. Kirby Collier, psychiatrist: "I have felt that A.A. is a group unto themselves and their best results can be had under their own guidance, as a result of their philosophy. Any therapeutic or philosophic procedure which can prove a recovery rate of 50% to 60% must merit our consideration."

Dr. Harry M. Tiebout, psychiatrist: "As a psychiatrist, I have thought a great deal about the relationship of my specialty to A.A. and I have come to the conclusion that our particular function can very often lie in preparing the way for the patient to accept any sort of treatment or outside help. I now conceive the psychiatrist's job to be the task of breaking down the patient's inner resistance so that which is inside him will flower, as under the activity of the A.A. program."

Dr. W. W. Bauer, broadcasting under the auspices of The American Medical Association in 1946, over the NBC network, said, in part: "Alcoholics Anonymous are no crusaders; not a temperance society.

They know that they must never drink. They help others with similar problems. In this atmosphere the alcoholic often overcomes his excessive concentration upon himself. Learning to depend upon a higher power and absorb himself in his work with other alcoholics, he remains sober day by day. The days add up into weeks, the weeks into months and years."

Dr. John F. Stouffer, Chief Psychiatrist, Philadelphia General Hospital, citing his experience with A.A., said:

"The alcoholics we get here at Philadelphia General are mostly those who cannot afford private treatment, and A.A. is by far the greatest thing we have been able to offer them. Even among those who occasionally land back in here again, we observe a profound change in personality. You would hardly recognize them."

The American Psychiatric Association requested, in 1949, that a paper be prepared by one of the older members of Alcoholics Anonymous to be read at the Association's annual meeting of that year. This was done, and the paper was printed in the American Journal of Psychiatry for November, 1949.

This address was published under the title "Three Talks to Medical Societies by Bill W." —formerly called "Bill on Alcoholism" and earlier "Alcoholism the Illness."

THE LASKER AWARD

In 1951 the Lasker Award was given Alcoholics Anonymous. The citation reads in part as follows: The American Public Health Association presents a Lasker Group Award 1951 to Alcoholics Anonymous in recognition of its unique and highly successful approach to that age-old public health and social problem, alcoholism. In emphasizing alcoholism as an illness, the social stigma associated with this condition is being blotted out. Historians may one day recognize Alcoholics Anonymous to have been a great venture in social pioneering which forged a new instrument for social action; a new therapy based on the kinship of common suffering; one having vast a potential for the myriad other ills of mankind.

THE RELIGIOUS VIEW ON A.A.

Clergymen of practically every denomination have given A.A. their blessing.

Edward Dowling, S.J., of the Queen's Work staff says, "Alcoholics Anonymous is natural; it is natural at the point where nature comes closest to the supernatural, namely in humiliations and in consequent humility. There is something spiritual about an art museum or a symphony, and the Catholic Church approves of our use of them. There is something spiritual about A.A. too, and Catholic participation in it almost invariably results in poor Catholics becoming better Catholics."

The Episcopal magazine, *The Living Church*, observes editorially: "The basis of the technique of Alcoholics Anonymous is the truly Christian principle that a man cannot help himself except by helping others. The A.A. plan is described by the members themselves as self-insurance. This self-insurance has resulted in the restoration of physical, mental and spiritual health and self-respect to hundreds of men and women who would be hopelessly down and out without its unique but effective therapy."

Speaking at a dinner given by Mr. John D. Rockefeller to introduce Alcoholics Anonymous to some of his friends, Dr. Harry Emerson Fosdick remarked: "I think that psychologically speaking there is a point of advantage in the approach that is being made in this movement that cannot be duplicated. I suspect that if it is wisely handled—and it seems to be in wise and prudent hands—there are doors of opportunity ahead of this project that may surpass our capacities to imagine."

HEARD IN THE ROOMS

I was given my first one and one-half pound, hard-cover Big Book at the very first meeting I attended in A.A. in 2006. It remains a cherished possession, and is crammed full of an assortment of notes and sayings I've heard in the rooms of A.A. since I've been sober.

The first thing I wrote in the book was my full name, where I was given the book and my sobriety date—none of which has changed.

The second item in the book was a drawing of the A.A. circle and triangle, with the words Recovery (Steps), Unity (Traditions) and Service (Concepts) written on the sides of the triangle.

Here is what is pasted and written on the pages throughout my original Big Book:

A.A. Preamble

Alcoholics Anonymous is a fellowship of men and women who share their experience, strength and hope with each other that they may solve their common problem and help others to recover from alcoholism. The only requirement for membership is a desire to stop drinking. There are no dues or fees for A.A. membership; we are self-supporting through our own contributions. A.A. is not allied with any sect, denomination, politics, organization or institution; does not wish to engage in any controversy; neither endorses nor opposes any causes. Our primary purpose is to stay sober and help other alcoholics to achieve sobriety.

A.A. Responsibility Statement

I am responsible. When anyone, anywhere, reaches out for help, I want the hand of A.A. always to be there. And for that: I am responsible.

Acceptance Is The Answer

And acceptance is the answer to all my problems today. When I am disturbed, it is because I find some person, place, thing, or situation—some fact of my life—unacceptable to me, and I can find no serenity until I accept that person, place, thing, or situation as being exactly the way it is supposed to be at this moment. Nothing, absolutely nothing, happens in God's world by mistake. Until I could accept my alcoholism, I could not stay sober; unless I accept life completely on life's terms, I cannot be happy. I need to concentrate not so much on what needs to be changed in the world as on what needs to be changed in me and in my attitudes. [Big Book, p.417]

The Real Alcoholic

If, when you honestly want to, you find you cannot quit entirely, or if when drinking, you have little control over the amount you take, you are probably alcoholic. If that be the case, you may be suffering from an illness which only a spiritual experience will conquer. [Big Book, p.44]

The A.A. Six-Pack:

1) don't drink, no matter what, 2) go to meetings, 3) ask for help, 4) get a sponsor, 5) join a home group and 6) get active in A.A. service work.

Days In The Week

July 29: There are two days in every week about which we should not worry, two days which should be kept from fear and apprehension. One of these days is *yesterday*, with its mistakes and cares, its faults and blunders, its aches and pains. Yesterday has passed forever beyond our control. All the money in the world cannot bring back yesterday. We cannot undo a single act we performed. We cannot erase a single word we said. Yesterday is gone beyond recall. Do I still worry about what happened yesterday?

July 30: The other day we should not worry about is *tomorrow*, with its possible adversities, its burdens, its large promise, and perhaps its poor performance. Tomorrow is also beyond our immediate control. Tomorrow's sun will rise, either in splendor or behind a mask of clouds, but it will rise. Until it does, we have no stake in tomorrow, for it is as yet unborn. Do I still worry too much about tomorrow?

July 31: This leaves only one day—*today*. Anyone can fight the battles of just one day. It is only when you and I add the burden of those two awful eternities, yesterday and tomorrow, that we break down. It is not the experience of today that drives us mad. It is the remorse or bitterness for something which happened yesterday or the dread of what tomorrow may bring. Let us therefore do our best to live but one day at a time. Am I living one day at a time? [Twenty-Four Hours A Day, July 29,30,31]

If you're a real alcoholic you *will* stop drinking someday, but it's better to be alive when it happens. [Bill P., Drop the Rock, p.6]

We have two authorities. There is God, our Father, who very simply says, "I am waiting for you to do my will." The other authority is named John Barleycorn and he says "You had better do God's will or I will kill you." [A.A. Comes of Age, p.105]

It is a spiritual axiom that every time we are disturbed, no matter what the cause, there is something wrong with us. [Twelve Steps and Twelve Traditions, Step 10, p.90]

The Four Paradoxes

We surrender to win, we give away to keep, we suffer to heal and we die to live.

The Elimination Of Slips

The majority who slip after periods of sobriety, says Dr. Silkworth, have double-crossed themselves into thinking that somehow they can have the unopened bottle and drink it, too. Even though they have been in A.A. and going to meetings, and following parts of the program, they have accepted it with reservations somewhere. They actually have been one step ahead of a drink. Then they began playing around with the notion they can drink a little and still have the good things of A.A. The outcome is as inevitable as the bottle becoming empty once it has been opened by the alcoholic. Slips are not the fault of A.A. I have heard patients complain, when brought in for another drying out, that A.A. failed them.

The truth, of course, is that they failed A.A. But this mental maneuvering to transfer the blame is obviously another indication of fallacious thinking. It is another symptom of the disease... First, he explains, let's remember the cause. The A.A. who slips has not accepted the A.A. program in its entirety. He has a reservation, or reservations. He's tried to make a compromise. Frequently, of course, he will say he doesn't know why he reverted to a drink. He means that sincerely and, as a matter of fact, he may not be aware of any reason. But if his thoughts can be probed deeply enough a reason can usually be found in the form of a reservation. The preventive, therefore, is acceptance of the A.A. program and A.A. principles without any reservations. This brings us to what I call the moral issue and to what I have always believed from the first to be the essence of A.A... In my opinion, the key principle which makes A.A. work where other plans have proved inadequate is the way of life it proposes based upon the belief of the individual in a Power greater than himself and the faith that this Power is all sufficient to destroy the obsession which possessed him and was destroying him mentally and physically. [The Elimination of Slips, A.A. Grapevine, June 1945]

- There are two powers we need in A.A.: the *human* power of the *Fellowship* (sponsor, sponsees, meetings, home group, service work) and the *spiritual* power of the *Design For Living* (Big Book and 12 Steps).

- Remember—it's the obsession and the allergy.

- We know loneliness such as few do—we have reached the jumping off place.

- His Majesty the Baby.

- When your mouth is running, your ears don't work.

- If drinking is causing you problems, maybe you have a drinking problem.

- If you don't have a sobriety date yet, we suggest you get one. If you have one, we suggest you keep it.

- Booze is liquid duct tape—it fixes everything.

- If faith without works is dead, willingness without action is fantasy.

- Don't drink, go to meetings, read the Big Book, do the Steps.

- If you have no Home Group you're homeless. If you have no sponsor you're clueless.

- How to be happy: show up, be present now, tell the truth and watch your expectations.

- The obsession of the mind that drives me to drink and the allergy of the body that drives me to death.

- Trust God, clean house, prayer, help others.

- Look back and thank God, look forward and trust God, look around and serve God, look within and find God.

- Nice to sober up rather than coming to.

- We turned our will over to the bottle, so why not to God?

- For the temptation to drink: picture a cute girl. Underneath is written "No matter how good she looks now, someone, somewhere, is sick of her shit."

- Alcoholism is a disease of *Denial* – I don't have it; of *Delusion* – I can fix it myself and of *Defiance* – I don't need anyone's help.

- When I feel B-A-D (Boredom, Apathy, Depression), I use my G-P-S (Gratitude, Prayer, Service) to get back on the Broad Highway.

- Keep your heart in A.A. and A.A. in your heart.

- Ask not for a lighter burden, but for broader shoulders.

- It's OK to look back; just don't stare.

- Uncover to recover.

- Enjoy life today; it's not a dress rehearsal.

- If you want to change who you are, change what you do.

- Hitting bottom is an inside job, not an outside circumstance.

- Results of wanting my way: In the past = resentment. In the present = anger. In the future = fear.

- Put on your bathroom mirror: "You are looking at your biggest problem today."

On the Beam / Off the Beam

Honesty / Dishonesty
Faith / Fear
Considerate / Inconsiderate
Humility / Pride
Giving / Greedy
Calm / Anger
Grateful / Envy
Patience / Impatience
Tolerance / Intolerance
Forgiveness / Resentment
Love / Hate
Self-Forgetfulness / Self-Pity
Humility / Self-Justification
Modesty / Self-Importance
Self-Forgiveness / Self-Condemnation
Trust / Suspicion
Moderation / Gluttony
Action / Sloth

The Seven Deadly Sins

Pride is the excessive belief in one's own abilities that interferes with the individual's recognition of the grace of God. It has been called the sin from which all others arise. Pride is also known as *Vanity*.

Envy is the desire for others' traits, status, abilities, or situation.

Gluttony is an inordinate desire to consume more than that which one requires, and is not limited to food.

Lust is an inordinate craving for the pleasures of the body.

Anger is manifested in the individual who spurns love and opts instead for fury. It is also known as *Wrath*.

Greed is the desire for material wealth or gain, ignoring the realm of the spiritual. It is also called *Avarice* or *Covetousness*.

Sloth is the avoidance of physical or spiritual work.

Post-Acute Withdrawal Syndrome (PAWS)

This medical condition can last six months to five years after abstinence. Symptoms include an intermittent loss of short term memory, sleep pattern disruption, poor simple problem solving and poor stress management.

Dr. Bob's Humility Plaque:

Humility is perpetual quietness of heart. It is to have no trouble. It is never to be fretted or vexed, irritable or sore; to wonder at nothing that is done to me, to feel nothing is done against me. It is to be at rest when nobody praises me, and when I am blamed or despised, it is to have a blessed home in myself where I can go in and shut the door and kneel to my Father in secret and be at peace, as in a deep sea of calmness, when all around and about is seeming trouble. [Inscription on Dr. Bob's desk plaque]

My Mom's Blessing

May you have enough happiness to make you sweet, enough trials to make you strong, enough sorrow to keep you human and enough hope to make you happy. [Cecile Gordon, 2006]

Third Step Prayer

God, I offer myself to Thee—to build with me and to do with me as Thou wilt. Relieve me of the bondage of self, that I may better do Thy will. Take away my difficulties, that victory over them may bear witness to those I would help of Thy Power, Thy Love, and Thy Way of Life. [Big Book, p.63]

Seventh Step Prayer

My Creator, I am now willing that you should have all of me, good and bad. I pray that you now remove from me every single defect of character which stands in the way of my usefulness to you and my fellows. Grant me strength, as I go out from here, to do Your bidding. [Big Book, p.76]

Eleventh Step Prayer

> This moving prayer is often attributed to St. Francis of Assisi, but he did not write it. In 1912, a small spiritual magazine based in Paris, France called La Clochette (Little Bell) printed the prayer, written anonymously, which was titled "A Beautiful Prayer to Say During the Mass." The magazine was published by the Catholic association La Ligue de la Sainte-Messe (The Holy Mass League), founded in 1901 by the French priest Father Esther Bouquerel (1855-1923).

Lord, make me a channel of thy peace--that where there is hatred, I may bring love--that where there is wrong, I may bring the spirit of forgiveness--that where there is discord, I may bring harmony--that where there is error, I may bring truth--that where there is doubt, I may bring faith--that where there is despair, I may bring hope--that where there are shadows, I may bring light--that where there is sadness, I may bring joy. Lord, grant that I may seek rather to comfort than to be comforted--to understand, than to be understood--to love, than to be loved. For it is by self-forgetting that one finds. It is by forgiving that one is forgiven. It is by dying that one awakens to Eternal Life. Amen. [Twelve Steps and Twelve Traditions, p.99]

The Merton Prayer

My Lord God, I have no idea where I am going. I do not see the road ahead of me. I cannot know for certain where it will end. Nor do I really know myself, and the fact that I think that I am following your will does not mean that I am actually doing so. But I believe that the desire to please you does in fact please you. And I hope I have that desire in all that I am doing. I hope that I will never do anything apart from that desire. And I know that if I do this you will lead me by the right road though I may know nothing about it. Therefore will I trust you always though I may seem to be lost and in the shadow of death. I will not fear, for you are ever with me, and you will never leave me to face my perils alone. [Thomas Merton, Thoughts in Solitude, Part Two, Chapter II]

Serenity Prayer

God, grant me the serenity to accept the things I cannot change, courage to change the things I can, and wisdom to know the difference. [Twelve Steps and Twelve Traditions, p.41]

God, give me grace to accept with serenity the things that cannot be changed, courage to change the things which should be changed, and the wisdom to distinguish the one from the other. Living one day at a time, enjoying one moment at a time, accepting hardship as a pathway to peace, taking, as Jesus did, this sinful world as it is, not as I would have it, trusting that You will make all things right, if I surrender to Your will, so that I may be reasonably happy in this life, and supremely happy with You forever in the next. Amen. [This original prayer was written by the Calvin theologian Reinhold Niebuhr in 1937]

Amazing Grace

Amazing grace! How sweet the sound that saved a wretch like me. I once was lost, but now am found; was blind, but now I see. Twas grace that taught my heart to fear, and grace my fears relieved; how precious did that grace appear the hour I first believed. Through many dangers, toils, and snares, I have already come; Tis grace hath brought me safe thus far, and grace will lead me home. The Lord has promised good to me, His Word my hope secures; He will my Shield and Portion be as long as life endures. Yea, when this flesh and heart shall fail, and mortal life shall cease, I shall possess, within the veil, a life of joy and peace. The earth shall soon dissolve like snow, the sun forbear to shine; but God, who called me here below, will be forever mine. When we've been there ten thousand years, bright shining as the sun, we've no less days to sing God's praise than when we'd first begun. [John Newton, 1779]

And God Said No

I asked God to take away my pride, and God said No. He said it was not for Him to take away, but for me to give up. I asked God to make my handicapped child whole, and God said No. He said her spirit is whole, her body is only temporary. I asked God to grant me patience, and God said No. He said that patience is a by-product of tribulation; it isn't granted, it's earned. I asked God to give me happiness, and God said No. He said He gives blessings, happiness is up to me. I asked God to spare me pain, and God said No. He said suffering draws you apart from worldly cares and brings you closer to me. I asked God to make my spirit grow, and He said No. He said I must grow on my own, but He will prune me to make me fruitful. I asked God to help me love others as much as He loves me, and God said, Ah, finally you have the idea! [Anonymous, 1980]

Twelve Simple Steps

1) The bottle has let me down—my life is a mess.
2) There is help.
3) I let a higher power take over.
4) I need to look at my life.
5) I admit I did wrong.
6) I want to be free.
7) I ask a higher power to help me be free.
8) I ask: who did I hurt? How can I fix it?
9) I try to fix things if I can.
10) I check up on myself and I am honest.
11) I ask a higher power for help to live the right way.
12) I live by these steps and get better. I try to help other alcoholics.

Other

- A.A. – Attitude Adjustment

- S.O.B.E.R. – Son Of a Bitch Everything's Real

- H.A.L.T. – Hungry, Angry, Lonely, Tired (relapse warning signs)

- H.O.P.E. – Hearing Other People's Experiences

- S.T.E.P.S. – Solution To Every Problem Solved

- U.F.T. – Unidentified Flying Thoughts

- D.E.N.I.A.L. – Don't Even Notice I Am Lying

- P.U.S.H. – Pray Until Something Happens

- S.L.I.P. – Sobriety Lost Its Priority

- N.U.T.S. – Not Using The Steps

- W.A.I.T. – Why Am I Talking?

- A.F.G.O. – Another F**king Growth Opportunity

- F.E.A.R. – False Evidence Appearing Real

- F.E.A.R. – F**k Everything And Run

- F.E.A.R. – Feelings Expressed Allowing Relief

Al-Anon Family Groups

It took a long time. but I finally realized that surrender does not mean submission—it means I'm willing to stop fighting reality, to stop trying to do God's part, and to do my own. [Courage to Change, Oct. 9]

Broken Dreams

As children bring their broken toys with tears for us to mend, I brought my broken dreams to God because He was my Friend. But then instead of leaving Him in peace to work alone, I hung around and tried to help with ways that were my own. At last I snatched them back and cried, "How could You be so slow?" "My child," He said, "What could I do? You never did let go." [Lauretta Burns, Broken Dreams]

BIG BOOK EIGHT WEEK STUDY GUIDE

WK	STEP	BIG BOOK CHAPTER READINGS	BB PGS
		STUDY GROUP ORIENTATION	
1	1	PREFACE, FOREWORDS, DOCTORS OPINION, BILLS STORY, THERE IS A SOLUTION, MORE ABOUT ALCOHOLISM	1 - 43
2	2,3	WE AGNOSTICS	44 - 64
3	4	HOW IT WORKS – Inventory: Grudge / Resentments	64 - 67
4	4	HOW IT WORKS – Inventory: Fears / Sex	67 - 71
5	5,6,7	INTO ACTION – Complete Fifth Step	72 - 76
6	8,9	INTO ACTION	76 - 84
7	10,11	INTO ACTION	84 - 88
8	12	WORKING WITH OTHERS	89 - 103

WEEK 0   (INTRODUCTION & ORIENTATION)

1) Appoint a Chairperson, which is usually the member that organized the Step Study.

2) Have each member introduce himself and BRIEFLY share their reasons for joining the Step Study.

3) Read the PURPOSE below.

4) Review the MATERIALS needed and make sure all members have a Sponsor.

5) Review the COMMITMENTS section. This is what is expected from each team member.

6) Agree on the meeting FORMAT.

7) Read the Assignment for the next meeting.

8) Choose a Chairperson for the next meeting.

PURPOSE

To complete the Twelve Steps of Alcoholics Anonymous, as outlined in the books *Alcoholics Anonymous* and the *Twelve Steps and Twelve Traditions*.

MATERIALS

1) Books: *Alcoholics Anonymous* (Big Book) and the *Twelve Steps & Twelve Traditions*

2) Get a <u>Notebook</u> for writing
3) Get a <u>Sponsor</u>

STRUCTURE

Remember that a Step Study Group is NOT an "A.A. meeting" under the formal definition of the Traditions, and therefore does NOT fall under AAWS guidelines. It is simply a group of alcoholics who have decided to meet for a few months to treat their illness.

1) Ideally, each group should be a mixture of experienced members and newer members.
2) The group members agree on a time and place for a weekly meeting and the length of the meeting.
3) The group usually exchanges full names, telephone numbers and e-mail addresses.
4) The group needs to decide if they will allow new members (late-comers) to join after the orientation meeting. It is usually inadvisable to admit new members late.
5) Each member will commit to completing the weekly assignment including the written work as outlined in the Step Study Guide.
6) For the written assignment, each member, in turn, will share <u>only from what they have written</u>. If you did not complete the written assignment we ask that you <u>not</u> participate in this part of the meeting.

YOUR RESPONSIBILITY & COMMITMENT

- I commit to attend each weekly meeting.
- If I am unable to attend a meeting due to unforeseen events, I will inform the meeting Chair or another group member prior to the meeting so as not to keep the group waiting.
- I commit to completing all the Steps, including the Fifth Step (the Fifth Step is not done with the group so details need not be revealed).
- I will communicate <u>regularly</u> with my sponsor during the study on my progress and activity.
- I am expected to prepare for the weekly meeting by completing the assignment for that week.
- If I <u>relapse</u> during the Step Study, I will withdraw and start over at Step One.

POSSIBLE MEETING FORMAT

1) Open meeting with a moment of silence or the Serenity Prayer.
2) Around the room introductions.
3) Review the COMMITMENTS.
4) Each member will read his assignment and then we will go around the room with other members reading their material.
5) Once all members have read their assignment and time permits, the Chair may ask if anyone wants to discuss anything from the Study Guide that calls for further attention.

Close discussion soon enough before the agreed end time in order to:

1) Read the assignment for next week.
2) Pick a Chairperson for the next meeting. No sobriety time requirement to chair.
3) Collect Tradition VII donations if needed.
4) Close the meeting with an optional prayer or reading of the Chairperson's choice.

WEEKLY ASSIGNMENTS

The Study Guide has a section for each week, and includes READING and WRITING assignments.

CONSIDERATIONS may be used to help you reflect on what you have read and guide your writing. Write as much as you want, but read only what you are comfortable reading at the meeting within the allowed timeframe. Depending on the size of the group and the time available, each member's reading may need to be limited to three minutes or so (use a timer if needed).

Suggestion: since writing requires focus and is best done when free of distraction, you may want to schedule at least an hour of "quiet time" each week to do your writing. Ensure your writings remain securely stored so that no one can read them without your permission, such as spouses, family members or friends.

WEEK 1

STEP 1

Step 1 -- *We admitted we were powerless over alcohol—that our lives had become unmanageable.*

READ from the beginning (Facepage) of *Alcoholics Anonymous* through "More About Alcoholism" (Chapter 3, p.43).

WRITE down your reactions to the readings as to how they apply to you and your illness, incorporating as much as possible of the considerations into your work. Think about:

- Any reservations you may have that in fact, you are powerless over alcohol.
- How the writings apply to your life.
- How you are powerless over alcohol and begin to consider what you can truly "manage" in your life.
- Have you listed those things you attempted to do to control your use of alcohol?
- Did you have a reservation of any kind or lurking notion that you will someday be immune to alcohol?

CONSIDERATIONS – Preface, Foreword, Doctors Opinion

1) Were you aware that your illness affected both your mind and your body?
2) Have you ever experienced the phenomena of "craving?" – p.xxviii?
3) Did you reach the point where you could not differentiate the "true" from the "false?"
4) Did your alcoholic life seem normal?
5) The Doctor seems to say that a "psychic change" must occur – What is a psychic change? (Spiritual Awakening)
6) Can you accept the fact that alcoholism "has never been, by any treatment with which we are familiar, permanently eradicated?"

CONSIDERATIONS – Bill's Story

1) Did you ever ask "Was I crazy?" – p.5

2) Did you ever feel the remorse, horror and hopelessness of the next morning? – p.6
3) Did your mind ever race uncontrollably? – p.6
4) Did you ever seek oblivion? – p.6
5) Did you ever feel lonely? – p.8
6) Did you ever feel fear? – p.8
7) What was your reaction to religion, the church and God? – p.10
8) Note what happened to Bill's prejudice against "their God" when he began to apply his own concept of God – p.12
9) Did you know that "nothing more was required of me" to make my beginning than "willingness," or a "willingness to believe?"
10) Doesn't Bill essentially take the First through the Eleventh Steps at this time? – p.13
11) Notice how Bill was instructed to find God's will and pray. – p.13
12) Has your common sense become "uncommon sense" in manner? – p.13
13) Bill really takes the Twelfth Step on p.14, doesn't he?
14) The Program worked in all of Bill's affairs. – p.15.
15) What was of particular significance to you in this chapter?
16) What did you find that you could not accept?

CONSIDERATIONS – There Is A Solution

1) What is your reaction to the membership of A.A.? -- p.17
2) Did your alcoholism "engulf all whose lives touched the sufferer's?" – p.18 What was their reaction?
3) Did you see how you can reach another alcoholic? – p.18
4) Note on p.20, the book answers the question, "What do I have to do?"
5) Have you been asked the questions of p.20 by yourself or other people? What were the answers?
6) From your examination of yourself in the past weeks and your reading of this chapter, are you a "real alcoholic?" – p.21 If not, why not?
7) Did you have control over alcohol? Did you do absurd and incredible and tragic things while drinking? Were you a Jekyll and Hyde?
8) Did the questions and observations on p.21 help you in answering the questions you have been writing and talking about?

For example:
- Why did we drink the way we did? – p.22
- Why do we take that one drink?
- Why can't we stay on the wagon?
- What has become of the common sense and the will power that we still sometimes display with respect to other matters?
- Did you ask yourself these questions?
- Had you lost the power of choice described on p.24?
- Have you ever said – "What's the use anyhow" or something similar?

9) Go to "There Is A Solution" (p.25). Read "The great fact is just this and nothing less: that we have had deep and effective spiritual experiences."

10) Read and understand the rest of this paragraph and "Appendix II" because it is an outstanding summary of what happens in the program.

11) Our alternative to the solution is to "go on blotting out the consciousness of our intolerable situation as best we could or to accept spiritual help" (p.25).

12) Note that "Appendix II" is referred to again on p.27.

CONSIDERATIONS – More About Alcoholism

1) Did you have the "great obsession?" -- p.30

2) Has your writing in your handbook listed those things you attempted to do to control your use of alcohol? -- p.33

3) Did you have a reservation of any kind or lurking notion that you will someday be immune to alcohol? -- p.33

4) Can you identify with the mental states that precede a relapse into drinking?

5) Do you understand that these mental states are the crux of the problem? -- p.35

6) Do you understand why an actual or potential alcoholic will be absolutely unable to stop drinking on the basis of self-knowledge? -- p.39.

7) Note the doctor's reaction to alcoholism on p.43.

8) Also note the solution at the top of p.43.

WEEK 2

STEPS 2 & 3

Step 2 -- *Came to believe that a power greater than ourselves could restore us to sanity.*

Step 3 -- *Made a decision to turn our will and our lives over to the care of God as we understood Him.*

READ "We Agnostics" and "How It Works" (Chapters 4 & 5, p.44-64), and "Appendix II—Spiritual Experience" (p.567)

WRITE down your reactions to the readings as to how they apply to you and your illness, incorporating as much as possible of the considerations into your work. Think about how the writings apply to your life.

- Write in your notebook what you can believe about a Power greater than yourself.
- Write on another page what you cannot believe about God.
- As you go forward from this point, it is those things which you believe or which fit into your conception of God which you will be using and you can be comforted in knowing that "our own conception, however inadequate, was sufficient to make the approach and to effect a contact with Him" – p.46

CONSIDERATIONS – We Agnostics, How It Works (Step 3 – through p.64) & Appendix II

1) Do you accept the fact that you have only two alternatives if you are an alcoholic – 1) an alcoholic death, or 2) to live a life on a spiritual basis?
2) Have you lacked power to manage life? – p.45
3) Note that the "main object of this book is to enable you to find a Power greater than yourself which will solve your problem" – p.45
4) Have you had honest doubts and prejudices about God? – p.45
5) What will he / she / it look like?
6) What will it be like when you find Him / Her / It?
7) Where did you get these ideas?

8) Had you abandoned the idea of God entirely? – p.45

9) Are you <u>willing</u> to lay aside your previous beliefs or prejudices and express a willingness to believe in a Power greater than yourself?

10) What is your concept of God? – p.46

11) Do you now believe or are you even willing to believe that there is a Power greater than yourself? – p.47

12) Do you recognize that when you can say "yes" to this question that you are "on the way" – p.47

13) Note the book once again refers you to "<u>Appendix II</u>" – p.47

14) What is it that "Appendix II" says that is indispensable?

15) Have you been open-minded or have you been obstinate, sensitive and unreasonably prejudiced about discussions about God?

16) What reservations do you have when you have completed this chapter?

17) Have you been biased and unreasonably prejudiced about the realm of the spirit? – p.51

18) Did your ideas work?

19) Will the God idea work? – p.52

20) Do you believe that "When we drew near to Him He disclosed Himself to us?" – p.57

21) Do you question whether you are <u>capable</u> of being honest with yourself?

22) Note the state of mind you are asked to have when you start the Steps: Honesty, Fearlessness, Thoroughness and a Willingness to go to any length. – p.58

23) What do <u>Half Measures</u> avail us? – p.59

24) Are you convinced that a life run on self-will can hardly be a success? – p.60

25) Can you see the effects of self-centeredness in your life?

26) How have you been self-centered? List examples in your notebook and discuss them with the group.

27) Did you know that you could not reduce self-centeredness much by wishing or trying on your own power? – p.62

ARE YOU REALLY READY TO:

- Fearlessly face and answer the proposition that "Either God is everything or he is nothing?"

- God either is or he isn't?
- What is your choice to be?

Remember what it says on p.28, "If what we have learned and felt and seen means anything at all, it means that all of us, whatever our race, creed, or color are the children of a living Creator with whom we may form a relationship upon simple and understandable terms as soon as we are willing and honest enough to try."

- Are you willing to take this step? -- STEP THREE
- Many groups at this point commit to one another that they are going to take this step and they recite the Third Step Prayer together as set forth on p.63.

3rd STEP PRAYER

God, I offer myself to Thee—to build with me and to do with me as Thou wilt. Relieve me of the bondage of self, that I may better do Thy will. Take away my difficulties, that victory over them may bear witness to those I would help of Thy Power, Thy Love, and Thy Way of life. May I do Thy will always! (p.63).

WEEK 3

STEP 4

Step 4 -- *Made a searching and fearless moral inventory of ourselves.*

<u>INTRODUCTION</u>

We come here with a huge load of stored up shame, guilt, and unresolved pain to be let go of. Step Four helps us lay bare the conflicts of the past so that we are no longer at their mercy.

Step Four gives us the means to find out who we are, and what we are not. It is about finding our assets as well as our defects of character. We discover that our problems began long before we took our first drink. We may have felt isolated and afraid, and it was our desire to change the way we felt that led to our drinking.

We have a disease. We are not responsible for being an alcoholic, any more than a diabetic is responsible for being diabetic. But now that we know we are an alcoholic, we are responsible for our recovery. There are no longer excuses, because we realize we must live the Steps daily or we will die spiritually, emotionally and physically. We are working on practices - things we do - that we will use every day of our lives to move us from being restless, irritable and discontented toward keeping us sober and having serenity and peace of mind.

Do Step Four as best as you reasonably can, and that is more than good enough. Watch out for paralysis from fear or perfectionism. Remember, it's your inventory, not someone else's.

<u>BEFORE THE MEETING</u>

<u>READ</u> the chapter "How It Works" (Chapter 5, <u>p.64-71</u>) and Step Four in the *Twelve Steps & Twelve Traditions.*

<u>WRITE</u> your "<u>Grudge List</u>" (Resentments of People, Institutions and Principles (<u>p.64</u>).

1) Complete Columnar Work on your Grudge List.

2) List your Faults, or character defects (shortcomings; Seven Deadly Sins).

3) Write your <u>Grudge List</u>, one list at a time top to bottom. Put down all the people, places, things, principles or institutions who you resent (feel bad about; are angry towards; harbor ill will towards, etc.) on a list.

4) Then make a brief note about how you "were hurt or threatened" (<u>p.65</u>), or where you had expectations of others, or others had expectations of you – where you were sore or were "burned up" (<u>p.65</u>).

DURING THE MEETING

Discuss any problems you are having. Exchange examples with one another.

<u>PROMPT</u>: before making a <u>Grudge list</u>, make a list of all people who "owe you something" – this gets to the issue of entitlement and will essentially be your resentment list.

<u>Why work a Grudge List?</u>

Resentments build us up to a drink. If we drink, we die. If we get rid of resentments, we are able to live life fully and be free of anger.

GRUDGE LIST EXAMPLE

PEOPLE

Spouse – always nags me
Employer – never satisfied with my work
Neighbor – always snooping, etc.

PRINCIPLES

Having to pay tax – I don't make enough to have to pay so much tax...
"You reap what you sow" – I never got a break in life...
"Your problems are of your own making" – it's not my fault I drink so much...

INSTITUTIONS
IRS – they won't leave me alone
Courts – if I could afford a good lawyer I wouldn't have all these problems
Creditors – they don't understand I don't have a job and can't make regular payments, etc.

COLUMNAR WORK

Transfer top 10 to 25 resentments from your Grudge list to column format. Make four Headings:

NAME (I'm resentful at)
CAUSE (Why I'm angry)
AFFECTS MY (What part of self)
MY PART (My Faults – where was I to blame?)

NAME: one of the names from your Grudge List

CAUSE: write a few words which describe each specific instance which caused you to feel bad about this person, institution or principle. This is an important part of the exercise. Be specific. Rather than write that "He lied," write "He told me he would pay me back and he didn't."

AFFECTS MY: list how each incident affected you. Often, the incident affects our self-esteem, security, pocketbook, ambition, or personal / sex relationships and created fear and worry.

THIRD COLUMN DEFINITIONS

Self-esteem - How I think of myself.

Security - General sense of emotional well-being.

Pocketbook - Basic desire for money, property and possessions.

Personal Relations - Our relations with other people.

Sex Relations - Basic drive for sexual intimacy.

Selfish, self-centered, egotistical - "It's all about me!"

Pride - How I think others view me.

Ambitions - Our goals, plans and designs for the future. Ambition deals with the things that we want. In examining our ambitions we notice that we have the following types:

a) Emotional ambitions - Our ambitions for Emotional Security. Our "feelings."

b) Material ambitions - Our ambitions for "Our pocketbook." Our ambitions towards physical and financial well-being.

c) Social ambitions - Our "place or position in the herd." Our ambitions of how others view us. Our ambitions towards what people think about us.

d) Sexual ambitions - Our ambitions for sex relations.

MY PART: leave *BLANK* for now.

NAME	CAUSE	AFFECTS MY	MY PART / FAULTS
MY MOTHER	Trying to control my feelings and actions. I say "I feel hungry," she says "You're not hungry."	Self-esteem; pride; personal relationship	
MY FATHER	Abandoned me as a child.	Self-esteem; personal relationship	

Make your Character Defect / Faults lists. If possible, order incidents or examples by age. Provide a short narrative describing examples of your faults. Be brief but specific. This is the self-analysis in which you will identify in the MY PART column your role in your resentments – where you were at fault (Grudge List). By doing this exercise, you will be relieved of the difficulty of forgiveness, and will be set free from your resentments.

MY PART: examples of common FAULTS	GRUDGE LIST: examples of common INSTITUTIONS	GRUDGE LIST: examples of common PRINCIPLES
Anger *or* Temper	Authority	God-Deity / Satan
Jealousy *or* Envy	Marriage	Certain Races
Pride *or* Vanity	Church	Religion
Selfish	Religion	Society
Frustration	Legal	Justice
Impatience	Government	Bible
Greed	Education System	Golden Rule
Gluttony *or* over-indulgence	Hospitals	Heaven / Hell
	DMV	Certain Lifestyles
Lust or excessive sexual appetite	Post Office	Life After Death
	Correctional System	Sin / Original Sin
Sloth *or* laziness	Welfare	Retribution
Dishonesty	IRS / Taxes	Adultery
Theft or Fraud	Health/Mental Health System	Ten Commandments
Vandalism		"Love, honor, obey"
Violence		"Can't be too thin"
Cheating		"Don't put off until tomorrow..."
Lying		
Criticism		"What goes around comes around"
Self–Pity		
Prejudice		
Intolerance		

Complete the Columnar Work. Fill in the <u>MY PART</u> column for each grudge or resentment, drawing on your Faults list.

List for each incident –

a) Where have I been at fault, to blame or doing wrong – selfish, dishonest, self-seeking or frightened?

b) What was the real issue?

c) What was the result – retaliation, fighting back, running away?

Did it help? Can you forgive?

NAME	CAUSE	AFFECTS MY	MY PART / MY ROLE / FAULTS
MY MOTHER	Trying to control my feelings and actions. I say "I feel hungry", she says "You're not hungry".	Self-esteem; pride; personal relationship	Responded in anger; resisted but often yielded; did not help. Real issue was my lack of adequate self-esteem. I can forgive. She did the best she could at the time.
MY FATHER	Abandoned me as a child.	Self-esteem; personal relationship	Responded in anger. Ran away from home. Refused to visit him after the divorce. Real issue was continued anger at him. Have not forgiven him.

WEEK 4

STEP 4

Step 4 -- *Made a searching and fearless moral inventory of ourselves.*

<u>BEFORE THE MEETING</u>

<u>READ</u> from the last paragraph on <u>p.68</u> of the Big Book (<u>SEX Relationships</u>) through the end of Chapter Five, "How It Works."

<u>WRITE</u> a list of the <u>FEARS</u> you have experienced throughout your life.

1) Go back to your analysis of your resentments to identify some of these fears.
2) With regard to each of these fears, write a short paragraph answering these questions:
a) When did this fear occur?
b) Why do I have this fear?
c) Did you feel you could handle the situation as you saw it?
d) If you could not handle the situation, who should you rely on?
3) After completing the FEAR list work, read page 68 in the Big Book, which gives us the solution to fear. We "ask Him to remove our fear and direct our attention to what He would have us be."

<u>WRITE</u> a list of names of persons (<u>SEX Relationships</u>) we were involved in, and describe how or why they ended. Describe where we had been selfish, dishonest or inconsiderate. Who did we hurt? Did we unjustifiably arouse jealousy, suspicion or bitterness? Where were we at fault, and what should have been done instead? (<u>p.69</u>)

- Crushes
- Steadies
- Wives or Partners
- Other

<u>DURING THE MEETING</u>

Discuss any problems you are having. Exchange examples with one another.

WEEK 5

STEPS 5, 6 & 7

Step 5 -- *Admitted to God, to ourselves, and to another human being the exact nature of our wrongs.*

Step 6 -- *Were entirely ready to have God remove all these defects of character.*

Step 7 -- *Humbly asked Him to remove our shortcomings.*

READ "Into Action" (Chapter Six - p.72-76)

WRITE down your reactions to the readings as to how they apply to you and your illness.

BEFORE THE MEETING

Find someone to take your Fifth Step with, and SET A SPECIFIC DATE for taking it with that person.

DURING THE MEETING

1) Discuss the Step Five process of Chapter Six.
2) Are there reservations about doing the Fifth Step and if so, what are they?
3) TAKE YOUR FIFTH STEP BEFORE THE NEXT MEETING!
Follow your Fifth Step with Steps Six and Seven as outlined in the Big Book.

STEP 6

"I...became willing..." (Bill's Story, p.13). Step Six is about NOT doing what you want to do. What are you willing to give up? Are you ready for change?"

We become willing to give up our bondage of self-absorption.

We are of the conviction that we are powerless over our addiction to alcohol, and that our lives are unmanageable. When we try to manage life, life becomes unmanageable.

Our compulsive physical cravings, our emotional obsessions, and our spiritual void leads us to be restless, irritable, and discontented. These all motivate us to react to life events with selfishness, dishonesty, self-seeking, and fear.

We are worn out.

We are dishonest when we do not see the reality of what is unfolding before us in true perspective and proportion. We are selfish and self-seeking in that our own self-centered desire, disinterest, or disgust are the criteria by which we judge and react to life. [12 & 12, p.92 - 93]

We are fearful as we anticipate the sense of loss that will happen if we do not get what we desire, or lose what we have, or we are found out for who we are and what we have done. [12 & 12, p.76]

We are exhausted. And we drink.

Or we act and think as though we have been drinking, on an emotional dry bender. Now we are exhausted with our way, we are worn out by our habitual choices; we are sick and tired of the consequences of doing things our way.

Our way *did not work*. (We Agnostics, p.52)

In Step Six, when these things become objectionable to us, we are ready to give them up. This is a gift of desperation. When we could not spot or note our thought-habits and behaviors, we could not get rid of them. Today, when we can see and name them, we can renounce them, turn them over and change.

STEP 7

...to have my new found Friend take them away, root and branch. (Bill's Story, p.13)

Step Seven is about DOING what you do not want to do. What are you going to do instead? Will you ask for help to make these changes?"

We may think of a shortcoming as falling short of our potential.

414

In Step 7 we are going to practice new things in our lives, and a personality change sufficient to bring about recovery; a conversion begins to take place. (Appendix II, p.567)

We are asking for help and strength from the power that we discover within us, through the discipline of the practice of working this program as understood by Alcoholics Anonymous. While we cannot. nor should not deny our instincts, we are asking the higher power of our understanding to remove that habitual and insatiable demand for the satisfaction of our instincts beyond our true needs.

The effort, or the act of working this Step, is in the asking. We are asking for help to have wisdom and clarity, to be made strong. How we go about asking – through prayer, through meditation or other spiritual practices, or by thinking it over – is up to us. We are not going to ask just once, we will ask again and again throughout our lifetime until in a moment of grace we find strength to go on without drinking or using. We need spiritual strength to go forth into the world and take those actions that are consistent with, and even demanded by, the understanding we have from our quiet time alone with our higher power. We take refuge in and cooperate with this inner knowing in the process of letting go, of opening ourselves to change. We have come to see that we are a part of, rather than apart from, this universal family. This true perspective of humility gives us peace of mind. [12 & 12, p.70]

WEEK 6

STEPS 8 & 9

Step 8 -- *Made a list of all persons we had harmed, and became willing to make amends to them all.*

Step 9 -- *Made direct amends to such people wherever possible, except when to do so would injure them or others.*

READ

Read Steps 8 and 9 on p.76 - 84 of the Big Book.

Read Steps 8 and 9 in the Twelve Steps & Twelve Traditions.

WRITE

Make a list of all people you have harmed (refer to your Step 4 Inventory sheets).

Amend: State not simply "I am sorry" but add "What can I do to make it up to you?"

NAME	SPECIFIC AMEND	NOTES
John	Three years ago, while drunk at work I stole construction site materials from the warehouse for my own use.	I now have a different job. Amend needs to be in person and cash payment made for stolen items.

Amends often involve Friends, Family, Employers, Creditors and the Deceased.

CONSIDERATIONS

1) Do you have any misgivings about these steps? p.76
2) Do you feel different about going to some of these people?
3) What is your real purpose? – p.77
4) Is timing important in this step?
5) Can you approach people on your Eighth Step list in a helpful and forgiving spirit? – p.77; also see p.66 & 67

416

6) Do you recognize that nothing worthwhile can be accomplished until you clean your side of the street? – p.78

7) Is it important that you be praised for your Ninth Step efforts? – p.78

8) Have you discussed with your sponsor any criminal offenses you may have committed and which may still be open? If not, you should do so. – p.79

9) Do you understand how your Ninth Step may harm other people? – p.79

10) Have you studied your domestic troubles and the harm that may have been caused in these areas?

11) Do you understand the importance of not causing further harm by creating jealousy and resentment in a "tell all" session? – p.81

12) What does the author mean when he says the spiritual life is not a theory, we have to live it? – p.83

13) Do you see that in taking the Ninth Step you should be sensible, tactful, considerate and humble without being servile or scraping? – p.83

14) Are you experiencing the Promises set forth on p.83 & 84?

WEEK 7

STEPS 10 & 11

Step 10 -- *Continued to take personal inventory and when we were wrong, promptly admitted it.*

Step 11 -- *Sought though prayer and meditation to improve our conscious contact with God as we understood Him, praying only for knowledge of His will for us and the power to carry that out.*

Continue making your Amends where appropriate.

READ

Read Steps 10 and 11 on p.84 - 88 (Chapter 6 – "Into Action") of the Big Book.

Read Steps 10 and 11 in the Twelve Steps & Twelve Traditions.

WRITE down your reactions to the readings as to how they apply to you and your illness, incorporating as much as possible of the considerations into your work. Think about:

CONSIDERATIONS

1) What are the specific instructions outlined for taking Step Ten?
2) What do we watch for? – p.84
3) Note that "By this time sanity will have been returned – we will seldom be interested in liquor" – p.84
4) Is this the sanity referred to in Step 2?
5) What is the proper use of will power? – p.85
6) What is a suggestion for taking the Eleventh Step on a daily basis?
7) Do you follow the procedure outlined on pgs.86 – 87 regarding your daily morning meditation and the way you proceed through the day?
8) Has your attitude about a Power greater than yourself changed since you studied the chapter "We Agnostics?"
9) Do you believe "It Works – It Really Does!"

WEEK 8

STEP 12

Step 12 -- *Having had a spiritual awakening as the result of these steps, we tried to carry this message to alcoholics and to practice these principles in all our affairs.*

READ

Read Chapter Seven – "Working with Others" (p.89 – 103).

Read Step 12 in the Twelve Steps & Twelve Traditions.

WRITE down your reactions to the readings as to how they apply to you and your illness, incorporating as much as possible of the considerations into your work. Think about:

CONSIDERATIONS

1) "Having had a spiritual awakening as a result of these steps." Can you again see the "entire psychic change" mentioned by Dr. Silkworth working in your life?
2) What are the step-by-step requirements for a Twelfth Step? Have you ever tried this? Share you experience with the group.
3) In cases where the alcoholic has not responded, have you worked with his family?
4) Did you offer them your way of life and what results did you have in that situation?
5) Do you believe that you should "Burn the idea into the consciousness of every man that he can get well regardless of anyone. The only condition is that he trust in God and clean house?" – p.98.
6) Is this the basis of the statement that this is a "selfish program?"
7) What are the principles we are to practice in all our affairs?
8) Why does Bill say "all our affairs?"
9) What does this mean to you?
10) How can you apply the Twelve Steps outside the meeting room? Do you do it?
11) What are some of your daily practices in life to maintain sobriety and to grow spiritually?

THE 12 STEPS of ALCOHOLICS ANONYMOUS

(with Spiritual Principles)

Step 1   We admitted we were powerless over alcohol—that our lives had become unmanageable.   [*Honesty*]

Step 2   Came to believe that a Power greater than ourselves could restore us to sanity.   [*Hope*]

Step 3   Made a decision to turn our will and our lives over to the care of God, *as we understood Him*.   [*Faith*]

Step 4   Made a searching and fearless moral inventory of ourselves.   [*Courage*]

Step 5   Admitted to God, to ourselves, and to another human being the exact nature of our wrongs.   [*Integrity*]

Step 6   Were entirely ready to have God remove all these defects of character.   [*Willingness*]

Step 7   Humbly asked Him to remove our shortcomings.   [*Humility*]

Step 8   Made a list of all persons we had harmed, and became willing to make amends to them all.   [*Forgiveness*]

Step 9   Made direct amends to such people wherever possible, except when to do so would injure them or others.   [*Justice*]

Step 10   Continued to take personal inventory and when we were wrong promptly admitted it.   [*Perseverance*]

Step 11   Sought through prayer and meditation to improve our conscious contact with God, *as we understood Him*, praying only for knowledge of His will for us and the power to carry that out.   [*Spiritual awareness*]

Step 12   Having had a spiritual awakening as the result of these steps, we tried to carry this message to alcoholics, and to practice these principles in all our affairs.   [*Service*]

TWELVE TRADITIONS

(Short Form)

1. Our common welfare should come first; personal recovery depends upon A.A. unity.

2. For our group purpose there is but one ultimate authority—a loving God as He may express Himself in our group conscience. Our leaders are but trusted servants; they do not govern.

3. The only requirement for A.A. membership is a desire to stop drinking.

4. Each group should be autonomous except in matters affecting other groups or A.A. as a whole.

5. Each group has but one primary purpose—to carry its message to the alcoholic who still suffers.

6. An A.A. group ought never endorse, finance, or lend the A.A. name to any related facility or outside enterprise, lest problems of money, property, and prestige divert us from our primary purpose.

7. Every A.A. group ought to be fully self-supporting, declining outside contributions.

8. Alcoholics Anonymous should remain forever nonprofessional, but our service centers may employ special workers.

9. A.A., as such, ought never be organized; but we may create service boards or committees directly responsible to those they serve.

10. Alcoholics Anonymous has no opinion on outside issues; hence the A.A. name ought never be drawn into public controversy.

11. Our public relations policy is based on attraction rather than promotion; we need always maintain personal anonymity at the level of press, radio, and films.

12. Anonymity is the spiritual foundation of all our Traditions, ever reminding us to place principles before personalities.

TWELVE TRADITIONS

(Long Form)

1. Each member of Alcoholics Anonymous is but a small part of a great whole. A.A. must continue to live or most of us will surely die. Hence our common welfare comes first. But individual welfare follows close afterward.

2. For our group purpose there is but one ultimate authority—a loving God as He may express Himself in our group conscience.

3. Our membership ought to include all who suffer from alcoholism. Hence we may refuse none who wish to recover. Nor ought A.A. membership ever depend upon money or conformity. Any two or three alcoholics gathered together for sobriety may call themselves an A.A. group, provided that, as a group, they have no other affiliation.

4. With respect to its own affairs, each A.A. group should be responsible to no other authority than its own conscience. But when its plans concern the welfare of neighboring groups also, those groups ought to be consulted. And no group, regional committee, or individual should ever take any action that might greatly affect A.A. as a whole without conferring with the trustees of the General Service Board. On such issues our common welfare is paramount.

5. Each Alcoholics Anonymous group ought to be a spiritual entity having but one primary purpose—that of carrying its message to the alcoholic who still suffers.

6. Problems of money, property, and authority may easily divert us from our primary spiritual aim. We think, therefore, that any considerable property of genuine use to A.A. should be separately incorporated and managed, thus dividing the material from the spiritual. An A.A. group, as such, should never go into business. Secondary aids to A.A., such as clubs or hospitals which require much property or administration, ought to be incorporated and so set apart that, if necessary, they can be freely discarded by the groups.

Hence such facilities ought not to use the A.A. name. Their management should be the sole responsibility of those people who financially support them. For clubs, A.A. managers are usually preferred. But hospitals, as well as other places of recuperation, ought to be well outside A.A.—and medically supervised. While an A.A. group may cooperate with anyone, such cooperation ought never go so far as affiliation or endorsement, actual or implied. An A.A. group can bind itself to no one.

7. The A.A. groups themselves ought to be fully supported by the voluntary contributions of their own members. We think that each group should soon achieve this ideal; that any public solicitation of funds using the name of Alcoholics Anonymous is highly dangerous, whether by groups, clubs, hospitals, or other outside agencies; that acceptance of large gifts from any source, or of contributions carrying any obligation whatever, is unwise. Then too, we view with much concern those A.A. treasuries which continue, beyond prudent reserves, to accumulate funds for no stated A.A. purpose. Experience has often warned us that nothing can so surely destroy our spiritual heritage as futile disputes over property, money, and authority.

8. Alcoholics Anonymous should remain forever non-professional. We define professionalism as the occupation of counseling alcoholics for fees or hire. But we may employ alcoholics where they are going to perform those services for which we may otherwise have to engage non-alcoholics. Such special services may be well recompensed. But our usual A.A. "12 Step" work is never to be paid for.

9. Each A.A. group needs the least possible organization. Rotating leadership is the best. The small group may elect its secretary, the large group its rotating committee, and the groups of a large metropolitan area their central or intergroup committee, which often employs a full-time secretary. The trustees of the General Service Board are, in effect, our A.A. General Service Committee. They are the custodians of our A.A. Tradition and the receivers of voluntary A.A. contributions by which we maintain our A.A. General Service Office at New York.

They are authorized by the groups to handle our over-all public relations and they guarantee the integrity of our principal newspaper, the A.A. Grapevine. All such representatives are to be guided in the spirit of service, for true leaders in A.A. are but trusted and experienced servants of the whole. They derive no real authority from their titles; they do not govern. Universal respect is the key to their usefulness.

10. No A.A. group or member should ever, in such a way as to implicate A.A., express any opinion on outside controversial issues—particularly those of politics, alcohol reform, or sectarian religion. The Alcoholics Anonymous groups oppose no one. Concerning such matters they can express no views whatever.

11. Our relations with the general public should be characterized by personal anonymity. We think A.A. ought to avoid sensational advertising. Our names and pictures as A.A. members ought not be broadcast, filmed, or publicly printed. Our public relations should be guided by the principle of attraction rather than promotion. There is never need to praise ourselves. We feel it better to let our friends recommend us.

12. And finally, we of Alcoholics Anonymous believe that the principle of anonymity has an immense spiritual significance. It reminds us that we are to place principles before personalities; that we are actually to practice a genuine humility. This to the end that our great blessings may never spoil us; that we shall forever live in thankful contemplation of Him who presides over us all.

THE TWELVE CONCEPTS FOR WORLD SERVICE

(Short Form)

The Twelve Concepts for World Service were written by A.A.'s co-founder Bill W., and were adopted by the General Service Conference of Alcoholics Anonymous in 1962. The Concepts are an interpretation of A.A.'s world service structure as it emerged through A.A.'s early history and experience. The short form of the Concepts reads:

1. Final responsibility and ultimate authority for A.A. world services should always reside in the collective conscience of our whole Fellowship.

2. The General Service Conference of A.A. has become, for nearly every practical purpose, the active voice and the effective conscience of our whole society in its world affairs.

3. To insure effective leadership, we should endow each element of A.A.—the Conference, the General Service Board and its service corporations, staffs, committees, and executives—with a traditional "Right of Decision."

4. At all responsible levels, we ought to maintain a traditional "Right of Participation," allowing a voting representation in reasonable proportion to the responsibility that each must discharge.

5. Throughout our structure, a traditional "Right of Appeal" ought to prevail, so that minority opinion will be heard and personal grievances receive careful consideration.

6. The Conference recognizes that the chief initiative and active responsibility in most world service matters should be exercised by the trustee members of the Conference acting as the General Service Board.

7. The Charter and Bylaws of the General Service Board are legal instruments, empowering the trustees to manage and conduct world service affairs. The Conference Charter is not a legal document; it relies upon tradition and the A.A. purse for final effectiveness.

8. The trustees are the principal planners and administrators of over-all policy and finance. They have custodial oversight of the separately incorporated and constantly active services, exercising this through their ability to elect all the directors of these entities.

9. Good service leadership at all levels is indispensable for our future functioning and safety. Primary world service leadership, once exercised by the founders, must necessarily be assumed by the trustees.

10. Every service responsibility should be matched by an equal service authority, with the scope of such authority well defined.

11. The trustees should always have the best possible committees, corporate service directors, executives, staffs, and consultants. Composition, qualifications, induction procedures, and rights and duties will always be matters of serious concern.

12. The Conference shall observe the spirit of A.A. tradition, taking care that it never becomes the seat of perilous wealth or power; that sufficient operating funds and reserve be its prudent financial principle; that it place none of its members in a position of unqualified authority over others; that it reach all important decisions by discussion, vote, and whenever possible, substantial unanimity; that its actions never be personally punitive nor an incitement to public controversy; that it never perform acts of government; that, like the Society it serves, it will always remain democratic in thought and action.

THE TWELVE CONCEPTS FOR WORLD SERVICE

(Long Form)

I. The final responsibility and ultimate authority for A.A. world services should always reside in the collective conscience of our whole Fellowship.

II. When, in 1955, the A.A. groups confirmed the permanent charter for their General Service Conference, they thereby delegated to the Conference complete authority for the active maintenance of our world services and thereby made the Conference—excepting for any change in the Twelve Traditions or in Article 12 of the Conference Charter—the actual voice and the effective conscience for our whole Society.

III. As a traditional means of creating and maintaining a clearly defined working relation between the groups, the Conference, the A.A. General Service Board and its several service corporations, staffs, committees and executives, and of thus insuring their effective leadership, it is here suggested that we endow each of these elements of world service with a traditional "Right of Decision."

IV. Throughout our Conference structure, we ought to maintain at all responsible levels a traditional "Right of Participation," taking care that each classification or group of our world servants shall be allowed a voting representation in reasonable proportion to the responsibility that each must discharge.

V. Throughout our world service structure, a traditional "Right of Appeal" ought to prevail, thus assuring us that minority opinion will be heard and that petitions for the redress of personal grievances will be carefully considered.

VI. On behalf of A.A. as a whole, our General Service Conference has the principal responsibility for the maintenance of our world services, and it traditionally has the final decision respecting large matters of general policy and finance.

But the Conference also recognizes that the chief initiative and the active responsibility in most of these matters should be exercised primarily by the Trustee members of the Conference when they act among themselves as the General Service Board of Alcoholics Anonymous.

VII. The Conference recognizes that the Charter and the Bylaws of the General Service Board are legal instruments: that the Trustees are thereby fully empowered to manage and conduct all of the world service affairs of Alcoholics Anonymous. It is further understood that the Conference Charter itself is not a legal document: that it relies instead upon the force of tradition and the power of the A.A. purse for its final effectiveness.

VIII. The Trustees of the General Service Board act in two primary capacities: (a) With respect to the larger matters of over-all policy and finance, they are the principal planners and administrators. They and their primary committees directly manage these affairs. (b) But with respect to our separately incorporated and constantly active services, the relation of the Trustees is mainly that of full stock ownership and of custodial oversight which they exercise through their ability to elect all directors of these entities.

IX. Good service leaders, together with sound and appropriate methods of choosing them, are at all levels indispensable for our future functioning and safety. The primary world service leadership once exercised by the founders of A.A. must necessarily be assumed by the Trustees of the General Service Board of Alcoholics Anonymous.

X. Every service responsibility should be matched by an equal service authority—the scope of such authority to be always well defined whether by tradition, by resolution, by specific job description or by appropriate charters and bylaws.

XI. While the Trustees hold final responsibility for A.A.'s world service administration, they should always have the assistance of the best possible standing committees, corporate service directors, executives, staffs, and consultants.

Therefore the composition of these underlying committees and service boards, the personal qualifications of their members, the manner of their induction into service, the systems of their rotation, the way in which they are related to each other, the special rights and duties of our executives, staffs, and consultants, together with a proper basis for the financial compensation of these special workers, will always be matters for serious care and concern.

XII. General Warranties of the Conference: in all its proceedings, the General Service Conference shall observe the spirit of the A.A. Tradition, taking great care that the Conference never becomes the seat of perilous wealth or power; that sufficient operating funds, plus an ample reserve, be its prudent financial principle; that none of the Conference Members shall ever be placed in a position of unqualified authority over any of the others; that all important decisions be reached by discussion, vote, and, whenever possible, by substantial unanimity; that no Conference action ever be personally punitive or an incitement to public controversy; that, though the Conference may act for the service of Alcoholics Anonymous, it shall never perform any acts of government; and that, like the Society of Alcoholics Anonymous which it serves, the Conference itself will always remain democratic in thought and action.

ABOUT THE AUTHOR

The author, Alex M., has published multiple articles and three other books about A.A.

Books

Daily Reprieve—A.A. for Atheists & Agnostics (October 2017). Amazon and/or BookBaby

Design For Living—Daily Meditations on the 12 Steps of A.A. for Atheists & Agnostics (March 2018). Amazon and/or BookBaby

Gods of Our Misunderstanding in A.A.—Not just for Atheists & Agnostics (October 2018). Amazon and/or BookBaby

Soft cover books and Kindle eBooks are available on Amazon and ePub format books are available on Bookbaby.

A.A. Grapevine Book

"God On Every Page" is included in the book *One Big Tent,* which is a collection of stories, originally published in the *A.A. Grapevine*, which represent the shared experience of secular A.A. members who have struggled with alcoholism, yet ultimately found a common solution in A.A.

A.A. Grapevine Articles

(as of April-2019)

Popping Up Everywhere (April 2019)

My GPS (February 2019)

Have Kit Will Travel (June 2018)

You're Under Arrest (April 2018)

Step Twelve (March 2018)

Lunch and Service (August 2017)

Yesterday's Mistakes (April 2017)

God On Every Page (October 2016)

Replay Resentment (February 2016)

Home But Not Alone (December 2015)

24-Hour Delivery (February 2014)

Cruising For A Boozing (October 2013)

AA Agnostica

Daily Reprieve

Design For Living

God On Every Page

Friend of Jim B. (published in *Do Tell! Stories by Atheists and Agnostics in A.A.*)

My Story

Facebook

Daily Reprieve

Design For Living

Gods of Our Misunderstanding in A.A.

The Author

Alex M. is a retired physician and life-long atheist living in the Bible Belt where he got sober in Alcoholics Anonymous in 2006. Since so many newcomers flee A.A. because of its God-centric focus, Alex believes his responsibility is to share his experience on how recovery can be attained through the A.A. Fellowship, its 12 Step program and the Big Book of Alcoholics Anonymous when one does not believe in God.

He has published three books about A.A.: *Gods of Our Misunderstanding In A.A.—Not Just for Atheists & Agnostics*, complements his previous two books, *Daily Reprieve—A.A. for Atheists & Agnostics*, which is a daily meditation book on the Big Book of Alcoholics Anonymous, and *Design For Living—Daily Meditations on the 12 Steps of A.A. for Atheists & Agnostics,* which is on A.A.'s 12 Steps.

The international *A.A. Grapevine* magazine has published twelve of Alex's submissions, including "God on Every Page" in the October 2016 special edition *A.A. Grapevine for Atheist & Agnostic Members*, and that article is also included in the 2018 Grapevine book *One Big Tent.*

He has also published in his A.A. Area Newsletter and an article called "A Friend of Jim B." was published in the book *Do Tell! Stories by Atheists & Agnostics in A.A.* by Roger C.

In 2010 he started a program which takes A.A. meetings to alcoholics in his community who are unable to attend their regular meetings due to medical conditions or legal restrictions. An article on this outreach service called "24 Hour Delivery" was published in the *A.A. Grapevine* in February, 2014.

His home group was the first atheist-agnostic A.A. group in his region. Service work remains the foundation of his recovery. He is active in A.A. sponsorship and volunteers for various service committees in his local Intergroup.

Alex is an Ivy League college English Major and avid reader, loves Pre-Code Hollywood films, relaxes by gardening and woodturning, and lives with two old headstrong rescue cats in a farmhouse built in 1842.

NOTES

Manufactured by Amazon.ca
Bolton, ON

25777978R00245